# Vancouver

"All you've got to do is decide to go
and the hardest part is over.

## So go!"

TONY WHEELER, COFOUNDER – LONELY PLANET

THIS EDITION WRITTEN AND RESEARCHED BY

John Lee

# Contents

## Plan Your Trip    4

## Explore Vancouver    46

## Understand Vancouver    223

## Survival Guide    241

## Vancouver Maps    264

(left) Sea wall walk at
Stanley Park (p54)

(above) View of
Granville Island from
Granville street bridge
(p97)

(right) Chinatown
parade (p79)

# Welcome to Vancouver

*Walkable neighborhoods, drink-and-dine delights and memorable cultural and outdoor activities framed by dramatic vistas; there's a glassful of great reasons to love this lotusland metropolis.*

## Neighborhood Villages

Downtown is just the start of Vancouver. Walk or hop transit and within minutes you'll be hanging with the locals in one of the city's many diverse and distinctive 'hoods. Whether you're discovering the coffee shops of Commercial Dr or the hipster haunts of Main St, the indie bars and restaurants of Gastown or the heritage-house beachfronts and browsable stores of Kitsilano, you'll find this city perfect for easy-access urban exploration. Just be sure to chat to the locals wherever you go; they might seem shy or aloof at first, but Vancouverites love talking up their town.

## Taste-Tripping

Don't tell Toronto or Montreal but Vancouver is the real culinary capital of Canada. Loosen your belt and dive right into North America's best Asian dining scene, from chatty Chinese restaurants to authentic *izakayas* (Japanese neighborhood pubs), or taste a rich smorgasbord of fresh-caught seafood, including seasonal spot prawns and juicy wild salmon. The farm-to-table movement has also revitalized the notion of West Coast cuisine – anyone for succulent Fraser Valley duck and a side dish of foraged morels? And we haven't even started on the nation-leading craft-beer scene, plus the city's emerging craft liquor producers.

## Creative Culture

As the city awaits its long-anticipated new Vancouver Art Gallery building, there's already a rich and ever-spreading canvas of cultural action to dive into around the city. Dig deeply and you'll uncover a diverse grassroots scene that operates like a locavore movement for culture-lovers. Mingle with the regulars at eclectic festivals, sparkling theatrical events, toe-tapping live music, waterfront Shakespeare shows and a camera-ready menagerie of public art – as well as the city's independent galleries and a huge, party-like open-house art crawl that lures locals and visitors to East Vancouver every November.

## Outdoor Wonderland

Those snow-dusted mountains that are peeking at you from between downtown's glass towers? They're less than 30 minutes away by car. Vancouverites really can ski in the morning and hit the beach in the afternoon – although it's far more relaxing to chill out and take your time. The North Shore nature doorstep offers snow sports, mountain biking and leisurely rainforest viewing, while the city itself is studded with sandy beaches, forest trails, kayaking routes, seawall bike lanes and Canada's urban green-space jewel, the mighty and highly beloved Stanley Park.

## Why I Love Vancouver

By John Lee, Writer

Eagles whirling overhead, sunset-framed beaches, and the unfurling ocean and mountain diorama from Stanley Park's breathtaking seawall. Although I moved here in the 1990s, I've never stopped gaping at Vancouver's natural charms. For me, it's this astonishing backdrop that sets the glass-towered metropolis apart. But I'm a city boy at heart and I'm also delighted that Vancouver is continuing to develop as it grows up. From amazing dining to a thriving art scene, this young West Coast city keeps moving forward – and I don't just mean the gratifying excellent craft-beer scene (although, personally, that really helps).

**For more about our writer, see p288**

Top: Vancouver cityscape

# Vancouver's
# Top 10

## Gastown (p79)

**1** The brick-paved, heritage-hugging neighborhood where 19th-century Vancouver began has seen a cool new wave of bars, restaurants and boutiques opening in recent years. But rather than building afresh, these independent businesses have restored and revitalized some of the city's oldest buildings. The former skid row 'old town' area is now a picturesque and popular balance of old and new: just ask the jaunty bronze statue of John 'Gassy Jack' Deighton in Maple Tree Sq, guarding the site where he built his first pub way back in 1867.

◉ *Gastown & Chinatown*

## Stanley Park Seawall (p54)

**2** Few cities have democratized their waterfront better than Vancouver: you can stroll or cycle along a tree-fringed, wave-lapped walkway all the way from Canada Place to Kitsilano and the University of British Columbia (UBC). But the highlight is the 8.8km stretch around Stanley Park. Like an immersive visual spa treatment, you'll encounter rippling ocean backed by looming mountains on one side and the gentle swish of dense forest and smiling cyclists on the other. It's a sigh-triggering reminder of how great life can be.

◉ *Downtown & West End*

### Craft Beer (p32)

**3** British Columbia (BC) has rapidly risen to become Canada's microbrewery capital in recent years with nearly 200 beermakers popping up across the province like cheery drunks at an open bar. Leading this boozy charge, Vancouver has dozens of intriguing options, most with inviting tasting lounges that feel like mini neighborhood pubs. There are walkable clusters on and around Main St and near the northern end of Commercial Dr, with hot producers such as Brassneck, Callister and Powell Street worth keeping your tastebuds primed for.

*Drinking & Nightlife*

### Granville Island Public Market (p99)

**4** Granville Island is packed with enticing backstreet studios and artsy little nooks, but the brimming Public Market lures everyone who comes here like a foodie-themed siren song. From pyramids of glistening fresh fruit to drool-triggering deli counters that inspire a picnicking approach to life, it's a taste-tripping wander for browsers as well as locals dropping in for their regular shop. Add a seat at the shoreline plaza outside, complete with cheery buskers and beady-eyed seagulls, and you've found what may be Vancouver's best afternoon out.

*Yaletown & Granville Island*

### Grouse Mountain (p181)

**5** Vancouver's favorite winter playground is a short drive from downtown. But Grouse isn't just for goggle-eyed powder nuts. In summer, you'll have great views over the city – shimmering in the water far below – plus the perfect excuse for a flower-studded alpine hike (take the steep Grouse Grind to reach the summit if you fancy working up a sweat or hop the scenic gondola ride instead). Either way, check out the grizzly bear enclosure: it's a great way to see sharp-toothed wildlife close up without wetting yourself.

*North Shore*

## Asian Dining *(p205)*

**6** Torn between visiting Canada or Asia? Come to Vancouver and try the richest, most authentic Asian dining scene in North America. From bustling dim-sum joints to cozy *izakayas* (Japanese neighborhood pubs), *pho* (Vietnamese soup) houses to superfresh sushi joints, Vancouver offers easy access to culinary adventure. For the especially epicurious, dive into the steam-shrouded food stands at the Hong Kong–style summer night markets in Richmond, the adjoining city that also has more Asian restaurants than you'll ever be able to visit.

✕ *Eating*

## Chinatown *(p79)*

**7** Not all Chinatowns are created equal. The largest in Canada (and also the third biggest in North America), Vancouver's still has the bustling feel of a vibrant community, from its busy apothecary shops to its steam-shrouded barbecue meat stores. The area is in transition, with a tasty menu of new eateries and coffee shops popping up in recent years, but the evocative older buildings remain in a neighborhood that has been designated a National Historic Site. A perfect urban explorer's excursion; ensure your camera is fully charged.

◉ *Gastown & Chinatown*

### Capilano Suspension Bridge
*(p181)*

**8** Arrive early to avoid the summer crowds and you'll have a great time inching over the swaying rope bridge that stretches across a roiling, tree-lined river canyon. Even the bravest find their legs turn to jelly here, but it's all in good fun. At least that's what you should tell yourself, as you'll have to cross back at some point. There's plenty to see in the surrounding temperate rainforest park: a series of canopy bridges, a glass-floored cliffside walkway and nature trails through the towering trees.

👁 *North Shore*

## Vancouver Art Gallery (p57)

**9** The city's leading showcase for art has been exhibiting local photo-conceptualist photographers, the nature-themed paintings of Emily Carr and an ever-changing roster of popular visiting exhibitions for many years, becoming Western Canada's most important art space in the process. And while plans are afoot to move from its downtown heritage building space to a landmark new joint just a few blocks away, some things will endure: including the regular FUSE evening events, when the gallery turns into a clubby late-night hangout for culture lovers.

**⊙** *Downtown & West End*

## Vancouver Aquarium (p55)

**10** There are few attractions that balance fun and education quite as well as this popular, family-friendly Stanley Park landmark. But while most parents bring their kids here to keep them occupied for a few hours, they end up having just as much fun. Don't miss the mesmerizing displays of alien-like jellyfish and the smile-inducing feeding demonstrations with perky dolphins and jocular otters (arguably the comedians of the aquatic animal world). And if you're fully enthralled, get close to the action with a brilliant behind-the-scenes trainer tour.

**⊙** *Downtown & West End*

# What's New

### East Vancouver Microbreweries

Clustered not far from the north end of Commercial Dr, 'Yeast Vancouver' has become Canada's hottest beer district, with a lip-smacking round of top microbrewery tasting rooms. Newbies include Off the Rail. (p121)

### Mobi Bike Share

Vancouver has finally introduced Mobi, its public bike share scheme. Look out for shiny new racks (and free-use helmets) dotted around the city. (p244)

### Catfe

Taking its cue from Tokyo, Western Canada's first cat cafe is a feline paradise of stroking, purring and java-sipping. (p89)

### Artisan Ice Cream

There's a sprinkle-topped explosion of independent ice cream makers popping up around the city. Among the lickable best is Earnest Ice Cream. (p135)

### Skwachàys Lodge

Western Canada's only First Nations art-themed boutique hotel, each room has a different but super-cool contemporary design. It's the city's most original new sleepover option. (p220)

### Railtown

A sliver of streets near Gastown, this once-grungy rail-yard area is Vancouver's next up-and-coming mini-district. Dine at Ask for Luigi to meet the locals. (p86)

### Craft Distilleries

Hot on the heels of Vancouver's craft-beer renaissance, artisan distilleries are popping up here. Dive into the scene at Granville Island's Liberty Distillery, especially during the cocktail happy hour. (p108)

### Eastside Flea

Finding a permanent home in a refurnished heritage building after many years in temporary digs, Vancouver's favorite hipster flea market is here to stay on Main St. (p94)

### Vij's

Moving into a swanky new space on Cambie St, the city's favorite Indian restaurant is bigger and bolder. But the celebrated lamb popsicles are still on the menu. (p152)

### Happy-Hour Dining

After a law change, Vancouver bars hopped on the happy hour wagon but restaurants have also joined in. Savvy locals know where to go for mid-afternoon appetizer deals. Start with Tacofino. (p83)

### BMO Theatre Centre

Vancouver's celebrated Art Club Theatre company has opened a new studio theater in the Olympic Village. Expect new and experimental works to hit the state-of-the-art stage. (p140)

### Silk Road Tea

Victoria's beloved tea emporium has dipped its leaves into the competitive Vancouver market, with a slick new Kitsilano store. Drop by for samples and suggestions for your new favorite tipple. (p176)

For more recommendations and reviews, see **lonelyplanet. com/canada/vancouver**

# Need to Know

**For more information, see Survival Guide (p241)**

## Currency
Canadian dollar ($)

## Language
English

## Visas
Not required for visitors from the US, the Commonwealth and most of Western Europe for stays up to 180 days. Required by those from more than 130 other countries.

## Money
ATMs are widely available around the city. Credit cards are accepted and widely used at all accommodation and almost all shops and restaurants.

## Cell Phones
Local SIM cards may be used with some international phones. Roaming can be expensive: check with your service provider.

## Time
Pacific Time (GMT/UTC minus eight hours)

## Tourist Information
The Tourism Vancouver Visitor Centre (Map p266) is a great resource for visitors, with a staff of helpful advisers ready to assist in planning your trip. Available here are free maps, visitor guides, half-priced theater tickets, accommodation and tour bookings, plus a host of glossy brochures on the city and the wider BC region.

## Daily Costs

### Budget:
### Less than $100
➡ Dorm bed: $35

➡ Food-court meal: $8; pizza slice: $2-3

➡ Happy-hour beer special: $5

➡ All-day transit pass: $9.75

### Midrange:
### $100–$250
➡ Double room in a standard hotel: $150

➡ Dinner for two in neighborhood restaurant: $40 (excl drinks)

➡ Craft beer for two: $15

➡ Museum entry: $15-25

### Top End:
### More than $250
➡ Four-star hotel room: from $250

➡ Fine-dining meal for two: $100

➡ Cocktails for two: $25

➡ Taxi trips around the city: $5 and up

## Advance Planning

**Three months before** Book summer-season hotel stays and sought-after tickets for popular shows and festivals. Buy your Vancouver Canucks tickets.

**One month before** Book car rental and reserve a table at a fancy restaurant. Book theater tickets via Tickets Tonight (www.ticketstonight.ca).

**One week before** Check the *Georgia Straight*'s online listings (www.straight.com) to see what events are coming up.

## Useful Websites

**Miss 604** (www.miss604.com) Vancouver's favorite blogger.

**Scout Magazine** (www.scoutmagazine.ca) Hip food and culture zine.

**Inside Vancouver** (www.insidevancouver.ca) What to do in and around the city.

**Vancouver Is Awesome** (www.vancouverisawesome.com) Online magazine showcasing the local scene.

**Tourism Vancouver** (www.tourismvancouver.com) Official tourism site.

**Lonely Planet** (www.lonelyplanets.com/canada/vancouver) Destination information, hotel bookings, traveler forums and more.

## WHEN TO GO

December to March for skiing. Summer crowds roll in from June to September. Spring and fall for great weather and reduced hotel rates.

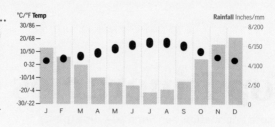

# Arriving in Vancouver

**Vancouver International Airport** Situated 13km south of the city in Richmond. Canada Line trains to downtown typically take around 25 minutes and cost $7.75 to $10.50, depending on the time of day. Alternatively, taxis cost up to $45.

**Pacific Central Station** Most trains and long-distance buses arrive from across Canada and the US at this station on the southern edge of Chinatown. Across the street is the Main St-Science World SkyTrain station. From there it's just five minutes to downtown ($2.75).

**BC Ferries** Services from Vancouver Island and the Gulf Islands arrive at Tsawwassen, one hour south of Vancouver, or Horseshoe Bay, 30 minutes from downtown in West Vancouver. Both are accessible by regular transit bus services.

For much more on **arrival** see p242

# Getting Around

Transit in Vancouver is cheap, extensive and generally efficient.

➡ **Bus** Extensive network in central areas with frequent services on many routes.

➡ **Train** SkyTrain system is fast but limited to only a few routes. Especially good for trips from the city center.

➡ **SeaBus** A popular transit ferry linking downtown Vancouver and North Vancouver.

For much more on **getting around** see p243

# Sleeping

With more than 25,000 hotels, B&B and hostel rooms on offer, you won't be short of somewhere to stay in Vancouver, especially in downtown. However as summer is the most popular time to visit, do make sure to book ahead.
Expect more expensive rates in July and August when visitor numbers are highest, or if you want a good deal, consider visiting in the spring or fall instead.

## Useful Websites

➡ **Tourism Vancouver** (www.tourismvancouver.com) Wide range of accommodation listings and package deals.

➡ **Hello BC** (www.hellobc.com) Official Destination British Columbia (BC) accommodation search engine.

➡ **BC Bed & Breakfast Innkeepers Guild** (www.bcsbestbnbs.com) Wide range of B&Bs in Vancouver and around the province.

➡ **Lonely Planet** (www.lonelyplanet.com/canada/vancouver/hotels) Recommendations and bookings.

For much more on **sleeping** see p212

# Top Itineraries

## Day One

### Gastown (p81)

 Start your wander around old town Gastown in **Maple Tree Square**. Admire the **'Gassy Jack' statue** and reflect on the fact that Vancouver might not be here today if it wasn't for the pub John Deighton built here. Since it's a little too early for a drink, peruse the cool shops along Water St, including **Orling & Wu** and **John Fluevog Shoes**.

>  **Lunch** Ever-popular Tacofino (p83) is one of the city's finest taco joints.

### Chinatown (p82)

 Your lunch spot is just a a few steps from Chinatown, another top historic 'hood. Spend some time winding around the kaleidoscopically hued streets. Don't miss the **Chinatown Millennium Gate** on Pender and the aromatic grocery and apothecary stores on Keefer St. Use your magnifying glass to sleuth out the **Vancouver Police Museum** before ending your afternoon at the delightfully tranquil **Dr Sun Yat-Sen Classical Chinese Garden**.

>  **Dinner** Head for contemporary Chinatown favorite Bao Bei (p86)

### Main St (p130)

 Walk south uphill on Main (or hop bus 3). Within a few minutes, you'll be at Brassneck (p137), Vancouver's favorite microbrewery. Drink deeply, and don't miss the Passive Aggressive pale ale.

## Day Two

### Main St (p133)

 Have a lazy late start then get moving with a hearty diner breakfast (plus copious coffee) at **Argo Cafe**. Then cross over Main St to explore the city's new gallery district, **the Flats**, colonizing a host of old industrial units. Next, hop on and off bus 3 southwards as you explore Main.

>  **Lunch** Dock Lunch (p135) feels just like dining in someone's home.

### Main St (p141)

 Bus to the 18th Ave intersection and hop off at the **Main Street Poodle** statue for some on-foot wandering. Check out Vancouver's best indie stores, from vinyl-loving **Neptoon Records** to the delightfully quirky **Regional Assemby of Text** stationery store. Back on the bus, backtrack north to the intersection with Broadway and transfer to the 99B Line express, heading east; you'll be at Commercial Dr in 10 minutes.

>  **Dinner** Head to Jamjar (p117) for excellent Lebanese comfort food.

### Commercial Drive (p120)

 Spend the evening bar - (or coffee house -) hopping along the Drive. Whatever you do, don't miss **Storm Crow Tavern**, Vancouver's original nerd pub; free the Vulcan of your dreams at the bar.

# Day Three

### Stanley Park (p54)

 Get here before the crowds to stroll the **seawall**, photograph the **totem poles** and nip into the **Vancouver Aquarium** to commune with the aquatic critters. Consider exploring the park by bike if you have time. You'll find some beady-eyed blue herons hanging out at **Lost Lagoon** – duck into the **Stanley Park Nature House** to find out more about them.

> **Lunch** Drop in to Stanley's Bar & Grill (p72) for a salmon burger and beer.

### West End (p61)

Fully explore the tree-lined West End neighborhood just outside the park, including Davie and Denman Sts. Save time for **English Bay Beach** and, a few blocks away, **Roedde House Museum**. There are also plenty of coffee and shopping spots to lure your attention.

> **Dinner** Dive into some locally sourced West Coast dishes at Forage (p66).

### West End (p72)

 Davie St is the center of Vancouver's gay nightlife scene, and the area has plenty of cool options for folks of all persuasions to hang with the locals. Consider a sunset-viewing cocktail at **Sylvia's Lounge** in the neighborhood's ivy-covered heritage hotel. Or dive into cantina-style **Lolita's** and drink yourself merry on cocktails.

# Day Four

### University of British Columbia (UBC) (p162)

 Start your day at the biggest university in British Columbia (BC), exploring a surprising wealth of attractions. The **Museum of Anthropology** and **Beaty Biodiversity Museum** are must-sees, while the green-thumbed should also check out the **UBC Botanical Garden** and the **Nitobe Memorial Garden**. Stick around and explore the waterfront campus: it's dotted with intriguing public artworks.

> **Lunch** Join the students at the ever-welcoming Koerner's Pub. (p174)

### Kitsilano (p162)

Hop bus 4 from UBC and you'll soon be on boutique-lined 4th Ave. You'll find plenty of cool independent shops and eateries here. Don't miss **Silk Road Tea**, **Zulu Records** and the travel-themed store, **Wanderlust**. Add coffee at **49th Parallel Coffee** or an ice cream at **Rain or Shine**.

> **Dinner** Tuck into a Thai feast at Maenam (p172).

### Granville Island (p103)

 Continue on to Granville Island for drinks at **Granville Island Brewing Taproom** before catching a raucous improv show at **Vancouver Theatresports League** (just remember: if you sit in the front, they'll likely pick on you).

# If You Like...

## Amazing Views

**Third Beach** Stanley Park's best sunset spot, with mesmerizing panoramic waterfront vistas. (p56)

**Vancouver Lookout** The city's lofty observation attraction, with 360-degree views over downtown Vancouver and its surroundings. (p60)

**Queen Elizabeth Park** Camera-ready signature vistas of the city backed by the looming North Shore mountains. (p147)

**Stanley Park Seawall** Stunning vistas of the ocean and mountains, backed by verdant rainforest. (p54)

**Sylvia's Lounge** Take in sunset views, with drink in hand, over the golden ripples of English Bay. (p61)

**Grouse Mountain** On a sunny day, spectacular view of the city shimmering in the water below. (p181)

## Beautiful Gardens

**VanDusen Botanical Garden** Manicured garden attraction with several themes. Don't miss the hedge maze. (p147)

**Dr Sun Yat-Sen Classical Chinese Garden** Tile-topped walls enclosing a symbolic Ming-style garden that's dripping with tranquility. (p82)

**Stanley Park** Among the nature trails and seafront views, look

Dr Sun Yat-Sen Classical Chinese Garden

out for the delightful rose and rhododendron gardens. (p54)

**Queen Elizabeth Park** Combining rustic, tree-lined areas with flower gardens. Save your photography urges for the top of the hill, where you'll find panoramic views across Vancouver. (p147)

**Bloedel Conservatory** A dome-covered tropical garden teeming with exotic birds, including some loudly vocal parrots. A perfect rainy-day hangout. (p147)

**UBC Botanical Garden** The university's greatest green space, with themed gardens, a forest canopy walk and – best of all – the annual Apple Festival. (p169)

**Nitobe Memorial Garden** Meticulous traditional Japanese garden with intricate symbolism, located at the University of BC. (p169)

## Fascinating History

**Gastown & Chinatown** Vancouver's National Historic neighborhoods recall the city's earliest days with buildings from just after the 1886 Great Fire. (p48)

**Museum of Vancouver** Documenting the city's colorful development, with especially evocative sections on the 1950s and 1960s plus a roomful of vintage neon signs from around the city. (p166)

**Roedde House Museum** This Victorian-era West End heritage mansion is lined with period artifacts and antiques and brings to life the world of well-to-do Vancouverites of the past. (p61)

**Vancouver Police Museum** Tracing the city's noirish past, including exhibits on unsolved murders. Don't miss the decom-

missioned mortuary room at the back. (p81)

**Forbidden Vancouver** Historic walking tours that illuminate the dark and sordid past of gritty old Vancouver. There are also behind-the-scenes tours of a downtown strip club. (p245)

**Engine 374 Pavilion** The engine that pulled the first transcontinental passenger train into Vancouver, carefully preserved in its own Yaletown home. (p101)

**Marine Building** The city's most beautiful art deco building is a soaring prewar fusion of aquatic motifs and late-1920s romanticism. Add City Hall for another deco landmark. (p59)

## First Nations Art

**Museum of Anthropology** Vancouver's best museum presents an amazing array of Pacific Northwest artifacts, as well as cultural treasures from around the world. (p164)

**Skwachays Lodge** A striking new boutique hotel with each room designed in collaboration with a First Nations artist. There's also a gallery and bookable First Nations experiences for guests. (p220)

**Bill Reid Gallery of Northwest Coast Art** Downtown's striking showcase of Haida artists and those they inspired, from carvings to jewelry. Check ahead for special exhibitions. (p59)

**Salmon n' Bannock** Vancouver's only authentic aboriginal restaurant is also lined with First Nations art. (p149)

**Stanley Park** The carvings and totem poles near Brockton Point are among the city's most photographed artworks. (p54)

**RBC Royal Bank** Head up the escalator to level two of this

main downtown bank to discover the gigantic 'Ksan Mural wood carving, one of the largest in Canada. (p58)

**Hill's Native Art** Gastown gallery with authentic art and crafts for sale. (p95)

## Neighborhood Festivals

**Eastside Culture Crawl** Hundreds of East Vancouver studios and galleries invite folks in to see their work. (p93)

**Car Free Day Vancouver** Streets across the city close to cars for a day of family-friendly partying. (p236)

**Khatsahlano Street Party** Kitsilano's 4th Ave comes to life with dozens of bands on alfresco stages. (p172)

**UBC Apple Festival** UBC's celebration of all things apple, from tastings to pies. (p175)

**Pride Week** The West End becomes party central with a week of events and a gigantic street parade. (p44)

**Chinese New Year** The city's Chinatown springs to life with food, stalls and a dragon parade. (p20)

**For more top Vancouver spots, see the following:**
→ Eating (p27)
→ Drinking & Nightlife (p31)
→ Entertainment (p35)
→ Shopping (p37)
→ Sports & Activities (p40)

PLAN YOUR TRIP IF YOU LIKE...

# Month By Month

**TOP EVENTS**

**Vancouver International Film Festival**, September

**Vancouver International Jazz Festival**, June

**Bard on the Beach**, June–September

**Pacific National Exhibition**, August

**Eastside Culture Crawl**, November

## January

**Vancouver's quietest month is usually cold, grey and dank weather-wise, with occasional sparkling blue skies to keep the locals from getting too miserable. Aside from the January 1 hangover cure, most happenings are indoors.**

### 🏃 Polar Bear Swim

This chilly New Year's Day affair has been taking place annually in English Bay since 1920. At around 2:30pm more than a thousand people charge into the ocean... and most usually leap out shivering a few seconds later.

### 🍴 Dine Out Vancouver

From around mid-January, restaurants across the city offer two weeks of great-value three-course tasting menus for $20, $30 or $40. Book ahead via the event's website (www.dineoutvancouver.com) – top spots always sell out.

### 🎭 PuSh Festival

A three-week season of innovative theater, music, opera and dance from around the world, or around the corner. Adventurous performance-art fans will love this unusual showcase (p35), staged at venues across the city from the third week of January.

## February

**There are still good off-peak hotel deals to be had here (except around Valentine's Day) and the weather may be warming a little – but don't count on it.**

### 🎭 Chinese New Year

This multiday celebration (www.vancouver-chinatown.com) in and around Chinatown can take place in January or February, but it always includes plenty of color, dancing and great food. Highlights are the Dragon Parade and fire-crackers.

### ☆ Winterruption

Granville Island chases away the winter blues with a warming weekend-long roster of live music, family-friendly events and walking tours of area booze makers at Winterruption (p98). Dress warmly – many happenings are outdoors.

## March

**Spring is beginning to bud around the city, which also means the rain is starting to kick in. Bring a waterproof jacket and complain about the relentless deluges and you'll fit right in.**

### 🎭 Vancouver International Dance Festival

Local, national and international hoofers come together for this calf-stretching spree of performances. The International Dance Festival (www.vidf.ca) showcases the city's credentials as a major dance capital.

### Vancouver International Wine Festival

The city's fave excuse for a drink – and one of North America's oldest wine fests – the week-long end-of-February wine fest (www.vanwinefest.ca) includes tastings, seminars and galas. Book ahead: many events sell out.

## April

**Dry spells become longer as the month progresses. Expect to see the city's blossom trees in full and fragrant glory, along with an attendant chorus of selfie-snappers.**

### ☆ Vancouver Fashion Week

If you feel like hitting the catwalk, or at least watching others on it, check out the first of two annual fashion weeks – the second is in September. Fashion Week (www.vanfashionweek.com) shows, galas and educational events highlight the work of regional and international designers.

### 🏃 Sun Run

One of North America's largest street races, the Sun Run lures 50,000 runners, speed walkers and wheezing wannabes for a spirited jaunt around the city in the fourth week of April.

## May

**The rain is intermittently forgotten as the promise of summer arrives. Several farmers markets start up for the season while pale-legged shorts-wearers** start gearing up for the arrival of some real sun.

### Vancouver Craft Beer Week

Reflecting a frothy surge in regional microbrewing, this ever-expanding late-May booze fest (www.vancouvercraftbeerweek.com) runs from pairing dinners to tasting events. Expect to rub shoulders with brewmeisters from Phillips to Four Winds plus some from the US; now's your chance to conduct an international taste-test.

### Vancouver International Children's Festival

Bristling with kid-friendly storytelling, performances and activities at venues around Granville Island, late-May's multiday Children's Festival (p25) is highly popular. Expect to be lured by face painters and balloon twisters while your ice cream-smeared kids run riot.

## June

**The summer good times roll as all Vancouverites shed some layers for the next three months. Neighborhood street parties also kick off and it's time to crank up the barbecue.**

### ☆ Bard on the Beach

Shakespeare performed the way it should be: in tents with the North Shore mountains peaking peacefully behind the stage. The four-play roster from Bard on the Beach (p175) runs from June to mid-September. Book ahead.

### Car Free Vancouver Day

An increasingly popular day-long event, Car Free Day Vancouver (p140) is held around mid-June, when the main streets of four neighborhoods – from Kitsilano to Commercial Drive– close to traffic and surrender to music, vendors, performers and food.

### Dragon Boat Festival

An epic weekend splashathon around mid-June, the colorful Dragon Boat Festival (www.dragonboatbc.ca) churns the normally placid waters of False Creek. Around 100,000 landlubbers turn up to cheer on close to 200 teams and partake of a minifestival of music, theater and food.

### Vancouver International Jazz Festival

Vancouver's Jazz Fest (www.coastaljazz.ca) is a huge multiday music party from late June that combines superstar performances (Oscar Peterson and Diana Krall in the past) with smile-triggering free outdoor shows around the city.

## July

**The city is in full-on beach-bumming mode, with the very idea of rain a distant memory (except when there's an occasional cracking thunder storm). Dress light and head outside for most of this month.**

### ✦ Canada Day Celebrations

Canada Place is the main Vancouver location for Canada Day celebrations marking the country's July 1 birthday. From 10am onwards expect food, live music, impromptu renditions of 'O Canada' and (eventually) fireworks. Granville Island also hosts smaller but equally proud celebrations.

### ✦ Vancouver Folk Music Festival

Kitsilano's Jericho Beach is the venue for the sunny, weekend-long Folk Music Festival (www.thefestival.bc.ca), featuring alfresco shows from folk to world music and beyond. Don your sun block and join the 30,000-odd hippies and hipsters at one of Vancouver's most enduring music events.

### ✦ Celebration of Light

One of North America's largest fireworks competitions, the Celebration of Light (www.thefestival.bc.ca) takes place in English Bay over three nights in late July and early August. Competing countries (different ones every year) put on their most spectacular displays.

## August

**It's the peak of summer, which means locals are in full sun-kissed patio mode and a tasty menu of local-grown fruit – from peaches to cherries – hits the city.**

### ✦ Pride Week

A multiday kaleidoscope of gay-, lesbian- and bisexual-friendly shows, parties and concerts culminating

(Top) Celebration of Light festival in English Bay
(Bottom) Dragon boat race at False Creek

JAN HOLAKOVSKY/500PX ©

VOLODYMYR KYRYLYUK/SHUTTERSTOCK ©

in Western Canada's largest pride parade (p44). Typically the first Sunday of August, this saucy West End mardi gras draws up to 500,000 people with its disco-beat floats and gyrating, scantily clad locals.

### ☆ Pacific National Exhibtion

From the third week of August onwards, this ever-popular country fair (p122) has evolved into a three-week community party of live music, family-friendly performances (check out the Superdogs) and artery-clogging food stands: miss the minidoughnuts at your peril. Don't forget the fairground, with its historic wooden roller coaster.

# September

**Summer is waning but there are usually still plenty of golden sunny days to go before the leaves start turning. The blue-skied end of the month especially is many Vancouverites' favorite time of year.**

### 🎭 Vancouver Fringe Festival

One of the city's biggest arts events, the Fringe (p109) features a lively 11-day roster of wacky theatrics from the second week of September, drawing thousands to large, small and unconventional Granville Island venues. Expect short plays and comedy revues, with tickets typically around the $10 mark.

### 🎭 Vancouver International Film Festival

This giant, highly popular film festival (p35)

celebrates smaller, art-house movies and international hidden gems. Its 17-day roster from late September covers hundreds of screenings of local, national and international films, and features gala events and industry schmoozes. Book ahead.

# October

**It's time to head inside as the rains roll back into town and locals rediscover their rainproof jackets for the rest of the year. Some sunny days remain though, illuminating the fading fall foliage.**

### 🎭 Vancouver Writers Fest

A six-day, late-October literary event, the Writers Fest (www.writersfest.bc.ca) offers Granville Island readings, workshops and forums with dozens of local and international scribblers. Past guests have included Salman Rushdie and Margaret Atwood.

### 🚶 Parade of Lost Souls

A spectral Day of the Dead celebration with a torch-lit procession of spookily dressed performers moving through the streets of East Vancouver. The Parade of Lost Souls (www.dusty flowerpotcabaret.com) is Vancouver's main Halloween event.

# November

**Wrap up if you want to partake of the events around the city this month. Scarves and umbrellas**

**are often a good idea in November.**

### ☆ Eastside Culture Crawl

Hundreds of local artists in Vancouver's Eastside open their private or shared studios to visitors at this excellent four-day showcase (p93) in mid-November. Expect to come across a wild and wacky array of works, from found art installations to woodblock prints of marauding crows.

### ◉ Bright Nights in Stanley Park

Indicating that Christmas is on its way, this month-long event sees a swath of the park covered in fairy lights, Yuletide displays and elfish dioramas. There's also a Christmas-themed train ride. Bright Nights (www. vancouver.ca/parks/events/ brightnights) is Vancouver's most popular seasonal attraction, so book ahead.

# December

**Time to embrace the winter by either going into hibernation or adding a few extra layers of clothing. Events-wise, it's all about Christmas for the rest of the year.**

### 🚶 Santa Claus Parade

Rivaling the Pride Parade for spectator numbers, this giant Christmas procession (p25) in the first week of December is a family favorite. Expect youth orchestras, carol-singing floats and, right at the end, the great man himself. And, yes, he's the real one.

# With Kids

*Family-friendly Vancouver is stuffed with activities and attractions for kids, including interactive science centers, animal encounters and plenty of outdoor activities to tire them out before bed. Several festivals are especially kid-tastic, and local transport experiences, including SeaBus and SkyTrain, are highlights for many youngsters.*

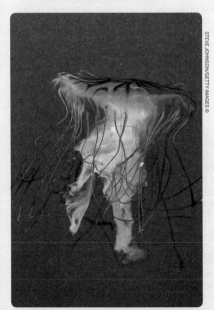

Jellyfish at Vancouver Aquarium

STEVE JOHNSON/GETTY IMAGES ©

## Animal Encounters

**Grouse Mountain** (p181) is home to resident grizzly bears in their own enclosure; there are also summertime bird-of-prey displays.

**Maplewood Farm** (p181) is ideal for younger kids who can't wait to hangout with the goats and chickens.

**Vancouver Aquarium** (p55) offers otters, iridescent jellyfish and dolphins to view, plus trainer encounters if your kids are keen on behind-the-scenes tours.

**Bloedel Conservatory** (p147) provides a delightful way to commune with hundreds of exotic birds; ask nicely and staff will let your child feed several at once from a bowl.

## Science & Nature

**Science World** (p132), packed with hands-on activities, has mastered the art of teaching kids through an abundance of fun. Its outdoor area is the city's favorite summertime hangout for children, especially under-10s.

**HR MacMillan Space Centre** (p166) is perfect for astronomically-minded children, with plenty of push-button games and activities.

**Capilano Suspension Bridge Park** (p181) offers a great way to learn about the local outdoors. After inching over the canyon on the (deliberately) wobbly wooden bridge, take some short trails through the forest to learn about the towering trees and local critters.

**Stanley Park Nature House** (p55) gives kids the opportunity to quiz friendly volunteers about the park's flora and fauna and partake of birdwatching tours, especially in summer.

## Outdoor Action

**Second Beach Pool** (p77) in Stanley Park, is one of the city's best summertime hangouts for kids who love to swim. This side of the park also has a popular playground, as does the Lumberman's Arch area, where you'll also find an outdoor water park.

**Granville Island Water Park** (p114) is even bigger and not far from the ever-popular **Kids Market** (p103).

Kitsilano Beach (p166) is ideal if your children want to play on the sand; it's very popular with families.

## For History-Huggers

**Gulf of Georgia Cannery** (p205) provides an evocative, family-friendly way to see how people used to work; in Richmond.

**BC Sports Hall of Fame & Museum** (p101) traces the region's sporting past via kid-friendly displays and activities.

**Kidsbooks** (p176), Vancouver's biggest family bookstore, has tomes on everything – history included.

**Academie Duello** (p78) offers kid-friendly sword-play lessons – plus hugely popular Knight Camps.

## Festivals & Events

**Vancouver International Children's Festival** (www.childrensfestival.ca; ⊘late May; 🚼) is packed with entertainers and face-painting shenanigans,

**Pacific National Exhibition** (p122) is crammed with shows, activities and fairground rides for kids of all ages. Don't miss the piglet races.

**Car Free Day Vancouver** (p236) takes over several main thoroughfares around the city and has lots of family-friendly activities.

### NEED TO KNOW
...........................................
**Accommodation** Children can usually stay with parents at hotels for no extra charge. Some hostels have family rooms. Hotels can recommend trusted babysitting services.

**Equipment** Strollers, booster seats and toys can be rented from Wee Travel (www.weetravel.ca).

**Resources** Pick up the free *Kids' Guide Vancouver* around town and visit www.kidsvancouver.com for local tips, resources and family-focused events.

**Santa Claus Parade** (www.rogerssantaclausparade.com; ⊘early Dec; 🚼) is Vancouver's best chance to see the big man himself, plus attendant floats, bands and music.

## Transport Fun

Kids of a certain age really enjoy getting around Vancouver. Taking the seat at the front of a SkyTrain (p243) is all about pretending to be the driver; while the front window seats on a SeaBus (p245) jaunt to North Vancouver are almost as coveted. Taking a bathtub-sized ferry around False Creek is also fun, while hopping aboard the Stanley Park Train (p56) is a must.

apilano Suspension Bridge Park

# For Free

*There are plenty of sights and activities to enjoy in Vancouver without opening your wallet. Follow the locals and check listings and you'll soon be perusing art shows, noodling around parks and taking in a gratis tour or two.*

Engine 374 Pavilion

LONELY PLANET/GETTY IMAGES ©

## Gratis Attractions

From nature to local history, there are several free places to visit in the city.

**Engine 374 Pavilion** (p101) preserves the locomotive that pulled the first transcontinental passenger train into Vancouver in its own Yale-town spot.

**Stanley Park Nature House** (p55) gives a fascinating introduction to the flora and fauna of the regional rainforest.

**The Marine Building** (p59) is Vancouver's favorite art deco masterpiece.

**Sun-Yat Sen Park**, the adjoining freebie alternative to the Dr Sun Yat-Sen Classical Chinese Garden (p82), has many of the same visual attributes.

**Lynn Canyon Ecology Centre** (p182) is the access point to a smaller alternative to Capilano Suspension Bridge.

## Discounts Galore

From cheap nights to free tours, there are several ways to keep your costs down.

**Vancouver Art Gallery** (p57) entry is by-donation on Tuesday evenings .

**Museum of Anthropology** (p164) entry is reduced to $10 on Tuesday evenings from 5pm to 9pm.

**Tickets Tonight** (Map p266, F1; ☎604-684-2787; www.ticketstonight.ca; 200 Burrard St) sells tickets for day-of-performance theater shows at half price.

**Vancouver Tour Guys** (p246) has four different gratuity-only (budget for $5 to $10) walking tours.

**Grouse Grind** (p183) gives access to the attractions atop Grouse Mountain via this free hiking route; it's $10 to get back down via the gondola, though.

### NEED TO KNOW

**Websites** Bored in Vancouver (www.boredinvancouver.com) has many suggestions for free events and activities.

**Discount Cards City Passport** (www.citypassports.com; $25) can be a good idea if you plan to visit many places.

**Happy Hour** Many bars and restaurants offer happy hour deals typically from 3pm to 6pm (often weekdays only).

BBQ teriyaki salmon

# Eating

Vancouver has an amazing array of generally great value dine-out options: top-drawer sushi joints, clamorous Chinese restaurants, inviting indie eateries, tempting food trucks and a fresh-picked farm-to-table scene are all on the menu. You don't have to be a local to indulge: just follow your tastebuds and dinner will become the most talked-about highlight of your Vancouver visit.

## NEED TO KNOW

### Price Ranges

The following prices are used in eating reviews:

**$** up to $15 per main dish

**$$** from $15 to $25 per main dish

**$$$** over $25 per main dish

### Opening Hours

➡ Restaurants generally open from 11:30am to 2pm for lunch and/or 5pm to 10pm (or later) for dinner.

➡ Breakfast is typically from 7am to 10am; later on weekends, when many places also serve brunch.

➡ Some restaurants close on Mondays in Vancouver, so check ahead before you leave your room.

### Reservations

Not every restaurant accepts reservations but call ahead for higher-end eateries. Many restos seat without bookings, especially for early dinners (from 5pm to 6pm). Note that Vancouver's restaurants dress code is generally relaxed; you'll spot jeans and fleeces at almost every dining level here.

### Taxes & Tipping

➡ GST (Goods & Services Tax) of 5% is added to restaurant bills for food.

➡ Alcohol attracts GST plus 10% PST (Provincial Sales Tax).

➡ Tipping is standard; typically it's 15% of the bill. Some restos add a tip automatically for large groups: check your bill carefully.

### Happy Hour

A recent rule change allowed Vancouver bars and restaurants to introduce happy-hour pricing. For restaurants, this typically means appetizer specials every afternoon, often between 3pm and 6pm. Locals have embraced the trend, with many eateries busier than ever at this time of the day.

### Seafood

One reason Vancouver has great sushi is the larder of top-table regional seafood

Dynamite roll sushi

available right off the boat. Given the length of British Columbia's coastline, it's no surprise most restaurants (whether Asian, Mexican, West Coast or French) find plenty of menu space for local goodies such as salmon, halibut, spot prawns and freshly shucked oysters. If you're a seafood fan, you'll be in your element; even fish and chips are typically excellent. Start your aquatic odyssey at Granville Island, where the Public Market has seafood vendors and Fisherman's Wharf is just along the seawall.

### Farm to Table

After decades of favoring imported ingredients over local, Vancouver now fully embraces regional food and farm producers. Restaurants can't wait to tell you about the Fraser Valley duck and foraged morels they've just discovered. Seasonal is key, and you'll see lots of local specials on menus; ask your server for insights. Adding to the feast, some restaurants showcase local cheese producers, and most have also taken their BC love affair to the drinks list: Okanagan wines have been a staple here for years but BC craft beer is the current darling of thirsty Vancouver locavores.

## Asian Smorgasbord

Vancouver is home to the best Asian dining scene outside Asia. From authentic sushi and ramen spots to Korean and Vietnamese street food and fine dining, as well as a richly varied Chinese scene that runs from dim sum to dragon's beard candy, you'll be spoilt for choice here. Adventurous foodies should dive into the local summer night-market scene for a full-on taste explosion.

## Street Food-a-Palooza

A late starter to the North American street-food movement, Vancouver now has the tastiest scene in Canada. The downtown core has the highest concentration of trucks. You'll find everything from Korean sliders to salmon tacos, Thai green curry to barbecued brisket sandwiches. A visit that doesn't include at least one street-food meal isn't really a visit at all. Catch as many trucks as you can at the annual summertime YVR Food Fest (www.yvrfoodfest.com).

## International Dining

You'd be forgiven for thinking Vancouver's ethnic cuisine scene begins and ends with Asia. In fact, locals know it's just the beginning. A city built on immigration, Vancouver's menu is a United Nations of dining options, from excellent Spanish and Italian eateries to highly popular Mexican joints. Follow the locals: they'll often lead you to unassuming family-run restaurants. Vancouver's dining is generally very reasonably priced, so this is a great city for trying something new.

## Farmers Markets

A tasty cornucopia of British Columbia (BC) farm produce hits Vancouver from May or June to September or October at more than half-a-dozen weekly farmers markets: a great way to stuff your face and meet the locals at the same time. Seasonal treats to look out for include crunchy apples, lush peaches and juicy blueberries, while home-baked cakes and treats are frequent accompaniments. Check locations and dates at www.eatlocal.org.

## Eating by Neighborhood

➡ **Downtown & West End** (p63) Food trucks and a full range of restaurants; many international midrange options in West End.

➡ **Gastown & Chinatown** (p82) Innovative independent eateries in Gastown; authentic Asian dining in Chinatown.

➡ **Yaletown & Granville Island** (p103) High-end restos in Yaletown; some good Granville Island seafood spots.

➡ **Commercial Drive** (p117) Brilliant neighborhood dining, with excellent patios.

➡ **Main Street** (p133) Quirky indie restaurants and neighborhood hangouts.

➡ **Fairview & South Granville** (p149) Fine dining and friendly neighborhood haunts.

➡ **Kitsilano & University of British Columbia (UBC)** (p170) Fine dining at midrange prices in Kits.

## Lonely Planet's Top Choices

**Vij's** (p152) Newly relocated, the city's favorite Indian restaurant.

**Ask for Luigi** (p86) Railtown charmer with delightful Italian dishes.

**Mr Red Cafe** (p170) Revelatory northern Vietnamse cuisine.

**Dock Lunch** (p135) Like dining in someone's house; food made with love.

**Forage** (p66) Showcase of farm-to-table West Coast dining.

**Fable Diner** (p136) Cool-ass reinvention of an old-school Mount Pleasant diner.

**Tacofino** (p83) West Coast taco hot spot in a great Gastown setting.

**Bistro 101** (p106) Great value prix-fixe lunches and dinners, prepared by celebrated cooking-school students.

**Bao Bei** (p88) Vibe-tastic contemporary Chinese bistro.

**Fish Counter** (p136) Vancouver's best fish and chips; prepare to queue.

## Best by Budget

### $

**Wakwak Burger** (p63) Great-value burger at downtown cart.

**Hawkers Delight** (p133) Heaping Malaysian street-food dishes.

### $$

**Dock Lunch** (p135) Homestyle dining among the Main St locals.

**Forage** (p66) Lip-smacking farm-to-table dishes.

### $$$

**Vij's** (p152) Elevated modern Indian cuisine.

**Chambar** (p65) Candlelit Belgian-influenced West Coast dining.

## Best Asian Dining

**Bao Bei** (p88) Supercool modern Chinese dining.

**Mr Red Cafe** (p170) Auethnic northern Vietnamese dishes.

**Phnom Penh** (p87) Taste-tripping Cambodian and Vietnamese dining.

**Hawkers Delight** (p133) Predominantly Malaysian street-food dishes.

**Maenam** (p172) Contemporary approach to Thai dining.

**Sushi Itoga** (p66) West End's freshest sushi spot

## Best Vegetarian

**Acorn** (p136) Cool modern veggie diner with a hipster vibe.

**Heirloom Vegetarian** (p152) Slick spot for a special dinner.

**MeeT in Gastown** (p85) Vegan comfort dishes in a chatty backstreet setting.

**Eternal Abundance** (p117) Hearty vegetarian and vegan dining and baked treats.

**Naam** (p173) Local vegetarian legend, open 24 hours.

**Vegan Pudding & Co** (p64) Delicious pudding cups from a downtown hole-in-the-wall.

## Best Breakfast

**Jam Cafe** (p65) Huge array of tempting breakfast and brunch dishes.

**Fable Diner** (p136) Modern reinvention of an old diner site, with top-notch fusion-esque menu.

**Cafe Medina** (p65) Amazing for waffles.

**Templeton** (p65) Diner joint with heaping breakfasts.

## Best Bakeries

**Purebread** (p83) Whistler's favorite treat purveyor with irresitable cakes and slices.

**Beaucoup Bakery & Cafe** (p152) Vancouver's best croissants and more.

**A Bread Affair** (p105) Brilliant bread and bakery treats on Granville island.

**Artisan Bake Shoppe** (p183) German-esque bakery with serious breads and strudel.

**Solly's Bagelry** (p149) Great bagels and traditional Jewish baked treats.

**Uprising Breads Bakery Cafe** (p117) Locals' loaf-loving favorite, just off Commercial Dr.

## Best Ice Cream

**Earnest Ice Cream** (p135) Heritage building setting for top-notch artisan ice cream.

**Rain or Shine** (p150) Purple-and-yellow-hued favorite with tons of great flavors.

**Bella Gelateria** (p67) Award-winning favorite, with line-ups to match.

## Best Happy-Hour Dining Deals

**Flying Pig** (p103) 4pm to 6pm daily.

**Tacofino** (p83) 3pm to 6pm daily.

**Jamjar** (p117) 4pm to 6pm daily.

**Reef** (p120) 9pm to close daily.

**Rodney's Oyster House** (p104) 3pm to 6pm Monday to Saturday.

## Best Romantic Dining

**L'Abattoir** (p86) Swish heritage-building setting with French-influenced fine dining.

**Picnix Al Fresco To Go** (p69) Order ahead for a perfectly prepared picnic in Stanley Park.

**Brix & Mortar** (p104) Large but intimate Yaletown restaurant with dual patios.

**Observatory** (p185) Grouse Mountain fine dining with views of the city below.

**Chambar** (p65) Candlelit redbrick restaurant with a warm and chatty vibe.

## Best Local Food Blogs

**Sherman's Food Adventures** (www.shermansfoodadventures.com)

**Vancouver Foodster** (www.vancouverfoodster.com)

**Food Gays** (www.foodgays.com)

**Van Foodies** (www.vanfoodies.com)

**Follow Me Foodie** (www.followmefoodie.com)

Dining outdoors at Granville Island

# 🍷 Drinking & Nightlife

*Vancouverites spend a lot of time drinking. And while British Columbia (BC) has a tasty wine sector and is undergoing an artisan distilling surge, it's the regional craft-beer scene that keeps many quaffers merry. For a night out with local-made libations as your side dish, join savvy drinkers supping in the bars of Gastown, on Main St and around Commercial Drive.*

## NEED TO KNOW

### Opening Hours

Pubs and bars serving lunch usually open before midday, with swankier operations waiting until 5pm. Most bars close sometime between 11pm and 2am, although some stay open to 4am. Nightclubs usually open at 9pm (although they don't really get going until 11pm) and most stay open until 3am or 4am.

### How Much?

➡ It's $5 to $8 for a large glass of beer here, but always ask about daily specials.

➡ A glass of wine costs anything over $7, cocktails up to $15.

➡ Your bill will include 10% Provincial Sales Tax (PST).

➡ Entry to clubs is $5 to $20, with weekends particularly expensive.

### Tipping

Table servers expect $1 per drink, or 15% when you're buying a round. Even if you order and pick up your beverage at the bar, consider dropping your change in the prominently placed tips glass.

Bellini

## Craft Beer

BC is Canada's craft-beer capital, with almost 200 beer producers dotted around the province, including dozens in Vancouver. You can plan an easy stroll (or stumble) around inviting clusters of microbrewery tasting rooms on and around Main St, as well as around the northern end of Commercial Dr. You'll also find bars around the city falling over themselves to showcase intriguing regional brews.

Ask your server what's local and/or seasonal on the draft list, and be sure to look out for favorite Vancouver-area beer makers including Four Winds, Brassneck, Powell Street, Central City and Main Street. For more information on the city's beery happenings, visit www.camravancouver.ca.

## Wine & Liquor

It's not just beer that's raised the bar recently in Vancouver. The city's drinking scene has improved immeasurably from the days when a badly made Manhattan was the height of sophistication. Grape-based quaffing kicked off the revolution, and several cool wine bars have popped up in recent years to satisfy thirsty oenophiles. Wine fans will now find plenty to crow about at bars around town. Cocktails are also impressing, with a selection of drinking joints, from traditional to quirky, joining the nightlife fray. Craft distilleries are the latest wave; look out for recently opened spots on your visit. And don't forget that the new happy-hour rules mean you can afford to be adventurous.

## Happening Happy Hours

One of the legacy laws that was recently repealed in this region was the one that banned happy hours in local bars. With the 2015 rule change, bars around the city now offer booze deals (typically from 3pm to 6pm on weekdays; sometimes on weekends as well). This usually means drinks reduced by a dollar or two. A tasty offshoot, though, has been the emergence of the restaurant happy hour, which has become wildly popular across the city. Time your visit well and you'll find great deals on appetisers or small plates, many of which are mentioned in the restaurant reviews in our neighborhood sections.

## Clubbing

While downtown's Granville Strip draws the barely clad booties of mainstream clubbers, there are other, less limelight-hogging areas catering to just about every peccadillo. Cover charges run from $5 to $20 ('the ladies' often get in free before

11pm) and dress codes are frequently smart-casual – ripped jeans and sportswear will not endear you to the bouncers who are just looking for people to send home. Bring ID: most clubs accept over-19s but some want you to be over 25. You can put yourself on the VIP list (no waiting, no cover) at the websites of individual clubs or via www.clubzone.com.

### Alternative Night Out

Pick up a copy of the free *Georgia Straight* weekly, the city's best listings newspaper, for additional night-out ideas. If you're stuck, consider the quarterly FUSE party night (p58) at the Vancouver Art Gallery; the monthly Green Drinks social mixer at Steamworks Brew Pub (p90); the pinball room at grungy Pub 340 (p92); Grandview Lanes bowling (p125) on Commercial Dr; playing board games at Storm Crow Alehouse (p155); or the delightful letter-writing club at the Regional Assembly of Text (p141).

## Drinking & Nightlife by Neighborhood

➡ **Downtown & West End** (p69) Granville Strip is lined with party-hard clubs and bars, while the West End's Davie St is gay nightlife central.

➡ **Gastown & Chinatown** (p88) Craft-beer taverns as well as indie bars and clubs.

➡ **Yaletown & Granville Island** (p106) Yaletown has some slick bars and a huge brewpub, while Granville Island is fine for pre-theater drinks.

➡ **Commercial Drive** (p120) Neighborhood pubs and old-school coffee bars abound; plus try the nearby 'Yeast Van' microbreweries.

➡ **Main Street** (p137) Where in-the-know hipsters drink at some of the city's best indie bars and microbrew tasting rooms.

PLAN YOUR TRIP DRINKING & NIGHTLIFE

Granville Island craft beer

## Lonely Planet's Top Choices

**Brassneck Brewery** (p137) Vancouver's favorite microbrewery tasting room.

**Storm Crow Alehouse** (p155) Large nerd pub with board games and sci-fi props on the walls.

**Alibi Room** (p88) Superb BC and beyond craft-beer selection wrapped in a friendly tavern vibe

**Brickhouse** (p92) Denlike locals' secret with eclectic decor.

**Shameful Tiki Room** (p137) Evocative, cavelike cocktail haunt.

**Callister Brewing Company** (p121) Adventurous operation shared by several nano-breweries.

**Narrow Lounge** (p138) Gemlike subterranean hideaway with secret back garden.

**Liberty Distillery** (p108) Craft liquor maker with a top tasting room.

**Whip** (p138) Neighborhood hangout where locals sup great BC beers.

**Cascade Room** (p139) Popular Mt Pleasant tavern with great food.

## Best Microbrewery Tasting Rooms

**Brassneck Brewery** (p137) Wood-lined tasting room with ever-changing beer line-up.

**Callister Brewing Company** (p121) Beer-making operation shared by several intriguing nano-breweries.

**Powell Street Craft Brewery** (p121) Popular producer with lively tasting room.

**Off the Rail** (p121) Upstairs tasting bar with a wide array of smooth libations.

**Main Street Brewing** (p138) Industrial chic room with top beer, including signature pilsner.

**Doan's Craft Brewing Company** (p121) Tiny, art-lined room with great vibe.

## Best Beer Bars

**Alibi Room** (p88) Vancouver's fave craft-beer tavern, with around 50 mostly BC drafts.

**Central City Brew Pub** (p106) Showcasing the beers of a celebrated regional producer, plus dozens of others

**Portland Craft** (p139) Main St bar with dozens of craft brews, mostly from the US.

**Devil's Elbow Ale & Smoke House** (p69) Top brews from Squamish's popular Howe Sound Brewing.

**St Augustine's** (p121) Sports-bar vibe with dozens of rare-for-Vancouver craft drafts.

**Whip** (p138) Laid-back neighborhood pub with good BC beer and a Sunday afternoon guest cask.

## Best Cocktail Joints

**Shameful Tiki Room** (p137) Windowless tiki-themed cave with strong concoctions.

**Liberty Distillery** (p108) Granville Island craft producer with a cool saloon-look bar.

**Diamond** (p89) Alluring upstairs room with perfect classic cocktails.

**Juniper** (p92) Gin flights and top-quality cocktails galore.

**Keefer Bar** (p92) Chinatown's fave lounge with great drinks and a cool-ass vibe.

## Best Bars for Live Music

**Guilt & Co** (p89) Subterranean bar with regular shows.

**Backstage Lounge** (p109) Granville Island bar hosting local bands.

**Uva Wine & Cocktail Bar** (p70) Live jazz on Saturday nights.

**Pat's Pub** (p93) Old-school bar with live jazz shows.

## Best Happy Hours

**Liberty Distillery** (p108) 3pm to 6pm Monday to Thursday.

**Uva Wine & Cocktail Bar** (p70) 2pm to 6pm daily.

**Cascade Room** (p139) 3pm to 6pm daily.

**Keefer Bar** (p92) 5pm to 7pm Sunday to Friday.

**Yaletown Brewing Company** (p108) 3pm to 6pm Sunday to Thursday.

## Best Bars for Food

**Irish Heather** (p90) Great place for sausage and mash with a pint of Guinness.

**Cascade Room** (p139) The Sunday roast is a local legend.

**Yaletown Brewing Company** (p108) Pizzas are the way to go at this popular Yaletown brewpub.

**Alibi Room** (p88) Don't miss the pork-belly sandwich.

**Whip** (p138) An enticing menu with plenty of gastropub flair.

# Entertainment

*You'll never run out of options if you're looking for a good time here. Vancouver is packed with activities from high- to lowbrow, perfect for those craving a play one night, a soccer match the next, and a rocking live music show to follow. Ask the locals for tips and they'll likely point out grassroots happenings you never knew existed.*

## Live Music

Superstar acts typically hit the stages at sports stadiums and downtown theaters (and with the big venue comes a big ticket price), while smaller indie bands crowd broom-closet-sized spaces at a rag-tag of local-fave venues around town. Local independent record stores will give you the lowdown on venues and Vancouver acts to catch; many of them also sell tickets to shows in the city. The scene here is not all about brooding indie bands: Vancouver has wide musical tastes and, with some digging, you'll find jazz, folk, classical and opera performances around the city, often with annual festivals to match.

## Film

While some independent movie theaters have closed in recent years, there are still plenty of places to catch blockbusters as well as a couple of downtown art-house cinemas for those who like subtitles rather than car chases: check out www.cinemaclock.com to see what's on while you're here. Visiting cinephiles will also be thrilled at the huge range of movie festivals. Consider the highly popular **Vancouver International Film Festival** (www.viff.org) in late September, as well as smaller film fests such as May's **DOXA Documentary Film Festival** (www.doxafestival.ca) and November's **Vancouver Asian Film Festival** (www.vaff.org).

## Theater

Vancouver has a long history of treading the boards. The **Arts Club Theatre Company** (604-687-1644; www.artsclub.com) is the city's leading troupe, with three stages dotted around Vancouver. Expect challenging shows and visiting companies at the Cultch (p124) and Firehall Arts Centre (p93). Depending on the time of your visit, catch January's **PuSh Festival** (www.pushfestival.ca; mid-Jan), September's Vancouver Fringe Festival (p109) or the summer-long Bard on the Beach (p175), where Shakespeare plays are performed in tents against a mountain backdrop.

## Entertainment by Neighborhood

⮕ **Downtown & West End** (p73) Home to top entertainment venues, from theaters to cinemas.

⮕ **Gastown & Chinatown** (p93) Location of several under-the-radar venues.

⮕ **Yaletown & Granville Island** (p109) The Island is a hotbed of theaters and festivals.

⮕ **Commercial Drive** (p124) Location of several locally loved performance spaces.

⮕ **Main Street** (p139) Home of some cool indie venues.

## NEED TO KNOW

### Costs

➡ Theater tickets typically start at $30.

➡ Cinema tickets start at $12, with matinees and Tuesday shows often cheaper.

➡ Live music shows are free or cheap in pubs and bars; from $30 in other live venues.

### Buying Tickets

➡ See www.ticketmaster.ca for live shows and events around Vancouver.

➡ See www.ticketstonight.ca for half-price deals available on the day.

### What's On?

➡ Pick up Thursday's freebie *Georgia Straight* (www.straight.com) for what's on in the week ahead.

➡ Head online to Live Van (www.livevan.com) for up-to-the-minute local gig listings.

## Lonely Planet's Top Choices

**Commodore Ballroom** (p73) Vancouver's fave band venue.

**Biltmore Cabaret** (p140) Great low-ceilinged spot to catch indie acts.

**Cultch** (p124) Brilliant theater space in a converted heritage building.

**Bard on the Beach** (p175) Shakespeare plays in waterfront tents.

**Pacific Cinémathèque** (p73) Art-house cinema.

## Best Live Music Venues

**Commodore** (p73) Springy-floored local legend.

**Biltmore Cabaret** (p140) Vancouver's favorite hipster venue.

**Rickshaw Theatre** (p93) Specializing in thrash and punk.

**Media Club** (p74) Local and visiting indie acts.

## Best Cinemas

**Pacific Cinémathèque** (p73) Long-established art-house cinema.

**Vancity Theatre** (p74) Slick downtown art-house cinema.

**Rio Theatre** (p124) Innovative independent cinema and live venue.

**Cineplex Odeon International Village Cinemas** (p94) Vancouver's favorite mainstream cinema venue.

**Cineplex Park Theatre** (p156) Screening classic movies and live theater broadcasts.

## Best Festivals

**Vancouver International Film Festival** (p35) Giant showcase for global movies.

**Vancouver Fringe Festival** (p109) Wacky shenanigans on Granville Island.

**Vancouver International Jazz Festival** (www.coastaljazz.ca) Massive array of shows, including many freebies.

**Bard on the Beach** (p175) Summer Shakespeare shows in a tented waterfront venue.

## Best Alternative Night Out Ideas

**Vancouver Poetry Slam** (p124) Commercial Drive fixture with a chance to perform your epic.

**Celluloid Social Club** (p140) Regular event where local movie-makers screen and discuss their work.

**Viva la Ukelucion** (p140) Monthly musical meet-up for ukulele fans.

**Bluegrass Jam Night** (p140) Regular music night for the bluegrass inclined.

**Jericho Folk Club** (p176) Long-running folkie night out.

## Best for Live Comedy

**Vancouver Theatresports League** (p111) Improv comedy troupe in a Granville Island theater.

**Hot Art Wet City** (p132) Regular comedy nights at this cool gallery.

**Yuk Yuk's Comedy Club** (p156) Traditional comedy venue with local and visiting stand-ups.

**Comedy Mix** (p75) Downtown stand-up live comedy club.

## Best Alternative Film Fests

**DOXA Documentary Film Festival** (www.doxafestival.ca)

**Vancouver Asian Film Festival** (www.vaff.org)

**Vancouver International Mountain Film Festival** (www.vimff.org)

**Vancouver Latin American Film Festival** (www.vlaff.org)

**Vancouver Queer Film Festival** (www.queerfilmfestival.ca)

Shopping on Commercial Drive

# Shopping

*Vancouver's retail scene has developed dramatically in recent years. Hit Robson St's mainstream chains, then discover the hip, independent shops of Gastown, Main St and Commercial Dr. Granville Island is stuffed with artsy stores and studios, while South Granville and Kitsilano's 4th Ave serve up a wide range of ever-tempting boutiques.*

### Independent Fashion

Vancouver has all the usual clothing chain suspects, but it also has a bulging shopping bag of independent stores with well-curated collections from local and international designers. Get off the beaten path to Main St and Commercial Dr for quirky vintage and artsy fashions. Or peruse the main drags of Gastown, South Granville and Kitsilano's 4th Ave for one-of-a-kind boutique gems. Keep your eyes peeled for pop-up shops and check the pages of *Vancouver* magazine and the *Georgia Straight* for retail happenings such as Gastown's 'shop hops' – seasonal evenings of late openings with a partylike vibe. Before you arrive, see Vancouver fashion blogs www. aliciafashionista.com and www.tovogueor-bust.com for the local lowdown.

### Arts & Crafts

The city's arts scene dovetails invitingly with its retail sector. There are dozens of intriguing private galleries, showcasing everything from contemporary Canadian art to authentic First Nations carvings and jewelry. Check out the Flats emerging gallery district just off Main St and the older gallery

## NEED TO KNOW

### Business Hours

Typical downtown retail hours are from 10am to 5pm or 6pm Monday to Saturday, and from noon to 5pm Sunday. Some stores and malls may stay open later on Fridays and Saturdays, especially during the Christmas season.

### Consumer Taxes

The price on most items in shops does not include tax, which is added when you take it to the cash register to pay. You will pay an extra 5% (GST) on most items, as well as an extra 7% (PST) on some.

Indigenous art

row on South Granville. There are also opportunities to buy art from indie galleries on Main and from the many artisan studios on Granville Island. In addition, there are dozens of arts and crafts fairs throughout the year – they're a great way to meet local producers and creative Vancouverites. Check local listings publications or www. gotcraft.com for upcoming events.

### Souvenirs

For decades, visitors to Vancouver have been returning home with suitcases full of maple-sugar cookies and vacuum-packed smoked salmon. You can still pick up these items, typically in the large souvenir stores lining the north side of Gastown's Water St. But it doesn't have to be this way. Consider consigning your Gastown-clock fridge magnet to the garbage and aiming for authentic First Nations art or silver jewelry; a book on Vancouver's eye-popping history (*Sensational Vancouver* by Eve Lazarus, for example); some delightful locally made pottery from Granville Island; or a quirky Vancouver-designed T-shirt from the fashion stores on Main St.

### Shop the Museums

The city's museums and galleries offer some unexpected buying opportunities. You don't have to see an exhibition to visit these shops, and keep in mind that you're helping to fund the institutions you're buying from. Perhaps the best of all the city's museum stores, the Museum of Anthropology (p164) shop has a fantastic array of First Nations and international

indigenous artworks, ranging from elegant silver jewelry to fascinating masks. Back downtown, the Vancouver Art Gallery (p57) gift shop is like a lifestyle store for artsy types, with clever contemporary knick-knacks and large art books to leave on your coffee table. And if you need to buy something cool for a kid back home, hit the Science World (p132) gift shop for all manner of intriguing educational goodies.

### Shopping by Neighborhood

➡ **Downtown & West End** (p73) Mainstream fashion boutiques on Robson St and in Pacific Centre mall.

➡ **Gastown & Chinatown** (p92) Independent fashion and homewares shops.

➡ **Yaletown & Granville Island** (p111) Swish boutiques in Yaletown; artisan studios on the island.

➡ **Commercial Drive** (p125) Eclectic fashions, vintage stores and hippy-esque shops.

➡ **Main Street** (p141) Local indie fashions, especially south of 18th Ave.

➡ **Fairview & South Granville** (p157) Independent stores on Cambie St; galleries and swish boutiques on South Granville.

➡ **Kitsilano & University of British Columbia (UBC)** (p176) Hit Kitsilano's West 4th Ave for boutiques and homewares.

## Lonely Planet's Top Choices

**Regional Assembly of Text** (p141) Creative stationery store with a little gallery nook.

**Mountain Equipment Co-op** (p141) Outdoor-gear and clothing megastore.

**Smoking Lily** (p142) Quirky fashions for the artistically minded.

**Neptoon Records** (p141) Old-school vinyl-hugging record shop.

**Paper Hound** (p75) Perfect little downtown used-book store.

**This Monkey's Gone to Heaven** (p142) Everything from taxidermy to critter-themed art.

**Eastside Flea** (p94) Regular used and vintage market on Main St.

**Urban Source** (p141) Favorite store of every hipster crafter in town.

**Erin Templeton** (p94) Bags and accessories made from recycled leather.

**Salmagundi West** (p94) Quirky array of used and new goods.

## Best Shopping Strips

**Main St** (p131)

**Commercial Dr** (p115)

**W 4th Ave** (p162)

**Water St** (p 79)

**Robson St** (p73)

## Best Vintage Shops

**Mintage** (p125) Perfectly curated array of classic old-school togs.

**Community Thrift & Vintage** (p94) Great selection of great vintage clothing.

**Attic Treasures** (p125) Vancouver's favorite mid-century antique store.

**Eastside Flea** (p94) New and used trinkets, crafts and clothes at this regular event.

**Front & Company** (p142) Hipster favorite with ironically cool used (plus new) clothing.

## Best Bookshops

**Paper Hound** (p75) Perfectly curated, mostly used, downtown bookstore.

**KidsBooks** (p176) Giant, child-focused bookshop.

**MacLeod's Books** (p75) Local legend crammed with teetering stacks of used tomes.

**Pulpfiction** (p142) Vancouver's favorite multibranch used-book store.

**Barbara-Jo's Books To Cooks** (p177) Recipe books and cuisine-related volumes.

## Best Record Shops

**Neptoon Records** (p141) Classic vinyl-focused store without hipster pretensions.

**Red Cat Records** (p142) Cool array of vinyl and CDs.

**Zulu Records** (p177) Giant vinyl selection in a *High Fidelity*–like setting.

**Sikora's Classical Records** (p75) Beloved downtown specialty music store.

**Audiopile** (p126) Well-priced new and used recordings, especially in the bargain racks.

## Best Outdoor Gear Stores

**Mountain Equipment Co-op** (p141) Western Canada's favorite outdoor gear department store.

**Arc'teryx** (p177) Top quality outerwear, made on the North Shore.

**Umbrella Shop** (p112) Near-legendary local umbrella maker.

**Sports Junkies** (p144) Great used gear and equipment.

**Tilley** (p177) Home of the famous Tilley travel hat.

## Best for Arts & Crafts

**Urban Source** (p141) Crafters' dream destination, crammed with possibility-triggering materials.

**Hot Art Wet City** (p132) Small gallery specializing in unusual well-priced artworks.

**Gallery of BC Ceramics** (p112) Excellent selection of locally made artisan pottery.

**Bird on a Wire Creations** (p143) Irresistible selection of artist-made goodies.

**Silk Weaving Studio** (p113) Beloved Granville Island pilgrimage spot for yarn fans.

## Best for Indie Designer Wear

**Smoking Lily** (p142) Cool clothes for the pale and interesting set.

**Oliver + Lilly's** (p158) Top togs for independent ladies.

**Lynn Steven Boutique** (p95) Select local and international designer gear.

**Barefoot Contessa** (p125) Classic vintage-influenced womenswear.

**John Fluevog Shoes** (p95) Funky footwear, designed in Vancouver.

# Sports & Activities

*Vancouver's variety of outdoorsy activities is a huge hook: you can ski in the morning and hit the beach in the afternoon; hike or bike scenic forests; windsurf along the coastline; or kayak to your heart's content – and it will be content, with grand mountain views as your backdrop. There's also a full menu of spectator sports to catch here.*

## Running

Vancouverites loves to jog. For heart-pounding runs (or even just a walk at arm-swinging speed), the 8.8km **Stanley Park Seawall** (📖19) is the city's number-one circuit. It's mostly flat, apart from a couple of uphill sections where you might want to hang onto a passing bike. The University of British Columbia (UBC) is another popular running destination, with tree-lined trails marked through Pacific Spirit Regional Park.

## Hiking

Hiking opportunities abound in local parks and Vancouverites are ever-keen to partake – especially on the infamous **Grouse Grind** (www.grousemountain.com; 📖236). Lighthouse Park and Whytecliff Park are also scenic gems with gentle trails to tramp around. If you're heading to any of the North Shore parks, be prepared for continually changing mountain conditions – the weather can alter suddenly here and a warm sunny day in the city might not mean it's going to be the same, or stay the same, in the mountains. For more information on area hiking trails, visit www.vancouvertrails.com.

## Cycling & Mountain Biking

Vancouver is a cycle-friendly city with a network of urban routes and a new public bike-share scheme. For maps and resources, see www.vancouver.ca/cycling. There's also a very active mountain-biking community on the North Shore; start your research via www.nsmba.ca and consider the forested runs at **Mt Seymour** (p182), including the 10km Seymour Valley Trailway. Good for first-timers, it has only a few uphills and offers great wilderness views – including the occasional deer.

## Skiing & Snowboarding

You'll find excellent alpine skiing and snowboarding areas as well as cross-country skiing trails less than 30 minutes from downtown – it's where you'll find most locals when the powder arrives. The season typically runs from late November to early April, and the main ski areas are **Grouse Mountain** (📞604-980-9311; www.grousemountain.com; 6400 Nancy Greene Way, North Vancouver; winter adult/child $58/25; ⊙9am-10pm mid-Nov–mid-Apr; 🚌; 📖236), **Cypress Mountain** (📞604-926-5612; www.cypressmountain.com; Cypress Bowl Rd, West Vancouver; lift ticket adult/youth/child $71/57/38; ⊙9am-10pm mid-Dec–Mar, 9am-4pm mid-Nov–mid-Dec & Apr) and Mt Seymour.

## Sports & Activities by Neighborhood

➡ **Downtown & West End** (p77) Adjoined by Stanley Park, Canada's favorite urban green space.

➡ **Kitsilano & University of British Columbia (UBC)** (178) Kits is the center of local watersports, along with beloved local beaches.

➡ **North Shore** (p186) A magnet for skiiers and snowboarders in winter plus hikers and mountainbikers in summer.

# Lonely Planet's Top Choices

**Stanley Park Seawall** (p54)
Breathtakingly scenic walking, jogging and cycling trail.

**Grouse Grind** (p183)Steep rite-of-passage hiking trail.

**Cypress Mountain** (p186)
Local-favorite ski and snowboard area.

**Ecomarine Paddlesport Centres** (p114) Perfect sunset paddling activity on False Creek.

**Mt Seymour** (p187) Ideal mountain-biking terrain.

## Best Places to Hike

**Grouse Grind** (p183)'Mother Nature's Stairmaster' is a steep climb to an attraction-packed lofty peak.

**Stanley Park** (p54) Swap the busy Seawall for the park's surfeit of tranquil interior trails.

**Mt Seymour** (p182) A verdant, sometimes steep climb with dramatic mountain and city vistas.

**Lighthouse Park** (p182) Transit-accessible North Shore trail through the forest to a craggy, picnic-friendly oceanfront.

**Lynn Canyon Park** (p182) Many great rainforest walks available, including the signature Baden Powell Trail.

# Best for Biking

**Mobi** (p244) New citywide public bike-share scheme.

**Cycle City Tours** (p246) Guided bike rides around Vancouver; rentals also available.

**Reckless Bike Stores** (p114) Popular bike-renting business, offering cruisers, mountain bikes and more.

**Spokes Bicycle Rentals** (p78) Kit out the family with various rental bikes; perfect for exploring nearby Stanley Park.

**Stanley Park Seawall** (p54) The city's favorite bike trail is 8.8km of forest and ocean delights.

**Pacific Spirit Regional Park** (p167) Tree-shaded trails in a nature-hugging 763-hectare park.

# Best Spectator Sports

**Vancouver Canucks** (p74) City's fave NHL hockey passion.

**BC Lions** (p111) Canadian Football League team, playing at BC Place.

**Vancouver Whitecaps** (p109) The city's MLS soccer team.

**Vancouver Canadians** (p156) Minor league fun at nostalgic old-school stadium.

## NEED TO KNOW

### Websites

➡ **Vancouver Parks & Recreation** (www.vancouver.ca/parks) Comprehensive listings and information on city facilities and green spaces.

➡ **Bike Hub** (www.bikehub.ca) Connect with the city's urban biking community.

➡ **MEC** (www.mec.ca) Gear and equipment rentals, plus area events and meet-ups.

➡ **Outdoor Vancouver** (www.outdoorvancouver.ca) Information on the local outdoorsy scene, including events and trail guides.

### Buying Tickets

Vancouver Cannucks hockey tickets are the hardest to snag; book far ahead via the team's website. It's easier – and cheaper to catch Whitecaps soccer matches or BC Lions Canadian football games, plus minor league Vancouver Canadians baseball. See individual team websites or Ticketmaster (www.ticketmaster.ca) for single tickets.

1. Grizzly bear 2. Kitsilano Beach Vancouver
3. Queen Elizabeth Park 4. Nitobe Memorial Garden at UBC

KEVIN MILLER/GETTY IMAGES ©

# 2 Vancouver Outdoors

Vancouver's sparkling natural setting is a key reason many visitors fall in love with this city. Plunge in at beaches, mountain promontories and perfect trails, both urban and on the city's tree-lined fringes.

## Beaches

You're never far from great beaches in Vancouver, such as the busy, sandy swathes of Kits Beach and English Bay Beach or more tranquil gems such as Stanley Park's Third Beach and rustic Spanish Banks. Consider a picnic and plan for a sunset vista.

## Grouse Mountain

It's hard not to take a deep breath when you step onto the smile-triggering summit of Grouse. Alpine trails, a grizzly bear refuge and some of the most spectacular natural views of the city shimming in the water far below will have you itching to click that camera.

## Queen Elizabeth Park

Stunning Stanley Park is hard to measure up to, but don't overlook these manicured gardens, jaw-dropping panoramic views of the city framed by mountains, and a tropical botanical garden teeming with beady-eyed, neon-hued birds.

## False Creek Seawall

Vancouver's shimmering waterfront has a spectacular seawall trail linking more than 20km of coastline, from downtown through Stanley Park and out to UBC. Don't miss the False Creek stretch; it's crammed with public art and water-to-city views.

## Parks & Gardens of UBC

Pacific Spirit Regional Park rivals Stanley Park for stature and tree-hugging glory but it's UBC's manicured green spaces that attract the crowds. From a symbolic traditional Japanese garden to the verdant themed areas of the huge Botanical Garden, green-thumbed visitors will have a ball here.

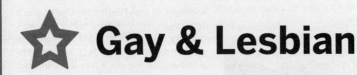 # Gay & Lesbian

*Vancouver's gay and lesbian scene is part of the city's culture rather than a subsection of it. The legalization of same-sex marriage here makes it a popular spot for those who want to tie the knot in scenic style. But if you just want to kick back and have a good time, this is also Canada's top gay-tastic party city.*

## West End

The West End's Davie St is the center of Vancouver's gay scene. Sometimes called the Gay Village, this is Canada's largest 'gayborhood' and is marked by rainbow flags, hand-holding locals and pink-painted bus shelters. There's a full menu of scene-specific pubs and bars, and it's a warm and welcoming district for everyone, gay or straight. Find the perfect spot sitting at a street-side cafe pretending to check your phone while actually checking out the passing talent; you can expect to make friends pretty quickly here. Vancouver's Commercial Dr is a traditional center of the lesbian scene. The city is highly gay-friendly, so you can expect events and happenings all around the city.

## Nightlife

You're unlikely to run out of places to hang with the locals in Vancouver's lively gay scene. Davie St, in particular, is home to a full bar-crawl of diverse gay-driven watering holes, from pubby haunts to slick lounge bars. You'll also find places to shake your thang on the dance floor here. But it's not all about the West End: look out for gay-friendly nights at clubs and bars around the city. Peruse some options at www.gayvancouver. net/nightlife.

## Pride Week

Showing how far the scene has progressed since the days when Vancouver's gay community was forced to stay in the closet, **Pride Week** (www.vancouverpride.ca) is now Canada's biggest annual gay celebration. Staged around the first week of August, the centerpiece is the parade – a huge street fiesta of disco-pumping floats, drum-beating marching bands and gyrating, barely clad locals dancing through the streets as if they've been waiting all year for the opportunity. In 2016 Justin Trudeau marched in the parade, becoming the first Canadian prime minister to do so. The parade is only the most visual evidence of Pride Week; this is also the time to dive into galas, drag contests, all-night parties and a popular queer film fest. Book your area hotel far in advance, since this is a highly popular event for visitors. During the same week, East Vancouver's annual Dyke March concludes with a festival and beer garden in Grandview Park on Commercial Dr.

## Gay & Lesbian by Neighborhood

➡ **Downtown & West End** (p50) West End's Davie St is Vancouver's gay scene central.

➡ **Commercial Drive** (p115) Traditional center of Vancouver's lesbian community.

## Lonely Planet's Top Choices

**Pride Week** Canada's best pride celebration, with a rocking street parade.

**Fountainhead Pub** (p73) Laid-back, beer-friendly gay community pub.

**1181** (p72) Smooth lounge bar; great spot to see and be seen.

**Little Sister's Book & Art Emporium** (p77) Long-time 'gayborhood' legend, stocking books and beyond.

## Best Gay Bars

**Fountainhead Pub** (p73) Popular community pub with a lively patio.

**Pumpjack Pub** (p73) Sometimes raucous spot, great for making new friends.

**1181** (p72) Smooth lounge bar with slick clientele.

## Best Places to Watch the Pride Parade

**Delany's Coffee House** (p73) Denman St coffee shop with street-side tables.

**Fountainhead Pub** (p73) From the patio, wolf-whistling the passing locals.

**Pumpjack Pub** (p73) Watch the show through the window.

**Vancouver Pride Society Float** Catch it all from the back of a float.

## Best Places to Recover After a Night Out

**Little Sister's Book & Art Emporium** (p77) Calm down and catch up on your reading.

**Delany's Coffee House** (p73) Grab a strong caffeine hit.

**Stanley Park Seawall** (p54) Blow away the cobwebs with a jog, bike or hangover-busting walk.

### NEED TO KNOW

➡ Check the online directory of the Gay & Lesbian Business Association of BC (www.loudbusiness.com) for all manner of local businesses, from dentists to spas and hotels.

➡ For local events and the inside track on the community, check www.gayvancouver.net and www.gayvan.com.

➡ Head to www.superdyke.com for insights on the local lesbian scene.

➡ For support and resources of all kinds, Qmunity (www.qmunity.ca) provides discussion groups, a health clinic and advice for lesbians, gays, bisexuals and the transgendered.

➡ Contact Vancouver Pride Society (www.vancouverpride.ca) for the latest info on the Pride festival.

PLAN YOUR TRIP GAY & LESBIAN

# Explore
# Vancouver

# VANCOUVER'S TOP SIGHTS

# Neighborhoods at a Glance

## 1 Downtown & West End p50

The heart of Vancouver occupies a jutting, ocean-fringed peninsula that's easily divided into three: the grid-pattern city center streets of shops, restaurants and businesses radiating from the intersection of Granville and West Georgia Sts; the well-maintained 1950s towers and dense residential side streets of the West End (also home to Vancouver's gay district); and Canada's finest urban green space, spectacular Stanley Park.

## 2 Gastown & Chinatown p79

The neighborhood where the city began, Gastown is Vancouver's cobbled old-town district. Rapidly transforming in recent years, its heritage buildings are now home to some of the city's best independent shops, bars and restaurants. Almost as old, historic Chinatown is one of Canada's largest and most vibrant and has recently begun gentrifying at an even faster rate.

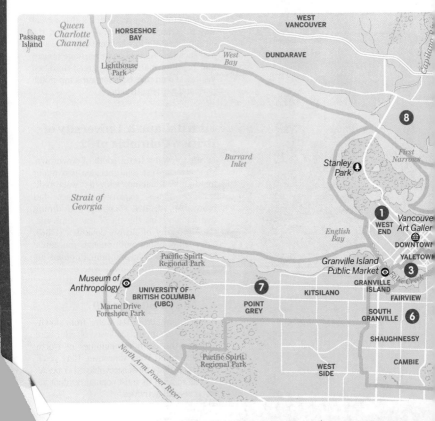

### ③ Yaletown & Granville Island p97

Straddling False Creek, these opposite shore-line neighborhoods exemplify Vancouver's development in recent decades. A former rail-yard and warehouse district on the edge of downtown, Yaletown is lined with chic restaurants and boutiques. Across the water, Granville Island was a grungy industrial area before being transformed in the 1970s into a haven of theaters, artisan studios and the best public market in Western Canada.

### ④ Commercial Drive p115

Colonized by European, mostly Italian, immigrants in the 1950s and by counter-culture types in the 1960s, this is one of the city's liveliest and most eclectic neighbor-hoods. Eschewing chains, the main drag is studded with quirky stores and coffee shops, each with their own distinctive but welcom-ing character. A great dining strip, it's also a short hop to Vancouver's (and perhaps Cana-da's) best microbrewery district.

### ⑤ Main Street p130

The skinny-jeaned heart of Vancouver's hip-ster scene, Main has become the city's cool-est 'hood, with many of its best independent cafes, shops, bars and restaurants. Expect lots of changes here; this area is developing rapidly. And that includes the Olympic Vil-lage, a waterfront neighborhood just around the False Creek corner from Science World that's continuing to add new places to eat and drink.

### ⑥ Fairview & South Granville p145

Combining the boutiques and restaurants of well-to-do South Granville with Fairview's busy Broadway thoroughfare and the cozy Cambie Village area, this Vancouver swath has something for everyone. It's also a great way to scratch beneath the surface of the city and meet the locals where they live, shop and socialize. As well as its heritage houses and bustling main streets, green-thumbed visitors should save time for some top-notch park and garden attractions.

### ⑦ Kitsilano & University of British Columbia p162

Across the water to the south of downtown, Vancouver's West Side includes two major highlights: Kitsilano, with its wood-built heritage homes, expansive beaches and browsable 4th Ave shopping and dining district; and, on the tip of the peninsula, the University of British Columbia (UBC), a verdant campus with enough museums, galleries, attractions and dining options for a great day out from downtown.

### ⑧ North Shore p179

A quick hop across the water from down-town, the mountain-shadowed North Shore includes the main communities of North Vancouver and West Vancouver. Here you'll find the region's most accessible ski slopes as well as some of its most popular outdoor at-tractions and activities.

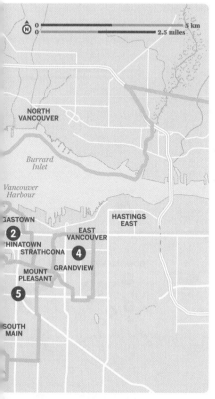

# Downtown & West End

## Neighborhood Top Five

**1 Stanley Park Seawall** (p54) Strolling or cycling the winding perimeter pathway for sigh-triggering views of the forest-fringed ocean, including a multi-hued Third Beach sunset.

**2 Vancouver Art Gallery** (p57) Rubbing shoulders with a crowd of arsty locals

at a partylike evening FUSE event.

**3 Commodore Ballroom** (p73) Catching a great show and bouncing on the famous dance floor at downtown's favorite live venue.

**4 Japadog** (p64) Scoffing a nori-topped Terimayo hot dog from one of the stands

or the ever-busy storefront location on Robson St.

**5 Theatre Under the Stars** (p74) Watching an energetic, smile-triggering musical on Stanley Park's outdoor stage, while the occasional heron flies over-head toward the water.

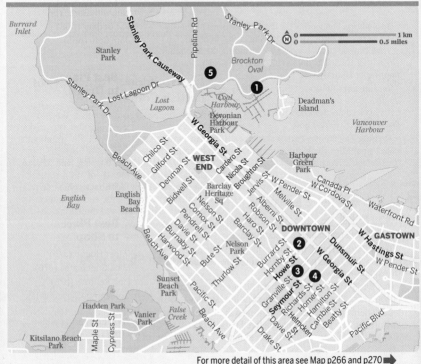

For more detail of this area see Map p266 and p270 ➡

# Explore Downtown & West End

Radiating from the intersection of Granville and Georgia Sts, Vancouver's downtown core is easily walkable. Consider starting a few blocks north on the waterfront at Canada Place heading slightly uphill, with the mountains at your back, along Burrard or Granville Sts. You'll pass plenty of stores and cafes before reaching Robson St, the city's main shopping promenade. Wander along for an hour or so (ducking into shops en route) before arriving at the intersection of Robson and Denman.

Explore the West End and its menu of midrange restaurants, side-street wooden heritage homes and the friendly 'gayborhood' vibe. Davie St is the West End's main strip, and both Denman and Davie Sts lead to English Bay Beach, one of Vancouver's most popular summer hangouts. From either end of Denman St, you can stroll into Stanley Park. Hitting the seawall here is the perfect way to commune with nature. It'll take you several hours to loop the entire park via this 8.8km pathway but there are a couple of ways to just dip your toes in: walk the seawall from Georgia St to the park's photogenic totem poles and back or take an easy nature-spotting stroll around Lost Lagoon where you'll almost certainly see raccoons, herons and possibly a sun-dappled turtle or two.

## Local Life

→**Bookshops** Hang out with local bookworms at the intersection of Richards and W Pender Sts, home to several browse-tastic bookstores, including the legendary old-school Macleod's Books (p75) and the nearby young pup, Paper Hound (p75).

→**Restaurants** Robson St is always lined with tourists, but locals are much more likely to be dining out at the better-priced neighborhood eateries on Denman and Davie Sts in the West End.

→**Jogging** The Stanley Park seawall (p54) is a vista-loving jogger's paradise. Avoid the summer crowds by hitting the trail early morning.

## Getting There & Away

→**Walk** Downtown's core is highly walkable with a grid street system that makes navigating easy.

→**Train** The SkyTrain's three lines meet at Waterfront Station while the Expo and Millenium Lines share tracks through downtown.

→**Bus** Bus 5 trundles along Robson St, bus 6 along Davie, bus 10 along Granville and bus 19 runs into Stanley Park.

→**Car** There are car parks and parking meters throughout downtown. The West End has metered parking and Stanley Park has pay-and-display parking.

## Lonely Planet's Top Tip

Downtown Vancouver is home to two art house cinemas and it's worth checking their eclectic schedules before you arrive. **Vancity Theatre** (p74) is the year-round home of the giant **Vancouver International Film Festival** (p35). But if you miss this 10-day late-September extravaganza, there's a full roster of movies throughout the year. The older but equally popular **Pacific Cinémathèque** (p73) is another film fans' fave; drop by in August for its film noir season when classic gritty flicks hit the big screen.

### Best Places to Eat

→ Forage (p66)
→ Royal Dinette (p64)
→ Guu with Garlic (p67)
→ Fat Badger (p68)
→ Jam Cafe (p65)

### Best Places to Drink

→ Uva Wine & Cocktail Bar (p70)
→ Devil's Elbow Ale & Smoke House (p69)
→ Stanley's Bar & Grill (p72)
→ 1181 (p72)
→ TAP Shack (p72)

### Best Places to Shop

→ Paper Hound (p75)
→ Mink Chocolates (p76)
→ Holt Renfrew (p76)
→ Golden Age Collectables (p76)
→ West End Farmers Market (p77)

# Stanley Park

## A HALF-DAY TOUR

It's easy to be overwhelmed by Stanley Park, one of North America's largest urban green spaces. But there are ways to explore this spectacular waterfront swathe – from its top sites to hidden gems – without popping any blisters.

From the Georgia St entrance, trace the seawall around the shoreline to Brockton Point's **totem poles** ❶. An early arrival means getting some snaps of these brightly painted carvings without fighting crowds.

From here, continue along the seawall. You'll pass a squat, striped lighthouse before reaching the Lumberman's Arch area. Duck under the road bridge and plunge into the park's tree-lined heart. Just ahead is **Vancouver Aquarium** ❷, the park's most popular attraction.

Next up, follow the path to the **Stanley Park Train** ❸. If you have kids in tow, take them for a trundle on this replica of the locomotive that pulled the first transcontinental passenger train into Vancouver.

From here, follow Pipeline Rd to the Tudoresque pavilion a few minutes away. In front is the **Malkin Bowl** ❹, a hidden outdoor theater. Poke around the nearby manicured gardens, then continue southwards to Lost Lagoon. Follow the shoreline clockwise to **Stanley Park Nature House** ❺, where you can learn about the park's flora and fauna.

Continue to the lagoon's western tip, then head to the ocean front ahead. Now on the park's rugged western side, follow the seawall northbound to **Third Beach** ❻. Find a log perch and prepare for Vancouver's best sunset.

### TOP TIPS

» When cycling the seawall, keep in mind that wheeled traffic is one-way only.

» The park is home to raccoons. Take pictures, but don't feed them.

» There are restaurants in the park if you're peckish.

» The meadow near Lumberman's Arch is a top picnic spot.

STUART DEE/GETTY IMAGES ©

**Third Beach**
Second Beach gets the crowds but Third Beach is where the savvy locals head. This is the perfect spot to drink in a sunset panorama over the lapping Pacific Ocean shoreline.

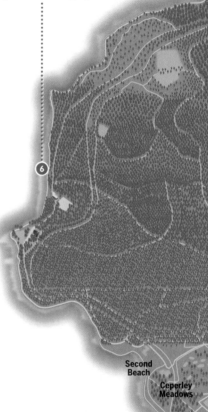

⑥

**Second Beach**

**Ceperley Meadows**

MARC STULKEN/SHUTTERSTOCK ©

**Stanley Park Nature House**
The freshwater Lost Lagoon was created when the Stanley Park Causeway was built. Its shoreline Nature House illuminates the park's plant and animal life and runs guided walks.

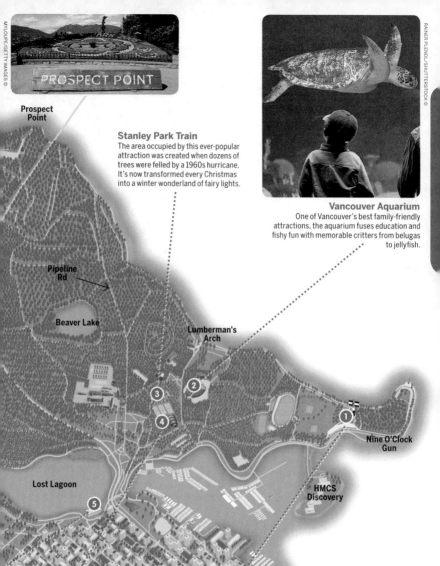

PROSPECT POINT

**Prospect Point**

**Stanley Park Train**
The area occupied by this ever-popular attraction was created when dozens of trees were felled by a 1960s hurricane. It's now transformed every Christmas into a winter wonderland of fairy lights.

**Vancouver Aquarium**
One of Vancouver's best family-friendly attractions, the aquarium fuses education and fishy fun with memorable critters from belugas to jellyfish.

**Pipeline Rd**

**Beaver Lake**

**Lumberman's Arch**

③

②

④

①

**Nine O'Clock Gun**

**Lost Lagoon**

⑤

**HMCS Discovery**

**Malkin Bowl**
Built by Vancouver mayor WH Malkin, this alfresco theater replaced an original bandstand. At the back of the seating area, you'll find a memorial statue to US president WG Harding.

**Totem Poles**
First Nations residents were still living here when Stanley Park was designated in 1888, but these poles were installed much later. The current poles are replicas of 1920s originals, carved in the 1980s.

*ALEXANDER HOWARD/LONELY PLANET ©*

# STANLEY PARK

One of North America's largest urban green spaces, Stanley Park is revered for its dramatic forest-and-mountain oceanfront views. But there's more to this 400-hectare woodland than looks. The park is studded with nature-hugging trails, family-friendly attractions, sunset-loving beaches and tasty places to eat. There's also the occasional unexpected sight to search for (besides the raccoons that call the place home).

## Seawall

Built in stages between 1917 and 1980, the park's 8.8km **seawall** (Map p287; 🚌19) trail is Vancouver's favorite outdoor hangout. Encircling the park, it offers spectacular waterfront vistas on one side and dense forest on the other. You can walk the whole thing in roughly three hours or rent a bike to cover the route far faster. Keep in mind: cyclists and in-line skaters must travel counterclockwise on the seawall, so there's no going back once you start your trundle. Also consider following the 24km of trails that crisscross the park's interior, including Siwash Rock Trail, Rawlings Trail and the popular Beaver Lake Trail (some routes are for foot traffic only). The Beaver Lake route is especially recommended; a family of beavers currently resides there and you'll likely spot them swimming around their large den.

The seawall also delivers you to some of the park's top highlights. You'll pass alongside the stately **HMCS Discovery** (Map p287; 1200 Stanley Park Dr, Stanley Park; 🚌19) naval station and a twee **cricket pavilion** (Map p287; Brockton Oval, Stanley Park; 🚌19) that looks like an interloper from Victorian England. About 1.5km from the W Georgia St entrance, you'll come to the ever-popular **totem poles** (Map p287; Brockton Point, Stanley Park; 🚌19). Remnants of an abandoned 1930s plan to create a First Nations 'theme village,' the bright-painted poles were joined by the addition of three exquisitely carved

## DON'T MISS

➡ Seawall
➡ Lost Lagoon
➡ Stanley Park Nature House
➡ Vancouver Aquarium
➡ Third Beach

## PRACTICALITIES

➡ Map p287, B2
➡ 🅿 ♿
➡ 🚌19

Coast Salish welcome arches a few years back. For the full First Nations story, consider a fascinating guided park walk with Talaysay Tours (p246).

Once you've taken your photos of the totems, continue on to the nearby **Nine O'Clock Gun** (Map p287; Seawall, Stanley Park; 🚍19) (it fires at 9pm every night) and **Lumberman's Arch** (Map p287; Seawall, Stanley Park; 🚍19), which is a good spot to see Alaska cruise ships sliding past. From here, you can cut into the park to the Vancouver Aquarium or continue around the seawall; it gets wilder and more scenic from here as you pass under the Lions Gate Bridge and face down the Pacific Ocean.

## Natural Attractions

You don't have to be a child to enjoy Stanley Park's signature attraction. The **Vancouver Aquarium** (Map p287; ☎604-659-3400; www.vanaqua.org; 845 Avison Way; adult/child $31/22; ⊙9:30am-6pm Jul & Aug, 10am-5pm Sep-Jun; 🚻; 🚍19) combines exotic marine species with re-created local seascapes. Home to 9000 water-loving critters – including sharks, wolf eels, beluga whales and a somewhat shy octopus – it also has a small, walk-through rainforest of birds, turtles and a statue-still sloth. Also check out the mesmerizing iridescent jellyfish, and peruse the schedule for feeding times: there's almost always one hungry animal or another waiting for its dinner. If you're traveling with someone who really loves marine animals, consider an Animal Encounter tour (from $35). They'll get close to their chosen mammal and learn all about being a trainer: the sea otter encounter is recommended if you want to learn why they eat while lying on their backs, using their stomachs as dinner plates (always the best way to dine).

The aquarium isn't Stanley Park's only hot spot for flora and fauna fans. A few steps from the park's W Georgia St entrance lies **Lost Lagoon** (Map p287; 🚍19), which was originally part of Coal Harbour. After a causeway was built in 1916, the new body of water was renamed, transforming itself into a freshwater lake a few years later. Today it's a bird-beloved nature sanctuary – keep your eyes peeled for blue herons – and its perimeter pathway is a favored stroll for wildlife nuts. The **Stanley Park Nature House** (Map p287; ☎604-257-8544; www.stanleyparkecology.ca; north end of Alberni St, Lost Lagoon; ⊙10am-5pm Tue-Sun Jul & Aug, 10am-4pm Sat & Sun Sep-Jun; 🚻; 🚍19) FREE here has exhibits on the park's wildlife, history and ecology – ask about the fascinating and well-priced guided walks.

**DOWNTOWN & WEST END** STANLEY PARK

## PARK TIPS

It typically takes around three hours to walk the 8.8km Stanley Park seawall, but bike rentals are also available at nearby Denman St stores.

In summer, the seawall is packed with visitors; arrive early morning or early evening if tranquil nature-communing is your bag.

There are often summertime queues to enter the Vancouver Aquarium; try to make it one of your first stops when you arrive at the park.

There are several restaurants here but this is the perfect destination for picnicking: book a pre-packed alfresco lunch or dinner via Picnix (p69) and consider the grassy meadow area near Lumberman's Arch.

**The only person to be legally buried in Stanley Park is writer Pauline Johnson. A champion of First Nations culture, her book on Coast Salish legends was a bestseller. When she died in 1913, thousands of locals lined the streets to mark her passing. Her memorial is a few steps from the seawall's Siwash Rock landmark.**

## Beaches & Views

If it's sandy beaches you're after, the park has several alluring options. **Second Beach** is a family-friendly area on the park's western side, with a grassy playground, an ice cream-serving concession, and a huge outdoor swimming pool (p77). It's also close to **Ceperley Meadows**, where **Fresh Air Cinema** (www.freshaircinema.ca) FREE offers wildly popular free outdoor movie screenings in summer. But for a little more tranquility, try **Third Beach**. A sandy expanse with plenty of logs to sit against, this is a favored summer-evening destination for Vancouverites. The sky often comes alive with pyrotechnic color, while chilled-out locals munch through their picnics.

There's a plethora of additional vistas in the park, but perhaps the most popular is at **Prospect Point.** One of Vancouver's best lookouts, this lofty spot is located at the park's northern tip. In summer you'll be jostling for elbow room with tour parties; heading down the steep stairs to the viewing platform usually shakes them off. Also look out for scavenging raccoons here (don't pet them). The area's Prospect Point Cafe (p69) offers refreshments – aim for a deck table.

## For Kids

It doesn't take much to plan an entire day with children here. As well as the aquarium and the Nature House, there are a couple of additional must-dos for under-10s. Look out for the large **waterpark** (Map p287; Seawall, Stanley Park; 🚌19) FREE overlooking the waterfront near Lumberman's Arch. There's also a playground here. Dry the kids off with a trundle on the **Stanley Park Train** (Map p287; ☏604-257-8531; adult/child $6/4.75; ⏱10am-5pm mid-Jun–Aug, 10am-4pm Sat & Sun Apr & May, plus Easter, Halloween & Christmas; 🚼; 🚌19); just a short stroll from the aquarium, this popular replica of the first passenger train that rolled into Vancouver in 1887 is a firm family favorite. The ride assumes several additional incarnations during the year: at Halloween, it's dressed up for ghost fans; and from late November it becomes a Christmas-decorated theme ride that's the city's most popular family-friendly Yuletide activity.

If it's still light when you're leaving the park, visit the man behind the fun day you've just had. Take the ramp running parallel with the seawall near the W Georgia St entrance and you'll find an almost-hidden **statue of Lord Stanley** (Map p287; Stanley Park; 🚌19) with his arms outstretched, nestled in the trees. On his plinth are the words he used at the park's 1889 dedication ceremony: 'To the use and enjoyment of people of all colors, creeds and customs for all time.' It's a sentiment that still resonates loudly here today.

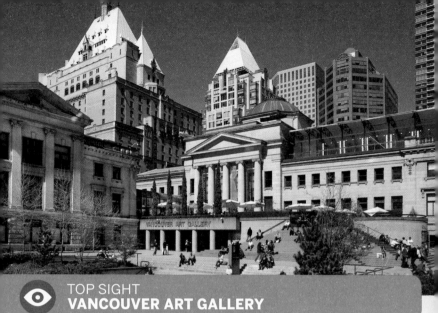

## TOP SIGHT
# VANCOUVER ART GALLERY

**Colonizing a heritage courthouse building, but aiming for a fancy new venue in the coming years, the VAG is the region's most important art gallery. Transforming itself in recent decades, it's also a vital part of the city's cultural scene. Contemporary exhibitions – often showcasing the Vancouver School of renowned photoconceptualists – are combined with blockbuster traveling shows from around the world.**

## VAG 101

Before you arrive at the VAG check online for details of the latest exhibition: the biggest shows of the year here are typically in summer and it's often a good idea to arrive early or late in the day to avoid the crush, especially at the beginning or end of an exhibition's run. But the VAG isn't just about blockbusters. If you have time, explore this landmark gallery's other offerings. Start on the top floor, where British Columbia's most famous painter is often showcased. Emily Carr (1871–1945) is celebrated for her swirling, nature-inspired paintings of regional landscapes and First Nations culture. Watercolors were her main approach, and the gallery has a large collection of her works.

The city's more recent contribution to art is conceptual and postconceptual photography – usually referred to jointly as photoconceptualism. As you work your way around the gallery, you'll likely spot more than a few examples of works in this genre by the Vancouver School, a group of local photo artists from the 1980s onwards who have achieved national and international recognition. These include Roy Arden, Rodney Graham, Stan Douglas and – the most famous of the bunch – Jeff Wall. The best way to learn about these artists and others on display at the gallery is to take a free guided tour: these are

### DON'T MISS

➡ Gallery tours
➡ FUSE
➡ Emily Carr paintings
➡ Gallery Café
➡ Gallery shop

### PRACTICALITIES

➡ VAG
➡ Map p266, E3
➡ ☎604-662-4700
➡ www.vanartgallery.bc.ca
➡ 750 Hornby St
➡ adult/child $20/6
➡ ⏰10am-5pm Wed-Mon, to 9pm Tue
➡ 🚌5

## GALLERY TIPS

If you're visiting in winter, you'll find the VAG's standard ticket prices reduced by a few dollars.

You can save on admission any time of the year on Tuesday evenings between 5pm and 9pm, when entry is by donation.

Seniors can also partake of by donation entry on the first Monday of every month between 10am and 1pm.

Check the VAG online calendar for in-depth curator tours; these are free with admission.

**With its columns and Trafalgar Sq–style lions, the handsome old 1907 gallery building was originally the Provincial Law Court. It was designed by Francis Rattenbury, who was responsible for many of the Colonial-era buildings that still exist in the towns and cities of British Columbia. His most famous constructions are in Victoria, the provincial capital, where the twin landmarks of the Parliament Buildings and the Empress Hotel still loom over the Inner Harbour – and most local postcards.**

usually held throughout the day on Thursdays, Saturdays and Sundays (especially in summer).

## Join the Locals

The gallery isn't just a place to geek out over cool art. In fact, locals treat it as an important part of their social calendar. Every few months, the VAG stages its regular **FUSE** (Map p266; ☎604-662-4700; www.vanartgallery.bc.ca/fuse; Vancouver Art Gallery; $24; ⊙8pm-midnight; 🚌5) socials, which transform the domed heritage venue into a highly popular evening event with DJs, bars, live performances and quirky gallery tours. Vancouverites dress up and treat the event as one of the highlights of the city's art scene; expect a clubby vibe to pervade proceedings. Take the chance to hang out with local chin-scratching creative types letting their hair down. You'll likely see some of the same crowd at the gallery's regular roster of lectures and art talks. There are also family FUSE events where arty kids can have some fun, usually with plenty of interactive shenanigans.

The Gallery Café (p64) is also one of downtown's most popular hangouts. Boasting the largest patio in the area, this cafe is the perfect spot to drink in the downtown vibe, even if you're not visiting an exhibition. On your way out, pop into the gallery shop: it's crammed with cool gadgets and artsy trinkets (and has a great collection of art books and cards).

## New Gallery

The VAG has been complaining about the limitations of its heritage building venue for many years and plans have recently been announced for a new and far larger purpose-built art museum a few blocks away on W Georgia St. At time of research, the architect-designed plans resembled a dramatic array of wooden blocks piled on top of each other in what will certainly be one of the city's most striking contemporary structures. Although it may be several years before a new gallery opens, a feverish fundraising drive has been under way for some time and the construction project is expected to break ground sometime in 2017. Check the VAG's website for the latest updates. And also mull the future of the existing gallery building, which many locals believe should become a new home for Vanier Park's Museum of Vancouver.

#  SIGHTS

You can easily spend a whole day exploring the attractions and natural sights of Stanley Park. But the downtown core and the West End have their own appeal, including art galleries, historic buildings and bustling main streets that are the city's de facto promenades.

# Downtown

**VANCOUVER ART GALLERY**     GALLERY

See p57.

**CANADA PLACE**     LANDMARK

Map p266 (☑604-775-7063; www.canadaplace.ca; 999 Canada Place Way; ℙ; ⑤Waterfront) Vancouver's version of the Sydney Opera House, judging by the number of postcards it appears on, this iconic landmark is shaped like sails jutting into the sky over the harbor. Both a cruise-ship terminal and convention center (next door's grass-roofed expansion opened in 2010), it's also a strollworthy pier, providing photogenic views of the North Shore mountains and some busy floatplane action.

Inside and outside the buildings, there are patriotic reminders of Canada's history and culture, from totem poles (inside) to the Canadian Trail (outside), a walking route illuminating the nation's 13 provinces and territories. If you have time, search for the pedestrian tunnel connecting the building to Waterfront Centre; it's lined with highly evocative large-format photos of yesteryear Vancouver. Here for July 1's Canada Day? This is the center of the city's festivities, with a day-long party of live music, faces painted with maple leaves and a fireworks finale around 10pm.

**MARINE BUILDING**     HISTORIC BUILDING

Map p266 (355 Burrard St; ⑤Burrard) Vancouver's most romantic old-school tower block, and also its best art deco building, the elegant 22-story Marine Building is a tribute to the city's maritime past. Check out the elaborate exterior of seahorses, lobsters and streamlined ships, then nip into the lobby where it's like a walk-through artwork. Stained-glass panels and a polished floor inlaid with signs of the zodiac await.

You should also peruse the inlaid wood interiors of the brass-doored elevators. The Marine Building was the tallest building in the British Empire when completed in 1930 and it's said to have bankrupted its original owners. It now houses offices.

**BILL REID GALLERY OF NORTHWEST COAST ART**     GALLERY

Map p266 (☑604-682-3455; www.billreidgallery.ca; 639 Hornby St; adult/child $10/5; ⊙11am-5pm mid-May–Sep, 11am-5pm Wed-Sun Oct–mid-May; ⑤Burrard) Showcasing carvings, paintings and jewelry from Canada's most revered Haida artist and many others, this tranquil gallery is lined with fascinating and exquisite works – plus handy touch-screens to tell you all about them. The space centres on the Great Hall, where there's often a carver at work. Be sure to also hit the mezzanine level: you'll come face to face with an 8.5m-long bronze of intertwined magical creatures, complete with impressively long tongues.

The gallery offers a comprehensive intro to the creative vision of Reid and his Haida co-creators, and also hosts occasional artist talks – especially when there's a new exhibition – that bring the works to life.

**CHRIST CHURCH CATHEDRAL**     CATHEDRAL

Map p266 (☑604-682-3848; www.thecathedral.ca; 690 Burrard St; ⊙10am-4pm; ⑤Burrard) Completed in 1895 and designated as a cathedral in 1929, the city's most attractive Gothic-style church is nestled incongruously alongside looming glass towers. It's home to a wide range of cultural events, including regular choir and chamber music recitals and the occasional Shakespeare reading. The roof was being replaced and a new stained-glass-accented bell tower was being added on our visit.

Peruse the kaleidoscopic array of stained-glass windows inside the cathedral as well. If you're short on time, head straight to the basement for a colorful, curlicue-patterned stained-glass window created by William Morris & Co. Save time to check out the church's dramatic hammerbeam ceiling, a rare construction that survived latter attempts to modernize it.

**FLYOVER CANADA**     THEATER

Map p266 (☑604-620-8455; www.flyovercanada.com; 999 Canada Pl; adult/child $22/14; ⊙10am-9pm, reduced hours in winter; ♿; ⑤Waterfront) Canada's Place's newest attraction, this breathtaking movie-screen simulator ride makes you feel as if you're swooping across the entire country, waggling your legs over grand landscapes and city landmarks from

**LOCAL KNOWLEDGE**

## HIDDEN ARTWORKS

Enter the lobby of the **RBC Royal Bank** (Map p266; ☑604-665-6991; www.rbcroyal
bank.com; 1025 W Georgia St; ⊘9am-5pm Mon-Fri; Ⓢ Burrard) at the corner of W Georgia
and Burrard Sts, and head up in the escalator that's directly in front of you. At the
top you'll find one of the largest First Nations artworks in western Canada. Measur-
ing 30m long and 2.5m high, the nine carved and painted red cedar panels of the
spectacular 'Ksan Mural dramatically cover an entire wall of the building. It took five
carvers three months to create in 1972, and it tells the story of Weget (or Man-Raven)
and his often mischievous exploits. Well worth a look, the artwork seems a world away
from the bustling streets outside. Continue your art crawl at the nearby **Vancouver
Art Gallery's offsite location** (Map p266; www.vanartgallery.bc.ca; 11 W Georgia St;
Ⓢ Burrard) FREE , a public art installation next to the Shangri-La Hotel that's changed
twice a year and is well worth a selfie or two.

coast to coast. En route, your seat will lurch,
your face will be sprayed and you'll likely
have a big smile on your face. And once the
short ride is over, you'll want to do it all again.

### JACK POOLE PLAZA                          PLAZA
Map p266 (Canada Pl; Ⓢ Waterfront) The
heart of Vancouver's 2010 Olympic Games
hosting duties, this handsome waterfront
public space is the permanent home of the
tripod-like Olympic Cauldron. The flame is
lit for special occasions (you can pay $5000
to have it switched on if you like). The plaza
offers great views of the mountain-backed
Burrard Inlet, and you can follow the shoreline walking trail around the Convention
Center West Building for public artworks
and historic plaques.

### VANCOUVER PUBLIC LIBRARY            LIBRARY
Map p266 (☑604-331-3603; www.vpl.ca; 350
W Georgia St; ⊘10am-9pm Mon-Thu, to 6pm
Fri & Sat, 11am-6pm Sun; ⓅⓇ⚐; Ⓢ Stadium-
Chinatown) This dramatic, Colosseum-like
building must be a temple to the great god
of libraries. If not, it's certainly one of the
world's most magnificent book-lending
facilities. Designed by Moshe Safdie and
opened in 1995, it contains 1.2 million
books and other items spread out over seven
levels, all of them seemingly populated by
language students silently learning English
from textbooks (and messaging each other).
There's free wi-fi available on-site, plus
computer terminals if you don't have your
laptop. The library hosts a lively roster of
free book readings and literary events. If
you're traveling with kids, the downstairs
children's section is an ideal hangout. Plans
were also being finalized on our visit to open

the library's rooftop garden and add a cafe
for visitors – ask at the front desk (quietly).

### ROGERS ARENA                         STADIUM
Map p266 (☑604-899-7400; www.rogersarena.
ca; 800 Griffiths Way; tours adult/child $12/6;
⊘tours 10:30am, noon & 1:30pm Wed-Sat, plus
Sun in summer; Ⓟ; Ⓢ Stadium-Chinatown) This
large multipurpose stadium hosts the National Hockey League's Vancouver Canucks.
On game nights, when the 20,000-capacity
venue heaves with fervent fans, you'll enjoy
the atmosphere even if the rules are a mys-
tery. It's also home to a large Canucks team
shop and is a favored arena for money-spin-
ning stadium rock acts. Behind-the-scenes
tours (75 minutes) take you into the hospi-
tality suites and the nosebleed press box up
in the rafters, and are popular with visiting
sports fans.

### VANCOUVER LOOKOUT                   VIEWPOINT
Map p266 (☑604-689-0421; www.vancouver-
lookout.com; 555 W Hastings St; adult/child
$16.25/8.25; ⊘8:30am-10:30pm mid-May–Sep,
9am-9pm Oct–mid-May; Ⓟ; Ⓢ Waterfront) Expect your lurching stomach to make a bid
for freedom as the glass elevator whisks you
169m to the apex of this needle-like viewing tower. Once up top, there's not much to
do but check out the awesome 360-degree
vistas of city, sea and mountains unfurling
around you. For context, peruse the historic
photo panels that show just how much the
downtown core has changed over the years.

### CONTEMPORARY ART GALLERY            GALLERY
Map p266 (☑604-681-2700; www.contemporar
yartgallery.ca; 555 Nelson St; suggested donation $5; ⊘noon-6pm Tue-Sun; ⊜10) Originally
the Greater Vancouver Artists' Gallery, this

small, off-the-beaten-path art space transformed itself into an independent gallery in 1996 and moved to a crisp, purpose-built facility a few years later. The gallery focuses on a wide range of modern art, and photography is particularly well represented here. Exhibitions are ever-changing and include local and international artists. Check the gallery's website for events and openings.

**PENDULUM GALLERY**     GALLERY

Map p266 (604-250-9682; www.pendulum gallery.bc.ca; HSBC Building, 885 W Georgia St; 9am-6pm Mon-Wed, to 9pm Thu & Fri, to 5pm Sat; Burrard) FREE A creative use for a cavernous bank building atrium, this gallery offers a varied roster of temporary exhibitions. It's mostly contemporary art and can range from striking paintings to challenging photographs and quirky arts and crafts. The space also houses one permanent exhibit: a gargantuan 27m-long buffed aluminum pendulum that will be swinging over your head throughout your visit.

# West End

**STANLEY PARK**     PARK
See p54.

**ENGLISH BAY BEACH**     BEACH
Map p270 (cnr Denman St & Beach Ave; 5) Wandering south on Denman St, you'll spot a clutch of palm trees ahead announcing one of Canada's best urban beaches. Then you'll see Vancouver's most popular public artwork (see below). There's a party atmosphere here in summer as locals catch rays and panoramic ocean views...or just ogle the volleyballers prancing around on the sand.

Be sure to snap a few photos of the beach's towering *inukshuk* (Inuit sculpture), south of the main area, or just continue along

the seawall into neighboring Stanley Park. The beach is a popular (but crowded) spot to catch the annual Celebration of Light (p22) fireworks festival, and it's also where the city's annual, wildly popular Polar Bear Swim takes place on January 1.

**ROEDDE HOUSE MUSEUM**     MUSEUM

Map p270 (604-684-7040; www.roeddehouse. org; 1415 Barclay St; $5; 11am-4pm Tue-Sat, 1-4pm Sun, reduced hours in winter; 5) For a glimpse of what the West End looked like before the apartment blocks arrived, drop by this handsome 1893 Queen Anne–style mansion, now a lovingly preserved museum. Designed by infamous British Columbia architect Francis Rattenbury, the house is packed with antiques and the garden is planted in period style. Admission comes with a guided tour while Sunday entry includes tour, tea and cookies for just $8.

The abode is the showpiece of Barclay Heritage Sq, a one-block site containing nine historic West End houses dating from 1890 to 1908. Pick up a free map covering the square's history highlights from Roedde House. Check the online events calendar for regular live music concerts here.

**ROBSON STREET**     AREA
Map p266 (www.robsonstreet.ca; Robson St; 5) Locals, tourists and recent immigrants – count the number of accents you catch as you stroll here – throng the eateries and shops of Robson St, Vancouver's de facto urban promenade. While most shops are of the ubiquitous chain-store variety, the strip is worth a wander for the urban vibe, especially on summer evenings when buskers and street cartoonists set up shop.

**COAL HARBOUR SEAWALL**     WATERFRONT
Map p270 (Canada Place to Stanley Park; Waterfront) An idyllic waterfront stroll from

---

## VANCOUVER'S FAVORITE PUBLIC ARTWORK

Head towards the West End's English Bay Beach and you'll be stopped in your tracks by 14 very tall **men** (Map p266; 6) – and the crowds of people snapping selfies with them. *A-maze-ing Laughter* by Yue Minjun comprises a gathering of oversized bronze figures permanently engaged in a hearty round of chuckling. It's impossible not to smile as you behold the spectacle but it's worth remembering that it's simply the most popular legacy from the **Vancouver Biennale** (www.vancouverbiennale.com), a festival that runs for two-year stretches in the city and brings large, sometimes challenging art installations to local streets. After the two-year run, some of these artworks remain as permanent fixtures. Check the Biennale's website for the the latest line-up of works around the city – and make sure your camera battery is fully charged.

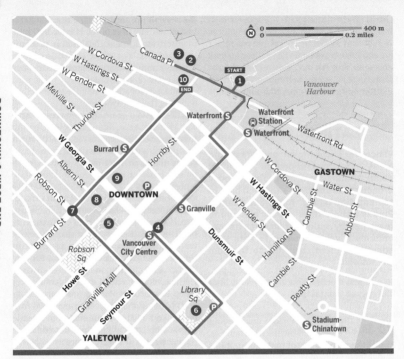

# Neighborhood Walk
# Downtown Grand Tour

**START** CANADA PLACE
**END** BELLA GELATARIA
**LENGTH** 3KM; ONE HOUR

Start at Vancouver's landmark **①Canada Place** (p59) and allow yourself time to walk along the outer promenade to watch the floatplanes diving onto the water. Next, stroll to the adjacent **②Convention Center West Building**. Peruse the outdoor artworks around its perimeter and check out the towering **③Olympic Cauldron**, a landmark reminder of the 2010 Games.

Head southwest along Howe St, turn left onto W Hastings St and then right onto bustling Granville St. Follow this uphill thoroughfare; it's one of the city's most important commercial streets. You'll pass coffee shops, clothing stores and the Pacific Centre, downtown's biggest mall. There's a large food court inside and also usually some food trucks on the street outside. Get your bearings at the busy intersection of **④Granville & W Georgia Sts**, in the heart of the downtown core. Check out the shops around here or nip across one block to the **⑤Vancouver Art Gallery** (p57) for a culture fix.

From here, stroll southeast a couple of blocks to the magnificent **⑥Vancouver Public Library** (p60). The glass-enclosed atrium is a perfect place to grab a coffee or you can check your email for free. Head northwest from here along Robson St, the city's mainstream shopping promenade, where you can wander to your credit card's content. There are also many restaurants here for a few dinner options.

Take a breather at the busy intersection of **⑦Robson & Burrard Sts**, then turn right and head along Burrard toward the mountain vista glinting ahead of you. Duck into the **⑧Fairmont Hotel Vancouver** (p216) to view the luxury lobby, then return to Burrard and continue downhill to **⑨Christ Church Cathedral** (p59). You'll soon be back at Canada Place...but have a treat at **⑩Bella Gelateria** (p67) first.

Canada Place to Stanley Park, this is a perfect way to spend a sunny afternoon. Along the 2km or so you'll take in the convention center art and history-paneled seawalk, the cooling grassy nook of Harbour Green Park and the *Light Shed* artwork – a replica of one of the marine sheds that once lined this area.

# EATING

**Vancouver's downtown and West End areas offer a jam-packed menu of dining options, from sushi joints to busy brunch spots and from sandwich bars to top-end fine dining. And while Stanley Park is a short stroll or easy bus hop to many nearby options, it also has its own eateries if you're looking to sate your appetite without straying too far from the seawall.**

## Downtown

You can't throw a Tim Hortons doughnut in the city center without hitting a restaurant. While there are plenty of midrange options and a smattering of celebrity-fave high-end locations radiating from Robson St, there are also some rewarding ethnic eateries and quirky backstreet joints hidden slightly off the beaten path.

### FINCH'S
CAFE **$**

Map p266 (☑604-899-4040; www.finchteahouse. com; 353 W Pender St; mains $5-10; ⊗9am-5pm Mon-Fri, 11am-4pm Sat; ☑; ☐4) For a coveted seat at one of the dinged old tables, arrive off-peak at this sunny corner cafe that has a 'granny-chic' look combining creaky wooden floors and junk-shop bric-a-brac. You'll be joining in-the-know hipsters and creative types who've been calling this their local for years. They come mainly for the freshly prepared baguette sandwiches (pear, brie, prosciutto and roasted walnuts recommended).

A quirky little hangout, it's a great spot for an afternoon cake and coffee, but be prepared to wait for a seat. Also a popular breakfast spot, Finch's boiled egg and soldiers is a good value option for just $4.75.

### TRACTOR
CANADIAN **$**

Map p266 (☑604-979-0550; www.tractorfoods. com; Marine Building, 335 Burrard St; ⊗7am-9:30pm Mon-Fri, 11am-9:30pm Sat & Sun; ☑; ⓢWaterfront) A healthy fast-food cafeteria tucked into the base of the Marine Building. Choose from 10 or so hearty mixed salads then add a half or whole grilled sandwich. Wholesome and satisfying housemade soups and stews are also available but make sure you add a lemonade as well; there's usually a tempting flavor or two.

This is also a great spot for vegetarians. The owners have high hopes of turning this concept into a chain; for now, there's a second restaurant on Kitsilano's 4th Ave if you're in that part of town.

### LA TAQUERIA
MEXICAN **$**

Map p266 (☑604-568-4406; www.lataqueria.ca; 322 W Hastings St; 4-taco combo $10.50; ⊗11am-5pm Mon-Sat; ☑; ☐14) Arrive off-peak at this tiny hole-in-the-wall to snag a seat at the turquoise-colored counter. Listening to the grassroots Mexican soundtrack and the kitchen staff chatting in Spanish is the perfect accompaniment to a few superbly prepared soft tacos: go for the four-part combo and choose from fillings such as grilled fish, pork cheeks and house-marinated beef, made with top-notch locally sourced ingredients.

Vegetarians also have some tasty choices such as the veggie combo (cheaper than the meat combo) and quesadillas. Save room for a glass of cinnamon-flavored *horchata* (a milkshake-style traditional beverage).

### WAKWAK BURGER
BURGERS **$**

Map p266 (511 Granville St; mains $3-6; ⊗11am-7pm Mon-Fri; ⓢWaterfront) Formerly known as Burger 2.85, the new name enabled this popular Japanese-influenced food truck to expand its menu beyond its signature $2.85 staple. Prices are still cheap, with burger and fries combos topping out at under $7. We recommend the crispy *mentchi-katsu* beef cutlet burger and, if you're lucky, you'll even be able to snag the bench alongside for sit-down dining. Cash only.

These burgers are more than a cut above the kind of fast-food aberrations your taste buds are typically tortured by at this price.

### CARTEMS DONUTERIE
DESSERTS **$**

Map p266 (☑778-708-0996; www.cartems. com; 534 W Pender St; doughnuts from $3.25; ⊗7am-8pm Mon-Thu, 7am-10pm Fri, 10am-10pm Sat, 10am-6pm Sun; ☜; ⓢGranville) Relocated from its original tiny corner spot a few blocks away, Vancouver's favorite hipster doughnut emporium offers a raft of fresh-made fusion treats with irresistible flavors including Earl Grey, salted caramel and the truly spectacular Canadian whiskey bacon, all served with a large dollop of smiley service.

**VEGAN PUDDING & CO** DESSERTS $

Mapp266(📞778-379-0545;www.veganpuddingco.com; 422 Richards St; dessert $3-5; ⏰11am-7pm; 📷; 📵14) 🌿 There's a cult-like following in Vancouver for this hole-in-the-wall take-out counter that serves utterly delicious custard-style puddings made from kabocha squash, coconut milk and flavors including strawberry, chocolate and matcha green tea. It's a silky-smooth revelation to those who think dairy is the only way. All ingredients are organic and you'll also find these puddings at green grocery stores around the city.

You are well advised to buy more than one pot since you'll want to start the next one as soon as you've finished the first.

**GALLERY CAFÉ** CAFE $

Map p266 (📞604-688-2233; www.thegallerycafe.ca; 750 Hornby St; mains $5-12; ⏰9am-9pm Mon-Fri, 9:30am-6pm Sat & Sun, reduced hours off-season; 📵5) The Vancouver Art Gallery's mezzanine-level cafe is a chatty indoordining area complemented by possibly downtown's best and biggest patio. The food is generally of the salad-and-sandwiches variety, but it's well worth stopping in for a drink, especially if you take your coffee (or bottled beer) out to the parasol-forested outdoor area to watch the Robson St action.

This is one of the city's favorite meeting places so it's often packed: arrive late in the afternoon for your pick of tables. And if you're sitting outside, keep your eyes on your grub: the local birds are especially bold here.

**FIELD & SOCIAL** CAFE $

Map p266 (📞778-379-6500; www.fieldandsocial.com; 415 Dunsmuir St; mains $12-13.50; ⏰11am-6pm Mon-Fri, 11am-4pm Sat; 📷; ⓈStadium) A salad-themed cafe with a menu of a half-dozen top-notch, fresh-tossed salads made with seasonal, regional ingredients, this is a great place to salve your conscience over all those Tim Hortons doughnuts you've been eating. Order at the end of the L-shaped counter – we recommend the delicious Rustic Orzo bowl – and find a communal table spot to dive in. Need additional cleansing? Add a glass of kombucha tea to the mix.

**JAPADOG** JAPANESE $

Map p266 (📞604-569-1158; www.japadog.com; 530 Robson St; mains $5-9; ⏰11am-10pm Mon-Thu, to 11pm Fri & Sat, to 9pm Sun; 📵10) You'll have spotted the lunchtime line-ups at the Japadog hotdog stands around town, but this was their first storefront, opening back in 2010. The ever-*genki* Japanese expats serve up a menu of irresistible wonder wieners – think turkey smokies with miso sauce and bratwursts with onion, daikon and soy – but there are also naughty seasoned fries (try the wasabi version). The tiny tables are usually taken, but the take-out window does a roaring trade.

**BIN 941** TAPAS $$

Map p266 (📞604-683-1246; www.bin941.ca; 941 Davie St; plates $5-23; ⏰5pm-1am Sun-Thu, to 2am Fri & Sat; 📵6) A hopping, intimate spot that's packed elbow-to-elbow most nights, cave-like Bin 941 kicked off Vancouver's share-plates fever a few years back. The inventive menu, based on local and seasonal ingredients, often includes international-influenced dishes such as lamb skewers, steamed mussels and mushroom risotto, but don't miss the addictive fried Navajo fry bread.

It's one of the best spots in town for late-night nibbles and a few glasses of wine with chatty friends – which will quickly include the people squeezed next to you at the small adjoining table. Reservations not accepted.

**ROYAL DINETTE** INTERNATIONAL $$

Map p266 (📞604-974-8077; www.royaldinette.ca; 905 Dunsmuir St; mains $15-34; ⏰11:30am-2pm & 5-10pm; ⓈBurrard) Seasonal and regional are the foundations of this smashing downtown restaurant but add friendly, unpretentious service and it becomes a winner. The lunchtime two- or three-course prix fixe ($30 or $35) is a good way to try the place out, but dinner is all about a lingering opportunity to savor international influences combined with local ingredients: the squid-ink spaghetti is our favorite.

## JAM CAFE
BREAKFAST **$$**

Map p266 (☑778-379-1992; www.jamcafes.com; 556 Beatty St; mains $11-16; ⊘8am-3pm; 🛜🍴; ⑤Stadium-Chinatown) The Vancouver outpost of Victoria's wildly popular breakfast and brunch superstar hit the ground running soon after opening here. It's typically packed: you'll have to wait for a table (reservations not accepted) unless you're smart enough to dine very off-peak. You'll find a white-walled room studded with Canadian knickknacks and a huge array of satisfying options, from chicken and waffles to red velvet pancakes.

Our favorite? The monumental BELTCH sandwich, with bacon, egg, lettuce, tomato, cheese and ham; you won't need to eat for the rest of the day after sinking your choppers into this.

## KYZOCK
JAPANESE **$$**

Map p266 (☑604-605-1625; 559 W Pender St; mains $8-18; ⊘11:30am-7pm Mon-Thu, to 8pm Fri; ⑤Granville) Fueling city-center office workers for years (which is why it's closed on weekends), this unassuming hole-in-the-wall serves some of the freshest, no-nonsense sushi in the downtown core. Prices are very reasonable (*nigiri* rolls cost $1.75 to $3.75, for example) and there's usually a special or two to entice you to try something other then your regular California rolls.

There's minimal seating, so consider taking your package to the waterfront and finding an alfresco spot with a view around Canada Pl, a 10-minute walk away.

## TEMPLETON
DINER **$$**

Map p266 (☑604-685-4612; www.thetempleton.ca; 1087 Granville St; mains $10-16; ⊘9am-11pm Mon-Wed, to 1am Thu-Sun; 🍴🍼; 🖥10) A chrome-and-vinyl '50s-look diner with a twist, Templeton serves up plus-sized organic burgers, addictive fries, vegetarian quesadillas and perhaps the best hangover cure in town – the 'Big Ass Breakfast.' Sadly, the mini jukeboxes on the tables don't work, but you can console yourself with a waistline-busting chocolate ice cream float. Avoid weekend peak times or you'll be queuing for ages.

The java here comes from Oso Negro, a legendary Nelson, BC, coffee roaster.

## INDIGO AGE CAFE
VEGAN **$$**

Map p266 (☑604-622-1797; www.indigoagecafe.com; 436 Richards St; mains $10-13; ⊘10am-8pm Mon-Thu, to 9pm Fri & Sat; 🛜🍴; 🖥14) 🌿 A cozy subterranean spot beloved of in-the-know Vancouver vegans and raw-food fans. Snag a log-slice table here and dive into a hearty array of housemade dishes. Pierogis, cabbage rolls and pizza have their fans here but we recommend the delicious zucchini pasta with portobello mushroom 'steak.'

It's also a chilled-out spot in the evening: quaff a few rounds of kombucha and share a slice of coconut-cream pie dessert. If someone at your table angrily refuses to share, it's just the kombucha talking.

## TWISTED FORK BISTRO
BISTRO **$$**

Map p266 (☑604-568-0749; www.twistedforkbistro.ca; 1147 Granville St; mains $14.50; ⊘8am-3pm; 🛜; 🖥10) Granville Strip's best brunch, this narrow, art-lined bistro feels as if it should be somewhere else. But even clubbers need to eat well sometimes. The menu is a well-curated array of classic and adventurous choices, which means choosing between endlessly tempting options. Go the croque monsieur route but make sure your dining partner has the eggs Benny so you can try that as well.

If you were out late the night before, there are five hair-of-the-dog cocktail options to salve your aching head.

## CAFE MEDINA
CAFE **$$**

Map p266 (☑604-879-3114; www.medinacafe.com; 780 Richards St; mains $8-19; ⊘8am-3pm Mon-Fri, 9am-3pm Sat & Sun; 🛜; ⑤Vancouver City Centre) At this lively breakfast-brunch cafe with bistro pretensions, finding a table can be tricky. But it's worth the wait if you're a Belgian-waffle fan: the light and fluffy treats come with gourmet toppings such as chocolate lavender and fig-orange marmalade. Alternatively, go the savory route: excellent paella and spicy tagines are available while the carnivorous Wolves Breakfast will fill you for a week.

## CHAMBAR
EUROPEAN **$$$**

Map p266 (☑604-879-7119; www.chambar.com; 562 Beatty St; mains $27-34; ⊘8am-3pm & 5-10pm; 🅿; ⑤Stadium-Chinatown) This giant, brick-lined cave is a great place for a romantic night out. The sophisticated Belgianesque menu includes perfectly delectable *moules et frites* (mussels and fries) and a braised lamb shank with figs that's a local dining legend. An impressive wine and cocktail list (try a blue fig martini) is also coupled with a great Belgian beer menu dripping with tripels and lambics.

Also consider dropping by just to hang out in the restaurant's front-room bar: grab a perch and work your merry way down the drinks list.

### HAWKSWORTH
WEST COAST $$$

Map p266 (☑604-673-7000; www.hawks worthrestaurant.com; 801 W Georgia St; mains $42-55; ☺6:30am-11pm; ℗; ⑤Vancouver City Centre) This chic, fine-dining anchor of the top-end Rosewood Hotel Georgia is a popular see-and-be-seen spot. Created by and named after one of the city's top local chefs, its menu fuses contemporary West Coast approaches with clever international influences, hence dishes such as soy-roasted sturgeon. The seasonal tasting menu is also heartily recommended. One of the city's best restaurants for a special night out; reservations are recommended.

### LE CROCODILE
FRENCH $$$

Map p266 (☑604-669-4298; www.lecrocodile restaurant.com; 909 Burrard St; mains $18.50-44; ☺11:30am-2:30pm Mon-Fri, 5:30-10:30pm Sat; ☐2) Tucked into a side street in an unassuming building resembling a shopping mall cast-off, this excellent Parisian-style dining room is up there with the city's top-end best. Instead of focusing on experimental shenanigans that only please the chefs, it's perfected a menu of classic French dishes, each prepared with consummate cooking skill and served by perfect, snob-free wait staff.

Try the sumptuous slow-braised lamb shank, washed down with a smashing bottle from the mother country, or treat yourself to the five-course chef's tasting menu ($85).

## ✖ West End

If you can walk along the West End's restaurant-packed streets without stopping to eat, you either have a newly installed stomach staple or the willpower of a particularly virtuous saint. But it's not just the sheer number of restaurants sardined along Denman, Davie and this end of Robson that is impressive; the vast variety and value of the eateries make this Vancouver's best mid-range dining 'hood. If you're a fan of Japanese and Korean food, you'll find plenty of authentic options radiating around the Robson and Denman intersection.

### DISH
CAFE $

Map p270 (☑604-689-0208; www.dishvan couver.com; 1068 Davie St; mains $6-9; ☺8am-8pm Mon-Fri, 9am-4pm Sat & Sun; ☎◢; ☐6) The place where locals fuel-up when they crave good, wholesome nosh without paying through the nose. Breakfast can be had here for well under $10 but the menu has lots of other options no matter what time of day you arrive; there are lots of vegetarian choices, too.

We love the rice bowls and turkey shepherd's pie, while the bulging sandwiches are perfect for picnicking.

### KINTARO RAMEN NOODLE
RAMEN $

Map p270 (788 Denman St; mains $6-10; ☺11:30am-11pm; ☐5) One of Vancouver's oldest noodle shops, fancy-free Kintaro feels like a bustling ramen spot in backstreet Tokyo. Arrive off-peak to avoid the queues and snag a counter seat to watch the steam-shrouded action. Miso ramen is recommended: a brimming bowl of sprouts, bamboo shoots and thick slices of barbecued pork. When you're done, walk off your noodle belly in nearby Stanley Park.

### SUSHI ITOGA
JAPANESE $

Map p270 (☑604-687-2422; www.itoga.com; 1686 Robson St; sushi combos $8-18; ☺11:30am-2pm & 5-8pm Mon-Sat, 5-8pm Sun; ☐5) You'll be rubbing shoulders with other diners at the large communal dining table here, one of the best spots in town for a superfresh sushi feast in a casual setting. Check the ever-changing blackboard showing what's available and then tuck into expertly prepared and well-priced shareable platters of all your fave *nigiri*, *maki* and sashimi treats. Udon dishes are also available.

### ★ FORAGE
WEST COAST $$

Map p270 (☑604-661-1400; www.forage-vancouver.com; 1300 Robson St; mains $16-29; ☺6:30-10am & 5pm-midnight Mon-Fri, 7am-2pm & 5pm-midnight Sat & Sun; ☐5) ◢ A champion of the local farm-to-table scene, this sustainability-friendly restaurant is the perfect way to sample the flavors of the region. Brunch has become a firm local favorite (turkey sausage hash recommended), and for dinner the idea is to sample an array of tasting plates. The menu is innovative and highly seasonal, but look out for the seafood chowder with quail's egg. Reservations recommended.

## DOWNTOWN'S BEST GELATO

You'd be forgiven for feeling skeptical about just how good North American gelato can be. After all, this isn't Italy. But that's before you've found the time to step into downtown's little **Bella Gelateria** (Map p266; 604-569-1010; www.bellagelateria.com; 1001 W Cordova St; 11am-10pm Sun-Thu, to 11pm Fri & Sat; Waterfront) and met James Coleridge. He learned his skills at a gelato university in Italy (yes, they *do* exist) and in 2012 he won a gold medal at the Florence Gelato Festival, the world's biggest such event. He was the first non-Italian to win.

But since the proof of the pudding is in the eating, you need to judge for yourself. Dive into the dozens of ever-changing gelato and *sorbetto* flavors and you'll likely find eye-rollingly amazing treats such as Amerana cherry, Thai coconut and salted caramel. And if you get Coleridge talking, you'll be swept up in his enthusiasm for discovering new and classic concoctions. If you're lucky, the frankly astonishing Persian-rosewater-infused *faloudah sorbetto* will be available: it's like no other dessert you've ever tried.

If you're dining alone, the U-shaped central bar is ideal – and it's a good spot to faceplant into some BC beers and wine.

★GUU WITH GARLIC     JAPANESE $$
Map p270 (604-685-8678; www.guu-iza kaya.com; 1698 Robson St; small plates $4-9, mains $8-16; 11:30am-2:30pm & 5:30pm-12:30am Mon-Sat, till midnight Sun; 5) One of Vancouver's best *izakayas* (Japanese pubs), this welcoming, wood-lined joint is a cultural immersion. Hotpots and noodle bowls are available but it's best to experiment with some Japanese bar tapas, including black cod with miso mayo, deep-fried egg and pumpkin balls or finger-lickin' *tori-karaage* fried chicken. Garlic is liberally used in most dishes. It's best to arrive before opening time for a seat.

Drinks-wise, go for the house-brewed Guuu'd Ale: a sparkling and surprisingly good pale ale made by a local craft brewer. Finish the night with a shot of *shochu*, a traditional distilled spirit, and you'll be looking for the nearest karaoke bar as soon as you hit the street.

TIMBER     PUB FOOD $$
Map p270 (604-661-2166; www.timbervancou ver.com; 1300 Robson St; mains $10-19; 11am-1pm Mon-Thu, 10am-1pm Fri & Sat, 10am-midnight Sun; 5) One of two good dining options attached to the Listel Hotel, this resto-pub combines a great BC-focused craft-beer menu with a tongue-in-cheek array of Canadian comfort food. Snap some photos with the taxidermied beaver and Canada goose, then dive into bison burgers, ketchup-flavored potato chips (Canada's fave flavor) and deep-fried cheese curds. It's like a crash course in calorific Canadian grub.

The beer list is a greatest hits of BC microbreweries, including choice quaffs from Phillips, Hoyne and Powell Street Brewing; a $15, four-sample tasting flight is available. Happy hour is 3pm to 6pm daily; look out for deals on beer and snacks. And before you leave, order some 'Timber Bits' to go. They're the restaurant's knowing nod to a particular Tim Hortons treat.

SURA KOREAN CUISINE     KOREAN $$
Map p270 (604-687-7872; www.surakore ancuisine.com; 1518 Robson St; mains $10-20; 11am-4pm & 5-10:30pm; P; 5) From the 1400-block of Robson St on and around onto Denman and Davie Sts, you'll find a smorgasbord of authentic Korean and Japanese eateries. A cut above its ESL-student-luring siblings, slick Sura offers awesome Korean comfort dishes in a cosy, bistrolike setting. Try the spicy beef soup, kimchi pancakes and excellent *bibimbap*: beef, veggies and a still-cooking egg in a hot stone bowl.

The set-course lunches ($15 or $20; two-person minimum order) are a great deal if you want to try as many flavors as possible; each comes with lots of little plates to dip into. Reservations not accepted. Some free parking is available.

ESPANA     SPANISH $$
Map p270 (604-558-4040; www.espanar estaurant.ca; 1118 Denman St; plates $5-12; 5pm-1am Sun-Thu, to 2am Fri & Sat; 5) Reservations are not taken but it's worth queuing to get into one of Vancouver's most popular Spanish tapas joints. The tables are crammed close and the atmosphere is ever-welcoming in the long, narrow dining room that's warmed by a hubbub of food-related chatter. The crispy

## FOOD TRUCK FRENZY

Keen to emulate the legendary street-food scenes of Portland and Austin, Vancouver jumped on the kitchen-equipped bandwagon in 2011, launching a pilot scheme with 17 food carts. Things took off quickly and there are now dozens dotted around the city, serving everything from halibut tacos to Korean sliders, pulled-pork sandwiches to French crepes. Prices are typically $8 to $12 per entree.

While there are a number of experimental fusion trucks, several have quickly risen to the top; look out for local favorites Le Tigre, Kaboom Box, TacoFino, Soho Road, Mom's Grilled Cheese and Vij's Railway Express – plus Johnny's Pops artisan ice lollies. Locating the trucks can sometimes be challenging; there are usually a couple outside the Vancouver City Centre Canada Line station and on busy stretches of downtown arteries such as Georgia, Robson and around the Vancouver Art Gallery perimeter. Also look out for the trucks at city farmers markets and outside some microbreweries (you're allowed to eat your truck takeout in the brewery tasting rooms). For listings, opening hours and locations, the handy www.streetfoodapp.com/vancouver website tells you excatly where to go. Alternatively, **Vancouver Foodie Tours** (✆604-295-8844; www.foodietours.ca; tours from $50) offers a tasty guided walk that includes samples at four trucks.

But if you're keen to loosen your belt and sample as many as you can in one belly-busting afternoon, check out August's three-day-long **YVR Food Fest** (www.yvrfoodfest.com; Olympic Village; ⊘Aug; Ⓢ Main St-Science World), where dozens of food carts congregate to lure the deeply esurient. And if you fancy an easy trip from town, August's one-day **Columbia StrEat Food Truck Fest** in New Westminster (easily reached via SkyTrain) is also well worth checking out, with its 70+ trucks. See www.downtownnewwest.ca for details.

squid and the cod and potato croquettes are delish, while the crispy chickpeas dish is a revelation.

There's a small but authentic sherry list to consider, plus a good array of Spanish wines – why not go the Cava route and toast your lovely meal?

**MOTOMACHI SHOKUDO**   JAPANESE **$$**

Map p270 (✆604-609-0310; 740 Denman St; mains $9-14; ⊘noon-11pm Thu-Tue; ☐5) A West End favorite, this incredibly tiny ramen house – it has fewer than 20 seats – combines good service with perfect comfort dishes. First-timers should try the New Generation miso ramen, which comes brimming with bean sprouts, sweet corn, shredded cabbage and barbecued pork. An added plus is that most ingredients are organic. Note that only cash or debit cards are accepted here.

**LOLITA'S**   MEXICAN **$$**

Map p270 (✆604-696-9996; www.lolitasrestaurant.com; 1326 Davie St; mains $10-19; ⊘5pm-2am; ☐6) This small-but-lively cantina is popular with West Enders, for good reason. It's a great place to find yourself late at night, when the warm party

vibe makes you feel as if you're hanging with friends at a beach bar. Turn your taste buds on with some Matador Mojitos, and be sure to sample some spicy, fusion-esque nosh, including the chimichurri Atlantic cod tacos.

It's super-busy here most weekends, so if you want to hear yourself think, consider dropping by on a weeknight. Looking for happy hour? There's a special menu from 11pm every night.

**FAT BADGER**   BRITISH **$$$**

Map p270 (✆604-336-5577; www.fatbadger.ca; 1616 Alberni St; mains $20-38; ⊘5-11pm Tue-Sun; ☐5) A gourmet reinvention of a British pub in a gabled heritage house, the atmospheric dark-wood interior here is the ideal setting for hunkering in a corner on a rainy night and stuffing yourself with Scotch eggs, lamb-and-Guinness pie and the kind of sticky toffee pudding that might make you propose marriage to your dessert (again).

There are several draft Fuller's brews on tap plus a decent range of bottled beers and ciders from the mother country. Quite well hidden, this place is tucked along a back thoroughfare parallel to Robson St;

just look for the sign of the portly, mono-cled badger outside.

# ✖ Stanley Park

The park has several welcoming beaches and some tree-fringed grassy expanses ideal for alfresco noshing but, if you haven't brought a picnic with you, Vancouver's verdant green heart also has its own dining options. Wherever you eat, try for a window seat so you can enjoy a side dish of forest or panoramic sea-to-sky views.

### PROSPECT POINT
### CAFE & GRILL                    BURGERS, FAST FOOD $
Map p287 (☎604-669-2737; www.prospect point.com; 5601 Stanley Park Dr; mains $10-16; ⏰9am-7pm, reduced hours off-season; ➡19) Recently acquired by new owners and already being elevated with renovations and a revamped menu (including smoke pulled pork poutine), the coffee shop, ice cream station and sit-down grill here all rest on one unassailable draw: the vistas of the dense Stanley Park forest and the twinkling shoreline unfurling below. If you have time, take the steps down the cliffside for even better views.

Area racoons have also noticed the surfeit of dining opportunities here; don't feed them or they'll likely follow you back to your hotel, board your plane with you and expect to be fed in your kitchen for the rest of their lives.

### PICNIX AL FRESCO TO GO              DELI $$$
Map p270 (☎778-889-7706; www.picnix.ca; 1725 Davie St; meal $25-40; ⏰noon-3pm & 6-9pm; ➡5) The perfect way to dine in Stanley Park, this clever service enables you to book a picnic and pick it up near the park's information center. For $40 per person, you receive a wheeled wagon that unfolds into a little table and is crammed with goodies including cheese, charcuterie, salads and chocolate mousse. You'll have three hours to dine before returning your wagon.

Blankets and inflatable pillows are also included. Both lunch and dinner service are available. A lower-priced ($25 per person) basket option was also being introduced during our visit; you collect it from the Davie St HQ.

### TEAHOUSE
### IN STANLEY PARK              WEST COAST $$$
Map p287 (☎604-669-3281; www.vancouverdine. com; Ferguson Point, Stanley Park; mains $21-38; ⏰11:30am-10pm Mon-Fri, 10am-10pm Sat & Sun; ➡19) Occupying a gabled 1930s park building, this lovely spot serves contemporary West Coast classics such as roasted BC sablefish and Fraser Valley duck, along with jaw-dropping sunset patio views over Burrard Inlet. It's a good place for weekend brunch – shrimp and scallion omelet recommended. The park's Third Beach is a few steps away and is ideal for an evening stroll after dinner.

The wine list has some good BC bottles; here's your chance to dive into a tipple or two from popular regional wineries such as Blasted Church and Quail's Gate.

#  DRINKING & NIGHTLIFE

**The Granville Strip between Robson and Granville Bridge is lined with mainstream bars where partying, heavy boozing and occasional street brawling (especially on weekends) are the main attraction. A short walk away, you'll find more discerning options in the West End's neighborhood pubs and bars, including several gay-friendly haunts along Davie St. Even better, head to the superior nightlife of Gastown or Main St.**

# 🍷 Downtown

### ★MARIO'S COFFEE EXPRESS          COFFEE
Map p266 (595 Howe St; mains $4-8; ⏰6:30am-4pm Mon-Fri; ⓈBurrard) A java-lover's favorite that only downtown office workers seem to know about. You'll wake up and smell the coffee long before you make it through the door here. The rich aromatic brews served up by the man himself are the kind of ambrosia that makes Starbucks drinkers weep. You might even forgive the 1980s Italian pop percolating through the shop. Hidden in plain view, this is arguably downtown's best for a cup of coffee.

### DEVIL'S ELBOW
### ALE & SMOKE HOUSE                    PUB
Map p266 (☎604-559-0611; www.devilselbow alehouse.com; 562 Beatty St; ⏰11:30am-midnight Mon-Thu, 11:30am-1am Fri, 10am-1am Sat,

10am-midnight Sun; ⑤Stadium-Chinatown) A cavelike brick-and-art-lined pub that feels like a local secret, this is the place to combine barbecued grub with brews from one of BC's best microbreweries. It's owned by the team behind Squamish's Howe Sound Brewing. You'll find great ales to try, from Hopraiser IPA to Father John's Winter Ale. The weekday $15 beer-included lunch deal is recommended.

Think Guinness is the best stout around? Wait until you try Pothole Filler Imperial Stout, which puts hairs on the chests of everyone in the area, whether or not they're drinking it. There's also a weekday happy hour from 3pm to 5pm when beers and bar snacks are $6 each.

### UVA WINE & COCKTAIL BAR    LOUNGE

Map p266 (☏604-632-9560; www.uvavancouver.com; 900 Seymour St; ◷11:30am-2pm; 🚊10) This sexy nook fuses a heritage mosaic floor with a dash of mod class. But, despite the cool appearances, there's a snob-free approach that encourages taste-tripping through an extensive by-the-glass wine menu and some dangerously delicious cocktails – we love the Spellbound. Food is part of the mix (including shareable small plates) and the daily 2pm to 6pm happy hour is ideal for extended discount quaffing.

Just a block from the party-hard madness (especially on weekends) of the Granville Strip, this is a great alternative to staggering around on the street wondering where you left your pants.

### BELMONT    BAR

Map p266 (☏604-605-4340; www.belmontbar.com; 1006 Granville St; ◷5pm-2am Tue-Thu, to 3am Fri & Sat; 🚊10) The subterranean, rough-around-the-edges Cellar nightclub has been spruced up as a loungey moodlit bar with 7pm live music most nights. Food is also available but we suggest sticking to the drinks here, including the couple of dozen craft and mainstream beers (Phillips Blue Buck recommended). It's often jam-packed on weekend late-nights when the DJ dance club approach returns.

A handsome room for a tipple or two, it's worth checking out during the week for a smoother vibe; there's a 5pm-to-7pm weekday happy hour, with $4 drinks, to help you do just that.

### JOHNNIE FOX'S IRISH SNUG    IRISH PUB

Map p266 (☏604-685-4946; www.johnniefox.ca; 1033 Granville St; ◷11:30am-1am Sun-Thu, to 2am Fri & Sat; 🚊10) A new glass front means you can now peer through the windows before committing to this small Granville St Irish pub. You'll find a gaggle of beer-swilling fellas having a grand old time to a soundtrack of live or recorded Celtic tunes. A lively spot for a Guinness (especially on weekends), it also has a menu of pub-grub classics (filled Yorkshire puddings recommended). There's live music of the toe-tapping variety four nights a week here, and Sunday evening's $12 roast dinner special is a good deal.

### CAFFÈ ARTIGIANO    COFFEE

Map p266 (☏604-694-7737; www.caffeartigiano.com; 763 Hornby St; ◷5:30am-9pm Mon-Fri, 6am-9pm Sat, 6am-8pm Sun; 🛜; 🚊5) An international award winner for its barista skills and latte art, Artigiano has the locals frothing at the mouth with its satisfyingly rich java beverages. The drinks appear with leaf designs adorning their foam and there's a good side attraction of gourmet sandwiches and cakes. The small patio here is almost always packed – grab a table quickly if you see one. If you can't sleep and really need a caffeine hit, this is one of the earliest-opening coffeehouses in town. The interior has a classy Tuscan look. There are several other outlets dotted around the city.

### ROXY    CLUB

Map p266 (☏604-331-7999; www.roxyvan.com; 932 Granville St; ◷8pm-3am; 🚊10) A raucous old-school nightclub that still has plenty of fans – including lots of partying youngsters who seem to be discovering it for the first time – this brazen old timer is downtown's least pretentious dance space. Expect to be shaking your booty next to near-teenage funsters, kid-escaping soccer moms and UBC students letting loose. If you really want to dive into the Granville Strip club scene, this is where to do it.

### VENUE    CLUB

Map p266 (☏604-646-0064; www.venuelive.ca; 881 Granville St; ◷9pm-3am Thu-Sat; 🚊8) Redesigned from its previous incarnation as the Plaza Club, Venue has a much larger dance floor since the removal of the obtrusive central bar. The music is of the mainstream variety – the weekly Good Fridays party is best – and the crowd includes plenty of non-locals in from Surrey and New Westminster

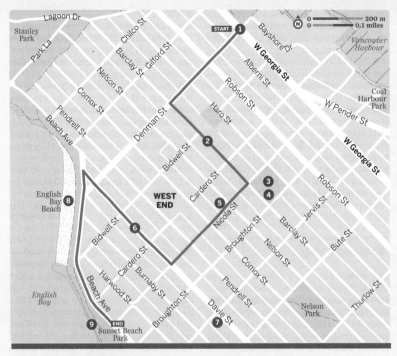

# Neighborhood Walk
## West End 'Hood & Heritage Stroll

**START** CNR OF W GEORGIA & DENMAN STS
**END** SUNSET BEACH
**LENGTH** 2KM; ONE HOUR

This urban walk takes you through one of Vancouver's most attractive residential areas, combining clapboard houses with art deco apartment buildings.

Start at the corner of W Georgia and Denman Sts and head south along **①Denman St**. You'll pass dozens of mid-priced restaurants and plenty of enticing shops to attract your wallet.

Turn left on **②Barclay St** and stroll through the residential heart of Vancouver's vibrant gay community. There are some smashing old heritage apartment buildings and wooden arts-and-crafts homes here. Continue until you reach the well-preserved plaza of historic houses at **③Barclay Heritage Square**, a reminder of how Vancouverites of yesteryear lived. Duck into what is perhaps the best-preserved of the bunch: lovely, antique-lined **④Roedde House**

**Museum** (p61); even better if you time your visit for Sunday's afternoon tea).

Head southwest along Nicola St and you'll come across the lovely brick-built 1907 **⑤Firehall No 6**. It's still in use but has the feel (and look) of a museum. There's often a shiny firetruck basking in the sun outside.

Continue on and turn right into **⑥Davie St**, a teeming area lined with shops and cafes that's also the commercial hub of the gay community. It's a popular place at night as it has plenty of bars and clubs. If you need a coffee break, **⑦Melriches Coffeehouse** (p73) is nearby.

When you reach the end of Davie St at **⑧English Bay beach** (p61), snap a few photos of the delightful *A-maze-ing Laughter* public artwork of 14 chuckling bronze figures then turn left and stroll along Beach Ave. This becomes the main promenade for **⑨Sunset Beach**, where you can sit on a grassy bank and watch the locals jog and skate by, or you can catch a miniferry to Granville Island which is winking at you just across the water.

for their weekly booze-fueled big night out. It is also a live-music venue some evenings – check the website to see what's coming up.

### BACCHUS LOUNGE
BAR

Map p266 (☑604-608-5319; www.wedgewood hotel.com; 845 Hornby St; ☺noon-midnight Sun-Wed, to 1am Thu-Sat; ☑5) A roaring hearth on a chilly day is the main attraction at Bacchus, a decadent bar with a gentleman's club ambience on the lobby level of the Wedgewood Hotel. Sink into a deep leather chair, adjust your monocle and listen to the piano player as you sip a signature Red Satin Slip martini of vodka, raspberry liqueur and cranberry juice. There's also a handy small-plate menu for the incurably hungry (go for the cheese).

## West End

### TAP SHACK
PUB

Map p270 (☑604-687-6455; www.tapshack.ca; 1199 W Cordova St; ☺11am-11pm Mon-Fri, 10am-11pm Sat & Sun; ⑤Waterfront) In summer, this place is all about the gigantic, red-parasol-studded patio that overlooks mountain-framed Burrard Inlet. Good pub grub of the pizza, brunch and Cajun club sandwich variety is available but the point here is to drink in the views and sample from more than a dozen BC craft beers, typically including top quaffs by Persephone, Yellow Dog and Four Winds.

There's also a popular fountain-studded kids' water park out front, so if you suddenly need to sober up you know where to go (just kidding).

### STANLEY'S BAR & GRILL
BAR

Map p287 (☑604-602-3088; www.stanleyparkpa vilion.com; 610 Pipeline Rd; ☺9am-8pm Jul & Aug, 9am-5pm Sep-Jun; ☑19) Tucked into one end of the handsome, century-old Stanley Park Pavilion. Snag a patio seat under the gigantic red parasols and grab a beery respite from your exhausting day of park exploring. There's a full range of Stanley Park Brewing tipples (not actually made in the park) plus some good pub grub; the barbecued salmon sandwich is especially recommended.

You'll be drinking among the trees here; keep your eyes peeled for passing eagles and herons plus a Douglas squirrel or two. And if you're heading for a show at Theatre Under the Stars (p74), this is a great spot to drink and dine beforehand.

### SYLVIA'S LOUNGE
BAR

Map p270 (☑604-681-9321; www.sylviahotel. com; 1154 Gilford St; ☺7am-11pm Sun-Thu, to midnight Fri & Sat; ☑5) Part of the permanently popular Sylvia Hotel, this was Vancouver's first cocktail bar when it opened in the mid-1950s. Now a comfy, wood-lined neighborhood bar favored by in-the-know locals (they're the ones hogging the window seats as the sun sets dramatically over English Bay), it's a great spot for an end-of-day wind down. There's live music here on Wednesdays and Thursdays.

Here's some scurrilous history for you: this is one of the bars Errol Flynn is reputed to have frequented during his booze-fueled final days, before dying in the city in 1959.

### CARDERO'S LIVE BAIT MARINE PUB
PUB

Map p270 (☑604-669-7666; www.vancouver dine.com; 1583 Coal Harbour Quay; ☺11:30am-midnight; ☑19) Nestled between Coal Harbour's bobbing boats, the restaurant here is fine but the little pub on the side is better. With cozy leather sofas, a wood-burning fireplace and great views of the marina, it has a decent menu of comfort food (we recommend the wok dishes and oyster burger) as well as drafts, from Strongbow to local Red Truck Lager. There's also live music, typically of the guitar-wielding singer-songwriter variety, every night.

### 1181
GAY

Map p270 (☑604-787-7130; www.1181.ca; 1181 Davie St; ☺6pm-3am; ☑6) A popular gay bar for those who like posing (or just looking), this loungy spot combines a sofa-strewn front space with a cozy back area that feels more intimate. Separating the two is a side bar staffed by cooler-than-you servers: this is also where the singletons sit, so you can expect to be the subject of some flirty attention if you prop yourself here. There's a good wine list and plenty of tempting cocktails. Davie's classiest gay bar.

### CELEBRITIES
GAY

Map p270 (☑604-568-1159; www.celebrities nightclub.com; 1022 Davie St; ☺9pm-3am Tue-Sat; ☑6) The city's fave gay club, recently revamped Celebrities has elevated its room to a new level of neon-lit cool. The club hosts a series of sparkling, sometimes sequined, event nights throughout the week, including a raucous Playhouse Saturday when everyone seems to hit the dance floor. If you're on a budget, Tuesday is cheap-ass $3 highball night.

### PUMPJACK PUB                                       GAY

Map p270 (www.pumpjackpub.com; 1167 Davie St; ☺1pm-2am; 🚇6) Glancing through the open window as you walk past on a summer night tells you all you need to know about this popular gay pub: it's a great place to meet leather-clad, often hairy locals ever-ready to make a new friend in town for a quick visit. Expect queues here on weekends as the local bears vie for a pick up or two. A long-time local favorite.

### MELRICHES COFFEEHOUSE                         COFFEE

Map p270 (📞604-689-5282; 1244 Davie St; ☺6am-9:30pm Mon-Sat, 7am-10pm Sun; 🛜; 🚇6) With its mismatched wooden tables, array of hearty cakes and crowd of journal-writing locals hunkered in every corner, this is an ideal rainy-day nook. Warm your hands on a pail-sized hot chocolate and press your face to the window to watch the Davie St locals bustling past. If you're hungry, the cookies are of the giant-sized variety here. This is the kind of place where Morrissey would hang out on a wet Monday afternoon to check his emails.

### DELANY'S COFFEE HOUSE                          COFFEE

Map p270 (📞604-662-3344; www.delanyscoffeehouse.com; 1105 Denman St; ☺6am-8pm Mon-Fri, 6:30am-8:30pm Sat & Sun; 🛜; 🚇5) A laid-back, wood-lined neighborhood coffee bar that's the java-hugging heart of the West End's gay community, Delany's is a good perch from which to catch the annual Pride Parade, although you'll have to get here early if you want a front-row seat. The usual array of cookies and muffins will keep you fortified while you wait. A good spot to pick up a take-out coffee for a stroll to nearby English Bay beach.

### FOUNTAINHEAD PUB                                 GAY

Map p270 (📞604-687-2222; www.thefountainheadpub.com; 1025 Davie St; ☺11am-1am Sun-Thu, 11am-2am Fri & Sat; 🚇6) The area's loudest and proudest gay neighborhood pub, this friendly joint is all about the patio, which spills onto Davie St like an overturned wine glass. Take part in the ongoing summer evening pastime of ogling passing locals or retreat to a quieter spot inside for a few lagers or a naughty cocktail: anyone for a Porn Star or a Red Stag Sour? Perfect place

to meet up before, during or after the Pride Parade.

 ## ENTERTAINMENT

**Studded with an eclectic mix of cinema, theater and live music options, Vancouver's downtown core has some great night-out entertainment options, plus a couple of unexpected suggestions beyond the city center.**

### ⭐COMMODORE BALLROOM          LIVE MUSIC

Map p266 (📞604-739-4550; www.commodoreballroom.com; 868 Granville St; 🚇10) Local bands know they've made it when they play Vancouver's best mid-sized venue, a restored art deco ballroom that still has the city's bounciest dance floor – courtesy of tires placed under its floorboards. If you need a break from your moshing, collapse at one of the tables lining the perimeter, catch your breath with a bottled Stella and then plunge back in.

The Commodore has been entertaining locals since 1929 and everyone from Count Basie to the Dead Kennedys has played here over the years (although they apparently weren't on the same bill).

### ⭐PACIFIC CINÉMATHÈQUE             CINEMA

Map p266 (📞604-688-3456; www.thecinematheque.ca; 1131 Howe St; tickets $11, double bills $16; 🚇10) This beloved cinema operates like an ongoing film festival with a daily-changing program of movies. A $3 annual membership is required – organize it at the door – before you can skulk in the dark with other chin-stroking movie buffs, who would probably name their children after Fellini and Bergman if they averted their gaze from the screen long enough to have a relationship. The high point of the year for some is August's annual classic film noir season.

### ORPHEUM THEATRE                         THEATER

Map p266 (📞604-665-3050; 601 Smithe St; 🚇10) Opened in 1927, Vancouver's grandest old-school theater venue has a gorgeous and beautifully maintained baroque interior, making it the perfect place to catch a rousing show with the Vancouver Symphony Orchestra, who calls this place home. There are frequent additional performers here throughout the year; check ahead to see what's on during your stay. The theater is

LOCAL KNOWLEDGE

## ARCADE ATTRACTION
........................................

Strolling along the neon-winking Granville Strip, avoiding the cheap pizza joints and staggering drunks, it's easy to walk past one spot that hasn't changed much since the 1970s. **Movieland Arcade** (Map p266; ☑604-681-6915; 906 Granville St; ⊗10am-1am; ⊠10) is lined with dozens of mostly retro pinball machines and video games (anyone for Miss Pacman?). Here you can relive the days of blowing your paper-route money pumping the flippers on that Addams Family machine.

also a National Historic Site. In summer, it also runs highly recommended behind-the-scenes tours. They're free but be sure to arrive early to beat the crowds.

### VANCITY THEATRE                              CINEMA
Map p266 (☑604-683-3456; www.viff.org/thea tre; 1181 Seymour St; tickets $12, double bills $18; ⊠10) The state-of-the-art headquarters of the Vancouver International Film Festival screens a wide array of movies throughout the year in the kind of auditorium that cinephiles dream of: generous legroom, wide armrests and great sight lines from each of its 175 seats. It's a place where you can watch a four-hour subtitled epic about a dripping tap and still feel comfortable. Check the ever-changing schedule for shows and special events, and remember that a $2 annual membership is mandatory.

### THEATRE
### UNDER THE STARS           PERFORMING ARTS
Map p287 (☑877-840-0457, 604-734-1917; www. tuts.ca; Malkin Bowl, Stanley Park, 610 Pipeline Rd; tickets from $29; ⊗Jul & Aug; ⊠19) The old-school Malkin Bowl is an atmospheric open-air venue for summertime shows. The season never gets too serious, usually featuring two enthusiastically performed Broadway musicals, but it's hard to beat the location, especially as the sun fades over the trees peeking from behind the stage.

### VOGUE THEATRE                         LIVE MUSIC
Map p266 (☑604-569-1144; www.voguethea tre.com; 918 Granville St; ⊠10) A 1940s heritage venue – check out the retro neon figure perched on the top of the streamlined exte-

rior – the Vogue was bought and refurbished a few years back. Happily the refurb didn't change much and this is a great old-school venue to see bands. It's an all-seater, though, which sometimes means tension between those who want to sit and those of the mosh-pit persuasion.

### DANCE CENTRE                    PERFORMING ARTS
Map p266 (☑604-606-6400; www.thedancecen tre.ca; 677 Davie St; ⊠10) Vancouver's dance headquarters, this cleverly reinvented old bank building offers a kaleidoscopic array of activities that arguably makes it Canada's foremost dance center. Home to resident companies – Ballet BC is based here – it also hosts classes, workshops, performances and events throughout the year: check the website calendar to see what's coming up.

### VANCOUVER CANUCKS                        HOCKEY
Map p266 (☑604-899-7400; canucks.nhl.com; Rogers Arena, 800 Griffiths Way; ⓢStadium-Chinatown) Vancouver's National Hockey League (NHL) team toyed with fans in 2011's Stanley Cup finals before losing Game 7 to the Boston Bruins, triggering riots across the city. But love runs deep and 'go Canucks go!' is still boomed out from a packed Rogers Arena at most games. Book your seat early or just head to a local bar for some raucous game-night atmosphere. There's a large team merchandise shop at the stadium, which is open even when there are no games on: it's a good spot to pick up cool souvenirs for sporting kids (and adults) back home.

### SCOTIABANK THEATRE                      CINEMA
Map p266 (www.cineplex.com; 900 Burrard St; ⊠2) Downtown's shiny multiplex is big enough to have its own corporate sponsor and it's the most likely theater to be screening the latest must-see blockbuster. In contrast, it also shows occasional live broadcast performances from major cultural institutions such as London's National Theatre and New York's Metropolitan Opera. Drop by on Tuesdays for discounted admission.

### MEDIA CLUB                            LIVE MUSIC
Map p266 (☑604-608-2871; www.themediaclub. ca; 695 Cambie St; ⓢStadium-Chinatown) This intimate, low-ceilinged indie space tucked underneath the back of the Queen Elizabeth Theatre books inventive local acts that mix and match the genres, so you may have the chance to see electro-symphonic or acoustic

metal groups alongside power pop, hip-hop and country bands – although probably not on the same night. There are shows here several times a week. An under-the-radar venue (except to those in the know), this is a great place for a loud night out...earplugs not supplied.

### COMEDY MIX
COMEDY

Map p266 (📞604-684-5050; www.thecomedymix.com; Century Plaza Hotel, 1015 Burrard St; ⏱shows 8:30pm Tue-Thu, 8pm & 10:30pm Fri & Sat; 🚇2) It may be hidden in a hotel basement, but this is one of Vancouver's most popular comedy venues; head here for some raucous belly laughs. Bigger acts strut their stuff on weekends when it's typically packed, but consider early in the week for a more chilled-out visit: Tuesday's ProAm Night includes a plethora of newbies trying to make you laugh without wetting themselves.

 # SHOPPING

## 🏠 Downtown

Centered on lively Robson St – Vancouver's leading mainstream shopping promenade and the home of most major chains – the downtown core is a strollable outdoor mall of grazing shoppers moving between their favorite stores with an ever-growing clutch of bags. High fashion, shoes and jewelry are the mainstays here, and there are also plenty of coffee shops if you need to stop and count your money. Head south along Granville St from the intersection with Robson St for urban streetwear shops: this is where you can pick up those limited-edition Converse runners you've always wanted. For luxe labels such as Tiffany, Burberry and Louis Vuitton, head to the area around the Burrard and Alberni Sts intersection.

### ⭐PAPER HOUND
BOOKS

Map p266 (📞604-428-1344; www.paperhound.ca; 344 W Pender St; ⏱10am-7pm Sun-Thu, 10am-8pm Fri & Sat; 🚇14) Proving the printed word is alive and kicking, this small but perfectly curated secondhand-book store opened a couple of years ago and has already become a dog-eared favorite among locals. It is a perfect spot for browsing your day away. You'll find tempting tomes (mostly used but some new) on everything from nature to poetry to chaos theory. Ask for recommendations; they really know their stuff here. The store is in the heart of a downtown area that has traditionally been known as Book Row. Once you're done here, check out the three or four other used bookstores that call this area home.

### MACLEOD'S BOOKS
BOOKS

Map p266 (📞604-681-7654; 455 W Pender St; ⏱10am-6pm Mon-Sat, 11am-6pm Sun; 🇸Granville) From its creaky floorboards to those skuzzy carpets and ever-teetering piles of books, this legendary locals' fave is a great place to peruse a cornucopia of used tomes. It's the ideal spot for a rainy-day browse through subjects from dance to the occult. Check the windows for posters of local readings and artsy happenings around the city. A few steps in from the door, look out for the travel section. It's ideal for picking up a guidebook to 1987 New York, just in case you're a time-traveller planning a trip.

### SIKORA'S CLASSICAL RECORDS
MUSIC

Map p266 (📞604-685-0625; www.sikorasclassical.com; 432 W Hastings St; ⏱10am-7pm Mon-Sat, noon-5pm Sun; 🇸Granville) Sikora's blows away the classical inventory of mainstream music stores with its giant selection of more than 25,000 CD/DVD titles, plus hundreds of LPs for all those traditionalists out there. Opera, organ, choral, chamber and early music are well represented, as are New Age and spoken word, and there's also a section devoted to celebrated and lesser-known Canadian musicians. The staff is highly knowledgeable and can point you to a hot Mahler or Rachmaninov recording at the drop of a hat.

### HUNTER & HARE
VINTAGE

Map p266 (📞604-559-4273; www.hunterandhare.com; 334 W Pender St; ⏱11am-7pm Mon-Sat, noon-6pm Sun; 🚇14) A lovely little store specializing in well-curated consignment clothing and accessories for women, this is the place to head if you've left your summer frock at home by mistake. Smiley staff can point you in the right direction and you'll find prices that are enticingly reasonable. It's not all used togs; there's also jewelry, greetings cards and beauty products from local artisan producers.

### VINYL RECORDS
MUSIC

Map p266 (📞604-488-1234; www.vinylrecords.ca; 319 W Hastings St; ⏱noon-6pm Mon-Sat, 1-5pm

Sun; 14) Recently relocated and now one of Vancouver's largest used (mostly) record shops. You'll need hours to sort through the higgledy-piggledy array of crates and cardboard boxes housing everything from polka to Pink Floyd. Make sure you know your prices since not everything is a bargain – most of the sale items are gathered near the front of the shop.

### VANCOUVER PEN
**SHOP**     FASHION & ACCESSORIES

Map p266 (604-681-1612; 512 W Hastings St; 9:30am-5:30pm Mon-Fri, 10am-5pm Sat; Waterfront) There are two things about this store that are pleasingly old-fashioned: the staff greet you when you walk in and ask how to help you, and the items they're selling harken back to a bygone age when fine pens and penmanship were important markers (no pun intended) of civilization. It's not all gold-nibbed fountain pens, though: there are writing tools for every budget here. If you're a real aficionado of the modern-day quill, check out the monthly meetings of the Vancouver Pen Club, staged at venues across the city (www.vancouverpenclub.com).

### GOLDEN AGE COLLECTABLES     BOOKS
Map p266 (604-683-2819; www.gacvan.com; 852 Granville St; 10am-9pm Mon-Sat, 11am-6pm Sun; 10) If you're missing your regular dose of *Emily the Strange* or you just want to blow your vacation budget on a highly detailed life-sized model of Ultra Man, head straight to this Aladdin's cave of the comic-book world. While the clientele is unsurprisingly dominated by males, the staff is friendly and welcoming – especially to wide-eyed kids buying their first *Archie*.

There are occasional signings by artists here. This is also the best place to be in the city on the annual Free Comic Book Day (first Saturday in May), when there's a party atmosphere and gratis goodies for all – whether or not you dress as Darth Vader (don't expect to get anything if you wear your Jar Jar Binks costume).

### MINK CHOCOLATES     FOOD
Map p266 (604-633-2451; www.minkchocolates.com; 863 W Hastings St; 7:30am-6pm Mon-Fri, 10am-6pm Sat & Sun; ; Waterfront) If chocolate is the main food group in your book, follow your candy-primed nose to this designer choccy shop in the downtown core. Select a handful of souvenir bonbons

– little edible artworks embossed with prints of trees and coffee cups – then hit the drinks bar for the best velvety hot choc you've ever tasted. Then have another. It's always a good idea to pick up a few souvenir chocolate bars for home while you're here, although it's likely you'll scoff them before they make it into your suitcase: ganache-filled key lime and high-tea varieties are superb.

### HOLT RENFREW     CLOTHING
Map p266 (604-681-3121; www.holtrenfrew.com; 737 Dunsmuir St; 10am-7pm Mon & Tue, 10am-9pm Wed-Fri, 10am-8pm Sat, 11am-7pm Sun; Granville) Vancouver's swankiest homegrown clothing and accessories department store. High-end-label lovers flock here to peruse the artfully presented D&G, Armani and Issey Miyake togs and accoutrements arrayed over several brightly lit floors. Service is personal from well-dressed staffers. The awesome end-of-season sales are recommended: racks of bargain clothes suddenly emerge on every floor, ripe for riffling.

Long regarded as Canada's answer to slick US chain Nordstrom, it now goes head-to-head with its rival in the city with the latter opening its own store nearby in 2015.

### ROOTS     CLOTHING
Map p266 (604-629-1300; www.roots.com; 1001 Robson St; 10am-6pm Mon-Fri, to 7pm Sat, to 5pm Sun; 5) Basically a maple-leaf-emblazoned version of the Gap, Roots designs athletic, plaid-accented streetwear that's unmistakably Canadian. Its retro-style jogging pants, hoodies and toques (if you don't know what that is, this is the place to find out) are ever-popular. There are additional outlets (usually in malls) throughout the city.

Check the sale rails for end-of-season deals. You might even pick up an ironic trappers hat for just a few bucks. If you're Australian you'll know the name of this store has naughty connotations back home; which means it's a good place to buy a T-shirt souvenir emblazoned with the Roots legend.

### LULULEMON ATHLETICA     CLOTHING
Map p266 (604-681-3118; www.lululemon.com; 970 Robson St; 10am-9pm Mon-Sat, 10am-8pm Sun; 5) Flagship downtown store of the Vancouver-based chain that made

ass-hugging yoga wear a mainstream fashion, this is the shop for that archetypal West Coast look. Sporty tops and stretchy pants for women are the collection's backbone, but menswear is also in the mix for those blokes in touch with their yoga side. The range has recently expanded to include cycling and jogging gear.

### PACIFIC CENTRE                    MALL

Map p266 (☏604-688-7235; www.pacificcentre.ca; cnr Howe & W Georgia Sts; ⊙10am-7pm Sat-Tue, 10am-9pm Wed-Fri, 11am-6pm Sun; ⑤Granville) If rain curtails your shopping activities, duck inside downtown Vancouver's main mall. You'll find all the usual chain and department store suspects, plus highlights such as H&M, Purdy's Chocolates and Harry Rosen. You can also check your email for free at the Apple Store. There's a large food court if you need a pit stop from all that retail therapy. Check the mall's website for an up-to-the-minute listing of sales and deals at the stores and eateries here.

### BIRKS                    JEWELLERY

Map p266 (☏604-669-3333; www.maisonbirks.com; 698 W Hastings St; ⊙10am-6pm Mon-Fri, 10am-5:30pm Sat, noon-5pm Sun; ⑤Waterfront) A Vancouver institution since 1879 – hence the landmark freestanding clock outside – Birks crafts exquisite heirloom jewelry and its signature line of timepieces. It's an upscale place, similar to Tiffany & Co in the US, and ideal for picking up that special something in a classy blue embossed box for a deserving someone back home.

## 🏠 West End

Not only a vibrant district of restaurants and coffee shops, the West End has more than a few stores worth nosing around in. The majority of the most distinctive businesses are on Davie St and are oriented toward the area's large gay community, but you can also expect bookstores, bakeries, wine shops and just about everything else along the way. The western end of Robson St delivers some interesting Asian stores: the perfect place to pick up oddball Japanese candies and those essential cans of Pocari Sweat.

### WEST END FARMERS MARKET      MARKET

Map p270 (☏604-879-3276; www.eatlocal.org; Comox St, btwn Bute & Thurlow Sts, Nelson Park; ⊙9am-2pm Sat Jun–mid-Oct; 🚌6) 🌿 Vancouver's most urban alfresco farmers market is in the heart of the West End. It runs during the sunniest months of the year (but doesn't stop for rain), and it's a great way to meet the locals. The strip of 30 or so stalls often includes baked treats, arts and crafts, and glistening piles of freshly picked, locally grown fruit and veg. Look out for seasonal blueberries, cherries, apricots and peaches, and expect a busker or two as you wander around gorging on your purchases.

### LITTLE SISTER'S
### BOOK & ART EMPORIUM   BOOKS, ACCESSORIES

Map p270 (☏604-669-1753; www.littlesisters.ca; 1238 Davie St; ⊙9am-11pm; 🚌6) One of the few gay bookshops in western Canada, Little Sister's is a large bazaar of queer-positive tomes, plus magazines, DVDs and toys of the adult type. If this is your first visit to Vancouver, it's a great place to network with the local 'gayborhood.' Check the notice boards for events and announcements from the wider community. There are also occasional events in the store, including launches and author readings.

### KONBINIYA JAPAN CENTRE        FOOD

Map p270 (www.konbiniya.com; 1238 Robson St; ⊙11am-1am; 🚌5) Situated at a point on Robson St where the generic chain stores dry up and the Asian businesses begin, this is the kind of colorful, chaotic, even tacky store frequently seen in Tokyo's bustling suburbs. It's the best place in town for Pocky chocolate sticks, wasabi-flavored Kit Kats and Melty Kiss candies, hence the homesick language students shuffling nostalgically around the aisles. If your accommodation are self-catering, this is a good place to pick up cheap instant noodles and Glico curry mixes – you can also buy some large bags of savory corn snacks for the road.

## 🏃 SPORTS & ACTIVITIES

### SECOND BEACH POOL          SWIMMING

Map p287 (☏604-257-8371; www.vancouverparks.ca; cnr N Lagoon Dr & Stanley Park Dr, Stanley Park; adult/child $5.86/2.95; ⊙10am-8:45pm mid-Jun–Aug, reduced hours off-season; ♿; 🚌19) This smashing outdoor pool shimmers like a gem right beside the ocean shoreline. It has lanes for laps but you'll be weaving past children on

## RIOTOUS BEHAVIOUR

When the 2010 Winter Olympics were staged in Vancouver, locals were surprised and delighted that the jam-packed nighttime streets never spilled over into trouble. So, when the Vancouver Canucks hockey team entered a play-off run in 2011, few were concerned that things might turn ugly – despite the distant memory of hockey riots here during a similar play-off run back in 1994.

On the night of June 15, 2011, however, just after the Canucks lost to the Boston Bruins, the downtown core rapidly descended into chaos. Hundreds of booze-fueled 'fans,' most of whom had been watching the game at an outdoor live-screening site, began rampaging through the city, smashing store windows, setting fire to police cars and looting dozens of shops, including the Bay and London Drugs. The police seemed unable to quell the rioters and control of the city center was lost for several hours. The region watched the unfolding events on its TV screens in horror.

The next day, after the violence had subsided, a different group of locals turned out on the streets. Armed with brooms and buckets, and rallied by a social media call-to-action that asked Vancouverites to show what the city was really all about, hundreds arrived to help with the clean-up. Interviewed on TV, many expressed their anger at what had happened the night before as well as their determination to help the recovery efforts. As for the rioters, many were outed and eventually charged by the police after posting photos of themselves on social media during the evening's flame-licked iniquity.

most summer days; the kids take over during school vacations, making it very hard to get anywhere near the waterslide (we've tried). If you're traveling with under-10s, they'll love the chance to hang with local kids.

### ACADEMIE DUELLO SWORDPLAY

Map p266 (☑604-568-9907; www.academieduello.com; 412 W Hastings St; ☺noon-8pm Mon-Fri, 10am-5pm Sat; ☂; ☐9) Perfect for finding your inner knight in ye olde Vancouver, this popular downtown sword-play school offers thrilling classes and workshops for kids and adults, showing you how to wield everything from rapiers to broadswords. If you're visiting the city with kids in July and August, book them into Knight Camp, a five-day favorite that's great fun and sells out every year.

### BAYSHORE RENTALS CYCLING

Map p270 (☑604-688-2453; www.bayshorebikerentals.ca; 745 Denman St; per hr/8hr $6/23.80; ☺9am-dusk; ☐5) One of several rival businesses taking advantage of their Stanley Park proximity, Bayshore will rent you just about anything to get you rolling around the nearby seawall. The mountain bikes are its bread and butter, but it also rents in-line skates, tandems (you know you want one) and rugged toddler bike-trailers so you can tow your kids like the royalty they are.

### SPOKES BICYCLE RENTALS CYCLING

Map p270 (☑604-688-5141; www.spokesbicyclerentals.com; 1798 W Georgia St; adult per hr/day

from $6.67/26.67; ☺8am-9pm, reduced hours off-season; ☐5) On the corner of W Georgia and Denman Sts, this is the biggest of the bike shops servicing the Stanley Park cycling trade. It can kit you and your family out with all manner of bikes, from cruisers to kiddie one-speeds. Ask for tips on riding the Seawall; it extends far beyond Stanley Park.

### CYCLE CITY TOURS TOURS

Map p266 (☑604-618-8626; www.cyclevancouver.com; 648 Hornby St; tours from $59, rentals per hr/day $8.50/34; ☺9am-6pm, reduced hours in winter; ⑤Burrard) Striped with an ever-increasing number of dedicated bike lanes, Vancouver is a good city for two-wheeled exploring. But if you're not great at navigating, consider a guided tour with this friendly operator. If you're a beer fan, aim for the Craft Beer Tour ($90), nine tasty samples included. Alternatively, go it alone with a rental; there's a bike lane right outside.

### HARBOUR CRUISES BOATING

Map p287 (☑604-688-7246; www.boatcruises.com; 501 Denman St; adult/child from $35/12; ☺May–mid-Oct; ☐19) View the city – and some unexpected wildlife – from the water on a 75-minute narrated harbor tour, weaving past Stanley Park, Lions Gate Bridge and the North Shore mountains. There's also a lovely 2½-hour sunset dinner cruise (adult/child $83/69) plus a long, languid lunch trek to lovely Indian Arm ($72) that makes you feel like you're a million miles from the city.

# Gastown & Chinatown

## Neighborhood Top Five

**❶ Catfe** (p89) Communing with a clutch of friendly felines and triggering a purr or two at British Columbia's first cat-themed cafe.

**❷ Alibi Room** (p88) Tucking into the city's best array of regional craft beers while rubbing shoulders with the locals at one of the long, can-

dlelit tables; small sampler glasses recommended.

**❸ Dr Sun Yat-Sen Classical Chinese Garden** (p82) Sinking into a state of calm while watching the bobbling turtles and admiring the gnarly bonsai trees.

**❹ Vancouver Police-Museum** (p81) Discovering the city's murky, sometimes murderous past at this hidden-gem museum.

**❺ Skwachays Lodge** (p220) Staying the night in Vancouver's artsy First Nations hotel; ground-floor art gallery recommended.

For more detail of this area see Map p272 and p273 ➡

## Lonely Planet's Top Tip

Gastown and Chinatown are part of the Downtown Eastside, which some locals will tell you is a dangerous area. These are generally locals who haven't been here. The neighborhood certainly has many social challenges and a high proportion of residents with addiction or mental-health issues. You're far more likely, however, to be asked for 'spare change' in the city center, and muggings here are rare. Stay street smart and avoid the fetid back alleys and side streets (especially at night).

### Best Places to Eat

➡ Tacofino (p83)

➡ Ask for Luigi (p86)

➡ Bao Bei (p88)

➡ Bestie (p86)

➡ Purebread (p83)

### Best Places to Drink

➡ Alibi Room (p88)

➡ Juniper (p92)

➡ Keefer Bar (p92)

➡ Brickhouse (p92)

➡ Catfe (p89)

### Best Places to Shop

➡ Eastside Flea (p94)

➡ Erin Templeton (p94)

➡ Community Thrift & Vintage (p94)

➡ Salmagundi West (p94)

➡ Lynn Steven Boutique (p95)

# Explore Gastown & Chinatown

Radiating from the jaunty Gassy Jack statue in brick-paved Maple Tree Sq, the main thoroughfares of compact Gastown are Powell, Water, Carrall and Alexander Sts. You'll find plenty of shops and restaurants on Water St, while its adjoining side streets are home to a more recent wave of hip bars, stores and coffee shops. Wandering southeast from Maple Tree Sq, you'll enter the heart of the Downtown Eastside, where many of the neighborhood's poorest residents reside. Hastings St runs across Carrall and is this rougher area's main drag. A block across is Chinatown, denoted by its flare-roofed buildings and dragon-topped street lamps. The entire Gastown and Chinatown district is easily explored on foot and makes for a fascinating afternoon of urban wandering. Couple this with an end-of-day drink or dinner in some of the city's best bars and restaurants.

# Local Life

➡**Bars** Avoid downtown's Granville Strip drunks on a bar crawl of Gastown's top watering holes. You'll find hipster locals as well as more BC craft beer than you can shake a merry stick at. Be sure to include the excellent Alibi Room (p88).

➡**Shops** Chinatown is teeming with traditional grocery stores, where looking is just as much fun as buying. You'll find interesting items such as lizards splayed on sticks. For a different scene, peruse the cool boutiques of Gastown.

➡**History** Vancouver's best heritage buildings line this area, from tile-topped apothecaries to handsome century-old stone edifices repurposed as cool bars and restaurants. Make sure you look higher than shop level for glimpses of this evocative past.

# Getting There & Away

➡**Train** SkyTrain's Waterfront Station is at the western edge of Gastown, near the start of Water St. Stadium-Chinatown Station is on the edge of Chinatown and a 10-minute stroll south of Gastown.

➡**Bus** Bus 14 heads northwards from downtown's Granville St then along Hastings, which makes it handy for both Gastown and Chinatown. Buses 3, 4, 7 and 8 also service the area.

➡**Car** There is metered parking throughout Gastown and Chinatown, with some non-metered parking east of Main St.

# ◉ SIGHTS

## ◉ Gastown

### VANCOUVER POLICE MUSEUM    MUSEUM

Map p273 (📞604-665-3346; www.vancouver
policemuseum.ca; 240 E Cordova St; adult/child
$12/8; ⊙9am-5pm Tue-Sat; 🚌4) Illuminating
the crime-and-vice-addled history of the region, this quirky museum is lined with confiscated weapons and counterfeit currency.
It also has a former mortuary room where
the walls are studded with preserved slivers
of human tissue – spot the bullet-damaged
brain slices. Consider adding a walking
tour ($20) to learn all about the area's sala-
cious olden days. And buy a toe-tag T-shirt
in the gift shop.

One of Vancouver's hidden-gem
museums, it has plenty of exhibits and
grainy photos covering a time when the city
was rougher than a 1950s X-rated film-noir
movie. Speaking of which, it also screens
apposite films once a month in the morgue
between September and May, often including shockers such as *Psycho*, *Silence of the
Lambs* and those later George Lucas *Star
Wars* debacles (just kidding).

### GASSY JACK STATUE    MONUMENT

Map p272 (Maple Tree Sq; 🚌4) It's amusing
to think that Vancouver's favorite statue
is a testament to the virtues of drink. At
least that's one interpretation of the John
'Gassy Jack' Deighton bronze, perched atop
a whiskey barrel here in Maple Tree Sq.
Erected in 1970, it recalls the time when
Deighton arrived here in 1867 and built a
pub, triggering a development that soon became Vancouver.

Rivaling the nearby Steam Clock for
most-photographed Gastown landmark,
the statue is roughly on the site of Deighton's first pub; he soon built a second,
grander one nearby.

### MAPLE TREE SQUARE    SQUARE

Map p272 (intersection of Alexander, Water, Powell & Carrall Sts; 🚌4) The intersection where
Vancouver began was the site of 'Gassy
Jack' Deighton's first pub, and the spot
where the inaugural city-council meeting
was held under a large maple tree. It drips
with old-town charm. Snap a photo of the
merry statue of Jack, plus the nearby, re-

cently restored Byrnes Block, the oldest
Vancouver building still in its original
location.

Gastown was designated a national historic site in 2010, in the main because of
this area. Stocked with historic buildings
completed a few years after the 1886 Great
Fire, Carrall St has some handsome historic architecture. Images from Vancouver's
early days (just after it was renamed from
the original moniker of 'Granville') show
that the first 'city hall' was actually a sag-
ging tent with a handwritten sign on it.

### WOODWARD'S    NOTABLE BUILDING

Map p272 (149 W Hastings St; 🚌14) The project that catalyzed recent Downtown Eastside redevelopment, this former landmark
department store was a derelict shell after closing in the early 1990s. Successive
plans to transform it failed until, in 2010,
it reopened as the home of new shops and
condos, a trigger for what many have la-
belled neighborhood gentrification. Check
out the monumental 'Gastown Riot' photo
montage inside.

The Woodward's W-shaped red neon
sign that stood atop the building for decades was replaced with a reproduction
when the new development was completed; the old one is preserved in a glass cabinet at ground level near the Cordova St
entrance. If you get the angle right (which
might mean lying on the sidewalk), you
can snap an image of both signs at the
same time.

### STEAM CLOCK    LANDMARK

Map p272 (cnr Water & Cambie Sts; Ⓢ Waterfront)
Halfway along Water St, this oddly popular tourist magnet lures the cameras with
its tooting steam whistle. Built in 1977, the
clock's mechanism is actually driven by
electricity; only the pipes on top are fueled
by steam (reveal it to the patiently waiting tourists and you might cause a riot). It
sounds every 15 minutes, and marks each
hour with little whistling symphonies.

Once you have taken the required photo, spend time exploring the rest of cobbled Water St. One of Vancouver's most
historic thoroughfares, its well-preserved
heritage buildings contain shops, galleries
and resto-bars. Be sure to cast your gaze
above entrance level for cool architectural
features.

**WORTH A DETOUR**

## JAPANTOWN

The Chinese weren't the only group to arrive from Asia in the early days of Vancouver. A couple of blocks east of Chinatown, Japantown was once home to many residences, shops and businesses that served the fledgling city's Japanese community. Centered on an area around **Oppenheimer Park**, this intriguing historic district is worth a wander if you're in the vicinity. You'll find some of the city's oldest small wooden homes, many of them time-capsule reminders of a sometimes forgotten period in Vancouver's past.

The best time to visit is late July or early August, when the park's unmissable week-end-long **Powell Street Festival** (www.powellstreetfestival.com) takes place, cel-ebrating Japanese heritage and culture. One of Vancouver's most popular community festivals, and bound to be a highlight of your trip, this sensory extravaganza includes traditional music, vibrant performances and inviting food stands (anyone for Spam sushi?) as well as a minimarket of authentic arts and crafts. The festival's **Omikoshi shrine procession** is a standout, a foot-stomping, camera-triggering happening that makes everyone stop what they're doing and rush over.

## ⊙ Chinatown

### CHINATOWN MILLENNIUM GATE
LANDMARK

Map p273 (cnr W Pender & Taylor Sts; ⑤Stadium-Chinatown) Inaugurated by Canadian Prime Minister Jean Chrétien in 2002, Chinatown's towering entrance is the landmark most visitors look for. Stand well back, since the decoration is mostly on its lofty upper reaches: an elaborately painted section topped with a terra-cotta-tiled roof. The characters inscribed on its eastern front implore you to 'Remember the past and look forward to the future.'

The gate sits on the same site as a previous temporary wooden one that was built here for a royal visit in 1912. The lions on either side of the Millennium Gate once had polished granite balls in their mouths, but they mysteriously disappeared soon after the gate was unveiled and have never been found.

### JACK CHOW BUILDING
NOTABLE BUILDING

Map p273 (www.jackchow.com; 8 W Pender St; ⑤Stadium-Chinatown) This spot, known for decades as the Sam Kee Building until Jack Chow Insurance changed the name and spruced it up, has been listed in the *Guinness Book of World Records* as the planet's shallowest commercial building. The new approach includes a Vegaslike musical light show on the outside of the structure.

It's interesting to note that this century-old building is only here as the result of a dispute. Chang Toy, the Sam Kee Co owner, bought land at this site in 1906, but in 1926 all but a 1.8m-wide strip was expropriated by the city to widen Pender St. Toy's revenge was to build anyway, and up sprang the unusual 'Slender on Pender' dwelling.

### DR SUN YAT-SEN CLASSICAL CHINESE GARDEN & PARK
GARDENS

Map p273 (✆604-662-3207; www.vancouverchinesegarden.com; 578 Carrall St; adult/child $14/10; ⊙9:30am-7pm mid-Jun–Aug, 10am-6pm Sep & May–mid-Jun, 10am-4:30pm Oct-Apr; ⑤Stadium-Chinatown) A tranquil break from clamorous Chinatown, this intimate 'garden of ease' reflects Taoist principles of balance and harmony. Entry includes a 45-minute guided tour, in which you'll learn about the symbolism behind the placement of the gnarled pine trees, winding covered pathways and ancient limestone forma-tions. Look out for the lazy turtles bobbing in the jade-colored water.

The adjacent **Dr Sun Yat-Sen Park** FREE isn't quite as elaborate as its sister, but this spot is also a pleasant oasis with whisper-ing grasses, a large fishpond and a small pagoda. Check the website for summer-time Friday-evening concerts in the mai Garden.

## ✕ EATING

After years of offering little more than boring tourist-trap eateries, Gastown's handsome heritage buildings are now stuffed with innovative gourmet hangouts and convivial comfort-food haunts. Things are changing rapidly, so keep your eyes peeled for new openings. In Chinatown, Pender and Keefer Sts (between Columbia St and Gore Ave) are your best bets for authentic Chinese dining, including some with contemporary fusion flourishes.

## ✗ Gastown

★**PUREBREAD** BAKERY

Map p272 (☑604-563-8060; www.purebread. ca; 159 W Hastings St; baked goods $3-6; ☺8:30am-5:30pm; ☏; 🚇14) When Whistler's favorite bakery opened here, salivating Vancouverites began flocking in en masse. Expect to stand slack-jawed in front of the glass panels as you try to choose from a cornucopia of cakes, pastries and bars. Cakewise, we love the coconut buttermilk loaf, but make sure you also pick up a crack bar or salted caramel bar to go (or preferably both).

And if you think power bars taste like the soles of old running shoes, sink your teeth into Purebread's velvet-soft go go bar, then walk it all off with a 50km stroll.

★**TACOFINO** MEXICAN $

Map p272 (☑604-899-7907; www.tacofino.com; 15 W Cordova St; tacos $6-12; @; 🚇14) Food-truck favorites Tacofino made an instant splash with this huge, handsome dining room (think stylish geometric-patterned floors and hive-like lampshades). The simple menu focuses on a handful of taco options (six at lunch, more at dinner) plus nachos, soups and a selection of beer, agave and naughty tequila flights. Fish tacos are the top-seller, but we love the super-tender lamb birria.

There are additional menu options at dinner time but consider dropping by for happy hour, from 3pm to 6pm daily, when you can scoff two tacos for $10.

**LOST + FOUND CAFE** CAFE $

Map p272 (☑604-559-7444; www.lostandfound cafe.com; 33 W Hastings St; mains $9; ☺8am-6pm Mon-Fri, 9am-5pm Sat & Sun; ☏; 🚇14) A cavernous room where comfy sofas lure

---

### DOWNTOWN EASTSIDE: REGENERATION OR GENTRIFICATION?

Radiating from the Main and Hastings Sts intersection, the Downtown Eastside was once Vancouver's primary business and shopping district. But by the 1970s the banks, flagship stores and neon-accented restaurants had moved across the city and the area had descended into a depressing ghetto of lives blighted by drugs and prostitution. The neighborhood that time forgot, though, has been on a swift upward curve in recent years.

The catalyst for change was the massive **Woodward's** (p81) redevelopment that opened in 2010, transforming a former department store that had stood empty and crumbling for more than a decade with new shops and condo units. It triggered the restoration of dozens of other old buildings in the neighborhood, many of them ironically still here because developers had treated this area as a no-go zone for decades while tearing down buildings of similar age in other parts of the city. Now handsomely renovated, these include the copper-colored **Dominion Building** (Map p272; 205 W Hastings St; 🚇14) and the beautifully upgraded **Flack Block** (Map p272; 163 W Hastings St; 🚇14). Don't stay too long outside the monumental-looking **Carnegie Centre** (Map p273; 401 Main St; 🚇3), though. The city's original public library is a lovely building – look out for its stained-glass window of Shakespeare, Spenser and Milton – but the milling crowds and barely concealed drug deals taking place outside can be overwhelming for some visitors.

Nostalgia fans should also keep their eyes peeled for heritage neon signs in this area, mostly along Hastings St. Look out for fine examples at the **Ovaltine Cafe** (251 E Hastings St) and **Save on Meats** (43 W Hastings St).

Not surprisingly, while many have praised efforts to restore and renovate the Downtown Eastside's historic look, accusations of gentrification have been strongly voiced. As hipster bars and boutique shops continue to pop up in old buildings here, the locals that have called the area home for decades are being priced out. It remains to be seen whether a balance can be found that pleases everyone.

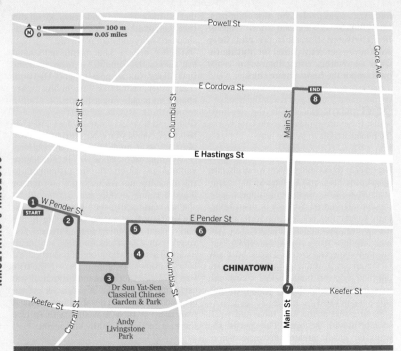

# Neighborhood Walk
## Chinatown History & Culture Crawl

**START** CHINATOWN MILLENNIUM GATE
**END** VANCOUVER POLICE MUSEUM
**LENGTH** 1.5KM; ONE HOUR

Stroll the streets of one of North America's largest Chinatown districts and immerse yourself in culture and heritage. Start near the intersection of W Pender and Taylor Sts, where the giant ❶**Chinatown Millennium Gate** (p82) dominates proceedings. Walk east under the gate and you'll come to the quirky ❷**Jack Chow Building** (p82), reputedly the world's narrowest office block. Peer in the windows and also notice the glass panels in the sidewalk, reminders of a subterranean public baths complex that once served area locals.

Turn right onto Carrall St. where the entrance to the lovely, landscaped ❸**Dr Sun Yat-Sen Classical Chinese Garden** (p82) will soon be on your left. Inside the garden, check out tranquil pools, intriguing limestone formations and gnarly pine and bonsai trees on a guided tour. Continue north towards

Pender St, noticing the ❹**bronze memorial** on the red tiles that commemorates the contribution of Chinese workers to building Canada's train system, and then see the white-paneled ❺**alternative Chinatown gate**, built for Expo '86 and moved here afterwards.

Turn right onto Pender and stroll east for a couple of blocks. You'll pass rows of antique Chinatown buildings – some of the city's oldest storefronts – as well as several dragon-topped street lamps; you're now entering the heart of historic Chinatown. ❻**Sai Woo** (p88) will be on your right next; it's a good spot to return to for dinner. Continue along Pender to Main St. Explore the traditional Chinese grocery and apothecary stores around Main here, especially one block south on ❼**Keefer St**. Then, return to Main, turn right and walk a couple of blocks north to Cordova St. Turn right onto Cordova and soon you'll reach the ❽**Vancouver Police Museum** (p81) where you can spend an hour exploring the city's past, from confiscated weapons to unsolved crimes.

lingering coffee quaffers, this laid-back eatery also serves good-value lunches. Inventive soups are made from scratch daily and they're perfectly paired with made-to-order sandwiches using their own lovely buns; go for the curry apricot chicken. Need a snack to go? Pick up a cinnamon bun and try not to eat it until you reach the door.

Save time to check out the art-lined walls; there are typically some cool works from local artists to peruse here.

### NELSON THE SEAGULL                    CAFE $

Map p272 (☑604-681-5776; www.nelsonthe seagull.com; 315 Carrall St; main $6-10; ⊘9am-5pm; 🛜🖋; ☐14) Gastown's hippest cafe, the mosaic-floored Seagull is also amazingly welcoming. Locals drop in to admire each other's MacBooks, lingering over flat-white coffees while indulging in the kind of wholesome treats that might be made by a gourmet grandma. Start the day with poached eggs on house-baked sourdough toast and return for the ploughman's lunch served on a board.

Grab a seat at the long table and you'll soon be in with the locals. Then peruse the walls for locally created artworks before taking a peek at the open kitchen at the back: if you're here when the bread's being baked, you'll be in culinary heaven (take-out loaves are available).

### MEAT & BREAD                    SANDWICHES $

Map p272 (www.meatandbread.ca; 370 Cambie St; mains $7-10; ⊘11am-5pm Mon-Sat; ☐14) Arrive early to sidestep the lunchtime line-ups at Vancouver's favorite sandwich shop and you might snag a seat. If not, hang with the locals at the long table, tucking into the daily-changing special or the ever-popular, nicely juicy porchetta sandwich. The finger-licking grilled cheese is also delicious, seriously challenging the hipsters trying to eat it without getting it on their beards. Wash it all down with a craft beer or glass of wine, and expect to come back: this place has an almost cult-like following.

### SAVE ON MEATS                    DINER $

Map p272 (☑604-569-3568; www.saveonmeats. ca; 43 W Hastings St; mains $5-15; ⊘7am-10pm Mon-Thu, 8am-10pm Fri & Sat, 8am-7pm Sun; 🍴; ☐14) A former old-school butcher shop, Save On Meats has been transformed into a popular hipster diner. But it's not just about looking cool. Slide into a booth or take a perch at the long counter and tuck into comfort

dishes, including a good-value $5 all-day breakfast plus a menu of basic faves such as shepherd's pie, and mac 'n' cheese.

There's also a kids menu here. And ask about the innovative token scheme that allows you to help support the local community instead of just giving 'spare change' to people who ask for it.

### ACME CAFE                    DINER $$

Map p272 (☑604-569-1022; www.acmecafe.ca; 51 W Hastings St; mains $10-16; ⊘8am-9pm Mon-Fri, 9am-9pm Sat & Sun; ☐14) The black-and-white deco-style interior here is enough to warm up anyone on a rainy day – or maybe it's the comfy booths and retro-cool U-shaped counter. Hipsters have been flocking here since day one for hearty breakfasts and heaping comfort-food lunches flavored with a gourmet flourish: the meatloaf, chicken club and 'high-falutin' grilled cheese sandwiches alone are worth the trip.

A great spot for weekend brunch (if you can avoid the crowds), it's also perfect for afternoon coffee and a slab of house-baked fruit pie. For those traveling with sprogs, there's a good and healthy kids menu.

### MEET IN GASTOWN                    VEGAN $$

Map p272 (☑604-688-3399; www.eatmeet.ca; 12 Water St; mains $7-15; ⊘11am-11pm Sun-Thu, to 1am Fri & Sat; 🖋; Ⓜ Waterfront) Bringing great vegan comfort dishes to locals without the worthy rabbit-food approach, this wildly popular spot can be clamorously busy at times. But it's worth the wait for a wide-ranging array of herbivore- and carnivore-pleasing dishes, from rice bowls to mac 'n' cheese (made from vegan nut 'cheese') and from portobello mushroom burgers to poutine-like fries slathered in cashew gravy (our recommendation).

In a cool courtyard area just off Water St (the city's tiny original jail once stood nearby), it also has a shaded outside patio for balmy day dining. This is the second branch of MeeT; the original, more intimate spot is on Main St and is worth visiting if you're in that part of town.

### NUBA                    MIDDLE EASTERN $$

Map p272 (☑604-688-1655; www.nuba.ca; 207 W Hastings St; mains $9-30; ⊘11:30am-10pm Mon-Fri, noon-10pm Sat, 5-10pm Sun; 🖋; ☐14) Tucked under the landmark Dominion Building, this Lebanese restaurant attracts budget noshers and cool hipsters in equal measure. If you're not sure what to go for, split some tasty, surprisingly filling meze dishes including excellent hummus and falafel, or just dive straight into a shareable La Feast for two ($38) that covers all the bases (including the inevitable doggie bag takeout).

There are plenty of vegetarian options here as well as a homey, fresh-made feel to the food. Consider taking a photo of the building on your way out: the copper-topped edifice is among the most iconic old buildings in the city and was once one of the tallest.

### WILDEBEEST                                   WEST COAST $$

Map p272 (☑604-687-6880; www.wildebeest. ca; 120 W Hastings St; mains $14-39; ⊘5pm-late daily, brunch 10am-2pm Sat & Sun; ☑14) This moodlit, bi-level joint is a carnivore's dream, but there are plenty of options for vegetarians here, too. Find a table among the chattering classes – or better still at the communal long table downstairs – and tuck into short ribs, pork jowl or the juiciest roast chicken you'll ever eat. Add a bone-marrow small plate for fun.

Drop by on weekends for a meaty brunch that will fill you up for a week. And don't miss the drinks list: far from being an afterthought, there's an excellent array of well-made cocktails here.

### DEACON'S CORNER                                 DINER $$

Map p272 (☑604-684-1555; www.deacon scorner.ca; 101 Main St; mains $8-16; ⊘8am-6pm Mon-Fri, 9am-6pm Sat, 9am-8pm Sun; ☑4) This lively, no-nonsense diner opened a few years back and immediately started luring Vancouverites to a grubby part of town they'd previously avoided. They come for the hulking, hangover-busting breakfasts (biscuits with eggs, chicken and gravy is recommended if you want your weekly calorific intake in a single meal), while lunches include good-value grilled sandwiches and bulging steak and cheese quesadilla.

Avoid the peak weekend breakfast period; the place can be packed and finding a seat (even at the counter) can be hard. Weekdays you'll have your pick of the perches. This is the ideal spot to fill your belly and then walk it off with a wander around the historic neighborhood.

### ★ASK FOR LUIGI                               ITALIAN $$$

Map p272 (☑604-428-2544; www.askforluigi. com; 305 Alexander St; mains $22-24; ⊘11:30am-2:30pm & 5:30-10:30pm Tue-Fri, 9:30am-2:30pm & 5:30-11pm Sat, 9:30am-2:30pm & 5:30-9:30pm Sun; ☑4) Consider an off-peak lunch if you don't want to wait too long for a table at this white clapboard, shack-look little charmer (reservations are not accepted). Inside, you'll find a checkerboard floor and teak-lined interior crammed with tables and delighted diners tucking into (and sharing) plates of scratch-made pasta that mama never used to make; think bison tagliatelle and borage-and-ricotta ravioli.

Despite the top-notch dishes, this Railtown hot spot never feels snobbish, especially during the weekend brunch service when the room is animated with lively local chatter.

### L'ABATTOIR                                     FRENCH $$$

Map p272 (☑604-568-1701; www.labattoir.ca; 217 Carrall St; mains $35-44; ⊘5:30-10pm Sun-Thu, to 10:30pm Fri & Sat, brunch 10am-2pm Sat & Sun; ☑4) Gastown's most romantic top-end restaurant, this candlelit, brick-lined spot makes an art of attending to every detail. Be careful not to fill up on the warm bread before you tuck into a menu of French-influenced West Coast dishes. We recommend the lamb leg with spicy merguez sausage. Reservations are suggested: ask for a table in the delightful window-walled back room.

Whatever you end up eating, save some room for a perfect cocktail; this restaurant is celebrated for its dedication to the libation gods. There's also a popular weekend brunch service if you want to start the day off in style.

## ✖ Chinatown

### BESTIE                                          GERMAN

Map p273 (☑604-620-1175; www.bestie.ca; 105 E Pender St; mains $4-11; ⊘11:30am-10pm Sun-Thu, to midnight Fri & Sat; 🐾; ☑3) Like a food truck with a permanent home, this while-walled hole-in-the-wall specializes in Berlin-style currywursts – hearty sausages slathered in curry sauce, served with crunchy fries. It's popular with passing hipsters so arrive off-peak for a chance of snagging the little cubby-hole window table: the best in the house. There's always a small but well-curated array of local craft beers to add to the fun.

### RAMEN BUTCHER                                  RAMEN $

Map p273 (☑604-806-4646; www.theramen butcher.com; 223 E Georgia St; mains $10-12; ⊘11am-3pm & 5-10pm Tue-Thu, 11am-10pm Fri-

## VANCOUVER'S OLDEST STREET

Just a few weeks after renaming itself Vancouver (no-one liked the original name 'Granville,' nor the insalubrious 'Gastown' slang name that preceded it), the fledgling city of around 1000 homes burnt almost to the ground in just minutes in what was termed the Great Fire. But the locals weren't about to jump on the next boat out of town. Within days, plans were drawn up for a new city. And this time brick and stone would be favored over wood.

The first buildings to be erected radiated from Maple Tree Sq, in particular along Carrall St. This thoroughfare (which is also one of the shortest streets in Vancouver) still exists today and it links the historic center of Gastown to Chinatown. Take a stroll south along Carrall from Maple Tree Sq and you'll spot some grand buildings from the early days of the city. Perhaps due to an abundance of caution, they are also some of the sturdiest structures around and will likely survive for many years to come, whether or not there's another fire.

If you'd visited 30 years ago, however, you would have seen many of these buildings seemingly on their last legs. This part of Vancouver hadn't attracted any new development or investment for years and Carrall St's old, paint-peeled taverns, hotels and storefronts were spiraling into skid-row degradation. Two things changed the inevitable: firstly historians and heritage fans banded together to draw attention to the area's important role in the founding years of the city, a campaign that finally culminated in a national historic site designation in 2010. Secondly, gentrification took hold. With few neighborhoods around the city still left to enhance, the developers finally came back here. While gentrification has many vocal detractors in this area, an undeniable positive is that it has preserved and protected Gastown's historic buildings for decades to come. The brick and stone landmarks that once lined Carrall have, for the most part, been sympathetically restored and renovated, giving the area a new lease on life beyond its heritage designation.

Sun; ⬚3) One of several new Asian-themed restaurants arriving in Chinatown in recent years, this is the first North American foray of a well-known Japanese ramen franchise. The signature thin noddles come in several brothy bowl varieties with slabs of slow-cooked pork; we recommend the garlicky Red Ramen. Still have some soup in your bowl? They'll toss in a second serving of noodles for free.

It's mostly about the ramen here, but there are also several gyoza varieties to fill you up (including a pork-and-cheese version).

### NEW TOWN
#### BAKERY & RESTAURANT                    CHINESE $
Map p273 (☏604-689-7835; www.newtown bakery.ca; 148 E Pender St; dishes $8-15; ☺6:30am-8:30pm; ⏚; ⬚3) It's the glass cabinets of baked treats that lure most people through the door of this longtime Chinatown fixture; pop in for a well-priced prawn turnover or barbecued pork steamed bun to go. The takeout is the point of this place but if you're hungry for more, snag a table in the busy dining area at the back and dive into dim sum.

#### PHNOM PENH            VIETNAMESE, CAMBODIAN $$
Map p273 (☏603-682-5777; 244 E Georgia St; mains $8-18; ☺10am-9pm Mon-Thu, to 11pm Fri-Sun; ⬚3) The dishes at this bustling joint are split between Cambodian and Vietnamese soul-food classics. It's the highly addictive chicken wings and their lovely pepper sauce that keep regulars loyal. Once you've piled up the bones, dive back in for round two: papaya salad, butter beef and spring rolls show just how good a street-food-inspired Asian menu can be.

Don't leave without sampling a steamed rice cake, stuffed with pork, shrimp, coconut and scallions, and washed down with an ice-cold bottle of Tsingtao. This is the kind of place that makes Vancouver Canada's most authentic ethnic-food city.

#### CAMPAGNOLO                           ITALIAN $$
Map p273 (☏604-484-6018; www.cam pagnolorestaurant.ca; 1020 Main St; mains $15-22; ☺11:30am-2:30pm Mon-Fri & 5-10pm daily; ⬚3) Eyebrows were raised when this contemporary, rustic-style Italian restaurant opened in a hitherto sketchy part of town. But Campagnolo has lured locals and inspired a mini-wave of other restaurants in

the area. Reserve ahead and dive into freshly reinvented dishes such as smoked chicken cannelloni and a fennel sausage-topped pizza that may induce you to eat your body weight in thin-crust.

Save some room for a buzz-triggering after-dinner glass of grappa and plan to drop by for weekend brunch, served in the even more intimate upstairs nook. There's also a commitment to local produce here – Campagnolo cures its own meat.

### BODEGA                                      SPANISH $$

Map p273 (☑604-565-8815; www.bodegaonmain.com; 1014 Main St; small plates $7-20; ⊙11am-midnight Mon-Fri, 4:30pm-midnight Sat & Sun; ☑3) The newest of several recently arrived restaurants in this once-sketchy Main St stretch is actually the relocated reincarnation of one of Vancouver's oldest Spanish eateries. A downtown mainstay for decades, the new Bodega is a sumptuous room of bordello-red seats and paintings evoking the old country, plus a menu of lovely tapas favorites such as meatballs, grilled octopus and slow-roasted rabbit.

The daily sandwich lunch special ($9) is a good deal, but hang on for the weekday 3pm to 6pm happy hour when five tapas items are reduced by a couple of dollars each. And if you're a paella fan, there are two eye-rollingly delicious feast-like options available here (they need 30 minutes preparation time, though).

### SAI WOO                                        ASIAN $$

Map p273 (☑604-568-1117; www.saiwoo.ca; 158 E Pender; mains $12-18; ⊙4:30pm-midnight Tue-Sat, 11am-3pm Sun; ☑3) There's a film-set look to the exterior of this new Chinatown eatery that makes it feel like a replica of an old Asian restaurant. But the long, slender interior is a great candlelit cave with a lounge like vibe. You'll find fusion dishes such as chop suey and soy-flavored ginger chicken; consider the 4:30pm to 6pm happy hour with $6 dim sum specials and $5 beer and wine deals.

Sai Woo also runs a monthly speaker series where local movers and shakers trigger conversations and network. Entry is $20, which includes a drink and something to nibble on. Book ahead via the website.

### BAO BEI                                       CHINESE $$

Map p273 (☑604-688-0876; www.bao-bei.ca; 163 Keefer St; small plates $5-19; ⊙5:30pm-midnight Mon-Sat, 5:30-11pm Sun; ☑; ☑3)

Reinterpreting a Chinatown heritage building interior with hipsteresque flourishes, this Chinese brasserie is the area's most seductive dinner destination. Bringing a contemporary edge to Asian tapas-sized, MSG-free dishes such as *shao bing* (stuffed Chinese flatbread), duck salad and steamed pork belly buns, it also offers an inventive cocktail array to keep you occupied if you have to wait at the bar for your table.

Top-notch organic meat and sustainable seafood are used as much as possible, and the vegetarian options are never an afterthought. Reservations are not accepted so try to avoid peak 7pm to 9pm dining times.

# 🍷 DRINKING & NIGHTLIFE

**Home to some of Vancouver's best bars, Gastown's atmospheric old brick buildings have been revitalized with distinctive watering holes in recent years, making this an ideal spot for an easy pub crawl. And don't forget about Chinatown, which also has a choice bar or two of its own.**

## 🍷 Gastown

### ★ALIBI ROOM                                      PUB

Map p272 (☑604-623-3383; www.alibi.ca; 157 Alexander St; ⊙5-11:30pm Mon-Thu, 5pm-12:30am Fri, 10am-12:30am Sat, 10am-11:30pm Sun; ☎; ☑4) Vancouver's best craft-beer tavern has an exposed-brick bar that stocks an interesting roster of around 50 drafts, mostly from celebrated BC breweries such as Driftwood, Four Winds and Yellow Dog. Adventurous taste-trippers – hipsters and veteran beer fans alike – enjoy the $11.50 'frat bat' of four samples: choose your own or ask to be surprised. Check the board for ever-changing guest casks.

Food-wise, go for a side order of skinny fries with chili garlic vinegar or the hearty barbecued pork-belly sandwich. There's a slender patio for alfresco summer quaffing, and the cavelike downstairs area is ideal for rainy-day hunkering and lingering taste-testing. Also ask about Brassneck (p137), Alibi's affiliated and arguably even more popular microbrewery location on Main St.

## CATS & CAPPUCCINOS

Japan has long been the bastion of cafes where coffee quaffers can stroke a few purring moggies while sipping their java. But it took a few years for Vancouver to catch up to the cat-loving trend with the recently opened **Catfe** (Map p273; ☑778-379-0060; www.catfe.ca; International Village Mall, 88 Pender St; with/without cafe purchase $5/8; ☺11am-9pm Fri- Wed; ⑤Stadium-Chinatown) on the edge of Chinatown. Visitors book online for their time slot (numbers are limited so the cats aren't overwhelmed); buy their coffee in the cafe nook next door; then push through the door to the large feline play room, where at least a dozen cats doze on shelves or in sunny windows, before winding around visitors' legs or seeking out a lap or two to curl up on.

The best part is that the cats are clearly in charge: there's a human-free room they can escape to for quiet time and visitors are not allowed to interrupt naps or pick them up. Even better, all the cats come from the local SPCA (Society for the Prevention of Cruelty to Animals) and are available for adoption via the SPCA's usual procedures. At time of writing, more than 150 cats had found forever homes through the Catfe – including Max, the handsome two-year-old ginger fella who came home with us a few days after our visit. The Catfe also received the seal of approval from pop superstar Adele, who visited in 2016 prior to playing a concert in Vancouver. Reports indicate she formed an instant rapport with a well-whiskered resident named Larry.

### SIX ACRES BAR

Map p272 (☑604-488-0110; www.sixacres.ca; 203 Carrall St; ☺11:30am-11:30pm Sun-Thu, 11:30am-12:30am Fri & Sat; ☎; ☐4) Gastown's coziest tavern: you can cover all the necessary food groups via the carefully chosen draft and bottled beer list here. There's a small, animated summer patio out front but inside (especially upstairs) is great for hiding in a chatty, candlelit corner and working your way through the brews – plus a shared small plate or three (sausage board recommended).

It seems right and proper to also have a whiskey here: that's Gassy Jack's statue outside, perched atop a barrel, and he started the city with his first bar just a few steps from where you are now. The history doesn't end there, though. Six Acres is located in the Alhambra Building, one of the city's oldest structures.

### REVOLVER COFFEE

Map p272 (☑604-558-4444; www.revolvercoffee.ca; 325 Cambie St; ☺7:30am-6pm Mon-Fri, 9am-6pm Sat; ☎; ☐14) With all those new hipster coffee shops opening around town, Revolver feels like an elder statesman, despite only being a few years old itself. It's remained at the top of the Vancouver coffee-mug tree via a serious commitment to great java. Aim for a little booth table or, if they're taken (they usually are), hit the large communal table room next door.

### GUILT & CO BAR

Map p272 (www.guiltandcompany.com; 1 Alexander St; ☺7pm-late; ⑤Waterfront) This cavelike subterranean bar, beneath Gastown's brick-cobbled sidewalks, has a cult following among the kind of under-30s crowd that loves sipping Anchor Steam and playing Jenga at its tables (one of the many games available for imbibers to play). Avoid weekends when there are often line-ups and the place is crammed – drop by on a chilled-out weekday instead.

Along with the beer, there's an array of inventive cocktails to keep things lively. Check ahead for live music of the singer-songwriter variety, too.

### EAST VAN ROASTERS COFFEE

Map p272 (☑604-629-7562; www.eastvanroasters.com; 319 Carrall St; ☺10am-5pm Tue-Sat; ☎; ☐14) Blink and you'll miss the entrance to this small but perfectly formed cafe, which adjoins a busy coffee-roasting operation. It's worth popping in, though, and combing an excellent espresso with some delectable single-origin chocolate treats, also made on site. A social enterprise providing training and employment for women who live in this area, the service is sparklingly friendly. This is also a good spot to pick up cool-chocolate-bar souvenirs for home.

### DIAMOND COCKTAIL BAR

Map p272 (www.di6mond.com; 6 Powell St; ☺5:30pm-1am Mon-Thu, to 2am Fri & Sat, to midnight Sun; 🖵4) When you head upstairs via the unassuming entrance, you'll find yourself in one of Vancouver's warmest little cocktail bars. A renovated heritage room studded with sash windows – try for a view seat – it's popular with local coolsters but is rarely pretentious. A list of perfectly nailed premium cocktails ($10 to $14) helps, coupled with a tapas menu that includes lots of Japanese-influenced options.

Check out the lovely crystal chandeliers here, antiques from a bygone age, and try to spot the statue of Gassy Jack atop a whiskey barrel across the square. If you have enough to drink, he might even talk to you.

### DARBY'S GASTOWN                            BAR

Map p272 (☎604-558-4658; www.darbys gastown.pub; 16 W Hastings St; ⊙4pm-midnight; 🖵14) Reinvented from its former incarnation as Bitter Tasting Room, this brick-walled Gastown satellite of a popular Kitsilano beer bar has increased the draft menu to include offerings from some of the region's most talked-about producers. Sidle up to the C-shaped bar and taste-test tipples from Strange Fellows, Persephone, Tofino Brewing and Crannog Ales. Also ask about any special casks that might be available.

The food menu has also been beefed up, with meatball sliders and brisket sandwiches to keep you from imbibing too much. Alternatively, take a break from boozing with one of the free-use board games on the side table; unless Yahtzee drives you to drink, of course.

### IRISH HEATHER                            PUB

Map p272 (☎604-688-9779; www.irishheather. com; 210 Carrall St, Gastown; ⊙11:30am-midnight Sun-Thu, to 2am Fri & Sat; 🗺; 🖵4) Belying the clichés about expat Irish bars (except for its reclaimed Guinness barrel floor), the Heather is one of Vancouver's best gastropubs. Alongside lovingly prepared sausage and mash, and steak-and-ale pie, you'll find good craft beers and, of course, some well-poured stout. Looking for happy hour? Drop by between 3pm and 6pm daily for $5 booze specials.

Whiskey fans will also be gobsmacked by the array of tipples in the back-room **Shebeen** bar. It's the kind of place where you could settle for hours and still be there a week later, as merry as a giddy kipper.

### BLACK FROG                            PUB

Map p272 (☎604-602-0527; www.theblackfrog. ca; 108 Cambie St; ⊙11:30am-1am Mon-Thu, 11:30am-2am Fri, noon-2am Sat, noon-midnight Sun; 🗺; ⑤Waterfront) A few steps from the Steam Clock in a side-street blind spot, this bar does everything right, from friendly staff to no-nonsense pub grub. In summer, aim to bask on the deck (it's covered against rain) with an array of regional craft beers (be sure to ask what the daily special is). Food-wise, swap the burger route for a hearty plate of pierogis.

Black Frog is a great place to catch a live ice-hockey game on TV; you'll soon realize why the sport is often regarded as Canada's religion. In fact, this may be the only time you'll see locals openly weeping and plotting riots against the injustice of it all.

### STEAMWORKS BREW PUB                            BREWERY

Map p272 (☎604-689-2739; www.steam works.com; 375 Water St; ⊙11:30am-midnight Sun-Thu, to 1am Fri & Sat; ⑤Waterfront) This huge brewpub on the edge of Gastown serves several own-made beers, including pilsners, IPAs and pale ales. But the best of the bunch is the rich and velvety oatmeal stout. Popular with tourists and clocked-off office workers, Steamworks has an inviting pub-grub menu. Time your visit for the monthly Green Drinks night (www.greendrinks.org/bc/vancouver) when chatty enviro-types flirt with each other.

Ask about special seasonal brews (the summer wheat beers and hardy winter ales are best). There are outdoor tables for summer drinkers, but the best views across the water are from inside on the main floor, where several tables face the mountain-framed Burrard Inlet. There's also a liquor store here if you fancy a takeout.

### CAMBIE                            PUB

Map p272 (☎604-684-6466; www.cambiepubs. com; 300 Cambie St; ⊙7am-2am Mon-Thu, 7am-3am Fri, 8am-3am Sat, 8am-2am Sun; 🖵14) One of Gastown's remaining dive bars, the Cambie is a local legend that most Vancouverites fondly recall (perhaps hazily) visiting at least once. Summer nights on the raucous patio are grungy fun, but perching at a bench inside with a cheap drink special is a good way to have a blast without busting your budget.

Check out the tables; each is painted with a different original artwork. There's

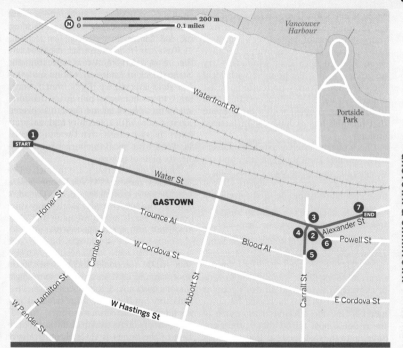

# 🏃 Neighborhood Walk
# Gastown Bar Crawl

**START** STEAMWORKS BREW PUB
**END** ALIBI ROOM
**LENGTH** 1KM (TIME DEPENDS ON HOW FAST YOU DRINK...)

This short walk will take you on a merry weave around Gastown's best watering holes and give you a glimpse of the city's nightlife scene.

Start your crawl at the western end of Gastown (near Waterfront SkyTrain station) with an oatmeal stout at **1 Steamworks Brew Pub** (p90), one of the city's few brewpubs. Enjoy the downhill slope east along Water St and you'll soon arrive at Maple Tree Sq. This is where Gassy Jack triggered the city by building his first saloon – tip your hat at the **2 statue** (p81) of him here, then duck underground to **3 Guilt & Co** (p89) for a bottled beer and a board game. Back outside, nip across the square to **4 Six Acres** (p89), one of the area's coziest hangouts. You'll be tempted to stick around, but the spirit of Gassy will be calling you back to the streets.

Stroll across Carrall St and duck into the **5 Irish Heather** (p90). The best spot in town for a Guinness, it also has a hidden whiskey bar out back where you can indulge your love of some of the top spirits from Ireland, Scotland and beyond. If you're still walking by this stage, head back onto Carrall, walk north for a few seconds and turn right onto Powell St. The street sign will point you to the unassuming stairwell that leads to the lovely **6 Diamond** (p89), a great spot to find a perfect cocktail. You'll likely still be able to spot Gassy's statue through the window, smiling at you across the square. If he doffs his hat and says 'hi', you've probably had too much to drink.

But if not, head back out and take Alexander St eastwards. Within a couple of minutes you'll be at the **7 Alibi Room** (p88). This is the city's favorite craft-beer bar and the best place in Vancouver to end your evening with a beery flourish; 'frat bat' of small sampler brews recommended.

## DON'T MISS: PINBALL WIZARD

One of the neighborhood's greasiest dive bars for decades, **Pub 340** (Map p272; ✆604-602-0644; www.pub340. ca; 340 Cambie St; ⊙9am-2am Mon-Thu, 9am-3am Fri & Sat; ☎; ▣14) has cleaned up its act somewhat in recent years. But it's not the cosmetic paint job, revamped menu and karaoke nights that have lured back some locals. It's the addition of arguably the city's best pinball room. A dozen or so shiny machines – from 1980s classics to new favorites – attract flipping fanatics. Regular tournaments welcome all-comers to show off their skills on machines including Terminator 2 and the Addams Family. Games cost $1 and, if you lose everything, you can cheer yourself up with a karaoke warble of that slightly well-worn Who song in the main bar area; a few glasses of Old Style Pilsner will help persuade you.

a beer-hall vibe in the main room but you can take a break from the noise in the arcade game area out back.

### SALT TASTING ROOM                    WINE BAR

Map p272 (✆604-633-1912; www.salttastingroom.com; 45 Blood Alley; ⊙4pm-midnight; ▣4) Sitting in a cobbled back alley reputedly named after the area's former butcher trade, this atmospheric little brick-lined wine bar offers dozens of interesting tipples, mostly available by the glass. From your communal table, peruse the large blackboard of house-cured meats and regional cheeses, then go for a $16 tasting plate of three, served with piquant condiments including Brit-style piccalilli.

## ⚘ Chinatown

### ★ BRICKHOUSE                          PUB

Map p273 (730 Main St; ⊙8pm-2am Mon-Sat, 8pm-midnight Sun; ▣3) Possibly Vancouver's most original pub, this old-school hidden gem is a welcoming, windowless tavern lined with Christmas lights, fish tanks and junk-shop couches. It's like hanging out in someone's den, and is popular with artsy locals and in-the-know young hipsters.

Grab an ale at the bar, slide onto a chair and start chatting: you're bound to meet someone interesting.

There's no food here (except chips) but the beloved Brickhouse is arguably the city's strongest claim to having its own Brit-style pub culture. Bicycle-shorts-wearing owner and barman Leo is committed to the idea that bars should be places where you hang out, socialize and connect. And play pool: there's a full-size table here as well.

### FORTUNE SOUND CLUB                    CLUB

Map p273 (✆604-569-1758; www.fortunesoundclub.com; 147 E Pender St; ⊙9:30pm-3am Fri & Sat, plus special events; ▣3) Vancouver's best club has transformed a tired Chinatown spot into a slick space with the kind of genuine staff and younger, hipster-cool crowd rarely seen in Vancouver venues. Slide inside and you'll find a giant dance floor popping with party-loving locals just out for a good time. Expect weekend queues, and check out Happy Ending Fridays, when you'll possibly dance your ass off.

Reputedly home to one of the city's best sound systems, Fortune also hosts a roster of regular bands.

### KEEFER BAR                          COCKTAIL BAR

Map p273 (✆604-688-1961; www.thekeeferbar.com; 135 Keefer St; ⊙5pm-midnight Mon, to 1am Tue-Thu & Sun, to 2am Fri & Sat; Ⓜ Stadium-Chinatown) This dark, narrow and atmospheric Chinatown bar was claimed by local cocktail-loving coolsters from day one. Drop in for a full evening of liquid taste-tripping and you'll have a blast. From perfectly prepared rosemary gimlets and Siamese slippers to an excellent whiskey menu and some tasty tapas (steam buns recommended), it offers up a great night out.

There are also cool extras here most nights – including Thursday's soul DJ – which are always combined with drinks specials. Cover charges for these are typically $5 to $8. In summer, grab one of the wood block seats outside and watch the Chinatown world go by.

### JUNIPER                             COCKTAIL BAR

Map p273 (✆604-681-1695; www.junipervancouver.com; 185 Keefer St; ⊙4pm-late; ▣3) A pilgrimage spot for gin fans. Head upstairs at this intimate mood-lit resto-bar and prepare for exquisite drinks that require serious savoring. There are several intriguing

## VANCOUVER'S BEST ART PARTY

Some locals claim that Vancouver doesn't have much of an arts scene. But if you're visiting in November and you know where to look, you'll have possibly the artiest weekend of your life. During the annual **Eastside Culture Crawl** (www.culturecrawl.ca; ⊘mid-Nov), more than 450 local artists open their studios, houses and workshops for free to art-loving visitors who wander from site to site, meeting the creators, hanging with artsy chums and even buying the occasional well-priced gem. Festival locations stretch eastwards from Main St and visitors spend their time walking the streets looking for the next hot spot, which is typically just around the corner.

You'll find full-time artists working on commissioned installations as well as artisans noodling away in their spare bedrooms. There's an almost partylike atmosphere in the streets during the weekend, especially if the rain holds off. Look out for the occasional street performer keeping things lively and incorporate a coffee-shop pit stop or two along the way. The event is a great opportunity to buy one-of-a-kind artwork souvenirs for that difficult person back home (you know the one).

Head to the website to plan your route, although we recommend just wandering and following the crowds to see what you find. Printed programs with maps are also available at most of the galleries involved in the event.

small-batch gins, available as top-notch G&Ts or lovingly crafted into delicious gin-based cocktails; try the tart East Van Bramble. There's also a food menu of seasonal dishes to distract you from the booze for a while.

If gin isn't your thing, there's a surprisingly good bottled-craft-beer array (go for anything by Four Winds).

### PAT'S PUB
LIVE MUSIC

Map p273 (☑604-255-4301; www.patspub. ca; 403 E Hastings St; ⊘11am-midnight Mon-Thu, to 1am Fri & Sat, to 10pm Sun; ☐14) The Downtown Eastside's most-accessible dive bar started a century ago and has recently dusted off the jazz chops that saw Jelly Roll Morton play here back in the day. Monday night sees no-cover jazz shows from 8pm, while there are often other cover-free jazz and blues happenings throughout the week. Check the pub's website calendar for events.

The good-value beer menu includes house-brewed Pat's Classic Lager. And the food is a cut above typical pub fare – pulled pork poutine and edamame, for example – with almost everything on the menu priced under $10.

## ⭐ ENTERTAINMENT

**Gastown is more about the bars but Chinatown is home to some decent entertainment options, including a couple of local-fave live venues. Converse with a few Vancouverites here and ask for recommendations about what's coming up and who's about to hit the stage.**

### RICKSHAW THEATRE
LIVE MUSIC

Map p273 (☑604-681-8915; www.liveatrick shaw.com; 254 E Hastings St; ☐14) Revamped from its grungy 1970s incarnation, the funky Rickshaw shows that Eastside gentrification can be positive. The stage of choice for many punk and indie acts, it's an excellent place to see a band. There's a huge mosh area near the stage and rows of theater-style seats at the back. Check the schedule to see who's on; many nights there are several bands on the roster.

### FIREHALL ARTS CENTRE
THEATER

Map p273 (☑604-689-0926; www.firehal lartscentre.ca; 280 E Cordova St; ☐4) One of the leading players in Vancouver's independent theater scene, this intimate, studio-sized venue is located inside a historic former fire station. It presents culturally diverse contemporary drama and dance, with an emphasis on emerging talent. A key venue during July's annual Dancing on the Edge festival (www.dancingontheedge. org), it also has a convivial licensed lounge on-site, where visiting drama fans can discuss the scene.

Check out the artworks lining the brick walls before you go in for your show: there's typically a focus on great local artists.

## COBALT
LIVE MUSIC, DANCE

Map p273 (www.thecobalt.ca; 917 Main St; ⊘9pm-2am; 🚇3) A favorite underground venue, the Cobalt has transformed from being a grungy live venue to being a grungy live venue with a good roster of underground acts and events, including many that serve the local gay scene. Alongside bands, you'll find a menu of karaoke and dance nights here.

## IMPERIAL
LIVE MUSIC

Map p272 (🖉604-428-2272; www.imperialvancouver.com; 319 Main St; 🚇3) An intimate live-music and club-night venue fusing tables and standing-room space, there's a revamped ballroom feel to this edge-of-Chinatown spot. Check the website to see what's coming up.

## CINEPLEX ODEON INTERNATIONAL VILLAGE CINEMAS
CINEMA

Map p273 (🖉604-806-0799; www.cineplex.com; 88 W Pender St; Ⓢ Stadium-Chinatown) Incongruously located on the 3rd floor of a usually half-empty Chinatown shopping mall, this popular Vancouver theater combines blockbuster and art-house offerings and is often used for film festivals. Comfy stadium seating is the norm here, and it's ideal for sheltering on a rainy Vancouver day with a large coffee and a case of Glosette Raisins.

 # SHOPPING

**Once lined with tacky souvenir stores (there are still a few here), Gastown has been increasingly colonized by designer boutiques, making this area a downtown rival to Main St in the indie shopping stakes. While Chinatown's multisensory, ever-colorful streets used to be more for looking at than actually shopping – how many live frogs do you usually buy? – it's also home to its own cool indie stores.**

### EASTSIDE FLEA
MARKET

Map p273 (www.eastsideflea.com; Ellis Building, 1014 Main St; $3; ⊘6-10pm Fri, 11am-5pm Sat & Sun, 3rd weekend of the month; 🚇3) Running for years at halls around the city, the monthly Flea's new Ellis Building location means 50 new and vintage vendors plus food trucks, live music and a highly inviting atmosphere. Arrive early so you can buy a top hat and swan around like the ironic out-of-time Victorian lady or gent you've always wanted to be.

On our visit, we spotted vendors hawking everything from old hockey jerseys to handmade Bill Murray magnets and from cold brew coffee to artisan doughnuts (the 'Homer Simpson' is recommended). It's $3 for entry but $5 buys you an all-weekend pass.

### COMMUNITY THRIFT & VINTAGE
VINTAGE

Map p272 (🖉604-682-1004; www.communitythriftandvintage.ca; 41 W Cordova St; ⊘11am-7pm Mon-Sat, noon-5pm Sun; 🚇14) There are two branches of this popular vintage clothing store just around the corner from each other. This one focuses on clothes for men and women, while the other (311 Carrall St) is dedicated to womenswear and is lined with dresses from every conceivable era. Here, though, you'll find shoes, tops and more to give your look that quirky retro lift you need.

This operation is a social enterprise supporting women who live and work in this part of town.

### ERIN TEMPLETON
FASHION & ACCESSORIES

Map p273 (🖉604-682-2451; www.erintempleton.com; 511 Carrall St; ⊘11am-6pm Wed-Sat; Ⓢ Stadium-Chinatown) Known for recycling leather into hip, super-supple bags, belts, hats and purses, this eponymous store has a cult following. Erin herself is often on hand and happy to chat about her creations (she trained in shoemaking at a London college). They're the kind of must-have, one-of-a-kind items that are hard to resist, no matter how many bags you already have back home.

The idea here is to marry form and functionality: locals rave about how long their purses last; and if anything does break, it's often fixed for free by Erin herself. Check the website for the full range and all her most recent designs.

### SALMAGUNDI WEST
VINTAGE

Map p272 (🖉604-681-4648; 321 W Cordova St; ⊘11am-6pm Mon-Sat, noon-5pm Sun; Ⓢ Waterfront) For that one stubborn person on your souvenir list who defies the usual salmon or maple cookies gifts from Canada, try this beloved local gem: a browser's paradise. You'll find everything from reproduction old-school toys to oddly alluring taxidermy and sparkling Edwardian-style jewelry. There's a mix of old and new (but old-looking) and it's easy to spend a rainy hour or so digging in.

### JOHN FLUEVOG SHOES SHOES

Map p272 (☏604-688-6228; www.fluevog.com; 65 Water St; ☺10am-7pm Mon-Wed & Sat, 10am-8pm Thu & Fri, noon-6pm Sun; ⑤Waterfront) Like an art gallery for shoes, this alluringly cavernous store showcases the famed footwear of local designer Fluevog, whose men's and women's boots and brogues are what Doc Martens would have become if they'd stayed interesting and cutting-edge. Pick up that pair of thigh-hugging dominatrix boots you've always wanted or settle on some designer loafers that would make anyone walk tall. Seasonal sales can be amazing and your new look will have everyone staring at your feet. Celebs such as Madonna have reputedly bought Fluevogs in the past.

### ORLING & WU HOMEWARES

Map p272 (☏604-568-6718; www.orlingandwu.com; 28 Water St; ☺10am-6pm Mon-Thu, 10am-7pm Fri & Sat, 11am-6pm Sun; ⑤Waterfront) With an irresistible array of chichi trinkets presented in a gallery-like space, it's hard to browse here without falling for something. From linen slippers and Japanese soaps to rubber stamp sets and wall clocks that will finally make you the coolest person in town, it puts your credit card constantly under pressure.

Alternatively, just make a list of everything you want and circulate it to your friends and family before Christmas: if they really love you, they'll buy you that Russian-style glassware tea set. And if they don't, it's time to cull your Christmas-card list.

### LYNN STEVEN BOUTIQUE CLOTHING

Map p272 (☏604-899-0808; www.lynnsteven.com; 225 Carrall St; ☺11am-6pm Mon-Sat, noon-5pm Sun; ☐4) An austere-looking white interior enlivened by a tower of paperbacks fashioned into a changing room, this excellent women's boutique is popular with an under-30s hip set looking for classic casual togs that stand the test of time. Tops and jeans from designers in Toronto, New York and LA dominate, but expect to also be tempted by the vegan bags from Montréal. Super-friendly service.

Look out for end-of-season sales, when dramatic savings can suddenly make that new outfit seem like the bargain of the year.

**WORTH A DETOUR**

### RAILTOWN RISING

Radiating six blocks east from the foot of Main St, a former gritty industrial area has rapidly become one of Vancouver's coolest new mini-hoods in recent years. Increasingly colonized by indie shops and restaurants, the old warehouses and workshops of Railtown are luring the hipsters to an area where few feared to tread just five years ago. If you're in Gastown or Chinatown, it's worth detouring for a quick wander around the area. Highlights to look out for here include **Vancouver Urban Winery** (☏604-566-9463; www.vancouverurbanwinery.com; 55 Dunlevy Ave; ☺11am-11pm Mon-Fri, 10am-11pm Sat & Sun; ☐4) and the locals' favorite restaurant, **Ask for Luigi** (p86).

### COASTAL PEOPLES
### FINE ARTS GALLERY ARTS & CRAFTS

Map p272 (☏604-684-9222; www.coastalpeoples.com; 312 Water St; ☺10am-7pm mid-Apr–mid-Oct, to 6pm mid-Oct–mid-Apr; ⑤Waterfront) This museum-like store showcases an excellent array of Inuit and Northwest Coast aboriginal jewelry, carvings and prints. On the high-art side of things, the exquisite items here are ideal if you're looking for a very special souvenir for someone back home. Don't worry: they can ship the totem poles if you can't fit them in your suitcase.

### BLIM ARTS & CRAFTS

Map p273 (☏604-872-8180; www.blim.ca; 115 E Pender St; ☺11am-9pm Mon-Sat; ☐14) Crammed with locally made bright-hued T-shirts, backpacks and ball caps (look out for resident cat Pounce, who likes to bolt for the door whenever possible), Blim's main business is the roster of classes on everything from line drawing to ceramic screen printing. Check to see what's on – or just buy someone else's handiwork from the shop. Blim also stages regular craft markets throughout the year at sites around the city; they're a great way to meet local artisans and pick up unique souvenirs. Check the website.

### HILL'S NATIVE ART ARTS & CRAFTS

Map p272 (☏604-685-4249; www.hills.ca; 165 Water St; ☺9am-9pm; ⑤Waterfront) Launched in 1946 as a small trading post

## SHOE FRENZY

If you're in Vancouver in April you may suddenly get itchy feet. But rather than a sudden desire to hit the road and start traveling, your tingling toes will be telling you the city's biggest sartorial event for feet is about to take place. When the **Army & Navy** (☑604-682-6644; www.armyandnavy.ca; 36 W Cordova St; ☺9:30am-6pm Mon-Sat, 10am-6pm Sun; ☑8) department store's annual multiday shoe sale kicks off, there's always a long, excited queue of hundreds of locals ready to get in. Those who've waited in line for hours have the chance to hit – usually at maximum velocity – the shiny pyramids of deeply discounted designer footwear from the likes of Guess, Christian Dior and Jimmy Choo. Delighted shoppers stagger around with armfuls of must-have shoes, while onlookers (typically of the male variety) hang in corners, wondering how they can escape.

on Vancouver Island, Hill's flagship store has many First Nations carvings, prints, ceremonial masks and cozy Cowichan sweaters, plus traditional music and books of historical interest. Artists are often found at work in the 3rd-floor gallery. This is a great spot to pick up some authentic aboriginal artworks for savoring at home.

There are many souvenir stores on Water St with First Nations goods but this is the one if you want to find something special.

**CANNABIS CULTURE
HEADQUARTERS**     FASHION & ACCESSORIES
Map p272 (☑604-682-1172; www.cannabiscul turehq.com; 307 W Hastings St; ☺10am-8pm Mon-Thu, 10am-10pm Fri & Sat, noon-8pm Sun; ☑14) For arguments in support of legalization, duck into the friendly shop and offices of the BC Marijuana Party, in a small pocket of the city sometimes called 'Vansterdam.' With books, hemp clothing and associated paraphernalia, this is the place to make some new, like-minded buddies during your visit. Also, nip next door to the New Amsterdam Cafe, a popular herbal smoking room.

You'll likely smell the aroma of 'naughty cigarettes' on streets around Vancouver: it's still illegal here, but the police don't generally bother with small-scale home users. You'll also likely notice many 'pot shops' throughout the region; Vancouver is currently going through a process to issue business licenses to establishments that sell medical marijuana, so long as they meet certain conditions.

**CANADIAN
MAPLE DELIGHTS**     GIFTS & SOUVENIRS
Map p272 (☑604-682-6175; www.maplede lights.com; 385 Water St; ☺8am-7pm Mon-Fri, 10am-7pm Sat & Sun; ⓢWaterfront) It might seem like a chore but if you have to pick up souvenirs for all those friends back home, this is an ideal one-stop shop. Canadian Maple Delights specializes in all manner of maple-syrup-flavored goodies (think maple sugar, maple tea, maple-leaf-shaped candy, maple-tree-growing kits etc). It also stocks vacuum-packed salmon for those who don't have a sweet tooth.

You'll find several additional large souvenir stores nearby if you want to get your list covered off in a single afternoon. Just don't buy the moose-dropping chocolate candies, go for a T-shirt that makes jokes about beavers instead; that's much more sophisticated.

# Yaletown & Granville Island

## Neighborhood Top Five

**1** **Granville Island Public Market** (p99) Wandering the deli stands and gathering some goodies before heading outside to catch a busker or two and watch the boats slide by in twinkling False Creek.

**2** **Gallery of BC Ceramics** (p112) Perusing the eclectic pottery and picking up a unique local-made souvenir; then wondering how to pack it for home.

**3** **Blue Water Cafe** (p104) Dining with Yaletown's professional socialites in a chichi setting while indulging in top-end seafood dishes.

**4** **Liberty Distillery** (p108) Diving into arti-san island-made liquor at the taste-tastic happy hour.

**5** **BC Lions** (p111) Catching all the razzmatazz of a Canadian Football game and cheering on the local team; face-painting optional.

For more detail of this area see Map p274 and p275 ➡

## Lonely Planet's Top Tip

Granville Island's off-season **Winterruption** (www.granvilleisland.com) festival runs every February and is a great way to hang out with the locals while enjoying a few eclectic events. Despite the cold, there's a party atmosphere with street performers and wandering groups of Vancouverites checking out art demonstrations, music shows and the ever-popular booze-tasting walking tour. Many events are free, with others bookable in advance; check the website for details.

 ### Best Places to Eat

➡ Bistro 101 (p106)

➡ Go Fish (p105)

➡ Edible Canada (p106)

➡ Blue Water Cafe (p104)

➡ Flying Pig (p103)

 ### Best Places to Drink

➡ Liberty Distillery (p108)

➡ Central City Brew Pub (p106)

➡ Granville Island Brewing Taproom (p108)

 ### Best Places to Shop

➡ Gallery of BC Ceramics (p112)

➡ Paper-Ya (p112)

➡ Granville Island Broom Company (p112)

➡ Xoxolat (p111)

➡ Umbrella Shop (p112)

# Explore Yaletown & Granville Island

Yaletown and Granville Island lie on opposite banks of False Creek but it's easy to see both on one day. Save most of your time for Granville Island with its unique shops and public market. Be sure to stroll the entire island, not just the Public Market end. Poking around the back alleys, you'll find cool artisan studios and you'll also escape the crowds that jam the market area in summer. Johnston St, Cartwright St and Railspur Alley are particularly worth exploring. The pedestrian and traffic entrance to Granville Island is under the south end of Granville Bridge. Here, Anderson St takes you right onto the island. Yaletown is a short miniferry ride from Granville Island. Compact and easy to explore, it primarily radiates a block or two either side of Hamilton St. There are some worthwhile shopping options here and, if you want to join the locals, stay for dinner. The city's renovated warehouse district is stuffed with dining options, a few of them among the city's finest dine-out options where you'll nosh with some of Vancouver's VIPs.

## Local Life

➡**Produce** The Granville Island Public Market (p99) is always stuffed with fruit and veg but the summertime farmers market – from June to October – is even better for fresh-picked local treats.

➡**Beer** Most Granville Island Brewing (p103) beverages are now produced in factory quantities off-site, but savvy locals know that the small-batch tipples still made on the island are superior. Hit the brewery's on-site liquor store and pick up a couple.

➡**Theater** Granville Island is the heart of Vancouver's theater scene. Locals save money on main-stage shows by checking the daily half-price deals at www.ticketstonight.ca.

## Getting There & Away

➡**Bus** Bus 50 runs from downtown and stops near Granville Island's entrance. Bus 10 is also popular and stops on the south side of Granville Bridge.

➡**Train** The Canada Line runs from downtown to Yaletown-Roundhouse Station, a short walk to all Yaletown's main attractions.

➡**Car** There is metered parking in Yaletown. There is free parking (up to three hours) on Granville Island but availability is severely limited at peak times.

➡**Miniferries** Granville Island is accessible by miniferry service from the West End and Yaletown side of False Creek.

## TOP SIGHT
# GRANVILLE ISLAND PUBLIC MARKET

A foodie extravaganza specializing in deli treats and pyramids of shiny fruit and vegetables, this is one of North America's finest public markets. It's ideal for whiling away an afternoon; snacking on goodies in the sun among the buskers outside or sheltering from the rain with a market tour. You'll also find side dishes of (admittedly inedible) arts and crafts.

## Taste-Tripping

Come hungry: there are dozens of food stands to weave your way around at the market. Among the must-see stands are **Oyama Sausage Company**, replete with hundreds of smoked sausages and cured meats; **Benton Brothers Fine Cheese**, with its full complement of amazing curdy goodies from British Columbia (BC) and around the world (look for anything by Farm House Natural Cheese from Agassiz, BC); and **Granville Island Tea Company** (Hawaiian rooibos recommended), with its tasting bar and more than 150 steep-tastic varieties to choose from. Baked goodies also abound: abandon your diet at **Lee's Donuts** and **Siegel's Bagels**, where the naughty cheese-stuffed baked bagels are not to be missed. And don't worry; there's always room for a wafer-thin album-sized 'cinnamon record' from **Stuart's Baked Goods**. French-themed **L'Epicerie Rotisserie and Gourmet Shop** has also been a popular addition to the market in recent years. It sells vinegars, olive oils and Bababapa pop bottles with delicious fresh-cooked, picnic-friendly take-out chicken and sausages.

In the unlikely event you're still hungry, there's also a small international food court: avoid off-peak dining if you want to snag a table and indulge in a good-value selection that runs from Indian curries to German sausages. And if you want to dive into some

## DON'T MISS

→ Oyama Sausage Company
→ Benton Brothers Fine Cheese
→ Granville Island Tea Company
→ Guided market tours
→ Summer farmers market

## PRACTICALITIES

→ Map p275, C1
→ ☏604-666-6655
→ www.granvilleisland. com/public-market
→ Johnston St
→ ⊙9am-7pm
→ ◻50, ⛴miniferries

## MARKET TIPS

➡In summer, arrive early to sidestep the crowds, which peak in the afternoons.

➡If you're driving, weekdays are the easiest times to find on-island parking.

➡The food court is the island's best-value dining. But tables are scarce at peak times.

➡Visiting bird-watcher? Look for the cormorants nesting under the the Granville Bridge span.

➡Gather a great picnic, then find a quiet spot to dine; the grassy knoll at the island's opposite end is ideal, while Vanier Park is a short stroll along the seawall.

➡Arrive in style; both **Aquabus** (Map p275) and **False Creek Ferries** (Map p275) operate miniferry services to the island.

**If you're out enjoying the buskers on the market's waterfront exterior, you'll notice your False Creek view is sandwiched between two of Vancouver's most famous bridges. Opened in 1954, the ironwork Granville Bridge is the third version of this bridge to span the inlet here. The more attractive art-deco Burrard Bridge, opened in 1932, is nearby. During its opening ceremony, a floatplane was daringly piloted under the bridge's main deck.**

regional seasonal produce, there's even a **farmers market** just outside the market building between June and October where you can, due to a recent law change, also sample BC-made booze.

## Arts & Crafts

Once you've eaten your fill, take a look at some of the market's other stands. There's a cool arts and crafts focus here, especially among the collection of **day vendors** that dot the market and which change every week. Hand-knitted hats, hand-painted ceramics, framed art photography and quirky carvings will make for excellent one-of-a-kind souvenirs. Further artisan stands are added to the roster in the run-up to Christmas, if you happen to be here at that time. For more information on the sorts of day vendors that appear at the market, visit www.gidva.org.

## Insider's Tour

If you're an incurable foodie, the delicious market tour organized by Vancouver Foodie Tours (p246) is the way to go. Taking about two hours to weave around the vendors and costing from $50, the morning-only guided amble includes tastings of regional foods and chef-approved tips on how to pair and prepare local ingredients. It caters to vegetarians if you mention it when you book and there's a $10 discount for epicurious children (aged three to 12). The company also runs culinary tours in other parts of the city if you're keen to keep eating; the Vancouver food truck tour is especially popular.

## Forgotten Past

The Public Market is the centerpiece of one of Canada's most impressive urban regeneration projects – and the main reason it has been so successful. Built as a district for small factories in the early part of the last century, Granville Island – which has also been called Mud Island and Industrial Island over the years – had declined into a paint-peeled no-go area by the 1960s. But the abandoned sheds began attracting artists and theater groups by the 1970s, and the old buildings slowly started springing back to life with some much-needed repairs and upgrades. Within a few years, new theaters, restaurants and studios had been built and the Public Market quickly became an instantly popular anchor tenant. One reason for the island's popularity? Only independent, one-of-a-kind businesses operate here.

# ◉ SIGHTS

## ◎ Yaletown

### BC PLACE STADIUM                                    STADIUM

Map p274 (☏604-669-2300; www.bcplacestadium.com; 777 Pacific Blvd; ℗; ⑤Stadium-Chinatown) Vancouver's main sports arena is home to two professional teams: the **BC Lions** Canadian Football League team and the **Vancouver Whitecaps** soccer team. Also used for major rock concerts and consumer shows, the renovated stadium – with its huge, crownlike retractable roof – hosted the opening and closing ceremonies for the 2010 Olympic and Paralymic Winter Games.

Check the website to see what's coming up at the stadium. And save time to check out the BC Sports Hall of Fame & Museum (p101) at Gate A.

### BC SPORTS HALL OF
### FAME & MUSEUM                                      MUSEUM

Map p274 (☏604-687-5520; www.bcsportshalloffame.com; Gate A, BC Place Stadium, 777 Pacific Blvd; adult/child $15/12; ◷10am-5pm; ⏃; ⑤Stadium-Chinatown) Inside BC Place Stadium, this small but perfectly formed attraction showcases top BC athletes, both amateur and professional, with galleries devoted to each decade in sports. There are medals, trophies and sporting memorabilia on display (judging by the size of their shirts, hockey players were much smaller in the old days), and tons of hands-on activities to tire the kids out.

You'll find plenty of info on the city's 2010 Olympic and Paralympic Winter Games, plus stirring exhibits on Terry Fox and his 'Marathon of Hope' run across Canada. Head outside the stadium for a cool **public artwork** by Douglas Coupland that also celebrates the nation's favorite hero.

### ENGINE 374 PAVILION                                MUSEUM

Map p274 (www.roundhouse.ca; Roundhouse Community Arts & Recreation Centre, 181 Roundhouse Mews; ◷10am-4pm, reduced hours off-season; ⏃; ⑤Yaletown-Roundhouse) **FREE** May 23, 1887 was an auspicious date for Vancouver. That's when Engine 374 pulled the very first transcontinental passenger train into the fledgling city, symbolically linking the country and kick-starting the eventual metropolis. Retired in 1945, the engine was (after many years of neglect) restored and placed in this splendid pavilion. The friendly volunteers here will show you the best angle for snapping the perfect photo of the engine.

Administered by the **West Coast Railway Heritage Park** in Squamish (a good excursion for rail buffs), the engine is kept in sparkling condition and is occasionally wheeled out onto the outside turntable, part of the beautifully restored heritage roundhouse building that recalls Yaletown's gritty rail history. Here around May 23? Check ahead for the Sunday anniversary that always includes free cake.

### ROUNDHOUSE COMMUNITY
### ARTS & RECREATION CENTRE          ARTS CENTER

Map p274 (☏604-713-1800; www.roundhouse.ca; 181 Roundhouse Mews, cnr Davie St & Pacific

*YALETOWN & GRANVILLE ISLAND* SIGHTS

---

### CANADA'S HERO

The most poignant gallery at the BC Sports Hall of Fame & Museum is dedicated to national legend Terry Fox, the young cancer sufferer whose one-legged 1980 Marathon of Hope run across Canada ended after 143 days and 5373km, when the disease spread to the Port Coquitlam resident's lungs. When Fox died the following year, the funeral was screened live across the country and the government ordered flags to be flown at half-mast. A memorial was later constructed outside BC Place Stadium but it was replaced in 2011 by a new and much more impressive one created by Vancouver artist and writer Douglas Coupland, who had already penned his own celebrated book, *Terry*, in tribute to Fox. The new statue has a series of running figures showing Fox in motion during his cross-country odyssey. When Fox started his run, he received very little attention, but by the time he was forced to stop it felt as if the entire country was behind him. Every year since his death, fundraising runs have been held in Canada and around the world to remember his bravery. The Terry Fox Foundation (www.terryfox.org) estimates that these have now raised more than $500 million for cancer research.

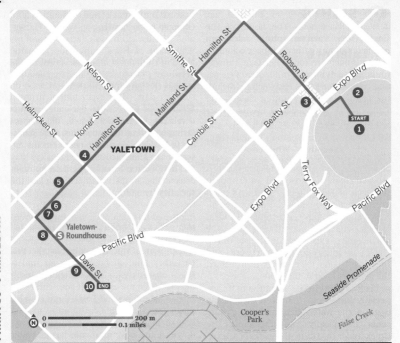

# Neighborhood Walk
## Yaletown Indulgence

**START** BC PLACE STADIUM
**END** ENGINE 374 PAVILION
**LENGTH** 2KM; 1 HOUR

Start at the city's largest sports venue, **1 BC Place Stadium** (p101), checking out the **2 BC Sports Hall of Fame & Museum** (p101) located inside and the Douglas Coupland **3 public artwork** outside – this celebration of Canadian hero Terry Fox is one of the neighborhood's most-photographed sights.

Next head up Robson St and turn left onto Hamilton. This is your chance to scope out options for dinner later. You'll pass the following: **4 Blue Water Café** (p104) (seafood), **5 Cioppino's** (p104) (Italian) and **6 Flying Pig** (p103) (gourmet comfort grub). Also notice the elevated redbrick sidewalks and old rails embedded in the roads. These are remnants of the neighborhood's former incarnation as a train yard and warehouse district. The area was reinvented after Expo'86; the world exposition

cleaned up and transformed the rundown district with temporary pavilions and exhibition spaces. Latter-day Yaletown isn't just about dining, though. Along Hamilton, you'll come to several stores that show how popular shopping is here, too. Among the best, **7 Goorin Bros Hat Shop** (p112) is the perfect spot to add a trendy sunhat to your day.

When you reach Davie St, turn left. If it's time for a pit stop, pop into **8 Caffe Artigiano** (p108) for a restorative latte and a pastry or two. It's in the Opus Hotel building, one of the city's trendiest boutique sleepovers: spot the beautiful people gliding around the lobby.

Continue your stroll along Davie, cross over Pacific Blvd and you'll spot the **9 Roundhouse Community Arts & Recreation Centre** (p101) just ahead. Attached to the side of the community center, **10 Engine 374 Pavilion** (p101) houses the handsomely restored steam engine that pulled the first passenger train into the city in 1887.

Blvd; ⊘9am-10pm Mon-Fri, to 5pm Sat & Sun; ⑤Yaletown-Roundhouse) The home of the Engine 374 Pavilion (p101), Yaletown's main community gathering space colonizes a handsomely restored heritage railway roundhouse. It offers a full roster of events and courses for locals and visitors, including popular drop-in running classes and Philosopher's Cafe debating events. Check the website calendar to see what's on.

### DAVID LAM PARK
                                                    PARK

Map p274 (www.vancouverparks.ca; cnr Drake St & Pacific Blvd; ⑤Yaletown-Roundhouse) A crooked elbow of landscaped waterfront at the neck of False Creek, Yaletown's main green space is sometimes used for free alfresco summer movie screenings. An ideal launch point for a seawall walk along the north bank of False Creek to Science World, you'll pass intriguing public artworks and the glass condo towers that transformed the neighborhood in the 1990s.

Look out for birdlife along the route, especially the herons that keep their beady eyes on the waters here and the cormorants who typically nest further along False Creek under the Granville Bridge.

## ◉ Granville Island

### GRANVILLE ISLAND
### PUBLIC MARKET
                                                    MARKET
See p99.

### GRANVILLE ISLAND
### BREWING
                                                    BREWERY

Map p275 (☎604-687-2739; www.gib.ca; 1441 Cartwright St; tours $9.75; ⊘tours 11:30am, 1pm, 2:30pm, 4pm & 5:30pm; ☒50) One of Canada's oldest microbreweries, GIB offers 30-minute tours in which smiling guides walk you through the tiny brewing nook, established in the olden days of 1984. The brewery has grown exponentially since then and most of its beers are now made off-site, although some tasty small-batch brews are still made here on the island. The tour concludes with three samples in the Taproom (p108).

You can also buy some takeout in the adjoining store; aim for the single bottles of small-batch beers since they're not easily available anywhere else. Need a souvenir for a beer fan back home? This is also a good spot to buy branded ball caps, T-shirts and bottle openers. The island is also home to another brewery, a distillery and even a

sake maker so it is a good destination for a compact booze crawl.

### RAILSPUR ALLEY
                                                    AREA

Map p275 (btwn Old Bridge & Cartwright Sts; ☒50) Seemingly far from the madding crowds of the Public Market – at least on summer days when every tourist in town seems to be there – this back-alley strip is a relaxing alternative. You'll find a short string of unique artisan stores, from painters to jewelers. Be sure to check out the Artisan Sake Maker (p108).

There's often a busker here on summer afternoons, so it's worth hanging around the alley for a bit.

### KIDS MARKET
                                                    MARKET

Map p275 (☎604-689-8447; www.kidsmarket. ca; 1496 Cartwright St; ⊘10am-6pm; ☒; ☒50) A nightmare if you stroll in by mistake, this two-story mini-shopping mall for under-10s is bustling with 25 kid-friendly stores, mostly of the toy variety. If your child's interests extend beyond Lego, there are also magic tricks, arts and crafts, and a menagerie of puppets for sale. Cool the sprogs down at the huge Granville Island Water Park (p114) out back.

## ✗ EATING

**A favored haunt for conspicuously wealthy Vancouverites, Yaletown has some good, splurge-worthy dining options, especially along Hamilton and Mainland Sts. But not everything here is worth the price, so choose carefully. Many of this area's restaurants also have patios. Granville Island has plenty of places to eat, too, but you'll need to do a little digging to avoid the tourist restaurants.**

## ✗ Yaletown

### FLYING PIG
                                        WEST COAST $$

Map p274 (☎604-568-1344; www.theflyingpig van.com; 1168 Hamilton St; mains $19-27; ⊘11am-midnight Mon-Fri, 10am-midnight Sat, 10am-11pm Sun; ⑤Yaletown-Roundhouse) Yaletown's best midrange restaurant is a warm, woodsy bistro that has mastered the art of friendly service and saliva-triggering gourmet comfort food. Dishes focus on seasonal local ingredients and are virtually guaranteed to make your belly smile. Wine-braised short ribs and roast chicken served with buttermilk mash top our to-eat list but it's best to arrive off-peak to avoid the crowds.

The Flying Pig offers an excellent and very popular weekend brunch (*croque madame* – a grilled ham-and-cheese sandwich topped with a fried egg – is recommended), but the best deal is the afternoon 'appy hour' menu (4pm to 6pm daily), when you can try a few tasty plates for around $6 a pop. Reservations are not accepted for dinner.

### RODNEY'S OYSTER HOUSE SEAFOOD $$
Map p274 (604-609-0080; www.rohvan.com; 1228 Hamilton St; mains $16-32; 11:30am-11pm; Yaletown-Roundhouse) Vancouver's favorite oyster eatery, Rodney's always has a buzz. And it's not just because of the convivial room with its nautical flourishes; these guys really know how to do seafood. While the fresh-shucked oysters with a huge array of sauces (try the spicy vodka) never fail to impress, everything from sweet mussels to superb Atlantic lobster is also available here.

Drop by from 3pm to 6pm weekdays for deals on oysters or warm up in winter with possibly the best New England clam chowder in the city.

### BLUE WATER CAFE SEAFOOD $$$
Map p274 (604-688-8078; www.bluewatercafe.net; 1095 Hamilton St; mains $29-48; 5-11pm; Yaletown-Roundhouse) Under celebrated executive chef Frank Pabst, this is one of Vancouver's best high-concept seafood restaurants. Gentle music fills the brick-lined, blue-hued interior, while top-notch char, sablefish and butter-soft scallops grace the tables inside and on the patio. Not a seafood fan? There's also a small array of meaty 'principal plates' to sate your carnivorous appetite, including Wagyu beef.

Service here is perfect; warm, gracious and ever-friendly. Reservations are required.

### WILDTALE COASTAL GRILL SEAFOOD $$$
Map p274 (604-428-9211; www.wildtale.ca; 1079 Mainland St; mains $22-29; 11am-midnight Mon-Fri, 10am-midnight Sat, to 11pm Sun; Yaletown-Roundhouse) A seafood restaurant with meaty extras (including a popular lamb-shank dinner). In-the-know locals have made this one of their favorite afternoon happy-hour destinations. Arrive early for

the 3pm to 6pm event and you'll find deals on fresh-shucked oysters, beef carpaccio and more. It's a great way to decide whether the solicitous service and white tablecloth patio will lure you back for dinner.

### BRIX & MORTAR CANADIAN $$$
Map p274 (604-915-9463; www.brixandmortar.ca; 1138 Homer St; mains $22-37; from 5pm; Yaletown-Roundhouse) A romantic heritage building with two large and contrasting patios, this sophisticated, recently renovated spot feels like a secret. The classy white-tablecloth setting is ideal for savoring contemporary international approaches to dishes such as duck confit and smoked sablefish gnocchi. There's also an excellent artisan cheese selection (three choices for $15).

There's a superior wine selection, including dozens of tempting tipples available by the glass.

### PROVENCE MARINASIDE FRENCH, SEAFOOD $$$
Map p274 (604-681-4144; www.provencevancouver.com; 1177 Marinaside Crescent; mains $24-42; 8am-3pm & 5-10pm Mon-Fri, 9am-3pm & 5-11pm Sat & Sun; Yaletown-Roundhouse) There's a serious seafood fixation at this French-approach restaurant just across from Yaletown's False Creek waterfront. But if you're not in the mood for marine-based treats, there are also chicken and beef dishes. If you're feeling aquatically inclined, faceplant into the feast-tastic seafood platter, including everything from prawns to pink scallops; it's simply prepared and delicious. Consider a patio table in summer.

At the weekend this becomes one of Yaletown's fave brunch spots; consider the crab-and-lobster omelet. Check the menu for dishes marked with the sustainable seafood symbol – sponsored by the Vancouver Aquarium.

### CIOPPINO'S MEDITERRANEAN GRILL ITALIAN $$$
Map p274 (604-688-7466; www.cioppinosyaletown.com; 1133 Hamilton St; mains $25-42; 5-10pm; Yaletown-Roundhouse) Not your standard fine-dining Italian joint, this popular Mediterranean eatery deploys the *cucina naturale* approach, revealing the delicate natural flavors of a range of regionally sourced ingredients. The warm wood and terra-cotta interior is the perfect surrounding for dipping into fine dishes

## VANCOUVER'S BRICK-BUILT SOHO

Aesthetically unlike any other Vancouver neighborhood, Yaletown has a trendy warehouse-district appearance today because it was built on a foundation of grungy, working-class history. Created almost entirely from red bricks, the area was crammed with railway sheds and goods warehouses in the late 1800s after the Canadian Pacific Railway (CPR) relocated its main western Canada operation from the British Columbia (BC) interior town of Yale. Along with the moniker, the workers brought something else with them: a tough-as-nails, hard-drinking approach that turned the waterfront area into one where the taverns usually served their liquor with a side order of fistfights. But at least the rough-and-ready workers kept the area alive: when the rail operations were closed down a few decades later, Yaletown descended into a half-empty mass squat filled with homeless locals and marauding rats. But that wasn't the end of the story.

When plans were drawn up for Vancouver to host the giant **Expo '86** world exposition, there were few areas of town with the space – and the absence of other businesses – to host it. But Yaletown fit the bill. The area became part of the planned Expo grounds along the north shoreline of False Creek, and was cleared, refurbished and given a new lease on life. After the summer-long fair, its newly noticed historic character made Yaletown the ideal spot for urban regeneration. Within a few years the old brick warehouses had been repaired, scrubbed clean and recolonized with a sparkling array of boutiques, fancy restaurants and swish bars – serving tipples that are a far cry from the punch-triggering beers that used to be downed here.

tweaked with Italian flourishes; try the lobster linguine or local duck served two ways: crispy breast plus velvety confit.

There's also a great wine list at your disposal here, with lots of rare vintages to keep your credit card fully deployed. In summer aim for a spot on the patio: there's often less noise from conversations than inside.

## ✖ Granville Island

### A BREAD AFFAIR
BAKERY **$**

Map p275 (☑604-695-0000; www.abreadaffair.com; 1680 Johnston St; sandwiches $9-11; ⊙8:30am-7pm Mon-Thu, to 7:30pm Fri-Sun; ☑50) A fire a few years back didn't kill this beloved organic bakery; it rose phoenixlike from the burned breadcrumbs. Alongside its sandwich bar (French ham and Havarti recommended) and racks of fresh-baked loaves, there's an irresistible array of treats, from cookies to croissants. Don't miss the hearty apple-cheddar-walnut galette; it's enough to feed two but that doesn't mean you have to.

Little free samples are offered up most days; consider donning disguises and returning at least 27 times. And if you find yourself at a farmers market around the city, you'll often spot this bakery's stalls; they're the ones with the line-ups.

### GO FISH
SEAFOOD **$**

Map p275 (☑604-730-5040; 1505 W 1st Ave; mains $8-14; ⊙11:30am-6:30pm Mon-Fri, noon-6:30pm Sat & Sun; ☑50) A short stroll westwards along the seawall from the Granville Island entrance, this almost-too-popular seafood stand is one of the city's fave fish-and-chip joints, offering halibut, salmon and cod encased in crispy golden batter. The smashing (and lighter) fish tacos are also recommended, while the changing daily specials – brought in by the nearby fishing boats – often include scallop burgers or ahi tuna sandwiches.

Expect long queues and sometimes oppressive waits in summer; arrive as off-peak as you can. The seating area has been expanded from its original limited selection but it's still best to continue along the seawall to **Vanier Park** for a sunset picnic alongside the ever-watchful seagulls.

### PUBLIC MARKET FOOD COURT
INTERNATIONAL **$**

Map p275 (1661 Duranleau St, Granville Island Public Market; mains $6-12; ⊙9am-7pm; ☑50) A great budget option but also very busy in summer: your table at the little Public Market food court could almost be auctioned off to the highest bidder when you're ready to leave (just kidding). Arrive off-peak to be sure of a seat and you'll have the pick of some excellent vendors hawking everything from German sausages to Mexican taco bowl salads.

Our favorite? The Indian food stand with its filling, well-priced combos, including good vegetarian options.

★BISTRO 101                    WEST COAST $$
Map p275 (☏604-724-4488; www.picachef.com; 1505 W 2nd Ave; ☺11:30am-2pm & 6-9pm Mon-Fri; 🚌50) Vancouver's best-value gourmet dining option, the training restaurant of the Pacific Institute of Culinary Arts is popular with in-the-know locals, especially at lunchtime when $22 gets you a delicious three-course meal (typically three options for each course) plus service that's earnestly solicitous. The dinner option costs $8 more and there's a buffet offering on the first Friday of the month. Reservations recommended.

Decor-wise, the restaurant is slightly dated, with a 1980s feel. But since you'll be fully focused on the food, that hardly matters. There's also a bakery cafe at the front if you're just passing by.

TONY'S FISH
& OYSTER CAFE               SEAFOOD $$
Map p275 (☏604-683-7127; www.tonysfishandoystercafe.com; 1511 Anderson St; mains $9-25; ☺11:30am-8:30pm, reduced hours in winter; 🚌50) A chatty spot where Vancouverites bring visitors when they take them to Granville Island, this tiny checkered-tablecloth joint serves great fish and chips, along with generous dollops of housemade coleslaw and tartar sauce. The food is good value, and it's not just about fish and chips: the BBQ-sauced oyster burger is almost a local legend. Service is fast and friendly.

Those seafood fans not craving the deep-fried route will also find some good fresh alternatives here, from hearty clam chowder to fresh-shucked oysters and steamed mussels. Appropriately, the beer selection includes Granville Island Brewing, which is just across the street.

EDIBLE CANADA              CANDIAN $$
Map p275 (☏604-682-6681; www.ediblecanada.com/bistro; 1596 Johnston St; mains $18-30; ☺11am-9pm Mon-Fri, 9am-10pm Sat & Sun; 🚌50) Granville Island's most popular bistro (book ahead) delivers a short but tempting menu of seasonal dishes, mostly from BC but also across Canada, often including ingredients such as elk tartare or Quebec cheeses. Consider sharing some small

plates if you're feeling adventurous and also add a selection from the all-Canadian wine list (including an ice-wine finale).

Check out the shop of artisan food treats at the back of the restaurant before you leave; the chocolate-bar array is always enticing. This is also a popular spot for brunch; avocado toast and poached eggs recommended.

# 🍷 DRINKING & NIGHTLIFE

**Yaletown is where the city's wealthy set comes to sip martinis and exchange lap-dog stories. You're sure to find something worth checking out amid the warehouse renos. Granville Island offers several bars perfect for winding down after a day spent weaving around the Public Market and artisan stores.**

# 🍷 Yaletown

SMALL VICTORY                    COFFEE
Map p274 (☏604-899-8892; www.smallvictory.ca; 1088 Homer St; ☺7:30am-6pm Mon-Fri, 8am-6pm Sat & Sun; 🚇; 🚊Yaletown-Roundhouse) The kind of austere, granite-countered coffee shop you might not feel cool enough to enter (or maybe that's just us), Small Victory is a favorite daytime hangout for hip Yaletowners. Sip your perfect cappuccino and standout flaky croissant (there's also an artful array of additional bakery treats) under the geometric wall-mounted artwork and you'll fit right in.

More substantial savory fare of the salads and sandwiches variety is also available if your sweet tooth has momentarily deserted you.

CENTRAL CITY BREW PUB     CRAFT BEER
Map p274 (☏778-379-2489; www.centralcitybrewing.com; 871 Beatty St; ☺11am-midnight Sun-Thu, to 1am Fri & Sat; 🚌17) Colonizing the site of former brewpub favorite Dix (that's their old sign on the wall inside), the downtown satellite of one of BC's most celebrated beermakers combines a passable pub-grub menu with a sparkling array of beers – its own as well as top picks from many other BC producers. Best Central City brews to try? Red Racer IPA and Red Racer India Red Ale.

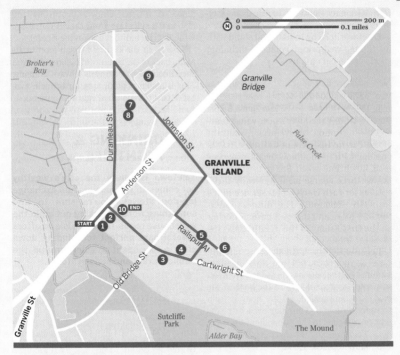

# 🏃 Neighborhood Walk
# Granville Island Artisan Trawl

**START** UMBRELLA SHOP
**END** GRANVILLE ISLAND BREWING
**LENGTH** 1 KM; ONE HOUR

This stroll takes you around some of Granville Island's favorite artisan studios and galleries, and ends with a well-deserved beer. Entering the island from the main entrance on Anderson St, nip into the ❶ **Umbrella Shop** (p112), especially if you need something to protect you from a passing deluge. Continue along Anderson to the corner of Cartwright St. Explore the ❷ **Kids Market** (p103) and consider one of the muppetlike puppets for sale here as a gift for a child back home.

Next weave eastwards along Cartwright. You'll see theaters and artisan shops. Take a look at two of the best artisan studios: ❸ **Crafthouse** (p113) gallery, which has plenty of regionally made arts and crafts to tempt you; and, opposite it, the ❹ **Gallery of BC Ceramics** (p112), which offers even more to choose from among its wide and eclectic range of locally made artisan pottery.

Duck along the little pathway beside the gallery and you'll hit the somewhat hidden ❺ **Railspur Alley** (p103). Peruse the excellent artsy stores here, including the ❻ **Artisan Sake Maker** (p108). Consider stopping for a few tastings or just ask some pertinent questions about the production process. Food pairing suggestions are also available.

Continue on via Old Bridge St and turn left onto Johnston St. Here you'll find the ❼ **Net Loft**. It's lined with arts and crafts stores, including the ever-popular ❽ **Paper-Ya** (p112). Diagonally across the street from here is the entrance to the ❾ **Public Market** (p99). Dominating the area, it specializes in deli-style food stalls – cheese-filled bagels recommended. When you've had your fill, weave southwards from the market along Duranleau St. Within a couple of minutes you'll be at the intersection with Cartwright St and the entrance to ❿ **Granville Island Brewing** (p103). Take a tour or hit the Taproom for a well-deserved pint.

Ask your server about the seasonal ale offerings here; there's usually an impressive selection.

### YALETOWN
### BREWING COMPANY
BREWERY

Map p274 (📞604-681-2739; www.drinkfresh beer.com; 1111 Mainland St; ⊙11:30am-midnight Sun-Wed, to 1am Thu, to 3am Fri & Sat; ⑤Yaletown-Roundhouse) There's a brick-lined brewpub on one side and a giant dining room on the other. Both serve pints of beer made on-site, but the restaurant adds a long menu of comfort foods. Check to see if there's an unusual small-batch beer on offer and, if there isn't, instead hit one of the mainstays: Brick & Beam IPA is recommended.

If you really want to try something out of the ordinary, ask about the eye-popping Oud Bruin sour beer. It's guaranteed to put hairs on your chest, but only if you finish it. In summer, the patio is a popular perch, but in winter a game of pool in the back of the bar is recommended. Happy hour is 3pm to 6pm Sunday to Thursday, which means $5 beer specials in the pub-side of the business. Beer fans should also drop by at 4pm Thursdays for cask night.

### CAFFE ARTIGIANO
COFFEE

Map p274 (📞604-336-4766; www.caffeart igiano.com; 302 Davie St; ⊙6am-8:30pm; 🛜; ⑤Yaletown-Roundhouse) One of Vancouver's most popular local coffee chains serves up arguably Yaletown's best java. Tucked into a corner of the Opus Hotel building, this ever-chatty spot takes pride in its drinks: go for a latte and they'll implant a nice little design into the foam (yes, we're easily pleased). There are also sandwiches and baked treats available if you need a fuel-up.

### BAR NONE
CLUB

Map p274 (📞604-689-7000; www.donnel lygroup.ca; 1222 Hamilton St; ⊙10pm-3am Fri & Sat; ⑤Yaletown-Roundhouse) Yaletown's longest-running haunt for club-loving professionals who want to let their hair down after a hard week has a scrubbed beatnik appearance. But within its exposed-brick-and-beam shell the main topics of conversation are perfect cocktails and real-estate prices. It's only open on Fridays and Saturdays, but it's the best spot in Yaletown to sip, sway and wish your were richer.

## 📍 Granville Island

### ★LIBERTY DISTILLERY
DISTILLERY

Map p275 (📞604-558-1998; www.thelibertydistillery.com; 1494 Old Bridge St; ⊙11am-8pm; 🚌50) Vancouver's most attractive craft distillery has a handsome saloonlike tasting room where you can gaze through windows at the shiny, steampunk-like booze-making equipment beyond. It's not all about looks, though. During the Monday-to-Thursday 3pm-to-6pm happy hour, sample gin made on-site, vodka and white whiskey plus great cocktails for just $6 a pop. Tours are available ($10; Saturdays and Sundays; 11:30am and 1:30pm).

The start of happy hour is announced by a steam whistle, so you'll know exactly when to start imbibing. Don't miss a hit or two of the aromatic Endeavour Pink Gin.

### ★ARTISAN SAKE MAKER
BREWERY

Map p275 (📞604-685-7253; www.artisansake maker.com; 1339 Railspur Alley; ⊙11:30am-6pm; 🚌50) This tiny sake producer uses locally grown rice – making it the first of its kind in Canada – and should be on everyone's Granville Island to-do list. Twinkle-eyed sake maker Masa Shiroki produces several tipples and you can dive in for a bargain $5 three-sake tasting. It's an eye-opening revelation to many drinkers who think sake is a harsh beverage. Take-out bottles are available.

Also consider buying a jar of kasu; the lees left over from the fermenting process are a great exotic cooking ingredient.

### GRANVILLE ISLAND
### BREWING TAPROOM
PUB

Map p275 (📞604-687-2739; www.gib.ca; 1441 Cartwright St; ⊙11am-9pm; 🚌50) You can sample the company's main beers in this pub-style room, although most are now made in a large out-of-town facility. Among these, Cypress Honey Lager, Lions Winter Ale and summertime False Creek Raspberry Ale are among the most popular. But the small-batch Black Notebook brews, made right here on the island, are even better: ask your server what's available.

Tours (p103) of the small brewery are also available and the food menu has also been seriously improved in recent years. Takeout is available in the souvenir and liquor store next door.

## BACKSTAGE LOUNGE BAR

Map p275 (☎604-687-1354; www.thebacksta
gelounge.com; 1585 Johnston St; ☺noon-2am
Mon-Sat, to midnight Sun; 🚌50) This dark,
under-the-bridge Granville Island hangout
has winning patio views and frequent local-
band live music. The bar is lined with more
than 20 mostly BC microbrew taps from the
likes of Driftwood, Phillips and Red Truck,
and there's always a bargain $2.75 special
on Tuesdays and Thursdays from Bowen
Island Brewing. The pub-grub food menu
includes good flatbread pizzas. This is a
popular spot for those attending the nearby
theaters.

## DOCKSIDE
BREWING COMPANY BAR

Map p275 (☎604-685-7070; www.dockside
brewing.com; Granville Island Hotel, 1253 Johnston
St; ☺11:30am-10pm; 🚌50) Often overshad-
owed by the other brewers in town (being
stuck on the quiet end of Granville Island
doesn't help), Dockside's beers are made on-
site and include the tasty, hibiscus-toned
Jamaican Lager. Sup on the excellent waterfront patio for tranquil views of False
Creek's boat traffic and you may have to be
forcibly removed by the end of the night.

If it's raining, stay indoors by the fireplace and sink into a leather couch. If
you're not sure which beer to have, try a
tasting flight. Dockside also offers free
brewery tours (4:30pm Thursdays) for
those who reserve ahead. If you're lucky,
it'll be led by the brewery's old-school German brewmeister, who certainly knows a
thing or two about great beer.

# ⭐ ENTERTAINMENT

**Granville Island is home to several
theaters and is a hotbed of performance
art and theatrical and cultural festivals.**

## GRANVILLE ISLAND STAGE THEATER

Map p275 (☎604-687-1644; www.artsclub.
com; 1585 Johnston St; tickets from $29; ☺Sep-
Jun; 🚌50) The Granville Island arm of
Vancouver's leading theater company, this
intimate, raked-seating venue is the perfect
spot to feel really connected to the action
on stage. Cutting-edge homegrown shows
as well as new versions of established hits
(especially blockbuster musicals in early
summer) populate the season here and
you're close to several restaurants if you
fancy a dinner-and-a-show night out.

If you're curious about West Coast theatrics, look out for plays by Morris Panych,
one of BC's favorite playwright sons.

## VANCOUVER WHITECAPS SOCCER

Map p274 (☎604-669-9283; www.whitecaps-
fc.com; BC Place Stadium, 777 Pacific Blvd; tickets $30-150; ☺Mar-Oct; ♿; Ⓢ Stadium-China-
town) Using BC Place Stadium as its home,
Vancouver's professional soccer team
plays in North America's top-tier Major
League Soccer (MLS). They've struggled a
little since being promoted to the league
in 2011, but have been finding their feet
(useful for soccer players) in recent sea-
sons. Save time for a souvenir soccer-shirt
purchase to impress everyone back home.

A good family-friendly activity, it's also
better value than taking everyone to a Vancouver Canucks NHL game.

---

## THE ISLAND'S BEST FEST

It might feel like an invasion but it's probably more accurate to call the 11-day **Vancouver Fringe Festival** (www.vancouverfringe.com; ☺mid-Sep) an energetic occupation of Granville Island. Running every September, the event includes a multitude of
enthusiastic performers from Canada and around the world staging approximately
700 shows – from comedy reviews to poignant dramas – at venues large and small.
Naturally, the island's surfeit of theaters is well utilized, but shows are also frequently
staged in less conventional venues, from floating miniferries to pop-up stages on
every street corner. Tickets hover around the $12 mark but deals are plentiful and
free shows are common. Book ahead for shows before you arrive, but note that just
strolling the island during the event can be equally entertaining, as buskers and fly-
posting performers try to catch your attention. Finally, consider hanging out with the
performers themselves: usually one bar is set aside during the festival for the thesps
to chill out with audience members between shows – it's the perfect opportunity for
you to dust off that searing reinterpretation of *Death of a Salesman* you've written that
just needs a producer (and a lyricist for the musical numbers).

# 🏃 Neighborhood Walk
# False Creek Seawall Stroll

**START** DAVID LAM PARK
**END** GRANVILLE ISLAND
**LENGTH** 6KM; 3 HOURS

Start on the north side of False Creek at Yaletown's **❶ David Lam Park** (p103) and head east alongside several intriguing public artworks before passing under **❷ Cambie Bridge**. Continue on and you'll come upon **❸ Expo '86**, the giant world exposition that put the city on the international map. From here to **❹ Science World** (p132), you'll pass reminders of the big event: the Plaza of Nations and, in the distance, the SkyTrain line.

Follow the seawall trail past Science World to the **❺ Olympic Village** (p132), the high-rise housing on the southeast corner of False Creek. Home to athletes during the 2010 Olympic and Paralympic Winter Games, it's now a new neighborhood containing hundreds of condos plus shops, bars and restaurants. If you need a break for lunch, **❻ Tap & Barrel** (p137) is a good pit stop and has a great patio overlooking the water.

Continue west along the seawall, passing over a steel pedestrian bridge shaped like a canoe, and you'll soon come to **❼ Habitat Island** – an artificially constructed tree-and-shrub-lined creation – a new inner-city sanctuary for passing cormorants and blue herons.

Pass under the Cambie Bridge again before reaching **❽ Leg-in-Boot Sq**. The cozy-looking neighborhood here is worth a quick poke around. Built in the 1980s, the low-rise homes are a stark contrast to the high-as-possible residential towers built within the last decade and now facing the area from the opposite shoreline.

Passing through the neighborhood and alongside **❾ Charleson Park**, you'll arrive at **❿ Spruce Harbour Marina**, a live-aboard boat community. Within a few minutes, **⓫ Granville Island** will appear on the shoreline ahead. You'll enter it from the hidden back route few visitors know about. Look out for the **⓬ totem pole** as you step onto the island. It was carved by hundreds of people and was erected in 1999, recalling the First Nations residents who once fished and lived in this area.

## BC LIONS
FOOTBALL

Map p274 (📞604-589-7627; www.bclions.com; BC Place Stadium, 777 Pacific Blvd; tickets from $35; ⊘Jun-Nov; 🚼; ⓢStadium-Chinatown) The Lions is Vancouver's team in the Canadian Football League (CFL), which is arguably more exciting than its US counterpart, the NFL. It's had some decent showings in recent years but hasn't won the all-important Grey Cup championship since 2011. Tickets are easy to come by unless the boys are laying into their arch enemies, the Calgary Stampeders.

The team relies on its jump-out-of-your-seat offense, and catching a game at the stadium includes plenty of schmaltzy razzamattaz, from cheerleaders to half-time shows. It's family friendly and a lot cheaper than catching an NHL hockey game.

### VANCOUVER
### THEATRESPORTS LEAGUE
COMEDY

Map p275 (📞604-738-7013; www.vtsl.com; The Improv Centre, 1502 Duranleau St; tickets $15-22; ⊘Wed-Sun; ☐50) The city's most popular improv group stages energetic romps – sometimes connected to themes such as Shakespeare or *Game of Thrones* – at this purpose-fitted theater. Whatever the theme, the approach is the same: if you're sitting near the front, expect to be picked on. The 11:15pm Friday and Saturday shows are commendably ribald. Check www.ticketstonight.ca for day-of half price tickets.

If you fancy your skills as a performer, try not to rush the stage. Theatresports offers regular drop-in Saturday afternoon workshops ($15) for those keen to give improv a try – you'll likely find out it's much harder than it looks.

### CAROUSEL THEATRE
THEATER

Map p275 (📞604-669-3410; www.carouseltheatre.ca; Waterfront Theatre; tickets adult/child $35/18; 🚼; ☐50) Mostly performing at Granville Island's Waterfront Theatre, this smashing child-focused drama company stages some great, wide-eyed productions that adults often enjoy just as much as their kids. Adaptations of children's classics such as *The Wind in the Willows* have featured in the past, with clever reinterpretations of Shakespearean works added to the mix for older children.

It also hosts an excellent kids' drama camps in summer if you're traveling with a young thesp.

# SHOPPING

Colonizing the area's evocative old brick warehouses, chichi Yaletown has some interesting stores and designer boutiques. But for craft fans, it has to be Granville Island. It's teeming with studios where artisans throw clay, blow glass and silversmith jewelry. Head to the Net Loft, Railspur Alley or Public Market if you're lacking direction, but make sure you explore as much as possible and duck along the back alleys to see artists at work in their studios. Buskers also hang out here on summer afternoons, making this Vancouver's most convivial shopping area.

# Yaletown

### XOXOLAT
CHOCOLATE

Map p274 (📞604-733-2462; www.xoxolat.com; 1271 Homer St; ⊘10:30am-6pm Tue-Sat, noon-5pm Sun & Mon; ⓢYaletown-Roundhouse) Pronounced *sho-sho-la*, one of Vancouver's finest chocolate shops lured a whole new sticky-fingered audience when it moved from a tiny across-town spot a few years back. The larger space enabled it to increase its racks of top-notch gourmet chocolate bars from around the world as well as displaying more of its own-made truffles, slabs and signature chocolate shoes.

There are also regular $25 chocolate tasting events at the counter toward the back of the store; check the website and book ahead before you arrive.

### CROSS
HOMEWARES

Map p274 (📞604-689-2900; www.thecrossdesign.com; 1198 Homer St; ⊘10am-6pm Mon-Sat, 11am-5pm Sun; ⓢYaletown-Roundhouse) Not everything is white at this large, high-ceilinged interior store but it certainly veers towards the pastel. From perfect wine glasses to cool linens, there's a continental, vintage-chic feel to the collection. It's ideal for a rainy-day browse, but be careful: you'll almost certainly find something you want to buy, which could mean blowing your baggage allowance on the way home.

Aside from furnishings and kitchenware, you'll also discover some cool design books and even jewelry.

YALETOWN & GRANVILLE ISLAND SHOPPING

### GOORIN BROS HAT SHOP                    HATS

Map p274 (☏604-683-1895; www.goorin.
com; 1188 Hamilton St; ⊘10am-7pm Mon-Thu,
10am-8pm Fri & Sat, 11am-7pm Sun; ⑤Yaletown-
Roundhouse) This welcoming hat emporium
can transform your tired old look in an
instant. An outlet of a funky US family-
run business, it caters to men and women,
and the store feels like an old-fashioned
haberdashers. Styles mix the classics with
the latest looks; you can't go wrong with a
straw fedora, and you'll be up there with
Yaletown's most fashionable when you step
outside.

### BROOKLYN CLOTHING                    CLOTHING

Map p274 (☏604-683-2929; www.brooklyn
clothing.com; 418 Davie St; ⊘10am-9pm Mon-
Sat, 11am-7pm Sun; ⑤Yaletown-Roundhouse)
Proving that Yaletown men are just as
aesthetically focused as women, this hip
menswear boutique is the perfect spot
to upgrade your style from that sad goth
look you've been sporting since 1985. Local designers are well represented – check
out the achingly cool T-shirts – and there
are dozens of jeans styles so you can finally
nail that perfect fit. Drop by on Sunday
night when it's quiet and you can try on
everything in the store. Twice.

## 🏛 Granville Island

### ★ GALLERY OF
### BC CERAMICS                         ARTS & CRAFTS

Map p275 (☏604-669-3606; www.bcpotters.
com; 1359 Cartwright St; ⊘10:30am-5:30pm;
🚌50) The star of Granville Island's arts-
and-crafts shops and the public face of
the Potters Guild of BC, this excellent spot
exhibits and sells the striking works of its
member artists. You can pick up one-of-a-
kind ceramic tankards or swirly painted
soup bowls; the hot items are the cool ramen noodle cups, complete with holes for
chopsticks. It's well-priced art for everyone.

There's a bristling stand of unique mugs
in the back corner and there was also some
tempting ceramic jewelry on our visit. Before you leave, peruse the site's art gallery
space with its ever-changing exhibits of
eye-catching creations.

### ★ PAPER-YA                          ARTS & CRAFTS

Map p275 (☏604-684-2534; www.paper-ya.
com; 1666 Johnston St, Net Loft; ⊘10am-7pm;
🚌50) A magnet for slavering stationery

fetishists (you know who you are), this
store's treasure trove of trinkets ranges
from natty pens to traditional washi paper. It's not all writing-related ephemera,
though. Whoever does the buying also
curates an eclectic, changing roster of
hard-to-resist treats including cool watches, adult coloring books and well-priced
animal-themed earrings (we like the bats
and cat heads).

There's also a back wall of seals and seal-
ing wax if you happen to be corresponding
with someone from the Middle Ages.

### ★ GRANVILLE ISLAND
### BROOM COMPANY                        HOMEWARES

Map p275 (☏604-629-1141; www.broomcompa
ny.com; 1406 Old Bridge St; ⊘10am-6pm, reduced
hours off-season; 🚌50) Ever since Harry Pot-
ter happened, locals have been entranced by
this Granville Island fave, which makes its
own beautifully handcrafted Shaker-style
straw brooms right in the store (you can
watch the mesmerizing process in action).
But these gnarly-handled lovelies aren't just
for decoration. You can pick up cobwebbers,
golf-shoe brushes and car whisks that will
easily fit in your luggage.

And just in case you're wondering, the
brooms – which can take anywhere from
20 minutes to several hours to produce –
are all fashioned from broom corn, which
grows in Mexico.

### UMBRELLA SHOP              FASHION & ACCESSORIES

Map p275 (☏604-697-0919; www.theumbrel
lashop.com; 1550 Anderson St; ⊘10am-6pm;
🚌50) Perhaps the only outdoor gear you'll
need in Vancouver is a sturdy brolly to
fend off the relentless rain. This family-run
company started in 1935 and has just the
thing, with hundreds of bright and breezy
designs that should put a smile on the face
of any tempest-addled visitor. Duck inside,
choose a great umbrella, then launch yourself back into the storm.

In summer the window is taken over by
parasols; it's your duty to bring this old-
school approach to sunny weather back into
vogue. Make sure it's as frilly as possible.

### AINSWORTH
### CUSTOM DESIGN                        ARTS & CRAFTS

Map p275 (☏604-682-8838; www.ains
worthcustomdesign.com; 1243 Cartwright St;
⊘10am-6pm Mon-Fri, noon-6pm Sat, noon-
5pm Sun; 🚌50) Ostensibly a design studio
working to commission, its front-of-shop

## GRANVILLE ISLAND'S INDUSTRIAL EDGE

Many visitors spend their time on Granville Island at the Public Market end, nipping between the myriad shops and studios. But heading a few minutes along Johnston St offers some reminders of the time when this human-made peninsula (since it's joined to the mainland, it's not actually an island) was home to dozens of hard-toiling factories making everything from chains to iron hinges.

One million cubic yards of landfill was tipped into False Creek to create the island in the early 20th century, but almost all the reminders of its gritty first few years have been lost. Almost. The area's oldest tenant, **Ocean Concrete,** is a cement maker that began here in 1917 and now cranks out enough product to build a 10-story tower block every week. It also does a great job of being a good neighbor. A recent Vancouver Biennale initiative saw the company's six gigantic waterfront silos transformed into huge painted figures, while it's annual April **open house** event is hotly-anticipated by local families.

Continue along Johnston a little further and you'll come to a second monument to the past: a landmark **yellow dock crane** that's been preserved from the old days. Nip across to the waterfront here for a final 'hidden' Granville Island view: a string of large and comfy-looking **houseboats** that many Vancouverites wish they lived in.

area showcases a kaleidoscopic array of arts and crafts by mostly local artists. It's an amazing selection, with bright-colored cartoon-monster paintings competing for your attention with Mexican wrestler-mask purses. You'll also get lots of ideas for furnishing rooms that belong to the kind of cool, quirky kids who love Roald Dahl.

Prices are good on many of the paintings. Save time to nip upstairs to the mezzanine so you can check out even more.

**SILK WEAVING STUDIO** ARTS & CRAFTS

Map p275 (☑604-687-7455; www.silkweavingstudio.com; 1531 Johnston St; ☺10am-5pm; ☐50) Almost hidden in a back alley maze of buildings, this beloved local favorite is a crafter's delight. It's hard not to stroke every strand of silk in sight, with a rainbow of colored threads and yarns calling your name. Watch out for weaving demonstrations. You'll find this store tucked down a nameless alley immediately under the bridge.

If you're here in June, check out the annual exhibition of top weaving work.

**CRAFTHOUSE** ARTS & CRAFTS

Map p275 (☑604-687-7270; www.craftcouncilbc.ca; 1386 Cartwright St; ☺10am-6pm May-Aug, 10:30am-5:30pm Sep-Apr; ☐50) At this bright and friendly nonprofit gallery run by the Craft Council of British Columbia (CCBC), the shelves hold everything from glass goblets and woven scarves to French butter dishes and lathe-turned arbutus wood bowls – all produced by dozens of

artisans from across the region. It's a great place to pick up something different for friends and family back home.

On your way out, check the flyers near the door for more info on local gallery and art-scene happenings.

**CIRCLE CRAFT** ARTS & CRAFTS

Map p275 (☑604-669-8021; www.circlecraft.net; 1666 Johnston St, Net Loft; ☺10am-7pm Apr-Dec, to 6pm Jan-Mar; ☐50) This large cooperative gallery hawks a highly diverse array of BC arts and crafts, including sculptures made from twigs, quirky oversized ceramics and sleek jewelry, with hand-sewn puppets and dolls thrown in (not literally) for good measure. Prices vary considerably but there's usually something here to suit most budgets and just looking around is fun.

**ROGER'S CHOCOLATES** FOOD

Map p275 (☑778-371-7314; www.rogerschocolates.com; 1571 Johnston St; ☺10am-6pm; ☐50) This historic West Coast chocolate-making company is based in Victoria, but this is its flagship Vancouver store. Try not to lick the dark-wood shelves as you peruse boxes of delectable treats that will never make it back home as souvenirs. The rich Victoria Creams are the signature: maple, coconut and maraschino cherry are highly recommended.

You'll likely be offered a sample or two (especially if you look as if you need cheering up) and there's also ice cream if you want to pick up a cone for the road.

### SPORT GALLERY
CLOTHING, GIFTS

Map p275 (☑604-620-5834; www.thesportgal
lery.com; 1551 Johnston St; ⊙11am-7pm; ☑50)
With its cool array of retro sportswear and
art-gallery historic sports photography, this
is the perfect pit stop for sports nuts with
money to burn. It's a great place to pick up
a striking, claret-hued replica hockey jersey
recalling the Vancouver Millionaires, the
only local team (so far) to ever win the Stanley Cup, back in the good old days of 1915.

Class it up a little with some cufflinks
made from sections of old baseballs or
hockey pucks used in professional games.

### NEW-SMALL & STERLING
### STUDIO GLASS
ARTS & CRAFTS

Map p275 (☑604-681-6730; www.hotstudio
glass.com; 1440 Old Bridge St; ⊙10am-6pm Mon-
Sat, 11am-5pm Sun; ☑50) Peer through the
windows at this family-run artisan glass
studio and you can watch the team blow
and twirl their stuff. There are also plenty
of works to purchase in the adjoining store;
just remember that you'll need an effective
stratgey for transporting it home without
breaking it into a million pieces.

### MICHAEL DEAN JEWELLERY
JEWELLERY

Map p275 (☑604-684-3866; www.michaeldean
jewellery.com; 1808 Boatlift Lane; ⊙11am-5pm;
☑50) Pearls and Canadian diamonds feature prominently in the rings created by
local artisan Michael Dean, who works on
his shiny trinkets at this cozy little island
studio. Wife Carole also creates her own
jewelry and has a sparkling range of abstract designs on silver necklaces. If you're
looking for something extra special, start
here.

# 🏃 SPORTS & ACTIVITIES

### GRANVILLE ISLAND
### WATER PARK
WATER PARK

Map p275 (⊙summer; 📶; ☑50) **FREE** Vancouver's biggest and best water park is
conveniently located near Granville Island's Kids Market (p103), which means
you'll have the perfect lure for enticing your
sprogs away from the toy shops. There's also
a large pond nearby that's often filled with
friendly ducks and geese; in May and June,
you'll often spot fuzzy babies of the feathered variety here.

### ECOMARINE
### PADDLESPORT CENTRES
KAYAKING

Map p275 (☑604-689-7575; www.ecomarine.
com; 1668 Duranleau St; kayak/paddleboard per
2hrs $39/29; ⊙9am-9pm Jun & Jul, to 8pm Aug,
10am-6pm Sep-May; ☑50) Headquartered
on Granville Island, the friendly folks at
Ecomarine offer kayak and stand-up paddle board (SUP) rentals as well as popular
guided tours around the area. At the center's Jericho Beach branch (p178), events
and seminars are organized where you can
rub shoulders with local paddle nuts. Fancy
exploring further? They also arrange multiday tours around some of BC's most magi-
cal marine regions.

If you have time for just one guided
kayak tour, take the cool full-moon paddle
($69) from Jericho Beach or English Bay.
It's a memorable experience you'll be telling
everyone about when you get back home.

### RECKLESS BIKE STORES
CYCLING

Map p274 (☑604-648-2600; www.reck-
less.ca; 110 Davie St; per 2/5hr $22.50/34.50;
⊙9am-7pm Mon-Fri, to 7pm Sat & Sun; ⑤Yaletown-Roundhouse) Popular bike rental store
with three branches across the city. This
one also specializes in high-performance
road bikes. Rentals for these are from
$125 per 48-hour period but you'll look
cooler than a Tour de France veteran as
you zip around the region.

### ACCENT CRUISES
BOATING

Map p275 (☑604-688-6625; www.accent
cruises.ca; 1698 Duranleau St, Granville Island;
cruise from $39; ⊙May-Oct; ☑50) Popular
cruise along the coastlines of English Bay,
Stanley Park and Ambleside Beach in West
Vancouver. Departures are from Granville
Island and it's a relaxing way to spend
your evening after a long day trawling the
sights on foot. An onboard dinner option
is also available.

# Commercial Drive

## Neighborhood Top Five

❶ **Havana** (p120) Spending a summer evening drinking and dining on the Drive's best patio.

❷ **Rio Theatre** (p124) Making new friends while hanging out with the locals at a late-night cult movie screening; costume and singing along optional.

❸ **Mintage** (p125) Rummaging the multitudinous racks for that perfect vintage prom dress, plus matching sunglasses and floppy hat.

❹ **Jamjar** (p117) Craving, ordering and then failing to share the delicious serving of deep-fried cauliflower with your dining partner.

❺ **Cafe Deux Soleils** (p123) Taking the stage (after a few beers) and regaling the locals with your flowery magnum opus at the city's favorite poetry slam night.

For more detail of this area see Map p276 ➡

## Lonely Planet's Top Tip

While you're walking up and down the Drive, make sure you glance along the side streets. Almost every building just off the main drag seems to have an eye-popping mural to entice your camera. There's an especially excellent one – a huge crow (a popular East Vancouver visual symbol) – just around the corner on Venables St.

###  Best Places to Eat

➡ Jamjar (p117)

➡ Tangent Cafe (p117)

➡ Kishimoto Japanese Kitchen (p118)

➡ Carthage Cafe (p120)

➡ Eternal Abundance (p117)

### Best Places to Drink

➡ Storm Crow Tavern (p120)

➡ St Augustine's (p121)

➡ Café Calabria (p123)

➡ Bump n Grind (p121)

➡ Prado (p122)

### Best Places to Shop

➡ Mintage (p125)

➡ Attic Treasures (p125)

➡ Licorice Parlour (p125)

➡ Canterbury Tales (p126)

➡ Barefoot Contessa (p125)

## Explore Commercial Drive

Take SkyTrain's Expo or Millennium line from downtown, and when you hop off at Commercial-Broadway station a few minutes later the Drive will be just along the street. Walk north toward the mountains and everything will unfold in a linear fashion: the Drive's main stores, restaurants and bars run on either side for about 17 blocks until the intersection with Venables. If it's too far to walk, bus 20 trundles along much of the main drag so you can jump aboard when you feel tired. Better still, just take a coffee-shop pit stop and you'll be back on your feet in no time. If you're exploring both of East Vancouver's two top thoroughfares – Main St and Commercial – take the 99B-Line express bus along Broadway: it links the two streets in around 10 minutes.

A lively, colorful strip, the Drive is said by some to be at its best on sunny summer afternoons. In fact, it's a perfectly relaxing half-day excursion from the city center. For others, it's languid summer evenings when the Drive thrives. This is the time when its abundant patios are at their most animated. If you're planning to eat here, make sure you wander along the strip for a few blocks before you settle on a place that truly whets your appetite. The same goes for the chatty bars and coffee shops, where you'll meet everyone from pixie-chick bohemians to chin-stroking poets and old-school dope smokers.

## Local Life

➡**People Watching** From locals with naughty cigarettes to hand-holding same-sex lovers strolling past: just taking a sidewalk cafe seat or a Grandview Park (p117) perch and watching the Drive go by is recommended.

➡**Shopping** The opposite of Robson St's slick chain stores, the Drive is teeming with one-of-a-kind indie shops always worth perusing.

➡**Dining** Like a far tastier, food-based version of the UN, it often seems as if every cuisine on the planet is available here, and the locals tuck right in.

## Getting There & Away

➡**Train** Board the Expo/Millennium line from downtown to Commercial-Broadway station.

➡**Bus** The 99B-Line express and the regular bus 9 both stop at the intersection of Broadway and Commercial, while bus 20 trundles along much of the Drive.

➡**Car** There is metered parking on the Drive and some nonmetered parking on its residential side streets.

#  SIGHTS

### GRANDVIEW PARK
PARK

Map p276 (Commercial Dr, btwn Charles & William Sts; 📵20) The Drive's alfresco neighborhood hangout is named after the smashing views peeking between its trees: to the north are the North Shore mountains, while to the west is a cityscape vista of twinkling towers. Teeming with buskers, dreadlocked drummers and impromptu sidewalk sales, the park is a big summertime lure for nearby locals.

# ✕ EATING

**The Drive is a strollable smorgasbord of independent and adventurous dining options. Fusing ethnic soul-food joints, cheap-but-good pizza spots, chatty street-side cafes and the kind of convivial pub-style hangouts that give the concept of 'neighborhood bar' a very good name, this is the city's most sociable dine-out district. It's also Vancouver's patio capital, so if the weather's good, drop by for an alfresco meal.**

### ★JAMJAR
LEBANESE $

Map p276 (☑604-252-3957; www.jamjaron thedrive.com; 2280 Commercial Dr; small plates $6-12; mains $17-22; ⊙11:30am-10pm; ✍; 📵20) This super-friendly cafe-style joint has a rustic-chic interior and a folk Lebanese menu of ethically sourced ingredients and lots of vegetarian options. You don't have to be a veggie to love the crispy falafel balls or the utterly irresistible deep-fried cauliflower stalks that will have you fighting for the last morsel if you made the mistake of ordering to share.

Drop by between 4pm and 6pm for happy-hour specials (usually including the cauliflower dish) and add a minty housemade lemonade to the mix.

### ★CANNIBAL CAFÉ
BURGERS $

Map p276 (☑604-558-4199; www.cannibalcafe. ca; 1818 Commercial Dr; mains $11-16; ⊙11:30am-10pm Mon-Thu, 11:30am-midnight Fri, 10am-midnight Sat, 10am-10pm Sun; 📵20) This is a punk-tastic diner for fans of seriously real burgers. You'll find an inventive array, from classics to the recommended Korean BBQ burger, all made with love. Top-notch ingredients will ensure you never slink into

a fast-food chain again. Check the board outside for daily specials and keep in mind there are happy-hour deals from 3pm to 6pm weekdays.

Grab a swivel stool at the counter and try to resist all the shiny beer taps staring back at you. Better still, work your way from left to right and see if you're still standing in the morning. There's also a downtown branch of this popular local spot.

### TANGENT CAFE
DINER $

Map p276 (☑604-558-4641; www.tangentcafe.ca; 2095 Commercial Dr; mains $11-14; ⊙8am-3pm Mon & Tue, to midnight Wed & Thu, to 1am Fri & Sat, to 10pm Sun; 🛜; 📵20) Lined with 1970s-style wood-paneling, this popular hangout combines comfort classic BLTs and burgers with several Malaysian curry options. But breakfast (served until mid-afternoon) is when most locals roll in, often to cure hangovers founded right here the night before. A great craft-beer menu (check the corner chalkboard) and live music (mostly jazz) three nights a week make this a popular nighttime haunt.

The side patio is busy here in summer. It's the perfect spot for sampling brews from BC ale-making darlings such as Persephone, Brassneck and Four Winds.

### ETERNAL ABUNDANCE
VEGAN $

Map p276 (☑604-707-0088; www.eternalabundance.ca; 1025 Commercial Dr; mains $7-17; ⊙9am-9pm Mon-Sat, to 8pm Sun; ✍; 📵20) 🍃 Organic and vegan are the watchwords at this grocery store and hemp-hugging eatery where you'll feel healthier just by walking through the door. Located in a little green ghetto of similar Drive businesses, tables in the small indoor and outdoor seating areas are typically topped with hearty plates of everything from beet burgers to zugghetti pasta, served in several tasty versions.

Pick up an amazing smoothie to go on your way out and you'll feel fueled for the rest of the Commercial Drive walk.

### UPRISING BREADS BAKERY CAFE
BAKERY $

Map p276 (☑604-254-5635; www.uprising breads.com; 1697 Venables St; mains $6-10; ⊙7am-7pm Mon-Fri, 7am-6pm Sat & Sun; 📵20) Vancouver's favorite bakery minichain has been satisfying the bread and cake cravings of locals for 30 years, but this East Side rustic-chic storefront is where it started. Perfect for coffee and treats any time of day (don't miss the ginger cookies), it's also a great lunch spot for a soup and sandwich, especially if it's warm enough to snag an outdoor table.

This is a good spot to pick up some fresh-baked take-out croissants or a loaf of bread – go for the hearty Finnish loaf.

### FIRE PIZZA
PIZZA $

Map p276 (☏604-253-5607; www.firepizza.ca; 1918 Commercial Dr; slices $2.75; ⊗11am-3am Sun-Thu, to 4am Fri & Sat; 🖋; 🚇20) The more popular of two side-by-side pizza joints (hence the line-ups). The generously-topped thin-crust slices here are the perfect way to salve your hunger pangs – especially late-night when you really need a comfort-grub fix. Peruse the glass cabinet for favorite varieties such as lamb, Mexican and maple pork. There's also a good array of vegetarian options (stir-fry veggie is recommended).

Slightly pricier than the dirt-cheap purveyors of greasy cardboardlike slices you'll see throughout the rest of the city, it's well-worth the extra few cents to eat here.

### LA CASA GELATO
ICE CREAM $

(☏604-251-3211; www.lacasagelato.com; 1033 Venables St; single scoops $4.50; ⊗11am-11pm; 🚇20) If you've been skiing, cycling, kayaking or just on your feet all day exploring the neighborhoods, it may be time to cool down with an ice-cold treat. A visit to Vancouver's fave traditional ice cream joint should hit the spot, although you'll likely get brain-freeze trying to choose from the bewildering kaleidoscope of flavors – 508 at last count.

### SWEET CHERUBIM
VEGETARIAN $

Map p276 (☏604-253-0969; www.sweetcherubim.com; 1105 Commercial Dr; mains $7-10; ⊗10am-10pm Mon-Sat, 11am-10pm Sun; 🖋; 🚇20) Many Drive restaurants offer vegetarian options but Sweet Cherubim goes the whole hog with a full-on vegan and veggie menu of hearty, well-priced comfort foods served at its red Formica tables. There's an Indian feel to much of the menu, with pakoras and chapati wraps proving justifiably popular. Go for the good-value thali combo to fuel up for the day.

The desserts are also worth dropping in for. Consider a mid-afternoon pit stop on the woodsy patio for a cheeky choc-dipped walnut hemp cookie or a not quite so cheeky raw hemp and blueberry smoothie. There's also a large health food store attached; the

perfect place to stock up if you're in self-catering accommodation.

### FRATELLI BAKING
BAKERY $

Map p276 (☏604-255-8926; www.fratellibakery.com; 1795 Commercial Dr; items from $3; ⊗9am-5:30pm Tue-Sat, 9am-4pm Sun & Mon; 🚇20) An authentic holdover from the Drive's Italian immigrant era, this ever-busy bakery is teeming with fresh-made treats – from loaves of warm asiago cheese bread to more cakes and pastries than you could possibly sample in a lifetime. No harm in trying, though: you might be surprised how far you get. Whatever you go for, don't miss a creamy Neapolitan slice (or three).

Consider starting the makings of a great picnic here and then combining it with some cheese and charcuterie at the Italian deli next door. Once your ad hoc lunch is fully gathered, weave north a few blocks and find a picnic spot in Grandview Park.

### KIN KAO THAI KITCHEN
THAI $$

Map p276 (☏604-558-1125; www.kinkao.ca; 903 Commercial Dr; mains $12-16; ⊗11:30am-3pm & 5-10pm Tue-Sat, 11:30am-3pm Sun, 5-10pm Mon; 🚇20) An austere, white-walled interior belies the warm service and spicy menu at this mod Thai restaurant. Share a few plates between you (don't miss the deep-fried crispy pork belly) or dive straight into the excellent red-curry duck, with its sweet pineapple and coconut flavors. Booze is not an afterthought here, either (hence the growlers on shelves behind the counter.)

Look out for beers from Townsite or Brassneck to pair with your grub. Reservations not accepted.

### KISHIMOTO
### JAPANESE KITCHEN
JAPANESE $$

Map p276 (☏604-255-5550; 2054 Commercial Dr; combo mains $9-14; ⊗5-9:45pm Tue-Sun; 🚇20) Reservations are not accepted at the Drive's best Japanese restaurant so arrive early to snag a table or expect to join a long line. Even if you have to queue, it'll be worth it: the sushi here uses fresh ingredients with exquisite presentation and attentive service. The salmon and OMG rolls are recommended but it also does an excellent *okonomiyaki* (Japanese pancake).

The menu is generally good value, but consider a combo bento box for the full stomach-stuffing effect. If pine-mushroom

# Neighborhood Walk
## Drive Drink & Dine

**START** ST AUGUSTINE'S
**END** UPRISING BREADS BAKERY CAFE
**LENGTH** 1KM; AN HOUR OR THREE (DEPENDING ON DRINKING)

From Commercial-Broadway SkyTrain station, walk north one block to **1 St Augustine's** (p121), a large local bar. You'll find one of the city's biggest arrays of draft microbrews from BC and beyond. If you haven't indulged too much, continue north on Commercial – don't worry, it's a straight line – and sober up with a coffee and a cookie at **2 Prado** (p122), one of many popular Drive coffee shops. And if it suddenly feels like time for a snooze, continue walking north towards the mountains and lie back in the grass at **3 Grandview Park** (p117) – but not before you've checked out the handsome vistas to the north (those craggy-topped mountains) and west (the twinkling downtown cityscape).

Then nip next door to Euro-style **4 Biercraft Tap & Tapas** (p123). Play it safe with a whiskey or work your way down the amazing menu of local and imported beers. Even better, forsake the booze and try a fortifying bowl of Belgian-style mussels. There's a side-patio here that's perfect on sunny days.

If you didn't eat at Biercraft, head across the road and drop into the cheery Caribbean-themed **5 Reef** (p120). The hearty soul food here is nicely spicy. And if you're keen to stay on an even keel, the tropical cocktails also come in handy nonalcoholic versions.

Stroll a few doors along to salivate over the eclectic little **6 Licorice Parlour** (p125). Aside from the dozens of imported varieties, it sells handmade hula-hoops (an ideal purchase unless your head is still reeling from the beer earlier.)

Continue north, making sure to check the murals painted on side-street walls on either side of you, and turn left onto Venables St. Within a minute or two, you'll come to **7 Uprising Breads Bakery Cafe** (p117), a local favorite. Sit down with a coffee and cake and consider all the dinner options you've passed along the Drive. Now's the time to make a decision.

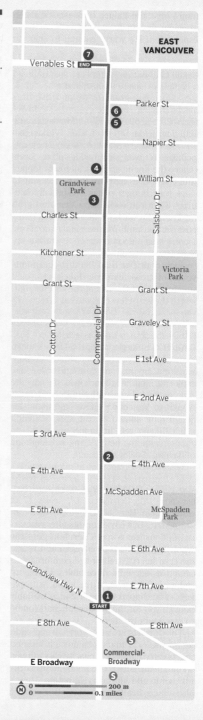

**COMMERCIAL DRIVE**

soup is available, slurp it up immediately: it's a seasonal house specialty.

### HAVANA
LATIN AMERICAN $$

Map p276 (☑604-253-9119; www.havanarestaurant.ca; 1212 Commercial Dr; mains $13-24; ⊙10am-11pm Sun-Thu, 10am-midnight Sat & Sun; ⊠20) The granddaddy of Drive dining buzzes on summer evenings when its patio – the area's biggest and best – is animated with clamorous chatter. With a couple of counter-culture holdovers (check the graffiti-scratched walls inside and the back gallery-theater combo), it's all about mojito pitchers and a comfort menu combining tacos, 'Cuban sandwiches' and jerk-chicken wraps. Go for the jambalaya.

Expect to wait for a park-view patio perch on peak summer evenings. And if you get one, hold onto it for dear life – or at least until the next round of drinks turns up. Comedy fan? There are Sunday and Monday night shows here every week.

### CARTHAGE CAFE
FRENCH $$

Map p276 (☑604-215-0661; www.carthage-cafe.com; 1851 Commercial Dr; mains $12-32; ⊙11:30am-3pm & 5-11pm Tue-Sat, 5-10pm Sun; ⊠20) This hidden gem is the Drive's most romantic European-style bistro. Hunker in a corner with your date and stare lovingly at a menu of French-Tunisian dishes that come to your candlelit table perfectly prepared. You can't go wrong with the spicy lamb shank on couscous but consider the mussels, too (coconutty Asian-style, recommended). Expect excellent, old-school service.

This is also a great spot to sample a tapas plate of escargot. They're served in traditional style, drenched in garlic butter.

### LA MEZCALERIA
MEXICAN $$

Map p276 (☑604-559-8226; www.lamezcaleria.ca; 1622 Commercial Dr; ⊙5-11pm Tue, 11am-11pm Wed & Thu, 11am-midnight Fri, 9am-midnight Sat, 9am-11pm Sun; ⊠20) Expect superb little soft tacos topped with delectable ingredients such as pork confit, zarandeado fish and braised beef cheeks. Take a seat at the long bar and you can also chat with the kind of servers who give friendliness a good name. And don't miss the drinks list: the eyebrow-raising mezcal and tequilla menu is serious. Handily, you can do tastings here so you can sip on Mexico's finest booze creations without your head swimming too much.

### REEF
CARIBBEAN $$

Map p276 (☑604-568-5375; www.thereefrestaurant.com; 1018 Commercial Dr; mains $14-19; ⊙11am-10pm Mon-Fri, 10am-11pm Sat & Sun; ⊠20) The bright beach-side cabana interior and Caribbean soul-food menu at this cheery joint can almost chase away the city's rainy-day blues. Stomach-lagging dishes like buttermilk fried chicken and eye-poppingly spicy curries help, but don't ignore the Jamaican patties (beef or tofu available), which will have you returning for more. Add a bucket of three Red Stripe bottles for the full effect.

### VIA TEVERE
PIZZA $$

Map p276 (☑604-336-1803; www.viateverepizzeria.com; 1190 Victoria Dr; mains $13-21; ⊙5-10pm Tue-Thu & Sun, 5-11pm Fri & Sat; ⊠20) Just two blocks east from the Drive, it's worth the five-minute walk for what may well be East Van's best pizza. Which is saying something, since the Drive is studded like an over-packed pepperoni pie with good pizza joints. Run by a family with true Neapolitan roots, check out the mosaic-tiled wood-fired oven then launch yourself into a feast. Capricciosa highly recommended.

There's a focus on simple but supremely well-made classic pizzas here, which means even the margherita is the perfect example of how amazing pizza should taste.

## 🍷 DRINKING & NIGHTLIFE

**If you like your drinks served with a frothy head of chatty locals, the Drive has some friendly neighborhood bars worth considering. Arguably even more enticing are the coffee joints that make this one of Vancouver's main java destinations. And don't forget the microbrewery district that's accessible from the north end of Commercial; it's the city's best.**

### ★ STORM CROW TAVERN
PUB

Map p276 (☑604-566-9669; www.stormcrowtavern.com; 1305 Commercial Dr; ⊙11am-1am Mon-Sat, 11am-midnight Sun; 🛜; ⊠20) Knowing the difference between Narnia and *Neverwhere* is not a prerequisite at this smashing Commercial Drive nerd pub. But if you do, you'll certainly make new friends. With displays of Dr Who fig-

## CRAWLING YEAST VANCOUVER

If you're a true ale nut, consider checking out a round of little, off-the-beaten-path 'Yeast Vancouver' microbreweries that together constitute one of Canada's best beer districts. Each has their own alluring tasting room and they also offer take-out growlers if you need libations to go.

Stay on the Drive and continue walking north for a few minutes past the intersection with Venables St and into an old industrial part of town (it's perfectly safe). When you come to Adanac St, turn left. Just ahead, you'll see **Bomber Brewing** (Map p276; ✆604-428-7457; www.bomberbrewing.com; 1488 Adanac St; ⊙noon-11pm; ☎; ⬚14), where the windowless little tasting room invites plenty of cozy quaffing; ESB recommended.

Back outside, continue west on Adanac for a couple of minutes; **Off the Rail** (Map p276; ✆604-563-5767; www.offtherailbrewing.com; 1351 Adanac St; ⊙noon-8pm Sun-Thu, to 10pm Fri & Sat; ⬚14) is nearby on the other side of the street. Climb the staircase and you'll find a convivial tasting room serving great beers made in the room next door.

Back on Adanac, continue to Clark Dr, turn right and walk for a few minutes on Clark until you reach Franklin St. Turn right on Franklin and you'll find red-fronted **Callister Brewing** (✆604-569-2739; www.callisterbrewing.com; 1338 Franklin St; ⊙2-9pm Mon-Thu, 2-10pm Fri, 1-10pm Sat, 1-8pm Sun; ⬚14), a shared facility where four excellent nano-breweries concoct their tasty wares.

Next, return to Clark, continue north and then turn right onto Powell St. Just ahead of you is the celebrated **Powell Street Craft Brewery** (www.powellbeer.com; 1357 Powell St; ⊙noon-9pm Mon-Thu, to 10pm Fri & Sat, to 8pm Sun; ⬚4). Consider the lip-smacking Dive Bomb Porter and Old Jalopy Pale Ale.

Continue east on Powell and, across the street, you'll find tiny **Doan's Craft Brewing Company** (✆604-559-0415; www.doanscraftbrewing.com; 1830 Powell St; ⊙2-9pm Mon-Thu, 2-11pm Fri, noon-11pm Sat, noon-9pm Sun; ☎; ⬚4), an art-lined little space serving an amazing American Rye Stout.

Finally, if you still have your wits about you, continue along Powell and turn right onto Victoria Dr then left on Triumph St. Here you'll find **Parallel 49 Brewing Company** (✆604-558-2739; www.parallel49brewing.com; 1950 Triumph St; ⊙11am-11pm; ☎; ⬚14) where the large tasting room serves a popular array of quirkily-named nipples, including Hoparazzi India Pale Lager and Gypsy Tears Ruby Red Ale. Need to know more? Pick-up a copy of *The Growler*, sold (for $2) at many of these breweries. It'll tell you all you need to know about the province's burgeoning beer scene.

ures and steampunk ray guns – plus a TV that seems to be always screening *Game of Thrones* – dive into the craft beer and settle in for a fun evening.

There's a small but perfectly formed menu of BC brews (plus some knowingly named cocktails including Romulan Ale and, of course, the Pan Galactic Gargle Blaster), while the grub is of the cheap-and-cheerful burgers and wraps variety. There are also role-play books and a wall of board games for the so-inclined (if you know what Elfenland is, that means you). And if a wizard winks at you from a corner table, wink right back.

### BUMP N GRIND
COFFEE

Map p276 (✆604-569-3362; www.bumpngrind cafe.com; 916 Commercial Dr; ⊙7am-7pm Mon-Fri, 8am-7pm Sat & Sun; ☎; ⬚20) Showing that Drive locals can never get enough

good java, this later addition to Commercial's coffeehouse culture has a loyal following, especially among devotees of the communal table out front. There's a strong commitment to great brews – not always the case among the area's highly competitive scene – founded on beans provided by popular local roaster 49th Parallel.

Friendly service is a byword here and there's also an array of good-value cakes, cookies, wraps and sandwiches if you can't live by coffee alone.

### ST AUGUSTINE'S
PUB

Map p276 (✆604-569-1911; www.staugustines vancouver.com; 2360 Commercial Dr; ⊙11am-1am Sun-Thu, to 2am Fri & Sat; ⓢCommercial-Broadway) It looks like a regular, sometimes overly loud, neighborhood sports bar from the outside, but step inside St Aug's and you'll find

## VANCOUVER'S UNMISSABLE SUMMER FAIR

Some of Vancouver's summer events and festivities have been around for several decades, but only one is still going strong after more than a century. Started in 1912, the **Pacific National Exhibition** (www.pne.ca; Hastings Park; ☉mid-Aug–Sep; 🚌) – known simply as the PNE by locals – is held just a few blocks from the northern end of Commercial Drive (hop the Hastings St bus 14 for faster access) and it's an August tradition for generations of Vancouverites. Starting life as an agricultural fair and community festival, the PNE has done a good job of updating itself over the years. It continues to be a popular, family-friendly day out, and a great way for visitors to rub shoulders with locals; it's hard to imagine an event that caters so well to such a diverse range of interests.

Plan ahead for a successful visit: check the website to see which entertainment you'd like to catch, then arrive as close to opening time as you can in the morning. This helps beat the crowds but also gives you the chance to see as much as possible. The parkland site is crammed with **exhibition halls** and **arenas**; take time to check out the market halls lined with vendors selling 'miracle' made-for-TV products. Then head to the **livestock barns**: the PNE is an important agricultural show for regional farmers, and the barns are lined for the duration with prize horses, cows, goats and sheep. To keep things lively, there are also **piglet races** that get the crowds roaring. There are **horse shows** in the domed stadium, which also give a you a chance to take a seat and plot the rest of your day using the printed program.

Included with your admission (typically around $17 but cheaper if bought via the PNE website) is a wide array of performances running all day. In recent years, these have included **Chinese acrobats**, **motorcycle stunts** and – the star attraction – the **SuperDogs** show. These talented mutts perform races and stunts for hollering crowds in what has become a PNE tradition. But they're not the only ones showing off: there's **live music** on alfresco stages throughout the day, especially in the evening, with nostalgic acts such as Foreigner and Culture Club adding to the party atmosphere in recent years.

Not everyone wants to stick around and watch their parents dance, though, and there are other attractions. The **Playland fairground** offers more than 50 rides, from dodgems to horror houses, but the top lure for thrill-seekers is the 1950s-built wooden **rollercoaster**. Coaster aficionados from across North America frequently eulogize this scream-triggering boneshaker, which reaches speeds of up to 75km an hour. It's usually a good idea to go on it before indulging in the final big attraction.

This is the one time of year when Vancouverites forget about their yoga-and-rice-cakes regimen, happily loosening their pants and stuffing themselves silly. The midway here is jam-packed with treats from **giant barbecued turkey legs** to **two-foot-long hotdogs**. Deep-fried everything is also a recent trend (from Oreo cookies to ice cream) while just about everyone will be sticking their hands into warm paper bags of **mini doughnuts** at some point during the day.

Don't spend all your money on food, though, because you'll need some for the big **lottery**. Take a walk through the show home, then enter the draw; you might win a brand new house, furnishings included. Try fitting that in your suitcase.

dozens of on-tap microbrews – one of the largest selections in the city. Most are from BC – look for highlights from Dageraad Brewing, 33 Acres and Central City – but there's an intriguing selection from south of the border as well.

If you're just not sure what to order, ask for the four-glass tasting flight. The food is of the standard pub-grub variety. Check the website to see what's on draft before you

arrive: it has a clever 'live beer menu' that shows how much of each brew is left.

### PRADO
COFFEE

Map p276 (☎604-255-5537; www.pradocafe vancouver.com; 1938 Commercial Dr; ☉7am-8pm Mon-Fri, 7am-7pm Sat, 8am-7pm Sun; 🛜; 🚌20) Eschewing the kitsch-heavy interiors of some Commercial Drive coffee shops, the comparatively austere Prado is the kind of place where minimalists sup in peace. But it's not just about aesthetics: the baristas here are serious about their fair-trade coffee, which – don't tell the Italians down the street – may be the best on the Drive. In summer, choose the on-road seating area out front.

Recent new owners have altered very little here and this is still the hippest coffee spot on the Drive, beloved of MacBook-wielding regulars quietly updating their multifarious social media accounts.

### CAFE DEUX SOLEILS                          CAFE

Map p276 (☑604-254-1195; www.cafedeuxs oleils.com; 2096 Commercial Dr; ◷8am-midnight Mon-Fri, 9am-midnight Sat & Sun; ☎; Ⓢ Commercial-Broadway) This rambling bohemian cafe is a hip and healthy Drive landmark. On sunny days, folks relax at the open windows with a beer, while acoustic musicians, performance poets and open-mike wannabes often take the stage in the evenings. There are plenty of good-value vegetarian eats here, but it's also just a great spot to chill with the counterculture locals.

Poetry slams are held on Monday nights ($6 to $10 cover charge) and shows start at 8pm (doors open 7pm). This is your big chance to regale the locals with your leotard-clad retelling of *The Rhyme of the Ancient Marine*r, perhaps while playing a lute.

### BIERCRAFT TAP & TAPAS                         BAR

Map p276 (☑604-254-2437; www.biercraft.com; 1191 Commercial Dr; ◷11am-11:30pm Mon, Tue & Fri, 11am-midnight Wed & Thu, 10am-1pm Sat, 10am-11:30pm Sun; ▣20) Originally founded on its eye-popping Belgian-beer menu (it still has some good overseas ales), Biercraft has recently shifted its boozy focus to the BC microbrew scene with dozens of drafts from the likes of Parallel 49 and Category 12. On sunny days, aim for a patio seat and keep drinking until you find your favorite new beer.

A hangover from its Belgian days, bowls of mussels are still a popular menu item here, while the weekend-only brunch is a local favorite.

### CAFÉ CALABRIA                          COFFEE

Map p276 (☑604-253-7017; www.cafecalabria.ca; 1745 Commercial Dr; sandwiches $6-10; ◷6am-10pm; ▣20) When Vancouverites tell you the Drive is the city's best coffee street, this is one of the places they're thinking about. It tops a healthy mugful of cafes founded here by Italian immigrants. Don't be put off

by the chandeliers-and-statues decor (not everyone likes a side order of statuesque genitalia); just order an espresso, sit outside and watch the Drive slide by.

If you really want to pretend you're in Italy, most of the area's old Italian dudes hang around all day outside Toscani coffee bar, a short walk away.

### RENZO'S                          COFFEE

Map p276 (1301 Commercial Dr; ◷8am-8pm; ☎; ▣20) Showing that not all the Drive's Italian coffee shops are traditional old haunts, this bright and perky corner spot is a breath of fresh air overlooking Grandview Park. Expect a jazzy soundtrack and art-lined walls – plus some excellent java made on a shiny machine that looks like the sibling of a Vespa.

Grab a seat on the mural-backed side patio and you'll likely be serenaded by the drummers kicking off in the park across the street.

### JJ BEAN                          COFFEE

Map p276 (☑604-254-3723; www.jjbeancof fee.com; 2206 Commercial Dr; ◷6am-10pm; ☎; Ⓢ Commercial-Broadway) Many Vancouver coffee bars close their doors too early for those who want to hang out at night. This JJ Bean, one of the oldest outlets of a popular citywide minichain, subverts that by opening into the wee hours (of 10pm). There's a cozy, almost neighborhood-pub, feel to this friendly joint and, befitting its Drive location, there's a chatty patio for summertime sipping.

JJ roasts its own quality beans, so consider picking up an apposite souvenir for coffee-loving friends back home: a bag of rich, earthy Eastside Blend.

### CHARLATAN                          PUB

Map p276 (☑604-253-2777; www.thecharlatan restaurant.com; 1447 Commercial Dr; ◷4pm-1am Mon-Thu, 4pm-2am Fri, 11am-2am Sat, 11am-1am Sun; ▣20) A longtime Drive fixture, this darkly-lit neighborhood bar is a perfect rainy-day hunker spot if you want to head to the wood-lined back room for beer specials and comfort pub grub. But in summer it becomes a different beast with its jam-packed and ever-popular patio plus open front windows.

Brunch is also popular here: the $10 traditional breakfast is arguably the best hair-of-the-dog recovery solution in the area.

**ROYAL CANADIAN LEGION**   BAR
Map p276 (☎604-253-1181; www.rclbranch179.ca; 2205 Commercial Dr; ☺noon-10pm Mon-Thu, noon-12:30am Fri & Sat; ☐20) Local hipsters have infiltrated this typically basic Legion social club, congregating outside to smoke, then nipping back in for cheap beers and a chatty ambiance. The old-timers seem happy the place is still being used and the darts board hasn't seen so much action in years. Perfect spot for a budget-friendly night out.

Even if you don't go in, snap a few photos of the Legion's dramatic exterior. One of the biggest murals on the Drive, it's an eye-opening wrap-around of memorial, sporting and community scenes.

# ★ ENTERTAINMENT

**The Drive is home to some of Vancouver's most eclectic night-out options, from poetry slams to retro bowling, plus one of the city's most popular independent theaters.**

★**CULTCH**   THEATER
Map p276 (Vancouver East Cultural Centre; ☎604-251-1363; www.thecultch.com; 1895 Venables St; ☐20) This once-abandoned church has been a gathering place for performers and audiences since being officially designated as a cultural space in 1973. Following comprehensive renovations a few years back, the beloved Cultch (as everyone calls it) is now one of Vancouver's entertainment jewels, with a busy roster of local, fringe and visiting theatrical shows staging everything from spoken word to touring Ibsen productions.

Check the online calendar to see what's on stage during your visit. And, after the show, hang around in the lobby bar to meet the locals and peruse the artwork displays that are changed every few weeks.

**RIO THEATRE**   CINEMA, THEATER
Map p276 (☎604-879-3456; www.riotheatre.ca; 1660 E Broadway; ⑤Commercial-Broadway) Vancouver's most eclectic cinema, this restored 1980s movie house is like a community rep theater staging everything from blockbuster and art-house movies to live music (there's an excellent sound system), improv comedy and saucy burlesque nights. Check the calendar to see what's on: the Gentlemen Heckler narrated movie screenings are recommended.

**VANCOUVER POETRY SLAM**   PERFORMING ARTS
Map p276 (www.cafedeuxsoleils.com; Cafe Deux Soleils, 2096 Commercial Dr; tickets $6-10; ☺7pm Mon; ⑤Commercial-Broadway) If you thought poetry was a tweedy, soporific experience, check out the events organized by the Vancouver Poetry House at Cafe Deux Soleils for a taste of high-speed, high-stakes slamming. The expert performers will blow your socks off with their verbal dexterity, which often bears more than a passing resemblance to rap. Every fourth Monday is also Youth Slam.

The venue itself offers vegetarian eats and local craft beers (down some Storm

---

## THE DRIVE'S BEST FESTS

In addition to the **Pacific National Exhibition** (p122) a few blocks away, consider celebrating Commercial Drive's rich Italian heritage at June's annual **Italian Day** (www.italianday.ca), an epic, jam-packed street party of music, bocce ball and plenty of food. Expect to see generations of Italian families flocking to the area during this day-long event, fostering a festive vibe that welcomes all. Check the website for exact dates and information.

Also in June and hugely popular, **Car Free Day** (p140) sees the street closed to traffic and turned into a massive fiesta of food, music, face-painting and stands selling or demonstrating artsy creations and local nonprofit initiatives.

Also look out for the city's finest homegrown Halloween happening if you're here in October. Staged by the Dusty Flowerpot Cabaret, the **Parade of Lost Souls** (www.dustyflowerpotcabaret.com) invites locals to dress up in their most ghoulish attire, stroll en masse with lanterns around the Commercial Drive area and congregate for spooky displays and performances that thrill, chill and entertain in equal measure. It's more fun than any self-respecting zombie could ever hope for.

Brewing ales and you'll soon be considering your own on-stage appearance).

### GRANDVIEW LANES BOWLING CENTRE BOWLING

Map p276 (☑604-253-2747; www.grandview bowling.com; 2195 Commercial Dr; ☉10am-11pm Mon-Wed, to midnight Thu, to 1am Fri & Sat, to 10pm Sun; ⑤Commercial-Broadway) For many, the Drive's best night out is to be had slipping on some rented shoes and hitting the lanes at this family-run, old-school gem. But it's not the regular 10-pin lanes upstairs that get everyone excited. Downstairs is home to a local nightlife legend: five-pin, glow-in-the-dark bowling that's as much fun as anyone can handle on a big night out.

### WISE HALL MUSIC, CABARET

Map p276 (☑604-254-5858; www.wisehall. ca; 1882 Adanac St; ⑤20) This comfortably grungy former church hall is a friendly neighborhood spot that's close to the heart of in-the-know locals who flock here to catch live ska, salsa, improv shows and the occasional hip-hop DJ night. Check the schedule for events or just hang out in the lounge (ask the bartender to sign you in as a guest).

It's a great place to mix with cool East Vancouverites; the bouncy floor brings out the mosh-pit desires in the most reluctant of dancers. There is also a popular flea market here on the last Sunday of every month.

# 🛍 SHOPPING

**Like a counterculture department store stretched along both sides of one street, the Drive is Vancouver's 'anti Robson.' You'll find dozens of interesting, independent shops, ranging from ethical clothing stores to intelligent-minded bookshops. If the area sounds a little too earnest, keep in mind that Commercial also has plenty of frivolous shopping outlets where you can pick up handmade candies and pop-culture gifts for your friends back home.**

### ★MINTAGE VINTAGE

Map p276 (☑604-646-8243; www.mintagevin tage.com; 1714 Commercial Dr; ☉10am-7pm Mon-Sat, 11am-6pm Sun; ⑤20) Where Drive

hipsters add a little vintage glam to their look, there's a Western saloon feel to the interior here. But don't be fooled; this is one of the city's most kaleidoscopically eclectic stores. Dominated by ladieswear, it has everything from saris to tutus, while the menswear at the back is ideal for finding a velour leisure suit with 'matching' Kenny Rogers T-shirt.

Don't miss the funky costume jewelry and check out the cleverly reworked clothes that give new life to old, otherwise unfashionable pieces.

### ★LICORICE PARLOUR FOOD

Map p276 (☑604-558-2422; 1002 Commercial Dr; ☉11am-6pm; ⑤20) Just when you think you'll never find that combination licorice and hula-hoop store you've been searching for all your life, here it is. A perky little spot with a serious commitment to the love-it-or-hate-it candy, it has dozens of varieties – including an entire row of salt licorice. Work off your candy belly with a hula-hoop: staff will even teach you a few moves.

Gelatin-free and gluten-free varieties, plus imported Italian licorice toothpaste, are also available and there were plans, on our visit, to add housemade chocolate to the tempting mix as well. Until then, buy a gnarly licorice root to go and chew on it outside while you wait.

### BAREFOOT CONTESSA CLOTHING

Map p276 (☑604-255-9035; www.thebarefoot contessa.com; 1928 Commercial Dr; ☉11am-6pm Mon-Sat, noon-5pm Sun; ⑤20) Vintage-look dresses and sparkling costume jewelry – plus a 1920s-style flapper hat or two – are the mainstays of this bright and inviting women's-wear boutique aimed at those who never want to be a clone of a chain-store mannequin. You'll find cute tops and accessories from Canadian and international designers, plus artsy-craftsy purses and laptop bags trimmed with lace. The staff here is famously friendly, with plenty of suggestions for the perfect new look.

### ATTIC TREASURES ANTIQUES

Map p276 (☑604-254-0220; www.attictreas uresvancouver.com; 944 Commercial Dr; ☉11am-6pm Tue & Thu-Sat, noon-5pm Sun; ⑤20) One of Vancouver's favorite antiques stores, this retro-cool double-room shop specializes in 1950s-to-1980s furniture and treasures. Peruse the candy-colored coffee pots and cocktail glasses and save time for the clutter room at the back, where bargains sometimes live. Much of the furniture has a Danish modern feel and there is often also German pottery and Finnish glassware to make your credit cards sweat.

Ask about vintage model kits so you can relive your halcyon days.

### KALI
CLOTHING, ACCESSORIES

Map p276 (✆604-215-4568; 1000 Commercial Dr; ⊙10am-6pm Sun-Tue, to 7pm Wed-Sat, 11am-6pm Sun; 📮20) Serving up a mixed array of women's clothing and crafty housewares and trinkets sourced from around the world, this popular browser's hangout is perfect for squandering a lazy hour or so before dinner. You'll find everything from summer hats to Buddha statues calling your name here. There's something for every budget.

### CANTERBURY TALES
BOOKS

Map p276 (✆604-568-3511; www.canterburytales.ca; 2010 Commercial Dr; ⊙10am-6pm Mon-Wed & Sat, 10am-7pm Thu & Fri, 11am-6pm Sun; 📮20) Serving the area's well-read bohemians, this used and new bookstore is one of several Drive literary nooks. It's a mini-labyrinth of floor-to-ceiling stacks bulging with titles, including some quirky staff picks near the entrance. Sci-fi and fantasy fans should also check the sections at the back of the store. Don't miss the well-curated literary travel section near the center of the stacks.

And consider picking up a Bukowski anthology or two: the infamous American author and poet gave a few notorious live readings on the Drive back in the day.

### MISCELLANY FINDS
VINTAGE

Map p276 (✆604-215-9970; www.miscellanyfinds.ca; 1029 Commercial Dr; ⊙10am-6pm Mon-Sat, noon-5pm Sun; 📮20) Like an explosion at a garage sale, this rambling used and vintage store invites serious perusing. The front room is packed with racks of mostly women's togs (plus some kids clothing and menswear) but the comfortably chaotic back area is crammed with just about everything else. From tartan suitcases to velour paintings, this is a fun place for treasure hunting.

There's also an intriguing used-book section in this room. It's the ideal place to find that first edition Lonely Planet *Canada* guide you need for that time-travelling trip to old-world Vancouver you've been planning.

### WOMYNS' WARE
ADULT

Map p276 (✆604-254-2543; www.womynsware.com; 896 Commercial Dr; ⊙11am-6pm Mon-Sat, 11:30am-6pm Sun; 📮20) Unlike any other sex shop, this friendly, ultra-welcoming spot is dedicated to female sexual empowerment. There's an eye-popping menu of sex toys and the helpful staff is happy to explain the workings of everything from the 'family jewels harness' to 'nun's habit flogger.' There's also a good array of books and games to put the fun back into your sexual shenanigans.

Fair-trade committed, the store is a great place for first-timers looking for tips and encouragement in a nonseedy, nonjudgmental setting.

### AUDIOPILE
MUSIC

Map p276 (✆604-253-7453; www.audiopile.ca; 2016 Commercial Dr; ⊙11am-7pm; 📮20) This local-fave record store takes a no-nonsense approach with basic racks of new and used vinyl and CD recordings. Perfect for that rare Joy Division (or not-so-rare New Order) album. Check the bargain $2.99 CDs and half-price vinyl near the entrance, plus the staff picks stand – how else are you going to find that Suzi Quatro record you've been looking for?

This is the perfect location for a rainy-day rummage and the staff really know their stuff; quiz them on Carter the Unstoppable Sex Machine albums and see if they flinch.

### PULPFICTION BOOKS EAST
BOOKS

Map p276 (✆604-251-4311; www.pulpfictionbooksvancouver.com; 1830 Commercial Dr; ⊙11am-7pm; 📮20) The smallest of Pulpfiction's mini-empire of three Vancouver bookstores, this spartan-looking shop has little decoration beyond its wood floors and well-stocked wooden bookshelves. And what that shows, of course, is that it really is all about the books here. An easy spot to while away an hour of browsing, it's almost impossible not to find something you want to buy.

And, if you're a fast reader, you can try to resell it back to the store before you leave for home: it has an active book-buying program (although apparently not very keen on anything by Dan Brown).

## DRIVE PAST

Strolling Commercial Drive today, it's easy to imagine the bohemians have ruled this strip forever. In reality, the street has an unexpected past as one of the city's most historic neighborhoods. Once part of the main transportation link between Vancouver and the city of New Westminster, streetcars trundled down the middle of the Drive from the 1890s, triggering the housing and storefront developments that remain here today. Many of these were later colonized by European families (mostly Italians as well as some Portuguese) who emigrated here in the 1950s. The handful of old-school coffee shops still here are an evocative reminder of this period.

But the Italians were a later chapter in the Drive's history. While main-drag storefronts catch the eye today, make sure you take a peek down the side streets. They're lined with gabled, wood-built homes constructed for Canadian Pacific Railway (CPR) workers in the first few years of the last century, and many have been restored in recent decades to their bright-painted clapboard glory. In fact, this neighborhood is home to one of the largest collections of **heritage homes** in Vancouver. Architecture fans will likely spot some well-known styles, including Edwardian, Queen Anne, Craftsman and arts-and-crafts.

In recent years, locals have begun to celebrate the area's rich past and a volunteer organization calling itself the **Grandview Heritage Group** (www.grandviewheritagegroup.org) has formed to help preserve the district's architectural treasures. The organization's annual **Centenary Signs Project** sees houses and buildings in the area that are more than 100 years old recognized with cool plaques. Walkers can then trawl the neighborhood spotting the best examples. There's a map of the included houses on the website, where you'll also find some evocative vintage images of the area's past.

### LA GROTTA DEL FORMAGGIO
FOOD & DRINKS

Map p276 (☑604-255-3911; www.lgdf.ca; 1791 Commercial Dr; ◌9am-6pm Mon-Thu & Sat, 9am-7pm Fri, 10am-5:30pm Sun; ▣20) If you insist on eating something other than chocolate or ice cream, hit this legendary old-school deli and sandwich shop, a family-run holdover from the days when this was Vancouver's 'Little Italy.' Peruse the lip-smacking cheese and charcuterie selections then check out the wall of marzipan, antipasti, olive oil and balsamic vinegar. Almost everything here has been imported from the mother country.

It's a good spot to gather the makings of a mighty fine picnic – prosciutto and smoked ricotta recommended – to scoff in nearby Grandview Park. But before you leave the store, check out the ceiling: it's painted with clouds, just like the Sistine Chapel (but better).

### WONDERBUCKS
HOMEWARES

Map p276 (☑604-253-0510; www.wonderbucks. com; 1803 Commercial Dr; ◌10am-6pm; ▣20) Dedicated to cut-price chic for homes that don't have million-dollar budgets, this store has everything from bargain art prints to mod journals. It's worth a peruse, especially if you have room in your luggage for that perfect floor-to-ceiling vase you've been looking for. There's an ever-changing array of goods so it's worth revisiting, and there are often excellent sales.

### PEOPLE'S CO-OP BOOKSTORE
BOOKS

Map p276 (www.peoplescoopbookstore.com; 1391 Commercial Dr; ◌11am-6pm Tue-Sun; ▣20) A Commercial Drive fixture for more than 70 years and a loud echo of the Drive's counter-culture heyday, this is the bookshop to pick up the latest copy of *Proletarian* magazine. But it's not all revolutionary fervor. The sky-blue stacks include art and cookery tomes – with new and used volumes mixed together – alongside the 'Labour' and 'Philosophy & Political Economy' sections.

Before you leave, peruse the noticeboard near the door for postings about area events, readings and edgy happenings. And check the website for the latest store hours, which were scheduled to be extended at the time of our visit.

TASHKA/GETTY IMAGES ©

### 1. Steam Clock, Gastown
Gastown's most photographed landmark marks each hour with whistling symphonies.

### 2. North Vancouver
Across the Capilano Suspension Bridge you'll find historic exhibits, totem poles and nature trails.

### 3. Stanley Park
This 400-hectare woodland is revered for its forest-and-mountain oceanfront views.

### 4. Yaletown and Burrard Bridge
A perfect spot to dine out if you feel like splurging and eating alongside wealthy Vancouverites.

# Main Street

## Neighborhood Top Five

**1** **Regional Assembly of Text** (p141) Composing pithy missives to your loved one on vintage typewriters at the legendary monthly letter-writing club.

**2** **Brassneck Brewery** (p137) Downing a Passive Aggressive pale ale or three at Vancouver's favorite neighborhood microbrewery; and adding a growler to go.

**3** **Gene Cafe** (p138) Sipping a creamy coffee with the plaid-shirted locals on a sun-baked wood-block perch, while overlooking the Mount Pleasant street scene.

**4** **Hot Art Wet City** (p132) Hanging with culture-hugging Mainsters at a gallery show opening, then buying some cool-ass art to take home.

**5** **Dock Lunch** (p135) Rubbing elbows with the regulars over a homestyle meal that feels like dining in a family friend's house.

For more detail of this area see Map p278 ➡

# Explore Main Street

After the north-end hub of Science World and the nearby Olympic Village, the main action on Main takes place further south in two key areas: around the intersection with Broadway and then further south from 18th Ave. These are the twin hearts of Vancouver's hipster scene. The first, the center of the Mount Pleasant neighborhood, is lined with independent bars and coffee shops, while the Riley Park area past 18th is perfect for airing your credit cards: it's full of one-of-a-kind fashion, arts and accessories stores. Consider an afternoon of window shopping here, followed by dinner and a few beers in either area. Handily, bus 3 runs along Main every few minutes from the Main St-Science World SkyTrain station, but make sure you hop off regularly for some on-foot exploration. If you're still hungry, stay on the bus south past 48th Ave where you'll find the Punjabi Market district, home to some of the region's best-value, all-you-can-eat curry restaurants.

## Local Life

➡**Coffee Shops** Locals spend more time hunched over laptops in cafes here than anywhere else in the city. Join them for a glimpse of what makes the area tick (ie great java).

➡**Microbreweries** Studded with some of Vancouver's best microbrewery tasting rooms, this is a great area for a hop-forward great night out with like-minded ale fans. Start at Brassneck (p137).

➡**Indie Shopping** The last place any major big box retailer would move to, browsing the surfeit of one-of-a-kind boutiques, bookstores and record shops keeps area locals busy.

## Getting There & Away

➡**Bus** Number 3 runs the length of Main St. The 99B-Line express bus connects Main and Commercial Dr along Broadway, as does the much slower bus 9.

➡**Train** SkyTrain connects to bus 3 services at Main St-Science World Station. But if you're on the Canada Line, alight at Broadway-City Hall and take the 99B-Line along Broadway to Main St.

➡**Car** There is some metered parking on Main St, plus lots of side-street parking the further south you drive.

###  Best Places to Eat

➡ Dock Lunch (p135)
➡ Fish Counter (p136)
➡ Trafiq (p135)
➡ Hawkers Delight (p133)
➡ Ernest Ice Cream (p135)

###  Best Places to Drink

➡ Brassneck Brewery (p137)
➡ Shameful Tiki Room (p137)
➡ Narrow Lounge (p138)
➡ Main Street Brewing (p138)
➡ Whip (p138)

### 🔒 Best Places to Shop

➡ Regional Assembly of Text (p141)
➡ Smoking Lily (p142)
➡ Urban Source (p141)
➡ Neptoon Records (p141)
➡ This Monkey's Gone To Heaven (p142)

MAIN STREET

# ◉ SIGHTS

Anchored by a geodesic-domed attraction loved by local families, this area's other main lures are its rich array of independent private galleries. Many are clustered just off Main around 2nd Ave, while others pop up around the area like splotches of fresh paint on a busy painter's palette.

★**SCIENCE WORLD**                    MUSEUM

Map p278 (☑604-443-7440; www.scienceworld.ca; 1455 Quebec St; adult/child $25.75/17.75; ◷10am-6pm, to 8pm Thu Jul & Aug, reduced hours off-season; 🅿 🚼; 🆂Main St-Science World) Under Vancouver's favorite geodesic dome (okay, its only one), this ever-popular science-and-nature showcase has tons of exhibition space and a cool outdoor park crammed with hands-on fun (yes, you *can* lift 2028kg). Inside, there are two floors of educational play, from a walk-in hamster wheel to an air-driven ball maze and, of course, a karilloscope.

Alongside the permanent galleries, there are changing visiting exhibitions and regular entertaining demonstrations of scientific principles for those who like to watch – the giant Omnimax Theatre takes that one step further. And if you fancy exploring without the kids (you know you do), check out the regular adults-only **After Dark** events, combining bar drinks and some live entertainment. These socials are staged every two months and are one of the city's cool nightlife secrets.

★**HOT ART WET CITY**                 GALLERY

Map p278 (☑604-764-2266; www.hotartwetcity.com; 2206 Main St; ◷noon-5pm Wed-Sat; 🚌3) **FREE** Possibly the most fun you can have at a private gallery in Vancouver. Trip up the stairs at this funky little space and you're guaranteed some eye-popping art to look at. Lowbrow and pop art are the usual focus, and mostly local artists are showcased. There's a new exhibition every month or so and past themes have ranged from art on bike saddles and beer bottles to the annual, highly popular, button art show.

Be sure to check the retail space in the corner for quirky, affordable souvenir ideas. There's also a lively roster of events, comedy nights and even yoga meet-ups.

**OLYMPIC VILLAGE**                    AREA

Map p278 (Athletes Way; 🆂Main St-Science World) Built as the home for 2800 athletes during the 2010 Olympic and Paralympic Winter Games, this glassy waterfront development became the city's newest neighborhood once the sporting types went home. It's taken a while to make the area feel like a community, but shops and restaurants – plus some cool public art – have helped. Worth a look on your seawall stroll. Don't forget to photograph the gigantic **bird sculptures** – preferably with the mountains behind them.

**EQUINOX GALLERY**                   GALLERY

Map p278 (☑604-736-2405; www.equinoxgallery.com; 525 Great Northern Way; ◷10am-5pm Tue-Sat; 🅿; 🚌3) **FREE** One of Vancouver's oldest established private galleries, Equinox pioneered this area's arty new credentials by being one of the first big names to move here. Look out for works by local and national artists – and if there's a show by Fred Hertzog, make sure you visit. His brightly colored yesteryear photos of vintage Vancouver are spectacular.

**WINSOR GALLERY**                    GALLERY

Map p278 (☑604-681-4870; www.winsorgallery.com; 258 E 1st Ave; ◷10am-6pm Tue-Fri, to 5pm Sat; 🅿; 🚌3) **FREE** Large-format photography and contemporary art from Canada, the US and the rest of the world are the specialties at this expansive, double-room space. Each room usually runs its own exhibition and recent shows have included works by local popular artists such as Attila Richard Lukacs and Brian Howell.

**CATRIONA JEFFRIES**                 GALLERY

Map p278 (☑604-736-1554; www.catrionajeffries.com; 274 E 1st Ave; ◷11am-5pm Tue-Sat; 🅿; 🚌3) **FREE** Transforming a former autoparts warehouse, this is another contemporary gallery migrant from a different part of town. The move has enabled more artworks to be displayed, but there remains a very strong focus on internationally renowned artists who reflect the city's rich conceptual art heritage.

**MONTE CLARK GALLERY**               GALLERY

Map p278 (☑604-730-5000; www.monteclarkgallery.com; 525 Great Northern Way; ◷10am-5:30pm Tue-Sat; 🚌3) **FREE** Joining its arty,

## GALLERY-HOPPING THE FLATS

Vancouver's newest gallery district, known as the Flats, is still a secret to many locals. But if you're a contemporary art fan, hop off bus 3 around Main and 2nd Ave (which joins to Great Northern Way) and you'll find 15 or so cool spaces colonizing the area's former industrial units. Among the highlights are the **Winsor** (p132), **Equinox** (p132) and **Catriona Jeffries** (p132).

This district is rapidly changing, with new college and university campuses enhancing the feel – especially the **Emily Carr University of Art + Design**, scheduled to move here from its original Granville Island base in 2017. The galleries first began moving to this district around 2010, lured by larger spaces and cheaper rents. Many have relocated from South Granville's once-dominant Gallery Row area.

Since arriving, the galleries have banded together to produce a free map of the area's arty hot spots – you can pick this up from any of them. Plan ahead and you can also partake of an exhibition opening night or two (make sure you pack your black polo-neck). Also be sure to check online before you visit: more galleries are opening here all the time. And if you're here in July, look out for the annual one-day **Block Party**, a neighborhood open house where Vancouverites wander the galleries while a street-party vibe ensues.

white-walled brethren here in 2013, Monte Clark is well worth a look. Past exhibitors have included photography by local-boy-made-good Jeff Wall, while works by celebrated artists including Roy Arden and Douglas Coupland have also graced the expansive space.

## ✖ EATING

Renowned for alternative shopping options plus its independent bar and coffeehouse scene, Main is also an intriguing area for eclectic, one-of-a-kind dining experiences. Many radiate from the intersection with Broadway, with additional pockets of tasty treats southwards as far as 48th Ave, where the city's Punjabi Market area offers cheap-and-cheerful curry buffets. Make sure you also peruse the local bar listings since many of the area's drinkeries also have worthwhile dining menus.

**HAWKERS DELIGHT**  ASIAN $

Map p278 (☑604-709-8188; 4127 Main St; mains $4-10; ⊗noon-9pm Mon-Sat; ✐; ☐3) It's easy to miss this cash-only hole-in-the-wall, but it's worth retracing your steps for authentic Malaysian and Singaporean street food, made from scratch at this family-run favorite. Prices are temptingly low, so order to share – from spicy mee pok to noodle-heavy mee goreng and prawn-packed laksa.

Check the counter when ordering for the addictive veggie fritters; just $1 for two.

One of the city's best and most enduring budget eats, there's not much room here, so consider arriving off-peak, unless you're planning a take-out picnic.

**BUDGIE'S BURRITOS**  TEX-MEX $

Map p278 (☑604-874-5408; www.budgiesburritos.com; 44 Kingsway; mains $7-10; ⊗11am-midnight; ✐; ☐8) It's a rare vegetarian eatery that has a loyal clientele of carnivores, but the bulging, good-value burritos at this quirky, well-hidden neighborhood haunt keep locals coming back for a seat among the Elvis and conquistador velour 'artworks.' First time here? Go for the tofu-sausage-packed Henry and snag a booth in the subterranean basement. Vegan options are also available.

If you're still hungry, chase it with a bowl of housemade tortilla soup. Finally, pick up a take-out menu on your way out and plan your next meal – you'll likely be back within a day or two, if only to confirm that the sad-eyed clown painting on the wall is actually real rather than something you had a nightmare about. It's often busy here, so arrive off-peak to avoid the line-ups.

**ARGO CAFE**  DINER $

Map p278 (☑604-876-3620; www.argocafe.ca; 1836 Ontario St; mains $7-16; ⊗7am-4pm Mon-Wed, 7am-4pm & 5-10pm Thur & Fri, 8am-2pm Sat; ☐3) One of Vancouver's last genuine diners has been souped up in recent years

# 🏃 Neighborhood Walk
# Main Street Hipster Stroll

**START** NEPTOON RECORDS
**END** SHAMEFUL TIKI ROOM
**LENGTH** 1KM, ONE TO THREE HOURS

Vancouver's hippest strip is ideal for those who like to browse around some of the city's coolest indie stores.

Hop off southbound bus 3 around 18th Ave. Start at indie-favorite **1 Neptoon Records** (p141) for some cool vinyl that's way more hip than you are. Then nip across the street to the smashing little designer shop **2 Smoking Lily** (p142) – especially if you're an intellectual clotheshorse. The staff here are friendly and they'll have plenty of additional suggestions for what to see on your walk.

Further south, you can dip into the vintage clothing racks at **3 Front & Company** (p142). If you've always wanted a 1950s crushed-velvet smoking jacket to wear with your jeans, this is the place to find it. But it's not only togs: the store does a cool line in kitsch giftware, too. At this point, you should also begin to notice your surroundings: check the painted murals on the sides of many buildings just off Main and look out for the steaming coffee-cup motifs etched into the sidewalk concrete.

From here, re-cross to the west side of the street and, if it's time to eat; join the throng at the **4 Fish Counter** (p136), home to arguably the city's best fish and chips. Grab a perch outside in the sun.

Across the street, a couple of minutes south, you'll find one of the city's most eclectic stores: the **5 Regional Assembly of Text** (p141) is where you can indulge your fetish for sumptuous writing paper, old-fashioned typewriters and all manner of stationery items. Pick the right day for your visit and join the hipsters at the monthly letter-writing social club.

Continue south to the area's other top indie record shop, **6 Red Cat Records** (p142). Peruse the CDs and vinyl and ask the staff for tips on bands to see in town – tickets are available here for many area shows. End your crawl with a cocktail at the delightful **7 Shameful Tiki Room** (p137).

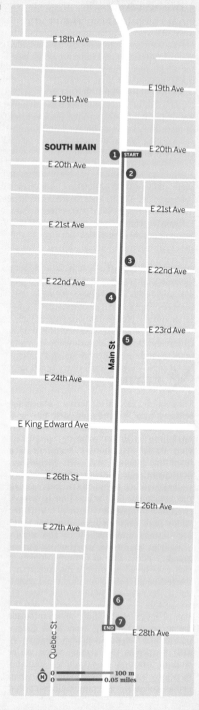

but it hasn't lost its gem like charm. Tucked inauspiciously in a light industrial part of town, it's worth searching out, especially if one of the comfy vinyl booths is available. You can still get a good value breakfast here for $6.95 but fancier fare includes well-made burgers and pasta dishes.

Keep in mind that it doesn't take credit cards (cash or debit only) and the drinks are of the non-booze variety. It's the kind of place that was built for the area's tough-ass working men and is now frequented by coolsters, and it isn't fazed by either.

### EARNEST ICE CREAM
ICE CREAM

Map p278 (☑778-379-0697; www.earnesticecream.com; 1829 Quebec St; ice cream from $5; ☺10am-10pm; ☐3) Vancouver's best artisan ice cream shop is slightly off-the-beaten-path in a redbrick heritage building near Olympic Village. But it's worth the hunt so you can dive into a dozen or so flavors, split between regulars including salted caramel and whiskey hazelnut and seasonals such as the utterly delicious rhubarb oat crumble. All are available in cone or cup form – plus naughty to-go pint jars.

There's plenty of seating here if you need to rest-up. Or you can grab your cone and walk towards a waterfront seat at the nearby Olympic Village; you'll likely finish long before you get there, though.

### TRAFIQ
CAFE $

Map p278 (☑604-648-2244; www.trafiq.ca; 4216 Main St; mains $7-9; ☺9am-6pm; ☑; ☐3) A local favorite, this sometimes clamorously busy French-influenced bakery cafe is a lunchtime magnet with its quesadillas, housemade soups and bulging grilled sandwiches (California club on cranberry pecan recommended). But the best time to come is off-peak when you can snag a table and take on one of the large, belly-busting cake slabs. Miss the salted caramel slice at your peril.

If there are two of you – or you're just greedy – add a slice of Chunky Monkey, a rich, cake-bread-pudding fusion combo that triggers equal feelings of delight and guilt.

### FRENCH MADE BAKING
BAKERY $

Map p278 (☑604-558-4880; www.frenchmadebaking.com; 81 Kingsway; mains $4-9; ☺8am-6pm Mon-Fri, 9am-6pm Sat, 10am-5pm Sun; ☐; ☐8) You know that feeling when you're walking around and you're suddenly struck by a maddening craving for *macaron* as well as the creeping realization that

you're thousands of miles from Paris? Don't worry, this tiny, easy-to-miss cafe has your back (and your bake). The delectable (and well-priced) treats are made to perfection here, along with an array of perfectly naughty pastries.

Stick around for coffee and a croissant (you may have to fight over the handful of seats). The fresh-made crepes here are also excellent and everything is highly authentic: hence the French-speaking staff. Like what you taste? Learn to make your own via the bakery's regular classes.

### SLICKITY JIM'S CHAT 'N' CHEW
DINER $

Map p278 (☑604-873-6760; www.skinnyfatjack.com; 3475 Main St; mains $8-14; ☺8:30am-4pm Mon & Tue, to 8pm Wed, Thur & Sun, to midnight Fri & Sat; ☑; ☐3) This local favorite gets jammed packed with bleary-eyed locals soothing their hangovers, but it's worth the wait for a quirky, darkened room lined with the kind of oddball art David Lynch probably favors in his house. Menu-wise, they've nailed breakfast here with traditional as well as inventive (and heaping) plates enlivened with quirky names like the Breakfast of Broken Dreams. Lunch and dinner is also available and there are plenty of vegetarian options too.

### LUCY'S EASTSIDE DINER
DINER $

Map p278 (☑604-568-1550; 2708 Main St; ☺24hr; ☎☑; ☐3) On those bleary-eyed mornings when only heaping comfort grub hits the spot, head to this popular retro-look diner which serves good value breakfasts, from traditional eggs and bacon to smoked salmon scrambles. The rest of the day, slide onto a counter perch and face-plant into burgers, fried chicken sandwiches or made-from-scratch soups.

### ★DOCK LUNCH
INTERNATIONAL $$

Map p278 (☑604-879-3625; 152 E 11th Ave; mains $10-14; ☺11:30am-5pm Mon-Fri, 11am-3pm Sat & Sun) Like dining in a cool hippy's home, this utterly charming room in a side street house serves a daily-changing menu of one or two soul food mains (think spicy tacos or heaping weekend brunches). Arrive early and aim for one of the two window seats and you'll soon be chatting with the locals or browsing the cookbooks and Huxley novels on the shelves.

One of Vancouver's most unusual eateries, this is as far from a restaurant

MAIN STREET EATING

dining experience as you can get. Expect to be talking about this place for weeks when you get back home. No reservations.

### FABLE DINER
DINER $$

Map p278 (☑604-563-3463; www.fablediner.com; 152 E Broadway; mains $7-18; ⊙7:30am-midnight Mon-Fri, 9:30am-midnight Sat & Sun; ▣9) Transforming a former greasy spoon in the landmark Lee Building into a new, more casual satellite of a popular Kitsilano restaurant, this modern diner has quickly become a favorite Mount Pleasant hangout. Snag a window booth or swivel chair at the kitchen-facing counter and dive into elevated all-day breakfasts and comfort grub, including the smashing roast duck and kimchi pancake.

Finish with a round of mini-doughnuts or dive into the weekly-changing milkshake special (especially recommended if you suddenly need an extra few thousand calories).

### TOSHI SUSHI
JAPANESE $$

Map p278 (☑604-874-5173; 181 E 16th Ave; mains $8-16; ⊙5-9:30pm Tue-Sat; ▣3) There are no reservations and the place is tiny, but this unassuming sushi joint just off Main is the best place in the neighborhood for Japanese dining. Expect to line up (try your best to arrive off-peak) before tucking into outstanding fresh-made dragon rolls, crunchy tempura and succulent sashimi platters: order a selection and everyone at the table will be delighted.

The service can be hit-and-miss – they're sometimes overwhelmed by the crowd – but this family-run joint is usually all smiles.

### FISH COUNTER
SEAFOOD $$

Map p278 (☑604-876-3474; www.thefishcounter.com; 3825 Main St; mains $10-22; ⊙10am-8pm; ▣3) Main's best fish and chips. This busy spot combines a seafood wet counter and a bustling fry operation. Order from the cashier in the middle, snag a spot at the stand-up table inside or sit-down benches outside and wait to be called. Battered halibut and cod are popular but we love the wild salmon, served with fries and a mound of 'slaw.

There's much more to the menu than fish and chips, though. Check the special on the handwritten poster under the cash desk (steamed halibut dumplings on our visit) or consider the fish tacos, oyster p'boys and a stomach-warming chowder that will fill you for a week. Add a beverage

from the excellent array of artisan pop bottles (anyone for dandelion and burdock?) and you'll be set.

### ACORN
VEGETARIAN $$

Map p278 (☑604-566-9001; www.theacornrestaurant.ca; 3995 Main St; mains $18-22; ⊙5:30-10pm Mon-Thu, 5:30pm-11pm Fri, 10am-2:30pm & 5:30-11pm Sat, 10am-2:30pm & 5:30pm-12am Sun; ✒; ▣3) One of Vancouver's hottest vegetarian restaurants – hence the sometimes long wait for tables – the Acorn is ideal for those craving something more inventive than mung-bean soup. Consider seasonal, artfully presented treats such as beer-battered haloumi or vanilla almond beet cake and stick around late-night: the bar serves until midnight if you need to pull up a stool, get tipsy and set the world to rights. At time of research, the team behind Acorn was planning an additional new venture a few doors away, a fast-food vegetarian diner. Check ahead to see if it's open yet.

### BURGOO BISTRO
WEST COAST $$

Map p278 (☑604-873-1441; www.burgoo.ca; 3096 Main St; mains $16-25; ⊙11am-11pm; ▣3) Hit Main's best patio in summer or hunker in the woodsy interior on those frequent Vancouver rainy days – either way, Burgoo has mastered the art of gourmet comfort dining. Always check the seasonal specials, then dive into a tasty fall-back position of jambalaya, butter chicken or irresistible cheddar-packed mac 'n' cheese. End with a glass of BC-made mead.

This is also a great spot for brunch: arrive early on weekends to beat the crowds and go for the cinnamon bun French toast. And if you really like this place, keep your eyes peeled around the city: there are additional Burgoo branches lurking around and each has a couple of distinctive specialties to keep things interesting.

### EAST IS EAST
MIDDLE EASTERN $$

Map p278 (☑604-565-4401; www.eastiseast.ca; 4433 Main St; mains $9-18; ⊙11:30am-4:30pm & from 5:30pm daily; ✒⏹; ▣3) Locals craving Indian and Middle Eastern comfort food plus a side dish of live music and international dance love this immersive, aromatic haven. Avoid weekends, when it can be overcrowded, and you'll have a much more pleasurable meal – especially with some roti rolls followed by the Chai Feast tasting menu. End with a round of the city's best Darjeeling masala chai. There are lots of vegetarian options here if you're that way inclined.

### SUN SUI WAH SEAFOOD RESTAURANT
CHINESE $$

Map p278 (☑604-872-8822; www.sunsuiwah. ca; 3888 Main St; mains $8-22; ☉10:30am-3pm & 5-10pm; ☲3) One of the best places in the city for dim sum, this large, chatty Hong Kong–style joint has been a deserved local favorite for years. Order an array of treats then sit back for the feast: although you should expect to be fighting over the Lazy Susan to see who gets the last mouthful. Seafood is a huge specialty here (hence the live tanks).

If it's a special occasion and you want to push out the boat, gorge on some king crab legs.

### BOB LIKES THAI FOOD
THAI $$

Map p278 (☑604-568-8538; www.bob likesthaifood.com; 3755 Main St; mains $12-16; ☉11:30am-2:30pm & 5-9pm Mon-Thu, to 10pm Fri & Sat; ☲3) Take a seat beneath the giant wooden spoon and fork paintings at this laid-back joint and tuck into satisfying Thai comfort grub. The papaya salad small plate and green-curry chicken main are hugely popular, but consider the exotic *miang kham* (six bites) starter dish, a cornucopia of flavors from peanut and ginger to lime and coconut shavings, all wrapped up in vine leaves.

### FOUNDATION
VEGETARIAN $$

Map p278 (☑604-708-0881; 2301 Main St; mains $9-18; ☉noon-1am Sun-Thu, to 2am Fri & Sat; ☑; ☲3) This lively vegetarian (mostly vegan) noshery is beloved of local coolsters, but it's sometimes too busy for its own good. Arrive off-peak for attentive service – they're sometimes rushed off their feet otherwise – and you'll have your pick of the retro-cool mismatched Formica tables. Among the hearty housemade soups and veggie burgers, the heaping nachos are the standout.

### TAP & BARREL
WEST COAST $$

Map p278 (☑604-685-2223; www.tapandbar rel.com; 1 Athletes Way; mains $15-22; ☉11am-midnight Mon-Fri, 10am-midnight Sat & Sun; ⑤Main St-Science World) In the heart of the Olympic Village, this popular neighborhood haunt serves gourmet comfort nosh such as Cajun chicken burgers and pork belly pizzas but, in summer, it's all about the views from

the expansive, mountain-facing waterfront patio (the area's best alfresco dining). Add some BC beer or wine and you'll have to be forcibly removed at the end of the night.

# 🍷 DRINKING & NIGHTLIFE

**Combining excellent microbrewery tasting rooms with independent bars and cozy coffeehouses, Main St is the kind of area where you can nurse a drink all afternoon while you type your latest travel blog entry on your tablet; don't spill any on the keyboard. Bus 3 makes bar-hopping easy here; the service runs every few minutes up and down Main and also links you to downtown Vancouver.**

### ★BRASSNECK BREWERY
MICROBREWERY

Map p278 (☑604-259-7686; 2184 Main St; ☉2-11pm Mon-Fri, noon-11pm Sat & Sun; ☲3) Vancouver's favourite microbrewery concocted more than 50 different beers in its first six months of operating and continues to win new fans with an ever-changing chalkboard of intriguing libations with names like Bivouac Bitter, Stockholm Syndrome and Magician's Assistant. Our recommendation? The delicious Passive Aggressive dry-hopped pale ale. Arrive early for a seat in the small tasting bar, especially on weekends,

Hungry? Couple your $8 sampler flight with a cured sausage or three from the jars on the counter. There's also a hidden table at the back of the room that's perfect for chatty shenanigans, and don't forget to peek through the holes punched in the wood-planked walls for a glimpse of the brewery beyond. A great pilgrimage spot for visiting beer fans. Pick up a Brassneck growler to go (filled of course) at the front; it'll keep you going for the rest of your visit.

### ★SHAMEFUL TIKI ROOM
BAR

Map p278 (www.shamefultikiroom.com; 4362 Main St; ☉5pm-midnight Sun-Thu, to 1am Fri & Sat; ☲3) This windowless snug instantly transports you to a Polynesian beach. The lighting – including glowing puffer-fish lampshades – is permanently set to dusk and the walls are lined with tiki masks and rattan coverings under a straw-shrouded ceiling. But it's the drinks that rock: seriously well-crafted classics from zombies to mai tais to a four-person Volcano Bowl (don't forget to share it).

Arrive early on weekends; there's only space for around 50 people. The worst thing about this perfect little tiki bar? When someone opens the door and lets the light in from the outside it reminds you that reality is waiting. Block it out with another Volcano Bowl.

### MAIN STREET BREWING MICROBREWERY

Map p278 (☑604-336-7711; www.mainstreet beer.ca; 261 E 7th Ave; ☺2-11pm Mon-Thu, noon-11pm Fri-Sun; ☐3) Tucked into an historic old brewery building, Main Street Brewing has a great, industrial-chic little tasting room and a booze roster divided into regular beers and casks. Start with a four-flight tasting sampler then dive in with a larger order. The Westminster Brown Ale is our favorite but there's usually an IPA or two worth quaffing here as well.

Main Street also has a larger food menu than most Vancouver microbreweries, ranging from pies and burgers to elevated bar snacks.

### NARROW LOUNGE BAR

Map p278 (www.narrowlounge.com; 1898 Main St; ☺5pm-1am Mon-Fri, to 2am Sat & Sun; ☐3) Enter through the doorway on 3rd Ave – the red light tells you if it's open or not – then descend the graffiti-lined stairway into Vancouver's coolest small bar. Little bigger than a train carriage and lined with moth-eaten taxidermy and junk-shop pictures, it's an atmospheric nook that always feels like midnight. In summer, try the hidden alfresco bar out back.

Mac 'n' cheese (go for the Guinness-infused version) is the fuel-up dish of choice here, or you can just have another whiskey and hope for the best – but if the mangy bear head on the wall starts talking to you, it's probably time to call it a night. Popular with Main St hipsters, this is a great location to spot local lads and their attempts to grow full-on Noah beards.

### KAFKA'S COFFEE

Map p278 (☑604-569-2967; www.kafkascof fee.ca; 2525 Main St; ☺7am-10pm Mon-Thu, 7am-8pm Fri, 8am-8pm Sat & Sun; ☎; ☐3) With more MacBooks than an Apple Store, locals fill the tables here silently updating their Facebook statuses as if their lives depended on it (which it does). But, despite appearances, this is a warm and welcoming

hangout. The single-origin coffee is excellent and there's a serious commitment to local artworks on the walls; it's like quaffing in a cool gallery.

All the art is for sale – making this the perfect spot to pick up a unique Vancouver souvenir that beats anything you'll find in the usual places. And if you're lucky, you might even meet the artist supping an espresso in the corner and trying to look nonchalant.

### GENE CAFE COFFEE

Map p278 (genecoffeebar.com; 2404 Main St; ☺7:30am-7pm Mon-Fri, 8:30am-7pm Sat & Sun; ☎; ☐3) Colonizing a flatiron wedge of concrete floors and expansive windows, slide onto a chunky cedar bench with your well-thumbed copy of *L'Etranger* and you might catch the eye of an available local. If not, console yourself with a perfectly made cappuccino and a chunky homebaked cookie (the fruit pies are recommended for additional consolation).

On sunny afternoons, bask on a wood-block perch in the sun outside and watch the Mount Pleasant locals strolling around the neighborhood as if they own the place. You might spot a regular: a little dog transported around by it's owner in a tiny bicycle sidecar that looks like the cockpit of a WWI German fighter plane (complete with fake machine gun).

### WHIP PUB

Map p278 (☑604-874-4687; www.thewhipres taurant.com; 209 E 6th Ave; ☺10am-1am Mon-Thu, 10am-2am Fri, 9am-2am Sat, 9am-1am Sun; ☐3) The laid-back, wood-floored Whip fuses the best in pub and lounge approaches. Hit the martini list with some yam *frites* or indulge in the excellent local beer list – check the specials board or order an excellent Fat Tug IPA. Better still, drop by at 4pm Sundays when they crack open a guest keg: perfect for a patio bask in the sun.

Arrive early on weekends when this spot is often heaving; you don't want to be lining up outside watching everyone else drink. And check out the artworks on the walls: the Whip has a strong commitment to showcasing local artists and the exhibitions are changed every few months. Thirsty for happy hour? There are $5 booze specials from 4pm to 6pm every weekday.

## THE RETURN OF BREWERY CREEK

Mainland Brewery, Red Star Brewery, San Francisco Brewery and, of course, Vancouver Brewery. The names of the city's long-gone beer producers recall a time when Brewery Creek – an area radiating from Main St around 7th Ave – concocted the suds quaffed by many ale-loving Vancouverites. The area was named after a rolling creek that once powered water wheels at area breweries, but there are now few reminders of this beer-making golden age. But don't despair: Brewery Creek is back, with a tasty crop of brand new microbreweries popping up in recent years. And all of them have highly inviting tasting rooms.

Tucked into a refurbished space at one of the few remaining Vancouver Brewery buildings, **Main Street Brewing** (p138) combines an industrial chic tasting room with a tempting roster of regular beers and ever-changing casks. Just around the corner on Main, **Brassneck Brewery** (p137) is many locals' number-one Vancouver beermaker; afternoons are a great time to avoid the crowds. A short walk away, **33 Acres Brewing Company** (p139) has a white-walled tasting room that may be the chattiest bar in town. But how does Vancouver-made beer compare to the rest of the Pacific Northwest? Conclude you beer crawl by hopping bus 3 south to **Portland Craft,** (p139) a bar specializing in great drafts from just south of the border.

### CASCADE ROOM                                             PUB

Map p278 (☏604-709-8650; www.thecascade.ca; 2616 Main St; ◷11am-1am Mon-Thu, to 2am Fri & Sat, to midnight Sun; ▣3) The perfect contemporary reinvention of a trad neighborhood bar, this is arguably Mount Pleasant's merriest watering hole. The ale list includes some great craft beers, including a healthy range of own-brand Main Street Brewing tipples produced just a few blocks away. Hungry on the weekend? Indulge in the area's best Sunday roast.

### 33 ACRES
### BREWING COMPANY                              MICROBREWERY

Map p278 (☏604-620-4589; www.33acresbrewing.com; 15 W 8th Ave; ◷9am-11pm Mon-Fri, 10am-11pm Sat & Sun; ▣9) Like a rec room for hipsters, this white-walled brewery bar is jam-packed and humming with extremely noisy chatter in the early evening when tech workers disgorge from their nearby offices. By 8pm, it's usually more mellow. Aim for a glass of lightly hoppy Ocean pale ale (a tumblerful is $5) and add a $45 souvenir T-shirt to show how cool you are.

Those in the know also save belly-room for the latest seasonals, which are often the brewery's most exciting libations.

### 49TH PARALLEL COFFEE                            COFFEE

Map p278 (☏604-872-4901; www.49thcoffee.com; 2902 Main St; ◷7am-10pm Mon-Sat, 7:30am-10pm Sun; ☏; ▣3) Attesting to Main's status as one Vancouver's independent coffeehouse capitals, when this large corner cafe opened in 2012 it was soon crammed with locals. It roasts its own coffee so the quality is high and you can also faceplant into a full selection of lovely Lucky's Doughnuts (apple-bacon fritter recommended). Avoid peak times: this place is often full to bursting.

### PORTLAND CRAFT                                      BAR

Map p278 (☏604-569-2494; www.portlandcraft.com; 3835 Main St; ◷11:30am-1am Mon-Thu, to 2am Fri & Sat, to midnight Sun; ▣3) With its extensive, unique-for-Vancouver draft list of mostly Western US beers, this convivial new resto-bar taps into the popularity of craft brews from Portland and beyond. You'll find Deschutes and New Belgium well represented here so, if you're a fan of super-hoppy IPAs, you'll soon be puckering your lips with pleasure. Arrive early on weekend evenings to snag a table.

## ☆ ENTERTAINMENT

### ★ FOX CABARET                                   LIVE MUSIC

Map p278 (www.foxcabaret.com; 2321 Main St; ▣3) Formerly one of North America's last-remaining porn cinemas, its new owners have transformed (and fully pressure-washed) this independent nightlife venue, ditching the dodgy flicks in favour of live music, DJ nights and regular events like Saturday's Alternative Dance Party and Sunday's popular comedy night. Check the

## MAIN'S BEST FEST

Stroll the streets here most days and you'll likely think that everyone who lives in this area is achingly hip. But if you make it to June's annual **Car Free Day** (www.carfree vancouver.org, ☉mid-Jun) – staged along Main St, south of the Broadway intersection, for at least 30 blocks – you'll realize there's much more diversity in this area than you thought. Taking over the streets for this family-friendly community fest, are live music, craft stalls, steaming food stands and a highly convivial atmosphere that makes for a partylike afternoon with the locals. And if you miss it? Consider checking out September's **Autumn Shift Festival** as well. It's just as much fun and has a sustainability theme.

online calendar before you arrive in town; there's always something different on stage in this narrow, high-ceilinged venue.

### BILTMORE CABARET
LIVE MUSIC

Map p278 (☎604-676-0541; www.biltmore cabaret.com; 2755 Prince Edward St; ☐9) One of Vancouver's best alt venues, the Biltmore is a firm favorite on the local indie scene. A low-ceilinged, good-vibe spot to mosh to local and touring musicians, it also has regular event nights: check the online calendar for upcoming happenings including the hugely popular **Kitty Nights Burlesque shows** (www.kittynights.com), which end with a full-on DJ dance party.

### BMO THEATRE CENTRE
THEATER

Map p278 (☎604-687-1644; www.artsclub. com; 162 W 1st Ave; ☐3) The newest addition to the city's Arts Club theater empire, this smaller, state-of-the-art purpose-built studio auditorium serves up more experimental fare. There are often three or four main shows here per year as well as on-stage readings of new works in progress, which are typically free; check the Art Club website for information on these.

### VIVA LA UKELUCION
LIVE MUSIC

Map p278 (www.vcn.bc.ca/vanukes; Our Town Cafe, 245 E Broadway; $5-10 donation; ☉7:30pm 4th Tuesday of the month; ☐9) If you haven't packed your uke, you can still drop by this Vancouver Ukelele Circle monthly strum-fest to watch dozens of locals of all skill levels. It's hard not to smile as they work through their songs and jam along to each other, often spilling out on to the street on summer evenings.

Arrive early for dinner and you'll also have the pick of the tables for when showtimes rolls around; the menu is of the hearty soup and sandwiches variety.

### CELLULOID SOCIAL CLUB
FILM

Map p278 (www.celluloidsocialclub.com; ANZA Club, 3 West 8th Ave; tickets $5-10; ☉7:30pm mid-month; ☐9) Visiting movie nuts with a penchant for making their own flicks – or just chewing the fat with those who do – should unspool their film at one of Vancouver's coolest underground hangouts. Held every month at the ANZA Club community hall, the club is a drop-in for local filmmakers and video artists who like showing their shorts to anyone who turns up.

The results – several mini-epics are shown over the course of a couple of hours – are always interesting, and the screenings are followed by a few beers and a chance to rub shoulders and chat with local auteurs.

### BLUEGRASS JAM NIGHT
LIVE MUSIC

Map p278 (www.pacificbluegrass.ca; ANZA Club, 3 W 8th Ave; $6; ☉7:30pm Mon; ☐9) A weekly public jam session for local and visiting bluegrass fans staged upstairs at the ANZA Club, where everyone is welcome to watch or join in. A great way to meet Vancouver fiddle-huggers, this footstomping night out is staged throughout the year, with a summer break to rest those weary plucking fingers. Also stages concerts throughout the year – check the website.

### ANZA CLUB
MUSIC, CABARET

Map p278 (☎604-876-7128; www.anzaclub. org; 3 W 8th Ave; ☐9) This wood-built community hall – which has the aesthetics of a worker's club without the edge – is popular with local cool kids as well as old-school hippies who've been coming here for years. Staging an eclectic roster of weekly events (many of them in the upstairs tiki lounge), it also has regular live shows and DJ nights.

# SHOPPING

This is Vancouver's must-see area for locally owned independent stores. Many showcase the exciting creative skills of hot regional designers, but there are also some tasty treats to scoff along the way, plus some perfect spots to buy that souvenir that no-one else will have back home. The two main shopping areas on Main are around the Broadway intersection and past the intersection with 18th Ave – this second area is full of options and is especially recommended.

### ★ REGIONAL ASSEMBLY OF TEXT
ARTS & CRAFTS

Map p278 (☑604-877-2247; www.assembly oftext.com; 3934 Main St; ⊙11am-6pm Mon-Sat, noon-5pm Sun; ☐3) This ironic antidote to the digital age lures ink-stained locals with its journals, handmade pencil boxes and T-shirts printed with typewriter motifs. Check out the tiny under-the-stairs gallery showcasing zines from around the world, and don't miss the monthly **Letter Writing Club** (7pm, first Thursday of every month), where you can hammer on vintage typewriters, crafting erudite missives to your far-way loved one.

If you have time, make your own pin badge or just browse the racks of hyper-cool greetings cards, mostly fashioned by the store's friendly art-school-grad co-owners. One of Vancouver's most original stores, it displays a little array of handmade self-published minibooks near the front window – where else can you read *One Shrew Too Few* and *Secret Thoughts of a Plain Yellow House*?

### ★ NEPTOON RECORDS
MUSIC

Map p278 (☑604-324-1229; www.neptoon. com; 3561 Main St; ⊙11am-6:30pm Mon-Sat, noon-5pm Sun; ☐3) Vancouver's oldest independent record store is still a major lure for music fans, with its *High Fidelity* ambiance and time-capsule feel. But it's not resting on its laurels: you'll find a well-priced array of new and used vinyl and CD recordings and some serious help with finding that obscure Sigue Sigue Sputnik recording you've been looking for.

Unlike some record stores, there's no attempt to be hip here, making it arguably the most comfortable spot in town for a browse, whether or not you're a geeky muso. It also sells tickets for shows around town; ask the knowledgeable staff for recommendations.

### ★ MOUNTAIN EQUIPMENT CO-OP
SPORTS & OUTDOORS

Map p278 (☑604-872-7858; www.mec.ca; 130 W Broadway; ⊙10am-9pm Mon-Fri, 9am-6pm Sat, 10am-6pm Sun, reduced hours off-season; ☐9) Grown hikers weep at the amazing selection of clothing, kayaks, sleeping bags and clever camping gadgets at this cavernous outdoors store: MEC has been encouraging fully fledged outdoor enthusiasts for years. You'll have to be a member to buy, but that's easy to arrange for just $5. Equipment – canoes, kayaks, camping gear etc – can be rented here.

There's also a good selection of regional and international maps and guidebooks, plus a climbing wall to test your new gear. And when it comes to Swiss Army knives: this is the place for that triple-blade-ice-pick-toaster combo. Check the notice board at the front of the store: it's a great place to see what the local hiking/biking brigade are up to. The clothing range has become increasingly more lifestyle-based in recent years, which means you can even buy jeans here now. The store was planning a move to a new flagship Olympic Village spot during our visit so check ahead before you set out.

### URBAN SOURCE
ARTS & CRAFTS

Map p278 (☑604-875-1611; www.urbansource. bc.ca; 3126 Main St; ⊙10am-5:30pm Mon-Sat; ♿; ☐3) ⚘ From used postcards to insect rubber stamps and from ladybug stickers to map pages from old books, this brilliant store offers a great melange of reclaimed materials and alternative arts and crafts supplies to a loyal band of locals. In this browser's paradise you'll suddenly be inspired to make an oversized pteradactyl model from glitter and discarded cassette tapes.

This is the perfect spot to gather all the supplies for making your own postcards. Your friends back home will be mightily impressed – or they may think you have too much time on your hands.

### BAKER'S DOZEN ANTIQUES
ANTIQUES

Map p278 (☑604-879-3348; 3520 Main St; ⊙11am-5:30pm Mon-Sat, noon-5pm Sun; ☐3) One of Vancouver's most interesting vintage and antique stores. Nose around the creaky-floored interior here and you'll

MAIN STREET SHOPPING

start to mentally redecorate your apartment with items to make you seem a whole lot cooler than you really are. From animal skulls to Edwardian children's books plus a smattering a cool-ass Bakelite goodness, this a great spot to browse on a rainy day.

### THIS MONKEY'S GONE TO HEAVEN ARTS & CRAFTS

Map p278 (☑778-379-9389; www.thismonkey.ca; 3957 Main St; ⊙11am-6pm Mon-Sat, noon-6pm Sun; ☑3) A fascinating menagerie of beady-eyed taxidermy greets you at this emporium of oddball trinkets and artifacts that almost feels like an art gallery. If you don't have room for a stuffed fox in your carry-on, there are also framed insects, mounted mammal skeletons and – best of all – knitted reproductions of dissected animals that would make the perfect gift (for some).

A fan of unusual taxidermy (as well as shops named after Pixies' songs)? This is the place to buy little stuffed mice dressed as Victorian ladies. Don't pretend you don't want one.

### PULPFICTION BOOKS BOOKS

Map p278 (☑604-876-4311; www.pulpfictionbooksvancouver.com; 2422 Main St; ⊙10am-8pm Mon-Wed, 10am-9pm Thu-Sat, 11am-7pm Sun; ☑3) One of the city's best used-bookstores (there are also plenty of new tomes, especially in the front room), this is the ideal haunt for the kind of serious browsing where you forget what time it is. You'll find good literature and biography sections, as well as a handy travel area at the back for planning your next big trip.

They also buy used books here so if you happen to be traveling with your personal library in several steamer trunks, this is the place offload it and cash it in for dinner. If they don't buy, just hang around the stacks for a few more hours looking morose.

### SMOKING LILY CLOTHING

Map p278 (☑604-873-5459; www.smokinglily.com; 3634 Main St; ⊙11am-6pm Mon-Sat, noon-5pm Sun; ☑3) Art-school cool rules at this mostly womenswear boutique, with skirts, belts and halter-tops whimsically accented with prints of insects, narwhals and the periodic table. Anatomically correct heart motifs are also popular, appearing on shirts, jewelry and cushion covers. And there's a great array of accessories, including quirky purses and shoulder bags beloved of the local pale and interesting set.All is designed and made in BC. Men's T-shirts are also a tiny but essential part of the mix, with fish, skull and tractor designs among the options. Expect super-friendly service.

### RED CAT RECORDS MUSIC

Map p278 (☑604-708-9422; www.redcat.ca; 4332 Main St; ⊙11am-7pm Mon-Thu, to 8pm Fri & Sat, to 6pm Sun; ☑3) The ideal destination to hang out on a Main St rainy day, Red Cat's wooden racks are home to a well-curated collection of new and used CDs and vinyl records in what is one of the coolest record stores in the city. It helps that it's co-owned by musicians; ask them for tips on who to see live on the local scene. You can also buy local show tickets and listen to your possible purchases before you buy. Looking for the Red Cat? His real name was Buddy and, although he passed away in 2006, he's fondly remembered here.

### VANCOUVER SPECIAL HOMEWARES

Map p278 (☑604-568-3673; www.vanspecial.com; 3612 Main St; ⊙11am-6pm Mon-Sat, noon-5pm Sun; ☑3) An irresistible, white-walled, double-sized store that appeals to design-minded individuals with its carefully chosen array of Tivoli radios, molded plastic side-tables and glossy architecture books. It's the kind of place you can easily spend an hour just browsing: the problem is you'll almost certainly find something – an Alessi cocktail set perhaps? – that you just can't live without.

### FRONT & COMPANY CLOTHING, ACCESSORIES

Map p278 (☑604-879-8431; www.frontandcompany.ca; 3772 Main St; ⊙11am-6:30pm; ☑3) A triple-fronted store where you could easily spend a couple of hours, its largest section contains trendy consignment clothing (where else can you find that vintage velvet smoking jacket?). Next door houses new, knowingly cool housewares, while the third area includes must-have gifts and accessories such as manga figures, peace-sign ice trays and nihilist chewing gum (flavorless, of course).

The ideal store to pick up a quirky souvenir for that difficult person back home who hates maple syrup (does such a person exist?); make sure you buy something cool for yourself as well.

## DON'T MISS THE MARKETS

Main Streeters love markets and there are several to keep them busy. The summertime **Main Street Station Farmers Market** (Map p278; www.eatlocal.org; 1100 Station St, Thornton Park; ⊙2-6pm Wed Jun-Sep; ⑤Main St-Science World) 🖋 is perfect for picking up seasonal BC-grown peaches, blueberries and luscious cherries. There are usually more than a few baked treats to indulge in while you're mulling your produce options. Purchases of the less edible variety are offered over in Olympic Village, where the quarterly **Portobello West** (Map p278; www.portobellowest.com; 1 Athletes Way, Creekside Community Recreation Centre; adult/child $2/free; ⊙11am-5pm Sat & Sun, 4 times per year; 🖪; ⑤Main St-Science World) weekend-long arts, crafts and fashion market colonizes the cavernous Creekside Community Centre. Expect an eclectic blend of handmade, one-of-a-kind goodies and locally designed togs to take back home, or just enjoy the live music and fresh-made treats.

Even more eclectic is the new permanent location for the monthly **Eastside Flea** (p94) which now calls the repurposed Ellis Building home after years of various locations. With space for 50 new and vintage vendors plus food trucks and live music, you'll be sure to have a good time.

But if you're determined to eat, track down the city's popular pop-up **Baker's Market** (www.bakersmarket.com). It typically runs on Sundays in spring and during the run-up to Christmas at a hall or community center not too far from Main. Check the website for dates and the current location details and be prepared to sample and buy everything from elaborately-topped cupcakes to dainty, rainbow-hued macarons, all made by local artisan cake-lovers who know exactly how to put temptation right in front of you.

### 8TH & MAIN · CLOTHING

Map p278 (📞604-559-5927; www.8main.ca; 2403 Main St; ⊙10am-9pm Mon-Sat, to 7pm Sun; 🚇3) Perhaps Vancouver's largest hipster clothing store, hence the Hershel daypacks and ironic high-top jeans, this huge store offers a cornucopia of men's and women's fashions as well as footwear and accessories. It's worth a visit if you're in the area; head to the back for the sale rails and you might find that neon-hued plaid mankini you've been searching for. There's a smaller satellite of this popular store on downtown's Granville St.

### MUCH & LITTLE · FASHION & ACCESSORIES

Map p278 (📞604-709-9034; www.muchandlittle.com; 2541 Main St; ⊙11am-6pm Mon-Sat, noon-5pm Sun; 🚇3) Proving that not all of Main St's best boutiques are clustered past 18th Ave, this smashing store is a must for artsy, indie types. With a perfectly curated array of superbly designed and ever-functional household goods, cute trinkets and irresistible accessories (plus an adjoining room of women's clothing), there's an artisan flare and a focus on small designers. Give yourself plenty of time to browse the selection, from badger pins to jars of East Van Jam. The staff is also superfriendly and more than happy to offer tips and suggestions for the perfect gift.

### BIRD ON A WIRE CREATIONS · ARTS & CRAFTS

Map p278 (📞604-315-1188; www.birdonawirecreations.com; 2535 Main St; ⊙10am-6pm Mon-Sat, 11am-5pm Sun; 🚇3) There's an eminently browsable, highly tempting and surprisingly diverse array of ever-tasteful handmade goodies at this cute and friendly store. Your credit cards will start to sweat as you move among the artisan jewelry, artsy T-shirts, ceramic craft-beer tankards and grinning monster kids' toys (that adults always want, too). But it's not just for show; there are regular craft classes here too.

Drop by for Friday night's hip Crafter's Club to hang with like-minded locals and start (or finish) a project or two. And if you're wondering where the store is on Main, just look out for the permanently yarn-bombed tree right outside

### REFIND · ANTIQUES

Map p278 (📞778-855-0969; www.refindhomefurnishings.com; 4609 Main St; ⊙noon-5pm Mon-Wed, to 7pm Thu-Sun; 🚇3) A new location further south on Main hasn't diminished the collection of tempting vintage offerings available here; think everything from Bakelite clocks to 1970s cocktail shakers. This is a highly browsable, retro-loving store, expect lots of nostalgic discoveries as you spot that old record player your dad used to have when you were a kid.

### GIVING GIFTS & COMPANY
ANTIQUES, ARTS & CRAFTS

Map p278 (☑604-831-7780; www.givinggifts.ca; 4570 Main St; ☺11am-6pm Mon-Fri, 10am-6pm Sat, noon-5pm Sun; ☐3) Despite the twee name, this is a five-room cooperative representing many local craft vendors and businesses under one roof. From Bakelite antiques to artisan chocolate bars and handmade kids wear, it's often well worth a look if you're in the neighborhood. The vendors are changed every few months to keep things lively, so there's almost always something tempting to buy. Keep your eyes peeled for vintage postcards of yesteryear Vancouver – then mail them home to show your friends that the city is still locked in 1947.

### NINETEEN TEN
HOMEWARES

Map p278 (☑604-558-0210; www.nineteenten.ca; 4366 Main St; ☺10am-6pm Mon-Sat, noon-5pm Sun; ☐3) There's a highly tempting array of must-haves at this whimsical, wood-floored housewares boutique. From crafty candle-holders to cutting boards shaped like British Columbia, you have to take your time to see everything here. But when you spot that ironwork fox-head coat hook you've been looking for all your life, it's time to get your credit card out. There's also a large and determinedly diverse array of quirky greetings cards to choose from.

### SPORTS JUNKIES
SPORTS & OUTDOORS

Map p278 (☑604-879-6000; www.sportsjunkies.com; 102 W Broadway; ☺10am-6pm Mon-Wed & Sat, 10am-8pm Thur & Fri, 10am-5pm Sun; ☐9) Along with the shelves of used boots and shoes near the door of this outdoor gear and sports equipment consignment store, you'll find racks of end-of-range new togs. Upstairs is a cornucopia of new and used equipment, from skis to snowshoes. If you know your prices, you can save a bundle here. If you're inspired to take to the city's surfeit of cycling lanes on your visit but don't want to rent, there's always a good selection of well-priced used bikes on offer here, including some good-value mountain bikes.

### BREWERY CREEK LIQUOR STORE
DRINKS

Map p278 (☑604-872-3373; www.brewerycreekliquorstore.com; 3045 Main St; ☺11am-11pm; ☐3) There's no denying that the bottled beer selection at this private liquor store (ie not run by the government, like many in the city) is among Vancouver's best. Alongside seasonal and stalwart favorites from celebrated BC brewers such as Driftwood and Hoyne, there's a jaw-dropping array of Belgian brews to keep you merry. There's also a good boutique selection of BC and international wines. A local favorite, the store is often busy with Main Streeters stocking up for their house parties (stick around and look alluring and you might even get an invite).

### TWIGG & HOTTIE
CLOTHING

Map p278 (☑604-879-8595; www.twiggandhottie.com; 3671 Main St; ☺11am-6pm Mon-Sat, noon-5pm Sun; ☐3) ✎ Named after owners Glencora Twigg and Christine Hotton, this wood-floored nook showcases distinctive garments (plus idiosyncratic jewelry) for women, from Canadian designers: it's *the* place to find something that nobody else is wearing back home. If you're in a budgeting mood, peruse the Steals and Deals rack at the back. There's also a real interest in using sustainable materials here, so feel free to ask about how those shoes you're salivating over were made.

### EUGENE CHOO
CLOTHING

Map p278 (☑604-873-8874; www.eugenechoo.com; 3683 Main St; ☺11am-6pm Mon-Thu & Sat, 11am-7pm Fri, noon-5pm Sun; ☐3) Behind the mustard-yellow facade of this Main St favorite beats the heart of a store that pioneered the emergence of this area as Vancouver's hip-wear capital. Once a grungy vintage-clothing shop, it's now a hotbed of designer duds for the city's slim-fit set – both men and women. They can't guarantee to make you cooler here, but they'll certainly have a good try.

# Fairview & South Granville

## Neighborhood Top Five

**❶ Queen Elizabeth Park**
(p147) Weaving uphill to snap some signature panoramic photos of Vancouver's dramatic, mountain-framed cityscape.

**❷ Vij's** (p152) Lining up with the locals and then faceplanting into Vancouver's (and maybe Canada's) finest Indian food; lamb popsicles included.

**❸ Vancouver Canadians**
(p156) Basking in the sun with a beer and a hot dog while catching an afternoon baseball game at Nat Bailey Stadium.

**❹ Bloedel Conservatory**
(p147) Feeding the twittering hordes of rainbow-hued tropical birds from a bowl as the parrots call loudly to each other around you.

**❺ Storm Crow Alehouse**
(p155) Practicing your Vulcan hand gestures while sipping a Romulan Ale or three, then beating everyone at a role-playing card game.

For more detail of this area see Map p280 ➡

## Lonely Planet's Top Tip

If your Vancouver visit is cursed with an overly generous serving of liquid sunshine and you're looking to escape it, head to Queen Elizabeth Park's **Bloedel Conservatory**. This glass-roofed, climate-controlled garden is a guaranteed warm-up spot on the wettest of Wet Coast days. Step inside and you'll find tropical flowers, a balmy climate and hundreds of bright-plumed birds flying and strutting about as if they own the place.

## Best Places to Eat

➤ Vij's (p152)

➤ Pronto (p150)

➤ Salmon n' Bannock (p149)

➤ La Taqueria Pinche Taco Shop (p149)

➤ Beaucoup Bakery & Cafe (p152)

## Best Places to Drink

➤ Storm Crow Alehouse (p155)

➤ Kino (p156)

➤ Marquis (p155)

➤ Biercraft Bistro (p155)

➤ Bump n Grind (p155)

## Best Places to Shop

➤ Walrus (p157)

➤ Bacci's (p158)

➤ Meinhardt Fine Foods (p158)

➤ Shop Cocoon (p158)

➤ Oliver + Lilly's (p158)

# Explore Fairview & South Granville

Start in Queen Elizabeth Park – the entrance is at 33rd Ave and Cambie St – and stroll north down Cambie St into the shop-and-restaurant-lined Cambie Village area. This is not a touristy district, so you'll get a good glimpse of local life. Check out the heritage houses on the side streets but catch bus 15 if you're in a hurry. Either way, you'll soon reach the super-busy intersection of Cambie and Broadway.

It's a 30-minute walk west along very busy Broadway to South Granville from here, the heart of Fairview. Alternatively, backtrack one block and walk in the same direction on more tranquil, tree-lined W 10th Ave. Or take the 99B-LIne express bus service that whisks passengers from here to South Granville in less than 10 minutes. The slower bus 9 covers the same route and is often less crowded.

At the intersection of Broadway and Granville St, turn right for an intriguing array of private galleries and an easy 10-minute stroll to Granville Island. Or turn left and explore South Granville's plethora of upmarket boutiques and enticing dining options. It's full of browseable fashion boutiques and homewares stores and has the feel of a shop-lined English high street.

From here, you can hop on bus 10 and you'll be back downtown in just a few minutes, via the Granville Bridge (scenic views included).

# Local Life

➤**Shopping** South Granville is busy with well-to-do locals buzzing around its designer boutiques, shopping bags in hand.

➤**Night Out** Cambie Village is popular for dinner at a local restaurant followed by an artsy flick at the one-screen Cineplex Park Theatre (p156).

➤**Parklife** Summertime cooling-down means Queen Elizabeth Park (p147), where you can picnic on the grass and feel as if you're far from the city.

# Getting There & Away

➤**Train** Cambie Village's shopping and dining area is sandwiched between the Canada Line SkyTrain stations at Broadway-City Hall and King Edward.

➤**Bus** Service 15 runs along Cambie St; bus 10 runs along South Granville. The two streets are linked along Broadway by the 99B-Line express service and the slower bus 9.

➤**Car** There is metered parking on Cambie and South Granville, with some limited street parking available throughout both areas.

# ⊙ SIGHTS

Parks and botanical attractions are the main visitor sights in this area and they're easily accessible via transit along Cambie St and Oak St.

★ BLOEDEL CONSERVATORY   GARDENS
Map p280 (☎604-257-8584; www.vanduse
ngarden.org; Queen Elizabeth Park, 4600 Cambie St; adult/child $6.75/3.25; ⊙9am-8pm Mon-
Fri, 10am-8pm Sat & Sun May-Aug, 10am-5pm
daily Sep-Apr; P🚻; 🚌15) Cresting the hill
in Queen Elizabeth Park, this balmy,
triodetic-domed conservatory is an ideal
rainy-day warm-up spot as well as Vancouver's best-value attraction. For little
more than the price of a latte, you'll find
tropical trees and plants bristling with
hundreds of free-flying, bright-plumaged
birds. Look for the resident parrots but
also keep your eyes peeled for rainbow-
hued Gouldian finches, shimmering Af-
rican superb starlings and maybe even a
sparkling Lady Amherst pheasant, snaking through the undergrowth. The attend-
ants might even let you feed the smaller
birds from a bowl.

Pick up a free bird-watcher's checklist
from the front desk and record how many
you see.

VANDUSEN
BOTANICAL GARDEN   GARDENS
Map p280 (☎604-257-8335; www.vanduse
ngarden.org; 5251 Oak St; adult/child Apr-Sep
$12.25/5.75; ⊙9am-8:30pm Jun-Aug, reduced
hours off-season; P🚻; 🚌17) The city's favorite green-thumbed tranquility break,
this 22-hectare, 255,000-plant idyll is a web
of paths weaving through many small, spe-
cialized gardens: the Rhododendron Walk
blazes with color in spring, while the Korean Pavilion is a focal point for a fascinating
Asian collection. Save time to get lost in the
maze and look out for the herons and turtles that call the ponds here home. Check
the online calendar for tours and events.

Pick up a free self-guided tour brochure
from the front desk; there's a different theme
each month. VanDusen is also one of Vancouver's top Christmastime destinations,
complete with thousands of twinkling fairy
lights illuminating the dormant plant life.

QUEEN ELIZABETH PARK   PARK
Map p280 (www.vancouverparks.ca; entrance
cnr W 33rd Ave & Cambie St; P; 🚌15) The city's
highest point – it's 167m above sea level
and has panoramic views of the mountain-
framed downtown skyscrapers – this
52-hectare park claims to house specimens
of every tree native to Canada. Sports fields,
manicured lawns and two formal gardens
keep the locals happy, and you'll likely also
see wide-eyed couples posing for their wed-
ding photos.

Check out the synchronized fountains
at the park's summit – home to the Bloedel Conservatory – where you'll also find a
hulking Henry Moore bronze called *Knife
Edge – Two Piece*. If you want to be taken
out to the ball game, the park's beloved Nat
Bailey Stadium is also a popular summer
hangout for baseball fans.

FAIRVIEW & SOUTH GRANVILLE SIGHTS

---

## BEHIND THE DECO FACADE

The Great Depression caused major belt-tightening among the regular folks of
1930s Vancouver. But despite the economic malaise, mayor Gerry McGeer spared
no expense when it came time to build a new **City Hall** (p148) in 1936 (50 years
after Vancouver was incorporated as a city). Defending the grand art-deco edifice
he planned as a make-work project for the idled construction industry, the $1 million
project (a very large sum for the time) was completed in just 12 months.

But while the jobs were appreciated by some locals, McGeer showed no additional
sympathy for the the city's working class. Believing that radicalism was taking hold
among out-of-work Vancouverites, he ordered that police officers should crack down
on protests whenever they emerged. When hundreds gathered to call for jobs in East
Vancouver's Victory Sq, McGeer turned up personally to read them the riot act. A few
weeks later, police and an estimated 1000 protesters fought a three-hour street battle with rocks, clubs and tear gas. Rumors at the time said the police were preparing
to use machine guns against the crowd when it began to disperse. The most famous
incident in Vancouver labor history, it was later named the **Battle of Ballantyne
Pier**.

## PARKLIFE

Vancouver's urban green spaces are home to a surprising array of critters. Many of them roam the city's streets after dark foraging for extra food. During your visit, you'll find **black squirrels** everywhere, but don't be surprised to also spot **raccoons**. Common in several parks, they are often bold enough to hang out on porches and root through garbage bins. **Skunks** are almost as common, but the only time you'll likely see them is after an unfortunate roadkill incident (a fairly common occurrence around area parks). But while squirrels, raccoons and skunks are regarded as urban nuisances, some animals in the city are much larger.

Every spring, several Vancouver neighborhoods post notices of **coyote** spottings (there are an estimated 3000 living in and around the city). This is the time of year when the wolf-like wild dogs build dens and raise pups, often in remote corners of city parks – and they become more protective of their territory in the process. This can lead to problems with domesticated pets. Vancouverites are warned to keep pets inside when coyotes are spotted in their neighborhoods, and report any sightings to authorities. Most locals will tell you they've only seen a coyote once or twice in their lives – the animals are mostly very adept at avoiding humans.

Animal encounters are an even bigger problem for areas that back directly on to wilderness regions. The North Shore is shadowed by a forest and mountain swath that's long been a traditional home for **bears** – mostly black bears. Residents in North Vancouver and West Vancouver know how to secure their garbage so as not to encourage bears to become habitualized to human food. But every year – often in spring when the hungry furballs are waking from hibernation – a few are trapped and relocated from the area.

At the other end of the scale, Vancouver is a great city for bird-spotters. In Queen Elizabeth Park, keep your eyes peeled for **bald eagles** whirling overhead. On Granville Island, glance up under Granville Bridge and you'll spot **cormorants** treating the girders like cliffside roosts. And if you're near a pond anywhere around the city, you might see **coots**, **wood ducks** and statue-still **blue herons** alongside the ubiquitous **Canada geese**. Head to Stanley Park's Lost Lagoon and you'll likely see them all in fairly short order.

It's not all about waterbirds, though. On streets around the city, look out for **Northern flicker woodpeckers** (known for their red cheeks and black-spotted plumage) as well as **finches**, **chickadees**, **American robins** and **Steller's jays**, a blue feathered friend that's also BC's provincial bird. If you're really fast, you'll even spot what many regard as an unlikely bird here: the delightful little **Anna's hummingbird** is a year-round resident in Vancouver. And, in spring and summer, it's joined by the migrating **rufous hummingbird**. They're the reason you'll spot sugar-water feeders on balconies across the city.

For more information on wildlife (and guided nature walks) in the city, click on www.stanleyparkecology.ca.

---

**CITY HALL**  HISTORIC BUILDING
Map p280 (www.vancouver.ca; 453 W 12th Ave, Fairview; ◉8:30am-5pm Mon-Fri; ⑤Broadway-City Hall) FREE Architecture fans should save time for a stroll through the marble-lined lobby of one of Vancouver's best art-deco buildings. Completed in 1936, its highlights include a mirrored ceiling, streamlined signs, cylindrical lanterns and embossed elevator doors. Duck inside one of the elevators to peruse the intricate inlaid-wood design, then check out the handsome heritage homes on surrounding Yukon St and W 12th Ave.

Exit the building on the north side and you'll find a statue of Captain Vancouver, not a superhero but the historic seafarer the city is named after. This is the spot to take your photo, with City Hall in the background. Glance at the far less elegant 1960s addition to the complex (slated for demolition in the coming years), then check out the rest of the neighborhood: many of the grand wooden heritage homes nearby were built for early mayors and merchants. If you're on a deco roll, also hit downtown's lovely Marine Building (p59).

#  EATING

Fairview and Cambie Village mostly offer welcoming casual eateries where the neighbors drop by to chill out, while higher-end South Granville has a couple of top spots as well as some good midrange options. Linking the two is Broadway, which is lined on both sides with good-value restaurants of every variety, from steaming *pho* (Vietnamese noodle soup) spots to fresh-serve sushi joints.

## ✗ Fairview

### ★LA TAQUERIA PINCHE TACO SHOP
MEXICAN $

Map p280 (✆604-558-2549; www.lataque ria.ca; 2549 Cambie St, Fairview; 4 tacos $8.50-10.50;⊘11am-8:30pmMon-Sat,noon-6pm Sun; ✐; Ⓢ Broadway-City Hall) This popular taco spot expanded from its tiny Hastings St location (which is still there) with this larger storefront. It's just as crowded but, luckily, many of the visitors are going the take-out route. Nab a brightly painted table, then order at the counter from a dozen or so meat or veggie soft tacos (take your pick or ask for a selection).

Service is warm and friendly here and the prices and quality ingredients are enough to keep you coming back: the tacos are $2.50 each or four for $10.50 (or just $8.50 if you take the vegetarian route). The braised beef-cheeks variety is always popular and there are bottles of housemade salsa to keep things lively. Before you order, check the specials board: there's usually something intriguing worth trying.

### MARULILU CAFE
BREAKFAST $

Map p280 (✆604-568-4211; 451 W Broadway, Fairview; mains $8-10; ⊘8:30am-6pm; Ⓢ Broadway City-Hall) A tiny, almost hole-in-the wall homestyle cafe specializing in good-value all-day breakfasts and brunches; snag your seat and then order at the counter. The extensive menu here ranges from traditional eggs and bacon to a wide array of Japanese options, such as oyaka rice bowls and katsu curry. Service is exceptionally friendly and you'll meet lots of loyal regulars.

This is a cozy, laid-back spot to hangout, just across the street from the Canada Line station.

### SOLLY'S BAGELRY
BAKERY $

Map p280 (✆604-675-9770; www.sollysba gelry.com; 368 W 7th Ave, Fairview; ⊘7am-7pm Mon-Fri, 8am-7pm Sat & Sun; Ⓢ Broadway-City Hall) The main branch of a three-store family-run Jewish bakery minichain, Solly's is the city's best bagel spot. Drop by for a breakfast schmear of cream cheese and smoked salmon on a toasted, fresh-made sesame and you'll likely leave an hour later with an armful of unanticipated treats for later in the day: potato knishs, chocolate babkas and deep-fried potato latkas recommended.

With a deli cabinet of cream-cheese tubs and jarred pickles, this is a great spot to create a picnic (there's a small park two blocks east). But if it's raining, stick around for lunch: chicken matzo-ball soup and a pastrami-on-rye sandwich is the way to go. And to be sure you don't look like a tourist, copy the locals by ordering from the right-hand end of the counter then paying at the left-hand end before picking up your order.

### K CAFE
CAFE $

Map p280 (✆778-737-9295; 2533 Heather St, Fairview; mains $6-9; ⊘7:30am-4pm Mon-Fri, 9am-2:30pm Sat; ☐9) Super-friendly family-run cafe loved by those working at nearby Vancouver General Hospital. You can grab a coffee on the run here or – better still – linger over lunch. The menu combines Korean comfort dishes such as *bibimbap* rice bowls with homemade soups and toasted chicken sandwiches made from off-the-bone cuts. Sitting on an off-Broadway side street, this is a great value option. Also a good spot for a traditional eggs-and-bacon breakfast if you're in the area.

### SALMON N' BANNOCK
WEST COAST $$

Map p280 (✆604-568-8971; www.salmonand bannock.net; 1128 W Broadway, Fairview; mains $14-24; ⊘11:30am-3pm & 5-9pm Mon-Thu, to 10pm Fri, 5-10pm Sat; ☐9) Vancouver's only First Nations restaurant is a delightful art-lined little bistro on an unassuming strip of Broadway shops. It's worth the bus trip, though, for fresh-made aboriginal-influenced dishes made with local ingredients. If lunching, try the signature (and juicy) salmon 'n' bannock burger, made with a traditional flatbread introduced by Scottish settlers that's now a staple of First Nations BC dining.

If you're planning dinner, go for the velvet-soft bison back ribs. Whatever you have, wash it down with a bottle of Nk'mip from BC's only First Nations winery.

### SHIZEN YA
JAPANESE $$

Map p280 (☎604-569-3721; www.shizenya. ca; 1102 W Broadway, Fairview; mains $8-16; ⊙11:30am-10pm; P 🚲; 🚇9) A cut above the area's humdrum cheap-and-cheerful sushi shops: the prices here are just as good but the quality and service make a huge difference. Only organic brown rice is used and there's a healthy approach which includes crispy fresh salads and quinoa specials. And while vegetarians are well looked after, the sushi is top-notch and the beef teriyaki is a local favorite.

It can get crowded on weekend evenings, so consider dropping in for lunch when the well-priced combo curry-rice or udon noodle deals (each usually under $10) are recommended.

### TOJO'S
JAPANESE $$$

Map p280 (☎604-872-8050; www.tojos.com; 1133 W Broadway, Fairview; mains $28-45; ⊙5-10pm Mon-Sat; 🚇9) Hidekazu Tojo's legendary skill with the sushi knife launched Vancouver's Japanese dining scene and his sleek restaurant is still a pilgrimage spot. Among his exquisite dishes are favorites such as lightly steamed monkfish, sautéed halibut cheeks and fried red tuna wrapped in seaweed and served with plum sauce. A sophisticated night out; book ahead for a seat at the *omakaze* sushi bar.

If Tojo is there on your visit, consider asking him about his Tojo tuna roll, created to introduce 1970s North American audiences to the pleasures of eating raw fish. Legend says that his creation later became known as the California roll. And the rest, of course, is sushi history.

## ✕ Cambie Village

### RAIN OR SHINE
ICE CREAM $

Map p280 (☎604-876-9986; www.rainorshi neicecream.com; 3382 Cambie St, Cambie Village; ⊙noon-10pm; 🚲; 🚇15) Under the gaze of a cone-crowned purple cow on the wall, you may have to queue at this finger-licking ice cream emporium. But that will give you time to mull the flavors, which range from – on our visit – crushed mint

to blueberry balsamic. All are made onsite and served in cups or cones, although perhaps staff will shovel it straight into your mouth if you ask nicely.

Alongside the flavor mainstays, there are always some seasonal additions to the roster, while glutinous milkshakes (Earl Grey lavender recommended) are also available if you still need a few thousand more calories to round-out your day. If you're in Kitsilano, find the original Rain or Shine on W 4th Ave.

### DUTCH WOODEN
### SHOE CAFE
BREAKFAST $$

Map p280 (☎604-874-0922; 3292 Cambie St, Cambie Village; mains $8-15; ⊙8am-2:30pm Mon-Fri, 8am-4pm Sat & Sun; 🚇15) Get your clogs on for the neighborhood's kitchest (and certainly Vancouver's most Dutch) homestyle eatery. Nothing has changed at this family-run joint in years: you'll still find the aforementioned signature footwear on the walls alongside faded photos of Netherlands' farm scenes. It feels like your grandma's house but the food – especially the *pannekoek* (Dutch pancake) – is comfort grub defined.

On a budget? Drop by on Tuesdays for the restaurant's regular buy-one-get-one-half-price pancake deal.

### ★PRONTO
ITALIAN $$

Map p280 (☎604-722-9331; www.prontocaffe.ca; 3473 Cambie St, Cambie Village; mains $14-22; ⊙11:30am-9pm Sun, Tue & Wed, 11:30am-10pm Thu-Sat; 🚇15) A delightful neighborhood eatery, this charming Cambie Village trattoria combines woodsy candlelit booths, perfectly prepared housemade pasta and the kind of welcoming service few restaurants manage to provide. Drop by for a lunchtime porchetta sandwich, or head here for dinner when the intimate, wood-floored space feels deliciously relaxed. Check the blackboard specials or head straight for the gnocchi with pesto and pancetta.

In summer, aim for a seat in the hidden back garden. And make sure you check out the eye-popping street-art bathrooms. Reservations are not accepted so dine off-peak or during the week. It also has a newer bar next door that has replicated the look of the original restaurant; you can dine here, too.

# Neighborhood Walk
## South Granville Stroll

**START** IAN TAN GALLERY
**END** BUMP N GRIND
**LENGTH** 1KM; ONE HOUR

Hop on bus 10 from downtown. After trundling over Granville Bridge, pull the bell and alight at the intersection with 7th Ave. On the right side of Granville St, nip into the **①Ian Tan Gallery** (p159) for a chin-rubbing look at some modern Canadian art. Don't buy anything too large or you'll have to carry it on the uphill southbound stretch accurately known as South Granville Rise. When you reach Broadway, cross over and continue south on Granville.

Also on the right side of the street, nose into **②Restoration Hardware** (p159), where you can pick up some design tips for your apartment back home. Continue south for a couple more blocks until you reach the intersection with W 11th Ave. On the corner you'll find Vancouver's favorite homegrown chocolate purveyor **③Purdy's Chocolates** (p158). Consider stopping for a well-deserved ice cream bar; or save your appetite for lunch and pick up some treats for later.

Cross over and head east on W 11th Ave for half a block. On your right you'll see **④Rangoli** (p152), the perfect pit stop for a tasty Indian curry pick-me-up. Once you've had your fill, rejoin Granville St and continue south. At the end of the block, you'll come to **⑤Bacci's** (p158); nip inside to peruse the funky homewares and trendy fashions. A couple more blocks delivers you to **⑥Meinhardt Fine Foods** (p158) where you can spend a giddy half-hour lusting after the posh groceries and tempting deli treats.

Finally, if all that strolling has your blisters throbbing, nip next door to **⑦Bump n Grind** (p155) for a restorative java and a muffin or two. From here, you can mull your options for dinner; there are several excellent spots to choose from nearby – which means you won't have to walk much further. And if you're aiming to head back downtown afterwards, you can hop the northbound bus 10 anywhere along Granville; you'll be back in the city center in minutes.

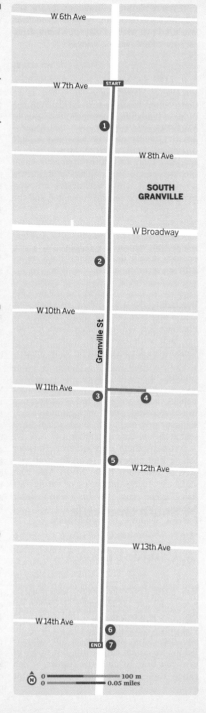

LANDMARK

### HOT POT HOUSE
CHINESE $$

Map p280 (✆604-872-2868; www.landmarkhot
pot.com; 4023 Cambie St, Cambie Village; mains
$8-22; ⏱5pm-2am; ⓈKing Edward) Pull up a
black-laquered chair and dive into the menu
at this Hong Kong–style hot-pot spot. It's a
surprisingly large, long-established place
that is often bustling with locals from the
Chinese-Canadian community – usually
a good sign of authenticity – and they're
mostly here for plates of meat and veggies
that you cook yourself at your table via a pot
of boiling broth.

A good place to come for a feast, this
is also an accessible introduction to the
city's traditional Chinese dining scene.

### ★VIJ'S
INDIAN $$$

Map p280 (✆604-736-6664; www.vijsrestau
rant.ca; 3106 Cambie St, Cambie Village; mains
$19-27; ⏱5:30-10pm; ☑; Ⓠ15) A sparkling
(and far larger) new location for Canada's favorite East Indian chef delivers a
warmly sumptuous lounge coupled with
a cavernous dining area and cool rooftop
patio. The menu, a high-water mark of
contemporary Indian cuisine, fuses BC
ingredients, global flourishes and classic
ethnic flavors to produce many inventive
dishes. Results range from signature 'lamb
popsicles' to savor-worthy meals such as
sablefish in yoghurt-tomato broth.

There are lots of delightful options for
vegetarians (jackfruit, cumin and car-
damom curry appetizer recommended).
Reservations are not accepted, which
sometimes means a long wait; soak it up
with a few spice-infused cocktails in the
lounge.

## ✖ South Granville

### ★BEAUCOUP BAKERY & CAFE
CAFE $

Map p280 (✆604-732-4222; www.beaucoupbak
ery.com; 2150 Fir St, South Granville; cakes &
sandwiches under $10; ⏱7am-5pm Mon-Fri,
8am-5pm Sat & Sun; Ⓠ4) Vancouverites used
to content themselves with humdrum
croissants and lame French pastries that
would be laughed off the counter in Paris
– until this amazing bakery opened. Now,
it's the pilgrimage spot of choice for eye-
rollingly amazing treats from cinnamon
scrolls to completely irresistible peanut-
butter-sandwich cookies. As for the crois-

sants, they're the best in the city: shatter-
ingly crisp with chewy-soft interiors.

This is a great place to make up a little
brown box of treats to go. On sunny days,
if the three little red tables outside are all
claimed, head across the street where a
new pocket-sized park also has a few tables. They also make sandwiches here: try
the vegetarian variety, complete with avo-
cado and Asian pear in a croissant.

### PAUL'S OMELETTERY
BREAKFAST $

Map p280 (✆604-737-2857; www.paulsome
lettery.com; 2211 Granville St, South Granville;
mains $8-14; ⏱7am-3pm; ☑🐾; Ⓠ10) You'll
be jostling for space with chatty moms at
this unassuming breakfast and lunch joint
near the south side of Granville Bridge. But
it's worth it: this cozy, super-friendly place
is superior to most bacon-and-eggs spots.
The menu is grounded on signature ome-
lets but it also does great eggs Benedict and
there are housemade burgers and sandwiches at lunch.

It's a perfect place to start the day before
a wander down to nearby Granville Island.
But be sure to arrive early on weekends
when there's often a line-up of bleary-eyed
locals looking for a hearty end-of-the-week
breakfast feast.

### RANGOLI
INDIAN $$

Map p280 (✆604-736-5711; www.vijsrangoli.ca;
1488 W 11th Ave, South Granville; mains $11-22;
⏱11am-10pm; ☑; Ⓠ10) This small, bistrolike
satellite of Cambie St's landmark Vij's res-
taurant is always popular. Service is brisk
and friendly and if you score a table on the
patio you'll soon be enjoying the hum of
conversation around you as you tuck into
top-notch dishes such as lamb in cumin
and cream curry. Add some naughty mogo
fries to share.

There's always a cool microbrew bottle or
two to keep your grub company (IPAs are a
great curry accompaniment) and the coco-
nut pudding dessert is enough to make any-
one smile. If you like what you've had (and
you're staying in a place with a kitchen),
you can also pick up ready-to-eat meals to
go from the cabinets near the front. And if
you're hungry for more, look out for the Vij's
Railway Express food truck around town.

### HEIRLOOM VEGETARIAN
VEGETARIAN $$

Map p280 (✆604-733-2231; www.heirloom
restaurant.ca; 1509 W 12th Ave, South Granville;
mains $14-20; ⏱9am-10pm; ☑; Ⓠ10) With a

white-walled cafeteria–meets–rustic arti-san look (hence the farm implements on the wall), this is one of Vancouver's tastiest vegetarian options, serving mostly BC and organic seasonal ingredients fused with international influences. Locals love the shiny-bunned Royale burger with its ad-dictive yam fries accompaniment. There's also a page of vegan options on the menu; we recommend the nicely spiced pineapple coconut curry.

Alongside a good wine, beer and cock-tail list, there's a diverse array of tempting nonalcoholic options; this is the place to have that restorative aloe-blossom beverage you've been craving.

### STABLE HOUSE BISTRO $$
Map p280 (☑604-736-1520; www.thestable house.ca; 1520 W 13th Ave, South Granville; mains $17-25; ☺11am-3pm Tue-Fri, dinner from 5pm daily; 🖳10) This is a modern reinvention of a European bistro that's quickly become a South Granville fixture since openng a cou-ple of years back. Try for the the weirdly-angular window table or slide onto a side perch for shareable plates of cheese and charcuterie or gourmet comfort dishes such as gnocchi or tuna loins. The lovely gruyere mushroom tart is our favorite; don't miss it.

The five-course chef's selection is a great route if you fancy pushing the boat out; but there's also a good-value lunch menu here if you want to sample the place without blowing your budget (go for the beef brisket Reuben).

### SUIKA JAPANESE $$
Map p280 (☑604-730-1678; www.suika-snack bar.com; 1626 W Broadway, Fairview; mains $8-22; ☺11:30am-2pm & 5:30-11:30pm Sun-Thu, 11:30am-2pm & 5:30-12:30am Fri & Sat; 🖳9) A contemporary *izakaya* (Japanese neigh-borhood pub) with a playful edge, Suika is all about sliding alongside a moodlit table under the sake-bottle chandelier and shar-ing dishes of rice balls, deep-fried *tori-yako* chicken (highly recommended) and the naughty-but-delicious Chinese poutine – fries topped with mozzarella and spicy ground-pork gravy. Drinks-wise, try a smashing oolong tea cocktail.

If you're a fan of Japanese pop culture, make sure your seat faces a TV screen so you can watch classic episodes of *Ultraman* to your heart's content – don't worry, your date will understand (or maybe not).

### OUISI BISTRO CAJUN $$
Map p280 (☑604-732-7550; www.ouisibis tro.com; 3014 Granville St, South Granville; mains $12-24; ☺11am-1pm Mon-Fri, 9am-2am Sat & Sun; 🖳10) Vancouver's most authentic Creole and Cajun dining in a casual, bar-style setting, Ouisi (as in 'Louisiana') serves up spice-tastic dishes such as voodoo ribs and seafood gum-bo; or consider a heaping jambalaya lunch. The weekend brunch offers hot fusion riffs on trad breakfast dishes. The large menu of accompanying malts and bourbons plus regular live jazz spice things up even more.

Drop back on Monday for the $11.50 burger-and-beer deal.

### WEST WEST COAST $$$
Map p280 (☑604-738-8938; www.westres taurant.com; 2881 Granville St, South Granville; mains $29-40; ☺11:30am-2:30pm daily, 5:30-10:30pm Sun-Thu, to 11pm Fri & Sat; 🖳10) This sleek but never snobbish fine-dining fa-vorite is committed to superb West Coast meals with ultra-attentive service and a great wine selection. Ideal for a classy night out, its seasonally changeable high-lights often include Cape Scott halibut and Fraser Valley pork, while the pastry chef delivers some of Vancouver's best desserts. Arrive early for a seat at the bar and sup some excellent cocktails.

If you're looking for a romantic dinner destination – and maybe a place to pop the question – West is ideal: you likely won't be the first to propose here.

### SHAUGHNESSY SWANK

If you're coming in from the airport along Granville St, watch for some extremely large heritage mansions hidden behind the towering hedges. When you're later ambling southbound up South Granville checking out the shops, continue past W 16th Ave and turn left up McRae Ave. Within a couple of minutes you'll be in the leafy heart of **Shaughnessy Heights**. Planned as a fat cats' neighborhood for the wealthi-est Vancouverites in the early 1900s, it's still lined with magnificent old piles that make it a wanderable museum of architectural styles. Look out for every-thing from revivalist Tudor and Georgian to colonial Dutch and Spanish. Then buy a lotto ticket so you can move right in.

**LOCAL KNOWLEDGE**

### TAKE ME OUT TO THE BALLGAME

If you can't get tickets to a **Vancouver Canucks** game, there's another local option to scratch your itch for spectator sports. It's a tradition for many Vancouverites to catch a summertime baseball game with the minor league **Vancouver Canadians** (p156), a farm-team affiliate of the Toronto Blue Jays. Tickets cost from just $11 to catch a game at the lovely, nostalgic **Nat Bailey Stadium** – an idyllic 1950s-built wooden stadium venue (capacity around 5000). Naturally, nosh is a big draw – especially if the action flags a little – and, for many, that means sitting in the stands munching on an impressive foot-long corn dog and gulping a few fizzy-but-cold brews. This being Vancouver, sushi is also available. Adding to the fun are the nonbaseball shenanigans, ranging from kiss cams trained on the crowd to mascot races. And, several times during the season, the nighttime action ends with a fun **fireworks** display. Catching a game here is arguably the most fun you can have at a spectator sport in Vancouver – and it's also one of the most budget-friendly options (depending on how many corn dogs you put away).

 # DRINKING & NIGHTLIFE

**Not renowned for its big-night-out credentials, this neighborhood has a couple of spots that are perfect for parking your thirst. Java-wise, there are also some excellent neighborhood coffeehouses dotted on the main drags of Cambie and South Granville, plus some hidden spots just off the beaten path.**

## Fairview

#### ELYSIAN COFFEE                    COFFEE

Map p280 (www.elysiancoffee.com; 590 W Broadway, Fairview; ⏱7am-7pm; 🛜; 🚍9) Just to show not all the hipsters hang out on Main St, this chatty neighborhood joint lures every skinny-jeaned local in its vicinity. They come for the excellent coffee (it's not just about looking cool here) plus a small array of baked treats and some very tempting home coffee-making paraphernalia. Take a seat at the front window and watch Broadway bustle past.

It's a handy pit stop if you're walking between South Granville and Cambie: you won't be the only one flicking through a copy of the *Georgia Straight* and planning your weekend here. In fact, there's a box just outside where you can pick up your free copy.

#### CAFFE CITTADELLA                   COFFEE

Map p280 (☎604-568-5909; www.caffecittadella.com; 2310 Ash St, Fairview; ⏱7am-7pm Mon-Fri, 8am-7pm Sat, 8am-6pm Sun; 🛜; 🚇Broadway-City Hall) Don't tell anyone you found this place, since the regulars will be very upset. A cute two-floored cafe tucked into a restored clappboard heritage home, it's ideal for a morning of java-supported newspaper-reading. There are some tables scattered around the building outside but on sunny days the doors are thrown open and it feels alfreso inside anyway.

Alongside the excellent array of housemade cakes and inventive treats (chocolate-lavender-cashew cluster bar recommended), it also serves locally roasted Parallel 49 coffee. And if you're still here at lunchtime, extend your stay by ordering from the panini sandwich menu. It can get packed here so, to ensure access to a table, it's best to avoid peak times.

#### PEKOE TEA LOUNGE                  TEAHOUSE

Map p280 (☎778-371-8343; www.pekoetealounge.com; 895 W Broadway, Fairview; ⏱7:30am-6pm Mon-Fri, 11am-6pm Sat & Sun; 🚍9) A restorative respite from busy Broadway, this locals' favorite is ideal for visiting tea nuts. Choose from dozens of varieties from around the world (nutcracker oolong recommended) then sink into a coveted sofa seat at the back of the store. Better still: go for the good-value pie-and-tea deal, which includes a bulging housemade slice (strawberry and rhubarb is best). Most pies are vegan and gluten-free. And if you enjoy your brew, consider a take-out tin for the road.

#### ROGUE KITCHEN & WET BAR               BAR

Map p280 (☎604-568-9400; www.roguewetbar.com; 602 W Broadway, Fairview; ⏱11:30am-11pm Sun & Mon, to midnight Tue-Thu, to 1am Fri

& Sat; 🖥9) Divided between a casual West Coast restaurant on one side and a funky lounge bar on the other, the main reason to visit this Broadway resto-bar is the excellent craft beer selection. Expect to find drafts from celebrated BC brewers including Hoyne, 33 Acres and Four Winds as well as US tipples by Oregon-based Deschutes, among many others.

Ask your server for the day's specials and consider accompanying your quaff with a Tempesta chili prawn pizza. Happy hour is 3pm to 6pm daily and there are usually beer deals of the $2-off-a-pitcher variety.

## 🍷 Cambie Village

### BIERCRAFT BISTRO                              BISTRO
Map p280 (🖉604-874-6900; www.bier craft.com; 3305 Cambie St, Cambie Village; ⊙11:30am-midnight Mon-Thu, 11:30am-1am Fri, 10am-1am Sat, 10am-midnight Sun; 🖥15) With a chatty, wood-lined interior plus two popular street-side patios, this beer-forward resto-bar is a great spot for ale aficionados. Dive into the astonishing array of Belgium tipples and compare them to some choice microbrews from BC and the US. Save time for food; the slightly pricey gastropub menu here ranges from steak *frites* to bowls of locally sourced mussels in several brothy iterations.

You'll see many of the same locals back here on the weekend enjoying brunch, which is served until 3:30pm. Poached eggs on cornbread is a popular choice.

## 🍷 South Granville

### ★STORM CROW ALEHOUSE                         PUB
Map p280 (🖉604-428-9670; www.stormcrow alehouse.com; 1619 W Broadway, South Granville; ⊙11am-1am Mon-Thu, 11am-2am Fri, 9am-2am Sat, 9am-1am Sun; 🖥9) The larger sibling of Commercial Drive's excellent nerd bar, this pub welcomes everyone from the Borg to beardy *Lord of the Rings* dwarfs. They come to peruse the memorabilia-studded walls (think Millennium Falcon models and a Tardis washroom door), play the board games and dive into apposite refreshments including Romulan Ale and Pangalactic Gargleblasters. Hungry? Miss the chunky chickpea fries at your peril.

It's not all about geek-based affectation here. This is a seriously good pub with an excellent array of great BC craft beers as well as a good-value menu of hearty pub fare. And if the drinkers at the next table happen to be speaking Klingon, it's probably best not to make eye contact.

### MARQUIS                                       BAR
Map p280 (🖉604-568-0670; www.themarquis. ca; 2666 Granville St, South Granville; ⊙4pm-2am Mon-Sat, to midnight Sun; 🖥10) Don't blink or you'll miss the entrance to this cozy hidden nook that's popular with locals meeting to start their night out or dropping by for a nightcap before bed. Find a perch at the high tables facing the bar and tuck into a menu of classic martinis and flirty cocktails (plus some nice bottled beer imports).

If you're in an adventurous mood, try a beer cocktail. There's also a small pub-grub food menu here: the spicy Cajun yam fries are recommended if you're feeling peckish.

### BUMP N GRIND                                  COFFEE
Map p280 (🖉604-558-4743; www.bumpngrind cafe.com; 3010 Granville St, South Granville; ⊙7am-7pm Mon-Fri, 8am-7pm Sat & Sun; 🖘; 🖥10) The South Granville branch of this two-outlet local coffeehouse chain has a great long table at the back where you can settle down with a java and peruse the tiny wall-mounted library of handmade zines. Alternatively, press your face against the glass cabinet of bakery treats at the front and try to levitate a curried butternut-squash muffin into your mouth.

This is a popular spot for local hipsters so there can be line-ups at peak times.

### DOSE ESPRESSO BAR                             COFFEE
Map p280 (🖉604-734-7711; 1517 W Broad way, South Granville; ⊙7am-4:30pm Mon-Fri, 9am-1pm Sat; 🖘; 🖥9) With beans roasted on Granville Island, there's a serious commitment to quality java at this tiny coffee nook and it's a great place to savor a proper espresso or excellent flat white while scribbling an impromptu ode to coffee in your journal. Take inspiration from the funky artwork on the walls, or just have another caffeine hit to get your poetic juices flowing.

Seating is tight here (it's tiny) so consider a coffee to go, then stroll down the hill to Granville Island.

# ENTERTAINMENT

**This area offers some laid-back entertainment options away from the crowds of downtown. You're much more likely to meet the locals at these events and there are plenty of nearby dining options if you want to add a meal to your big night out.**

### STANLEY THEATRE
THEATER

Map p280 (☑604-687-1644; www.artsclub.com; 2750 Granville St, South Granville; tickets from $29; ☺Sep-Jun; 🚇10) Popular musicals dominate early summer (usually the last show of the season) at this heritage theater, but the rest of the year sees new works and adaptations of contemporary hits from around the world. Officially called the Stanley Industrial Alliance Stage (a moniker that not a single Vancouverite uses), the Stanley is part of the Arts Club Theatre Company, Vancouver's biggest.

The 1200-seat theater was opened as a movie house and live venue in 1931, and it's interior is an unusual mix of the era's architectural fashions, from Moorish to art deco. And if you're reading this in 2107, it's time to open the time capsule of contemporary street photographs that was buried outside the theater.

### VANCOUVER CANADIANS
BASEBALL

Map p280 (☑604-872-5232; www.canadians baseball.com; Nat Bailey Stadium, 4601 Ontario St; tickets $11-25; ☺Jun-Sep; 🚇33, 🇸King Edward) Minor-league affiliates of the Toronto Blue Jays, the Canadians play at the charmingly old-school Nat Bailey Stadium. It's known as 'the prettiest ballpark in the world' thanks to its mountain backdrop. Afternoon games – called 'nooners' – are perfect for a nostalgic bask in the sun. Hot dogs and beer rule the menu, but there's also sushi and fruit – this is Vancouver, after all.

### KINO
CABARET

Map p280 (☑604-875-1998; www.thekino.ca; 3456 Cambie St, Cambie Village; ☺5pm-1am Mon-Fri, 3pm-1am Sat, to midnight Sun; 🚇15) Vancouver's only flamenco cafe is a great place to chill on a summer evening. If it's really warm, bask in the sun with a beer outside. But be sure to trip back in when the show starts: there's live dancing on the little wooden side stage from Wednesday to Saturday, with jazz, bluegrass and comedy rounding out the rest of the week.

Whether or not you think you like flamenco, it's hard not to be caught up in the energy of the performances and you'll likely be tapping your own toes on the hardwood floor within minutes. Order some tapas for your table to keep everyone in the mood. If you're here on Friday and Saturday, expect a crowd: this room can really buzz on weekends.

### PACIFIC THEATRE
THEATER

Map p280 (☑604-731-5518; www.pacifictheatre.org; 1140 W 12th Ave, South Granville; 🚇10) This unusual and well-hidden fringe-style venue stages a borad mixture of shows during its September-to-June season. There's usually a different one every month, ranging from contemporary retellings of Shakespeare to new or classic dramas. The intimate setting – the seats are configured 'alley style' on either side of the stage – can make for especially involving performances.

Tickets are around the $30 mark (discounted for weekdays and matinees). The Christmas show is usually the busiest of the year: it's typically an uplifting affair with plenty of Yuletide cheer.

### CINEPLEX PARK THEATRE
CINEMA

Map p280 (☑604-709-3456; www.cineplex.com; 3440 Cambie St, Cambie Village; 🚇15) Last holdout of a popular Vancouver independent movie theater chain, the Park succumbed to a takeover by the big boys a few years back. It's still a one-screen neighborhood charmer but has recently abandoned first-run movies in favor of a revolving roster of classic movies, one-off screenings and filmed productions from London's National Theatre and Moscow's Bolshoi Ballet, among others.

Be sure to check out the cool-ass deco-esque neon sign on top of the building.

### YUK YUK'S COMEDY CLUB
COMEDY

Map p280 (☑604-696-9857; www.yukyuks.com; 2837 Cambie St, Fairview; 🚇Broadway-City Hall) Although there are other comedy nights in bars and theaters around the city, Yuk Yuk's is one of Vancouver's few dedicated stand-up venues. Check ahead to see what's on: amateur nights are the best deal but there's also a roster of journeyman comedians rolling in from across Canada and the US. A small, windowless

**WHAT'S IN A NAME?**

In 1870, the Earl of Granville – otherwise known as George Leveson-Gower – generously lent his grand title to the search for a new name for the fledgling community that had grown up around Gassy Jack Leighton's bar on the banks of the Burrard Inlet (in what's now known as Maple Tree Sq). The locals had begun calling it 'Gastown' but the colonial administration wanted something of its own. Virtually no-one used the name 'Granville' to describe the settlement and it was abandoned after a year and replaced with 'Vancouver,' after the seafaring British captain who had set foot on the forested shoreline in 1792. 'Granville Street' was later adopted for the moniker of one of the city's busiest thoroughfares.

venue, it can feel overly crowded on busy nights.

Don't be put off by the unassuming exterior, which resembles the stage door at the back of a regular theater. Food-wise: stick to the drinks.

# 🔒 SHOPPING

**The main retailing activity here is along South Granville, which – especially between Broadway and 16th Ave – recalls a boutique-packed English high street in a well-to-do town. It makes for a pleasant hour or two of strolling as you nose around fashion stores and slick homeware emporiums. Art fans should also check out the handful of private galleries on Granville, mostly north of Broadway. Cambie Village is also worth a poke around, with some cool indie stores nestled between the restaurants and coffeehouses.**

## 🔒 Fairview

UMBRELLA SHOP     SPORTS & OUTDOORS

Map p280 (☑604-669-9444; www.theumbrellashop.com; 1106 W Broadway, Fairview; ☺10am-6pm Mon-Sat; ☑10) If you've lived for more than a few months in Vancouver (or if you've been unlucky with the weather on your visit), you'll know the value of a good umbrella. This family-owned local company does, too. This is its factory store and it makes and repairs its own brands here but also sells a wide selection of imported umbrellas.

Now's the time to stop buying a different umbrella every year, and leaving it in a crumbled heap of broken spokes after a few months. Expect to pay a few dollars more

and also ask the friendly staffers for some handy tips about longevity (it's all about how you put it away).

BOOK WAREHOUSE     BOOKS

Map p280 (☑604-872-5711; www.bookwarehouse.ca; 632 W Broadway, Fairview; ☺9am-8pm Mon & Tue, 9am-9pm Wed-Fri, 10am-8pm Sat, 10am-6pm Sun; ☑9) When Vancouver's beloved discount-book chain announced its closure a few years ago, locals were sad to see the end of an era. But at the last minute the final store was rescued and revived by another company (Black Bond Books). It kept the old name and the same approach: stacks of new books (bestsellers included) at discounted prices.

You'll find good selections of fiction and travel guides here. And this is also a great spot to pick up tomes covering local history (if your baggage limit allows, go for *The Chuck Davis History of Metropolitan Vancouver*) at the best price in the city.

## 🔒 Cambie Village

WALRUS     HOMEWARES

Map p280 (☑604-874-9770; www.walrushome.com; 3408 Cambie St, Cambie Village; ☺10am-7pm Mon-Fri, 10am-5pm Sat, noon-5pm Sun; ☑15) A small but perfectly curated store teeming with superbly designed homewares and accessories that are almost impossible to resist. Form meets function with everything on the shelves here, including excellent travel clocks, mod coffee pots with a knowing nod to the 1970s and must-have Mondaine watches for all you style mavens. Your credit card will soon be sweating.

Along with the usual designery suspects – that means you, Alessi – there are many lesser-known creators showcased here, including several contemporary Canadian designers. And be sure to check out the available art: there's usually something clever that would look great on your wall back home.

### SHOP COCOON
CLOTHING

Map p280 (☑778-232-8532; www.shopcocoon. com; 3345 Cambie St, Cambie Village; ☺11am-7pm Tue-Sat, 11am-6pm Sun; ☐15) A narrow, inviting little boutique showcasing a carefully chosen array of North American and international designer women's clothing, from natty summer dresses to flirty tops and cute jeans. A Cambie Village favorite, it also stocks extras such as locally made jewelry or handmade soap, artfully presented on antique bookcases. Ask the famously solicitous staff for tips on other stores to check out around the city.

### FABTABULOUS THRIFT 2.0
VINTAGE

Map p280 (☑604-428-1334; 2915 Cambie St, Cambie Village; ☺11am-7pm Mon-Sat, noon-6pm Sun; ☐15) A neighborhood thrift store that's not trying to be an antique emporium: everything is bargain-priced at this popular Cambie Village shop. Which means that, alongside the $3 T-shirts and $5 shoes, there are finds to be found – start with the clothing racks outside. Peruse the used DVDs and well-thumbed books piled high inside and watch out for sales with drastic reductions. It's always worth dropping back here a couple of times during your stay in the city: the selection (and the sales) changes constantly.

## 🔒 South Granville

### MEINHARDT FINE FOODS
FOOD

Map p280 (☑604-732-4405; www.meinhardt.com; 3002 Granville St, South Granville; ☺8am-9pm Mon-Sat, 9am-8pm Sun; ☐10) The culinary equivalent of a sex shop for food fans, this swanky deli and grocery emporium's narrow aisles are lined with international condiments, luxury canned goods and the kind of tempting treats that everyone should try at least once. Drop by for Christmas goodies or build your perfect picnic from the tempting bread, cheese and cold-cuts selections.

It's worth spending some time browsing the closely packed shelves for that unexpected item: where else are you going to find that essential jar of fig mustard, for ex-

ample? But it's not all sophisticated edibles: treat yourself to a smiley-face cookie and savor it as you stroll down the street.

### BACCI'S
HOMEWARES, CLOTHING

Map p280 (☑604-733-4933; www.baccis.ca; 2788 Granville St, South Granville; ☺9:45am-5:45pm Mon-Sat; ☐10) Combining designer women's clothing on one side with a room full of perfectly curated trinkets piled high on antique wooden tables on the other, Bacci's is a dangerous place to browse. Before you know it, you'll have an armful of chunky luxury soaps, embroidered cushions and picture-perfect coffee mugs to fit in your suitcase.

It's hard to miss the store from the outside: its side wall is adorned with an artsy mural that changes every few months.

### OLIVER + LILLY'S
CLOTHING

Map p280 (☑604-736-7774; www.oliveran dlillys.com; 1575 W 6th Ave, South Granville; ☺10am-6pm Tue-Fri, 10am-5pm Sat, noon-5pm Sun; ☐10) Sitting in a chi chi enclave of galleries and restaurants off South Granville, this small but well-curated women's clothing boutique is an oasis of great designer duds, from classic looks to more frivolous fun. You'll find stylish but casual jeans, summer dresses and halter tops from European and US designers plus occasional extras such as scented candles.

There are also often some local-made jewelry and accessory fourishes to accent your new look. Expect to spend some time here chatting with the smiley staff, who are more than happy to offer suggestions for other shopping options in and around the city.

### PURDY'S CHOCOLATES
FOOD

Map p280 (☑604-732-7003; www.purdys.com; 2705 Granville St, South Granville; ☺10am-6pm Mon-Sat, noon-5pm Sun; ☐10) Like a beacon to the weary, this purple-painted chocolate purveyor stands at the corner of Granville and W 11th Ave calling your name. It's a homegrown BC business with outlets dotted like candy sprinkles across the city, and it's hard not to pick up a few treats: go for chocolate hedgehogs, mint meltie bars or sweet Georgia browns – pecans in caramel and chocolate.

It's a great spot to pick up distinctive, Vancouver-made souvenirs for your friends and family back home; rush to the sales racks after Christmas and Valentine's Day for dramatic bargains. And on sunny days, drop in and treat yourself: the nut and chocolate–covered ice cream bars are a local legend.

### IAN TAN GALLERY
ARTS & CRAFTS

Map p280 (⚲604-738-1077; www.iantangal lery.com; 2321 Granville St, South Granville; ☺10am-6pm Mon-Sat; 🚌10) While some private galleries can seem intimidating (perhaps purposely), this popular stop on the city's one-time gallery row is the opposite. It recently relocated from its original premises across the street. Step inside for bold, often bright contemporary works. Canadian artists are the main focus here.

There's usually an intriguing mix of styles and approaches on display, including large paintings, smaller-scale photography (Vancouver is renowned for its contemporary photoconceptualism) and a plinth or two of ceramics or sculpted figures.

### BAU-XI GALLERY
ARTS & CRAFTS

Map p280 (⚲604-733-7011; www.bau-xi.com; 3045 Granville St, South Granville; ☺10am-5:30pm Mon-Sat, 11am-5:30pm Sun; 🚌10) One of the oldest-established of Vancouver's private galleries, Bau-xi – pronounced 'bo-she' – showcases the best in local artists and generally has prices to match its exalted position. The main gallery selection changes monthly and the focus is usually on original paintings – although prints, drawings and sculpture are also added to the mix on occasion.

Look out for works by favored Vancouver contemporary painters such as Jack Shadbolt, who is one of Canada's most collectible modern artists.

### RESTORATION HARDWARE
HOMEWARES

Map p280 (⚲604-731-3918; www.restoration hardware.com; 2555 Granville St, South Granville; ☺10am-7pm Mon-Sat, 11am-6pm Sun; 🚌10) Filled with furnishings and interior flourishes that you wish you had in your house, this upmarket favorite also carries occasional kitsch-tastic reproduction toys and old-school gadgets, especially at Christmastime. Even if you don't buy anything, it's a great place to poke around and get some ideas for your summer house in the south of France.

160

EYESPLASH IMAGES ARE CREATED IN CANADA/GETTY IMAGES ©

1. Celebration of Light festival 2. Denman St *izakaya* 3. Chinatown New Year Parade 4. Indigenous totem pole

ANNHFHUNG/GETTY IMAGES ©

# Multicultural Vancouver

Vancouver offers uncountable ways to dive into the food, traditions and artistic side of nations near and far. For many visitors, this rich international accessibility is a highlight of their trip.

## Festivals

From giant Chinese New Year parades to grass-roots events such as Greek Day, Italian Day, Caribbean Days and the Japanese-themed Powell Street Festival, it's hard not get swept up in Vancouver's heady mix of great cultural fests.

## Chinatown

Canada's largest historic Chinatown is in transition but it still remains a vital part of the city. The bustling grocery stores show that this neighborhood is grounded in tradition.

## Denman Street

This West End thoroughfare (p66) is crammed like a United Nations food court with Vancouver's best midrange dining from around the world. From authentic *izakayas* (Japanese neighbourhood pubs) and noodle shops to Mexican eateries and fancy French restaurants, you can eat in a different country here every night.

## Aboriginal Art

The region's first inhabitants have a rich heritage of creativity, which visitors have many opportunities to discover. From thrilling carvings at UBC's Museum of Anthropology (p164) to a stunning collection at the Bill Reid Gallery of Northwest Coast Art (p59), you'll also find aboriginal public art studding the streets and buildings around the city.

## Commercial Drive

Coffee is a way of life on the Drive, where generations of Italian families have been serving the city's best java since arriving in the 1950s. You'll find elderly Italian grandparents rubbing shoulders with cool-ass hipsters here; they're all after the same thing – that perfect cup to see them through the day.

# Kitsilano & University of British Columbia (UBC)

## Neighborhood Top Five

**①** **Museum of Anthropology** (p164) Taking a guided tour of Vancouver's best museum, with its immersive array of First Nations art and artifacts as well as fascinating, sometimes mysterious, exhibits from cultures around the world.

**②** **Bard on the Beach** (p175) Watching a Shakespeare show in a tented Vanier Park theater, as the sun sets over the mountains behind the stage.

**③** **West 4th Avenue** (p166) Shopping for yoga gear, vinyl records or great travel books, and stopping for artisan ice cream.

**④** **Museum of Vancouver** (p166) Noodling around the nostalgic displays illuminating the yesteryear city, before adding the two other nearby museums to your day out.

**⑤** **Kitsilano Beach** (p166) Sunning yourself with the locals on the area's best beach.

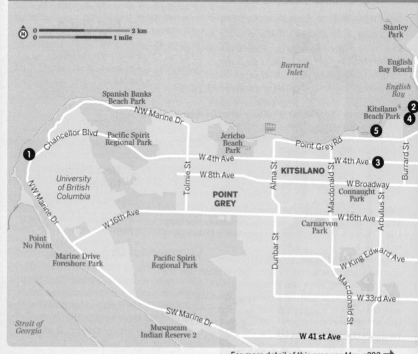

For more detail of this area see Map p282 ➡

# Explore Kitsilano & University of British Columbia (UBC)

Kitsilano and UBC occupy the same peninsula, but you'll hit Kits first when traveling from downtown. The number 4 bus will take you along West 4th Ave, which is Kitsilano's best shopping district. Walk five blocks north from West 4th and you'll come to Broadway, the other main Kitsilano thoroughfare. West of Trafalgar St this major Vancouver artery takes on a villagelike ambiance and is well stocked with restaurants and stores (including some excellent bookshops). A fun fusion of groovy patchouli and slick retail therapy, Kits is ideal for easy urban exploring – add the three museums in Vanier Park plus dinner on West 4th and you'll have a full day out.

From Kits you can hop back on a westbound bus (4, 9 or 99B-Line) and you'll soon arrive at the end of the peninsula on the sprawling UBC campus. An excellent half-day hangout, UBC has some great and often underrated attractions, including museums, galleries and gardens. It's also a tranquil break from the busy downtown streets and there are even live music and theater venues here if you fancy extending your visit. Don't forget the beaches, either: the peninsula is lined with great sandy hangouts, from summertime-packed Kits Beach to UBC's naturist Wreck Beach.

## Local Life

➡**Hangouts** On languid summer days, everyone in Vancouver seems to be soaking up the rays at Kitsilano Beach (p166). Arrive early to find a good spot.

➡**Sunsets** Watching the multi-hued evening sky from the Galley Patio & Grill (p174) is a popular Kits-area pastime.

➡**Free Shows** The summer-long Kitsilano Showboat (p175) is a beloved tradition. Snag a bleacherlike perch, meet the locals and watch grassroots acts from Morris dancers to brass bands.

## Getting There & Away

➡**Bus** Services 4 and 9 run through Kitsilano on West 4th Ave and Broadway respectively, eventually reaching UBC. The 99B-Line express also runs along Broadway to UBC.

➡**Train** Take the Canada Line SkyTrain service from downtown to Broadway-City Hall, then hop bus 9 or the 99B-Line express bus along Broadway to UBC.

➡**Car** There is also metered parking on West 4th and Broadway in Kitsilano as well as surrounding side streets. There is metered parking plus six public parkades (parking lots) at UBC.

## Lonely Planet's Top Tip

Many of Kitsilano's best restaurants are packed on weekends and finding a table can be a problem. Consider dining off-peak or coming on a weekday, when you'll have your pick of the best options. Breakfast and brunch are almost as popular as dinner among weekending locals, so follow the same rule for your first meal of the day; come early or late or wait for a weekday.

KITSILANO & UBC

### ✖ Best Places to Eat

➡ Mr Red Cafe (p170)
➡ Fable (p172)
➡ AnnaLena (p173)
➡ Naam (p173)
➡ Sophie's Cosmic Cafe (p173)

### ♆ Best Places to Drink

➡ Corduroy (p174)
➡ Galley Patio & Grill (p174)
➡ Koerner's Pub (p174)
➡ Fringe Cafe (p175)
➡ 49th Parallel Coffee (p174)

### 🔒 Best Places to Shop

➡ Silk Road Tea (p176)
➡ Stepback (p177)
➡ Kidsbooks (p176)
➡ Zulu Records (p177)
➡ Thomas Haas (p176)

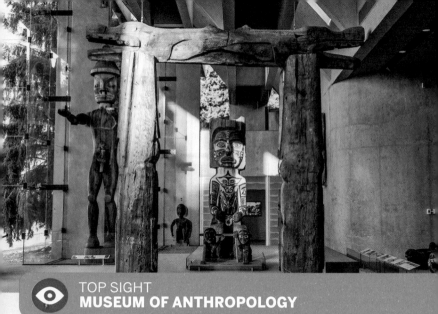

ALEXANDER HOWARD/LONELY PLANET ©

TOP SIGHT
# MUSEUM OF ANTHROPOLOGY

Vancouver's best museum is the main reason many visitors come to the the University of British Columbia campus. The MOA is home to one of Canada's finest and most important collections of Northwest Coast aboriginal art and artifacts. But that's just the start; the ambitious collection here goes way beyond local anthropological treasures, illuminating diverse cultures from around the world.

## MOA 101

The highlight of the Arthur Erickson–designed museum, the grand **Great Hall** is a forest of dozens of towering totem poles plus a menagerie of carved ceremonial figures, house posts and delicate exhibits – all set against a giant floor-to-ceiling window facing the waterfront and mountains. Many of the ornate carvings are surprisingly vibrantly colored: look out for some smiling masks as well as a life-size rowing boat containing two figures that look ready to head straight out to sea on an adventure. The Great Hall is everyone's introduction to the museum – it's the first part you stroll into after paying your admission – and it's also where the one-hour-long **free tours** depart from several times a day: these are highly recommended since they provide an excellent overview of what else there is to see here.

## Getting Lost

If you miss the tour or just want to go at your own pace, this is also a good museum in which to get lost. And, despite its reputation for only showcasing aboriginal culture, there is much more to be seen than you'd imagine. The renovation enabled more of the university's immense collection to be displayed in the jam-packed **Multiversity Galleries**. There are more than 10,000 fascinating and often eye-popping ethnographic artifacts from cultures

### DON'T MISS

→ Great Hall
→ Free tours
→ Multiversity Galleries
→ Live performances
→ MOA gift shop

### PRACTICALITIES

→ Map p286, A2
→ ☎ 604-822-5087
→ www.moa.ubc.ca
→ 6393 NW Marine Dr
→ adult/child $18/16
→ ⊙10am-5pm Wed-Sun, to 9pm Tue
→ P
→ 🚍99B-Line

around the world, closely packed into display cabinets. It's a sensory immersion: you'll find everything from Kenyan snuff bottles to Maori stone knives and from ancient Greek jugs to Navajo blankets from the US. A selection of ornate, brightly hued Asian opera costumes is also a highlight.

There's so much to see in this part of the museum that it can be a little overwhelming, but you can calm your brain in the soothing **European Ceramics Gallery**. Sometimes overlooked by visitors clambering to see the totem poles, it's a subtle stunner, created from a private collection of hundreds of pieces of delicately beautiful pottery and porcelain made between the 16th and 19th centuries. This gallery is rarely crowded, so you can usually peruse in relative tranquility: look out for detailed porcelain figures, ornate tea sets and a hulking tile-covered oven that once graced a busy kitchen.

## Value-Added Extras

Aside from the regular permanent galleries, there are some diverse temporary exhibitions during the year. Do not leave before you've checked these out. Recent visiting shows have included Buddhist art, Peruvian silverware and First Nations treasures from across BC and beyond. Check the MOA's website calendar before you arrive and you'll also find lectures, movies and presentations, as well as occasional live music performances, which are often staged in the grand Great Hall. Some shows and presentations are included with your admission, for others you'll have to pay extra.

## Before You Leave

The final part of anyone's visit – aside from a coffee-and-carrot-cake pit stop at the the courtyard cafe – should be the **gift shop**. While many museum stores are lame afterthoughts offering cheesy trinkets at inflated prices, the MOA's version is far superior. And while you can certainly pick up postcards and T-shirts here, the best purchases are the authentic aboriginal arts and crafts created by local artisans. Look out for rare and unique carved masks as well as intricately engraved gold and silver jewelry. There is also delicate Japanese pottery as well as intricate Tibetan paintings and South American beaded necklaces. In fact, you could start your own anthropology museum when you get back home.

## MOA TIPS

Admission is cut to $10 from 5pm to 9pm every Tuesday.

There are free 30-minute and 60-minute tours, included with entry, on most days. Check at the front desk for times.

The first Tuesday of every month includes a guided curator tour. It's in the early evening so can be combined with Tuesday's regular reduced-entry night.

There are several other attractions on campus. Add galleries, gardens and other museums for a full UBC day out.

**The museum was founded in the basement of the main campus library in 1949 but it moved to its current purpose-built space in 1976. Architect Arthur Erickson's design was inspired by traditional post-and-beam structures built by regional Northwest Coast Aboriginal communities. Since moving to its own space and undergoing two major renovations, the museum has almost doubled in size. Appropriately, it stands on traditional Musqueam land.**

KITSILANO & UBC MUSEUM OF ANTHROPOLOGY

# ⊙ SIGHTS

Kitsilano's Vanier Park is home to a triumvirate of museums, with some of the city's best beaches stretching from here along the shoreline to the University of BC. The campus itself has more than enough attractions of its own to justify an alternative day out from the city center.

# ⊙ Kitsilano

### MUSEUM OF VANCOUVER                    MUSEUM

Map p282 (☑604-736-4431; www.museumof vancouver.ca; 1100 Chestnut St; adult/child $15/5; ⊙10am-5pm, to 8pm Thu; P ♿; ☐22) The MOV has hugely improved in recent years, with cool temporary exhibitions and evening events aimed at culturally-minded adults. It hasn't changed everything, though. There are still superbly evocative displays on local 1950s pop culture and 1960s hippie counterculture – a reminder that Kits was once the grass-smoking center of Vancouver's flower-power movement – plus a shimmering gallery of vintage neon signs from around the city.

There's plenty of hands-on stuff for history-minded kids here, including weekend scavenger hunts and fun workshops. The museum is hoping to relocate to a downtown site in future years, so check the website for progress reports.

### HR MACMILLAN
### SPACE CENTRE                    MUSEUM

Map p282 (☑604-738-7827; www.spacecentre. ca; 1100 Chestnut St; adult/child $18/13; ⊙10am-5pm Jul-Aug, 10am-3pm Mon-Fri, 10am-5pm Sat & noon-5pm Sun Sep-Jun; P ♿; ☐22) Popular with schoolkids – expect to have to elbow them out of the way to push the flashing buttons – this slightly dated science center illuminates the world of space. There's plenty of fun to be had battling aliens, designing spacecraft or strapping yourself in for a simulator ride to Mars, plus movie presentations on all manner of spacey themes.

Drop by on Saturday evenings for a date with a difference: a planetarium presentation, a mini-lecture on a hot space topic and a visit to the observatory to peek at the stars – all for $13.

### VANCOUVER
### MARITIME MUSEUM                    MUSEUM

Map p282 (www.vancouvermaritimemuseum. com; 1905 Ogden Ave; adult/child $11/8.50; ⊙10am-5pm, to 8pm Thu, reduced hours off-season; P; ☐22) Combining dozens of intricate models, detailed re-created ship sections and some historic boats, the prize exhibit in this waterfront A-frame museum is the St Roch, a 1928 Royal Canadian Mounted Police Arctic patrol vessel that was the first to navigate the legendary Northwest Passage in both directions. On a budget? Thursday entry (after 5pm) is by donation.

The building was actually built around the St Roch (a protected National Historic Site). The museum has struggled slightly in recent years, with its non-city-center location making it hard to keep admission numbers up. But it has been adding some interesting temporary exhibitions to lure the locals – a recent one covered sailors' tattoos and naughty scrimshaw carvings.

### KITSILANO BEACH                    BEACH

Map p282 (cnr Cornwall Ave & Arbutus St; ☐22) Facing English Bay, Kits Beach is one of Vancouver's favorite summertime hangouts. The wide, sandy expanse attracts buff Frisbee tossers and giggling volleyball players, and those who just like to preen while catching the rays. The ocean is fine for a dip, though serious swimmers should consider the heated **Kitsilano Pool** (Map p282; ☑604-731-0011; www.van couverparks.ca; 2305 Cornwall Ave; adult/child $5.86/2.95; ⊙7am-evening mid-Jun–mid-Sep; ♿; ☐22), one of the world's largest outdoor saltwater pools.

Perch on a log on a summer afternoon and catch the breathtaking view here: one of Vancouver's signature panoramas. You'll be treated to shimmering seafront backed by the twinkling glass towers of downtown and the North Shore mountains beyond. It's one of those vistas that will have you considering your emigration options.

### WEST 4TH AVENUE                    AREA

Map p282 (www.shopwest4th.com; ☐4) This strollable smorgasbord of stores and restaurants may have your credit cards whimpering for mercy after a couple of hours. Since Kits is now a bit of a middle-class utopia, shops that once sold cheap groceries are now more likely to be hawking designer yoga gear, hundred-dollar hiking socks and exotic (and unfamiliar) fruits from around the world.

There are also some excellent bookstores and coffeehouses here, as well as the menagerie of well-maintained wooden heritage homes along almost every side street. The neighborhood is definitely worth a lazy afternoon of anyone's time – and you're never far from the beach if you need to cool off.

### JERICHO BEACH                    BEACH
Map p282 (north foot of Alma St; ☐4) An activity-lover's idyll, Jericho is great if you just want to putter along the beach, clamber over driftwood and catch stunning views of downtown. It's popular with locals on summer evenings, so expect impromptu but civilized beach gatherings where discreet coolers of beer may appear. Talk nicely to folk with your novelty foreign accent and they'll likely invite you over.

### VANIER PARK                    PARK
Map p282 (west of Burrard Bridge; ℗; ☐22) Winding around Kitsilano Point towards Kits Beach, waterfront Vanier Park is more a host than a destination. Home to three museums, it's also the venue for the tents of the annual Bard on the Beach Shakespeare Festival (p175). It's also a popular picnic spot: bring takeout from Granville Island (a 10-minute stroll away via the seawall) and watch the kite-flyers.

If you want to avoid the sweaty crush in English Bay during the Celebration of Light fireworks event (p22), bring your blanket and spread it out here. You'll have great views of the aerial display among a far more convivial and family-friendly crowd.

### OLD HASTINGS MILL
### STORE MUSEUM                  MUSEUM
Map p282 (☎604-734-1212; www.hastings-mill-museum.ca; 1575 Alma St; by donation; ☉1-4pm Tue-Sun mid-Jun–mid-Sep, 1-4pm Sat & Sun mid-Sep–Nov & mid-Feb–mid-Jun; ☐4) Built near Gastown in 1865, this wooden structure is Vancouver's oldest surviving building. Originally a store for sawmill workers, it survived the Great Fire of 1886 and was used as a makeshift morgue that fateful day. Saved from demolition by locals, it was floated here in the 1930s and now houses an eclectic array of pioneer-era and First Nations exhibits.

Staffed by volunteers, this charming little neighborhood museum is well worth

**KITSILANO & UBC** SIGHTS

a visit if you're in the area. Ask about the old kitchen chair: it also survived the Great Fire and is still on display.

### CITY FARMER                    GARDENS
Map p282 (☎604-736-2250; www.cityfarmer.info; 2150 Maple St; ☉9am-4pm, reduced hours off-season; ☐4) ✿FREE Home of the Vancouver Compost Demonstration Garden, this fragrant, flower-strewn urban garden site is just a two-block walk from W 4th Ave. It's divided into sections, including a biodiversity garden and climate-change garden: you can learn about composting and water-efficient horticulture (check the website for tours and classes) or just suck up the flowerage as you wander around.

Staffed by chatty volunteers, this is a good spot for green-thumbed visitors. The site also adjoins a disused rail corridor that, on our visit, was being transformed into the new **Arbutus Greenway Park**, a 9km tree-fringed linear walkway.

## ⊙ UBC

### MUSEUM OF ANTHROPOLOGY    MUSEUM
See p164.

### PACIFIC SPIRIT REGIONAL PARK    PARK
Map p286 (www.pacificspiritparksociety.org; cnr Blanca St & W 16th Ave; ℗; ☐99 B-Line) This stunning 763-hectare park stretches from Burrard Inlet to the North Arm of the Fraser River, a green buffer zone between

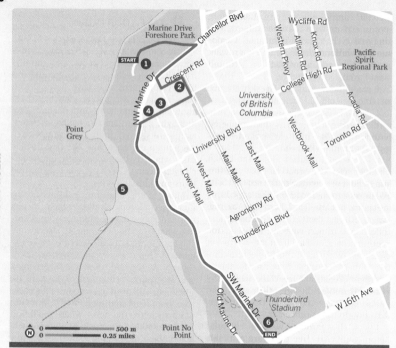

# Neighborhood Walk
# UBC Campus & Gardens Walk

**START** MUSEUM OF ANTHROPOLOGY
**END** UBC BOTANICAL GARDEN
**LENGTH** 3KM; 1.5 HOURS

This walk introduces you to UBC's leading cultural attractions and celebrated gardens.

Start at Vancouver's best museum, the ❶ **Museum of Anthropology** (p164), where you'll gain an appreciation for the culture and artistry of the region's original First Nations residents. Save time for the excellent but sometimes overlooked European ceramics gallery and take in the towering totem poles in the main atrium.

Cross NW Marine Dr and head down West Mall, turning left on Crescent Rd then right onto Main Mall. On your left is the free-entry ❷ **Morris and Helen Belkin Gallery**, which stages changing and sometimes challenging exhibitions of modern art.

Continue southwards along Main Mall, then turn right onto Memorial Rd. Continue downhill until you come to the rock garden of the ❸ **UBC Asian Centre** on your right.

The boulders here are inscribed with Confucian philosophies.

Continue along Memorial and ahead you will see the entrance to the oasislike, Japanese-themed ❹ **Nitobe Memorial Garden**. Spend time here immersing yourself in the site's subtle yet meaningful design. Tours are often available during the summer season and are highly recommended if you have time.

Return to NW Marine Dr and continue southeastwards for about 1km. If you're feeling adventurous, look for the signs for Trail 6 to the waterfront, where you can disrobe – you're on ❺ **Wreck Beach** (p170), Vancouver's official naturist beach. It's the only one in the region.

Continue along NW Marine Dr until it becomes SW Marine Dr. Near the intersection with W 16th Ave, you'll find ❻ **UBC Botanical Garden**. Wander through the garden areas here and save time for the Greenheart TreeWalk, an illuminating elevated stroll through the trees via platforms and suspension bridges.

the UBC campus and the city. A smashing spot to explore with 70km of walking, jogging and cycling trails, it includes **Camosun Bog wetland** (accessed by a boardwalk at 19th Ave and Camosun St), a bird and plant haven.

Some of the more dense forest trails give an indication of what Vancouver would have looked like before it was developed: a rich, verdant jungle of huge ferns, unencumbered birdlife (including bald eagles) and towering trees arching overhead.

UBC BOTANICAL GARDEN                    GARDENS

Map p286 (www.botanicalgarden.ubc.ca; 6804 SW Marine Dr; adult/child $9/5; ☺9:30am-4:30pm, to 8pm Thu mid-Mar–Oct, 9:30am-4pm Nov–mid-Mar; ➌99 B-Line, then C20) You'll find a giant collection of rhododendrons, a fascinating apothecary plot and a winter green space of off-season bloomers in this 28-hectare complex of themed gardens. Save time for the attraction's Greenheart TreeWalk, which lifts visitors 17m above the forest floor on a 308m guided eco tour. A combined botanical garden and walkway ticket costs $20.

Check the garden's website calendar before your visit: free tours are available on selected days and they provide a great introduction to the various garden areas. And make sure you drop into the gift shop before you leave, for its well-curated collection of green-thumbed books and trinkets. Here in October? The annual UBC Apple Fest is also staged right here; it's the highlight of the year for the kind of locals and visitors who love Cox's Orange Pippins.

GREENHEART TREEWALK                    LOOKOUT

Map p286 (☑604-822-4208; www.botanicalgarden.ubc.ca; UBC Botanical Garden, 6804 SW Marine Dr; adult/child $20/10; ☺10am-4:30pm daily, to 7:30pm Thu Apr-Oct; P⌖) One of the best ways to commune with nature is to pretend you're a squirrel. And while costumes are not required here (you may win a raised eyebrow if you chance it), visitors love swaying across the steel bridges and noodling around the wooden platforms high in this forest canopy walk located inside UBC Botanical Garden; admission also includes entry to that attraction.

Your ticket also includes a guided TreeWalk tour which illuminates the flora and fauna of the region.

BEATY BIODIVERSITY MUSEUM            MUSEUM

Map p286 (☑604-827-4955; www.beatymuseum.ubc.ca; 2212 Main Mall; adult/child $12/10; ☺10am-5pm Tue-Sun; ⌖; ➌99B-Line) UBC's newest museum is also its most family-friendly. It showcases two million natural history specimens that have never before been available for public viewing: there are fossil, fish and herbarium displays. The highlight is the 25m blue-whale skeleton, artfully displayed in the museum's two-story main entrance, plus the first display case, which is crammed with tooth-and-claw taxidermy. Check the schedule for free tours and kids activities.

Many of the museum's exhibits are in high-tech pullout draws, which means you can spend hours poking around seeing what's in the next one. It also means you have to work a little to really make the most of this museum; it's well worth it, though. At the end, there's a surprisingly well-stocked gift shop to look forward to. And if you still need to keep your kids occupied, search out the small **Pacific Museum of Earth** across the street, where you'll find fossils, gemlike minerals and a large duck-billed dinosaur skeleton.

NITOBE MEMORIAL GARDEN            GARDENS

Map p286 (www.nitobe.org; 1895 Lower Mall; adult/child $7/4; ☺11am-4:30pm, to 8pm Thu mid-Mar–Oct, 10am-2pm Mon-Fri Nov–mid-Mar; ➌99 B-Line, then C20) Exemplifying Japanese horticultural philosophies, this is a tranquil oasis of peaceful pathways, small traditional bridges and a large, moss-banked pond filled with plump koi carp. It's named after Dr Inazo Nitobe, a scholar whose mug appears on Japan's ¥5000 bill. Consider a springtime visit for the florid cherry-blossom displays.

MORRIS & HELEN BELKIN GALLERY            GALLERY

Map p286 (☑604-822-2759; www.belkin.ubc.ca; 1825 Main Mall; ☺10am-5pm Tue-Fri, noon-5pm Sat & Sun; ➌99 B-Line) FREE This great little gallery specializes in contemporary and often quite challenging pieces – which explains the billboard-style depiction of an Iraqi city outside, complete with the caption 'Because there was and there wasn't a city of Baghdad.' Inside, you can expect a revolving roster of traveling shows plus chin-stroking exhibits from a permanent collection of Canadian avant-garde works.

Although the gallery only opened in 1995, it replaced the UBC Fine Arts Gallery, which opened in 1948 and for many years was the only place where Vancouverites could view contemporary art.

### SPANISH BANKS                                BEACH

Map p286 (cnr NW Marine Dr & Blanca St; 🚌44, then C19) This tree-backed public beach is a popular locals' hangout – they're the ones jogging past in Lululemon outfits – and is a good spot to unpack a picnic and perch on a log to enjoy some sigh-triggering waterfront vistas. It was named after English Bay's 1792 meeting between British mariner Captain George Vancouver and his Spanish counterpart Dionisio Galiano.

While the two captains parted amicably, it was Vancouver's name that would eventually grace the city that he almost certainly did not imagine would rise out of the area's dense wilderness. As for Galiano, posterity remembered the Spaniard by naming a tiny Gulf Island after him.

### WRECK BEACH                                 BEACH

Map p286 (☑604-308-6336; www.wreckbeach. org; via Trail 6; 🚌99B-Line, then C20) Follow Trail 6 into the woods and down the steep steps to find Vancouver's only official naturist beach, complete with a motley crew of counterculture locals, independent vendors and sunburned regulars. The pants-free bunch are a generally welcoming group, so long as you're not just there to gawk; start your visit on the right foot by quickly peeling off in solidarity.

Time your visit well and you can take part in the annual **Bare Buns Fun Run**. And if you fancy connecting with other local naturists during your stay, check in with the Van Tan Nudist Club (www.vantan.ca) for events, including regular swimming meets at local pools.

## ✖️ EATING

**Kitsilano's two main arteries – West 4th Ave and Broadway – offer a healthy mix of eateries: it's well worth the trek here to lounge on a beach or stroll the shopping areas then end your day with a rewarding meal. The neighborhood's hippie past has left a legacy of vegetarian-friendly restaurants, but Kits' more recent wealth means there are also some top-notch high-end options well worth a splurge. If you're at UBC, there are some dining options available; alternatively, hop on a bus to nearby Kitsilano for a far superior selection.**

### ⭐MR RED CAFE                          VIETNAMESE $

Map p282 (☑604-559-6878; 2680 W Broadway; mains $6-14; ⏱11am-9pm; ▨; 🚌9) Serves authentic northern Vietnamese homestyle dishes that look and taste like there's a lovely old lady making them out back. Reservations are not accepted; dine off-peak to avoid waiting for the handful of tables, then dive into shareable gems such as pork baguette sandwiches, *cha ca han oi* (spicy grilled fish) and the ravishing pyramidical rice dumpling, stuffed with pork and a boiled quail's egg.

The Sunday night family dinner for two ($37.50) is a local favorite; arrive early for a table and you'll be the happiest diner in town. Cash or debit cards only are accepted here.

### CARTEMS DONUTERIE                     BAKERY

Map p282 (www.cartems.com; 3040 W Broadway; baked goods $3-4; ⏱8am-10pm Mon-Fri, 9am-10pm Sat, to 8pm Sun; 🚌9) The newest of a three-outlet gourmet doughnut mini-chain (the others are on Main St and downtown), this austere-looking L-shaped spot is all about indulging in that most vital of food groups: the treat. Snag a seat at the communal table and sink your choppers into salted caramel, Earl Grey or Canadian whiskey bacon varieties – or all three. Local-made Earnest Ice Cream is also served.

Before you leave, don't forget to make up a to-go box for the the road; try to resist scoffing them on the bus on your way home.

### SERANO GREEK PASTRY              BAKERY $

Map p282 (☑604-739-3181; 3185 W Broadway; pastries $2-6; ⏱9:30am-6pm Mon-Sat, noon-6pm Sun; 🚌9) You'll find it impossible to pass this fancy-free little Greek bakery, the baking aromas calling you like a siren song. Step inside and the temptation increases exponentially. Naturally, the spanakopita is fantastic, but this family-run joint is really all about old-school cakes, pastries and multi-hued meringues: the cream-filled korne makes the art of smiling and eating at the same time suddenly seem easy.

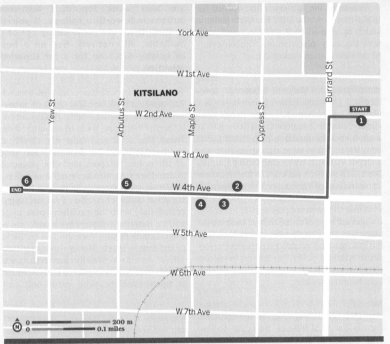

# Neighborhood Walk
# Kitsilano Food-for-Thought Hop

**START** BARBARA-JO'S BOOKS TO COOKS
**END** GRAVITY POPE
**LENGTH** 1KM; 1.5 HOURS

This walk will introduce you to the Kitsilano neighborhood and two of its main obsessions: shopping and dining.

Kick things off on W 2nd Ave (near the intersection with Burrard St) at the recipe-and-chef-themed bookshop **1 Barbara-Jo's Books to Cooks** (p177). You can pick up a tome or two from famed local star chefs such as Vikram Vij, Frank Pabst and John Bishop.

Stroll west to Burrard St, turn left and walk two blocks south until you reach W 4th Ave. Head up W 4th until you come to the city's biggest travel-book store **2 Wanderlust** (p177). Duck inside for some inspiring travel tomes and a can of mosquito repellent – not something you'll usually need in Vancouver.

Cross over and you'll be in front of one of the city's favorite indie shops, **3 Zulu Records** (p177). It's well worth a few

minutes to browse the vinyl among the local musos here. You should also ask the all-knowing staff to recommend some Vancouver bands.

You're in the heart of the Kits shopping district here, so spend some time checking out what's on offer. Once you've had your fill, continue westwards on W 4th and within a few steps you'll come to **4 Fable** (p172), one of the city's best farm-to-table restaurants. Consider nipping in here to make a dinner reservation for later in the day: it's usually the only way to avoid a long evening wait for a table. But if you're hungry right now, cross to the other side of W 4th and slide into **5 Sophie's Cosmic Café** (p173), a retro diner with a great line in heaping brunches and hearty comfort-food lunches.

After your fuel-up, continue west on the same side and salve your appetite for fashion, in particular the great range of shoes at **6 Gravity Pope** (p178).

Try to make this your first call of the day if you're exploring Kits. Every local in the area knows about this place and some treats quickly sell out.

## MODERNE BURGER
DINER $

Map p282 (☎604-739-0005; www.moderneburger.com; 2507 W Broadway; mains $9-16; ☺noon-7:30pm Tue-Sun; ☐9) Possibly Vancouver's best-looking retro diner. Slide into a green vinyl booth here and tuck into comfort-food heaven (but not before you've selected a track from the jukebox in the corner). Unlike some burger joints, this one hasn't gone for weird-ass combinations. Instead, you'll get well-made classics such as beef and turkey patties with cheese and bacon toppings.

The fries are of the fresh-made, plate-heaped variety and this is the place to indulge in that naughtily calorific ice-cream-packed coffee-mocha shake you've been dreaming about all your life.

## TERA V BURGER
VEGETARIAN $

Map p282 (☎604-336-3575; www.teravburger.com; 2961 W Broadway; mains $6-15; ☺11:30am-8pm Mon-Wed, to 8:30pm Thu & Sun, to 9pm Fri & Sat; ☕; ☐9) Aiming to convert meat-eaters into herbivores is the stated aim of this modern vegetarian burger bar. Which means hearty, meat-esque dishes such as grilled Tofurkey sandwiches and Thai 'chicken' salads. The burgers are the way to go, especially the barbecue tempeh burger with yam fries. Most dishes are available in vegan options and a fruit smoothie is the perfect accompaniment.

There's not much seating here – it echoes the layout of meatarian fast-food joints – so if you can't find a spot, pack your burger and head north. If you hotfoot it, you can be on the Kitsilano waterfront in 15 minutes.

## ★FABLE
WEST COAST $$

Map p282 (☎604-732-1322; www.fablekitchen.ca; 1944 W 4th Ave; mains $19-31; ☺11:30am-2pm Mon-Fri, 5:30-10pm Mon-Sat, brunch 10:30am-2pm Sat & Sun; ☐4) One of Vancouver's favorite farm-to-table restaurants is a lovely rustic-chic room of exposed brick, wood beams and prominently displayed red rooster logos. But looks are just part of the appeal. Expect perfectly prepared bistro dishes showcasing local seasonal ingredients such as duck, lamb and halibut. It's great gourmet comfort food with little pretension, hence the packed room most nights. Reservations recommended.

The lunch menu – including an excellent ploughman's lunch platter – is invitingly priced. And if you're lucky enough to snag a table for weekend brunch, go for the pulled-pork johnny cakes.

## MAENAM
THAI $$

Map p282 (☎604-730-5579; www.maenam.ca; 1938 W 4th Ave; mains $16-22; ☺noon-2pm Tue-Sat, 5-10pm daily; ☕; ☐4) Vancouver's best Thai restaurant is a contemporary reinvention of the concept, with subtle, complex influences flavoring the menu in a warm, wood-floored room with an inviting ambiance. You can start with the familiar (although even the pad Thai here is eye-poppingly different), but save room for something new, such as the utterly delicious black-pepper venison stir-fry.

The halibut green curry is also a local favorite. The mains here are surprisingly well

---

### BLAST FROM THE PAST

Kitsilano was named after Chief Khatsahlano, leader of the First Nations village of Sun'ahk, which occupied the area now designated as Vanier Park. In 1901 the local government displaced the entire community, sending some families to the Capilano Indian Reserve on the North Shore and others to Squamish.

The first Kits streetcar service in 1905 triggered an explosion of housing development, but by the 1960s many of these homes had been converted for university students, sparking the 'beatnik ghetto' that soon defined Kits. Fueled by pungent BC bud, counterculture political movements mushroomed – including a little group of antinuclear protesters that a few years later became Greenpeace. But Khatsahlano has not been completely forgotten: every July, the neighborhood's biggest community festival is a day-long celebration on 4th Ave featuring more than 50 live bands. The area's most popular (and well attended) event, it's called the Khatsahlano Street Party (www.khatsahlano.com).

priced, but why not feast like a king via the six-dish chef's menu for $45 (also available in a vegetarian version)?

### NAAM
VEGETARIAN $$

Map p282 (☑604-738-7151; www.thenaam.com; 2724 W 4th Ave; mains $9-16; ☺24hr; ☑; ☑4) An evocative relic of Kitsilano's hippie past, this vegetarian restaurant has the feel of a comfy farmhouse. It's not unusual to have to wait for a table at peak times, but it's worth it for the huge menu of hearty stir-fries, nightly curry specials, bulging quesadillas and ever-popular fries with miso gravy. It's the kind of veggie spot where carnivores delightedly dine.

There's nightly live music from around 7pm as well as good beers (go for Nelson Brewing's Organic IPA) and a popular patio – it's covered, so you can cozy up here and still enjoy the rain. Happy hour is 3pm to 6pm weekdays and typically includes good food specials.

### LA CIGALE BISTRO
FRENCH $$

Map p282 (☑604-732-0004; www.lacigale bistro.ca; 1961 W 4th Ave; mains $18-28; ☺11:30am-2:30pm Tue-Fri, 5-10pm Tue-Sun, 10:30am-2:30pm Sat & Sun; ☑4) A charming neighborhood bistro with a casual contemporary feel, its menu combines traditional French recipes with local ingredients and simple, flavor-revealing preparations. Expect hearty nosh including practically perfect filet mignon and velvet-soft braised lamb shoulder. We recommend the three-course Sunday-to-Thursday $32 prix-fixe special. In summer, the garagelike front windows are thrown open so it feels as if you're dining alfresco.

There's a small but well-curated French wine list, but if you want to bring your own bottle, the usual corkage fee is waived on Tuesdays.

### SOPHIE'S COSMIC CAFÉ
DINER $$

Map p282 (☑604-732-6810; www.sophiescos miccafe.com; 2095 West 4th Ave; mains $11-16; ☺8am-2:30pm Mon, 8am-8pm Tue-Sun; ☝; ☑4) Slide between the oversized knife and fork flanking the entrance and step into one of Vancouver's favorite retro-look diners, with a cornucopia of kitsch lining the walls. Burgers and big-ass milkshakes dominate the menu, but breakfast is the best reason to come. Expect weekend queues as you await your appointment

with a heaping plate of eggs and lamb mergeuz sausage.

To avoid line-ups, soak up the decor with an afternoon window seat – although you won't see much outside beyond the windowsill of junk-shop bowling trophies – coupled with a pyramid-sized apple pie slice (you can jog up and down the hill to and from the beach to work it off). There's also a good kids menu here.

### ANNALENA
CANADIAN $$$

Map p282 (☑778-379-4052; www.annalena.ca; 1809 W 1st Ave; mains $15-36; ☺5pm-late Tue-Sun; ☑22) Kitsilano's current 'it' spot is an elegant-but-casual resto-bar with some serious foodie chops. Its elongated lounge-like room (think monochrome decor and brushed concrete floors) is the setting for superbly prepared dishes, from seared tuna to buttermilk fried chicken to housemade ice cream. Add a top-notch cocktail plus a bottle from the excellent wine list (BC wines included). Reservations are highly recommended.

On summer evenings, the large front window is opened and you'll feel as if you're hanging out on a chic, almost European side street. Until it rains, of course. This is also a good spot to dine before hitting a show at Bard on the Beach (p175), a five-minute stroll away in Vanier Park.

### BISHOP'S
WEST COAST $$$

Map p282 (☑604-738-2025; www.bishopson line.com; 2183 W 4th Ave; mains $36-45; ☺5:30-11pm; ☑4) Behind its '80s-style beige exterior, Bishop's pioneered West Coast cuisine long before 'locavore' was a word. In fact, legendary chef-owner John Bishop is still at the top of his game, serving top-notch dishes in an elegant white-tableclothed room. The seasonally changing menu can include Fraser Valley lamb, Haida Gwaii halibut and succulent veggies that taste as if they've just been plucked from the ground.

The service here is pitch-perfect, so stay a little longer and indulge in dessert: if you're lucky, it'll be rhubarb and rosemary panna cotta. And look out for the man himself: he'll almost certainly drop by your table to say hi and will sign a copy of his cookbook *Fresh* if you wave it in front of him. Reservations recommended.

KITSILANO & UBC EATING

# 🍷 DRINKING & NIGHTLIFE

★ CORDUROY                                    BAR

Map p282 (📞604-733-0162; www.corduroyres
taurant.com; 1943 Cornwall Ave; ⊙4pm-2am Mon-
Sat, 4pm-midnight Sun; 🚌22) Handily located
near the first bus stop after the Burrard
Bridge (when coming from downtown), this
tiny spot is arguably Kitsilano's best haunt.
Slide onto a bench seat and peruse the
oddball artworks – junk-shop pictures and
carved masks – then order a house beer from
the shingle-covered bar: if you're lucky, it'll
be served in a boot-shaped glass.

Tempting cocktails are also offered at
this quirky spot and there are regular live
events include comedy and open-mike
nights.

KOERNER'S PUB                                  PUB

Map p286 (📞604-827-1443; www.koerners.
ca; 6371 Crescent Rd; ⊙11:30am-9pm Mon-
Wed, to midnight Thu & Fri summer, extended
hours in term time; 🚌99B-Line) UBC's best
pub welcomes with its communal tables,
tree-fringed garden and clientele of nerdy
professors and hipster regulars. There's an
excellent booze list; go for draft sake or a
craft-beer tasting flight dominated by BC
favorite Driftwood Brewing. Food-wise,
the Koerner Organic Burger is a staple
but also try the crunchy UBC Farm Salad,
largely sourced from the university's own
nearby farm.

UBC Farm is also planning to open its
own microbrewery, so check ahead when
you visit the campus. It's a bit hard to
find Koerner's; just head along West Mall
towards NW Marine Dr and you'll find the
entrance located up the slight incline on the
last driveway.

GALLEY PATIO & GRILL                           PUB

Map p282 (📞604-222-1331; www.thegalley.
ca; 1300 Discovery St, Jericho Sailing Centre;
⊙10am-10pm Mon-Fri, 9am-10pm Sat & Sun; 🚌4)
At sunset, plop down on one of the plastic
patio chairs then eyeball the sailboats steer-
ing toward shore as the pyrotechnic sky unfolds. There are usually a couple of BC wine
offerings, along with tasty local beers from
R&B Brewing (the Sun God Wheat Ale is
recommended in summer). Grub is of the
beer-battered fish and chips variety.

This is a family-friendly joint where
you'll mostly meet locals. They're always
up for a chat and you can quiz them about
other sunset-viewing spots around the
city (they'll likely mention Third Beach in
Stanley Park; p54).

BIMINI                                         PUB

Map p282 (📞604-733-7116; www.donnel-
lygroup.ca; 2010 W 4th Ave; ⊙11:30am-1am Sun-
Thu 11am-2am Fri & Sat; 🚌4) Packed on weekends with more of a nightclub feel, this is
a good pub to visit on weekday afternoons
for a sly ale and some fries in a darkened
corner (of which there are many). There's a
good array of craft beers, often including
tipples from BC darlings Phillips and Four
Winds. Check out the table football and arcade games near the entrance.

There are good booze specials on most
days. Monday's deal is best: $12 for a beer
and burger plus the added bonus of pub
quiz night. It also has its own liquor store
next door if you're craving takeout.

49TH PARALLEL COFFEE                        COFFEE

Map p282 (www.49thparallelroasters.com;
2198 W 4th Ave; ⊙7am-7pm Mon-Thu, to 8pm Fri-
Sun; 🔊; 🚌4) Kitsilano's favorite coffeeshop
hangout. Sit with the locals in the glass-
enclosed outdoor seating area (handy in
deluge-prone Raincouver) and slowly sip
your latte while scoffing as many own-
brand Luckys Doughnuts as you can man-
age; just because they're artisanal, doesn't
mean you should have only one. Need a
recommendation? Try an apple-bacon fritter. Or two.

This company also roasts its own beans,
which means you're unlikely to be disap-
pointed. The tables here are often dominated by fashionable young parents and their
strollers, so visit off-peak or stroll along
shop-lined W 4th with a take-out cup.

WOLF & HOUND                                   PUB

Map p282 (📞604-738-8909; www.wolfand-
hound.ca; 3617 W Broadway; ⊙4pm-midnight
Mon, noon-midnight Tue-Thu, noon-1am Fri & Sat,
11am-11pm Sun; 🚌4) The nearest good pub to
UBC and one of Vancouver's best Irish watering holes; you'll find plenty of students
avoiding their assignments here. They
come to watch sports in the denlike back
room or to catch free live music, often of the
Celtic persuasion, on most weekends. Harp
and Kilkenny join Ireland's fave stout on
the beer list alongside some good BC craft
brews.

## UBC'S BEST FEST

From Salish to Aurora Golden Gala and from Gravensteins to Cox's Orange Pippins, fans of the real king of fruit have plenty to bite into at the autumnal, weekend-long **UBC Apple Festival** (www.ubcbotanicalgarden.org/events; adult/child $4/free; ⊙mid-Oct). Staged every October at the **UBC Botanical Garden** (p169), it's one of Vancouver's most popular community events. Along with live music and demonstrations on grafting and cider-making, there are lots of smile-triggering children's activities. But the event's main lure is the chance to nibble on a vast array of around 18,000 kg of BC-grown treats that make most supermarket apples taste like hockey pucks. The best way to sample as many as possible is to pay an extra $5 and dive into the **Tasting Tent**. Here, 60 locally grown heritage and more recent varieties are available for considered scoffing, including rarities such as Crestons and Oaken Pins. Before you leave, follow your nose to the sweet aroma of perhaps the best apple pie you'll ever taste. A highlight of the festival, the deep-dish, golden-crusted slices for sale here are an indulgence you could happily eat until you explode – with an apple-flavored smile on your face.

KITSILANO & UBC ENTERTAINMENT

Go for the Hoyne Dark Matter; made in Victoria, it's arguably BC's best porterlike brew. Add a pint of Storm Brewing's Black Plague Stout and you'll soon be singing a merry ballad or two.

### FRINGE CAFÉ                               PUB
Map p282 (www.thefringecafe.com; 3124 W Broadway; ⊙3pm-1am Mon-Thu, 3pm-2am Fri & Sat; ☐9) A tiny reminder of Kitsilano's counterculture heritage, from its memorabilia-lined walls to its chatty, bar-propping regulars. The cheapest drafts are often Dirty Girl Lager and Ugly Boy Pale Ale but Fat Tug IPA is a far superior brew if you're picky (it's on special every Thursday). There's also a surprisingly large array of international bottled brews, including everything from Tuborg to Hobgoblin.

If you're hungry, there's the usual range of burgers and nachos plus nicely spicy Jamaican patties. Drop by on Monday for free-entry trivia night.

## ☆ ENTERTAINMENT

### ★ BARD ON THE BEACH        PERFORMING ARTS
Map p282 (☑604-739-0559; www.bardonthe beach.org; Vanier Park, 1695 Whyte Ave; tickets $20-57; ⊙Jun-Sep; ☐22) Watching Shakespeare performed while the sun sets against the mountains beyond the tented stage is a Vancouver summertime highlight. There are usually three Bard plays, plus one Bard-related work (*Rosencrantz and Guildenstern are Dead,* for example) to choose from during the run.

Q&A talks are staged after Tuesday-night performances, and there are opera, fireworks and wine-tasting nights throughout the season.

Expect Christopher Gaze – the festival's effervescent artistic director and public figurehead (and a popular local actor) – to hop up on stage to introduce the show. He's the kind of old-school actor-manager Shakespeare himself would have appreciated. And make sure you save time to hit the on-site Bard-related gift shop; the perfect place to pick up that Shakespearean insult T-shirt you've always wanted, *thou crusty batch of nature.*

### KITSILANO SHOWBOAT        CONCERT VENUE
Map p282 (☑604-734-7332; www.kitsilanoshow boat.com; 2300 Cornwall Ave; ⊙7pm Mon, Wed, Fri & Sat mid-Jun–mid-Aug; ☝; ☐22) FREE An 80-year-old tradition that generations of locals know and love, this alfresco waterfront stage near Kits Pool offers free shows and concerts in summer. Grab a bleacher-style seat facing the sunset-illuminating North Shore mountains and prepare for singers, musicians, dancers or more; check the online schedule to see what's coming up. A great way to mix and mingle with the chatty locals.

### CINEPLEX FIFTH AVENUE
### CINEMAS                          CINEMA
Map p282 (☑604-734-7469; www.cineplex. com; 2110 Burrard St; tickets $12.50; ☐44) Kitsilano's biggest movie house, popular Fifth Avenue screens indie films, foreign flicks and blockbuster Hollywood schlock (those

locals might look like intellectuals, but they enjoy *Star Wars* as much as anyone else). This is one of Cineplex's newly adult-focused cinemas, which means there's an on-site bar and you must be over 19 to watch a movie here.

Check out the loveseats: you can lift the padded divider and snuggle up with your movie buddy. Tuesday admission is reduced to $7.99 per ticket.

### JERICHO FOLK CLUB                    WORLD MUSIC

Map p282 (www.jerichofolkclub.ca; 1300 Discovery St, Jericho Sailing Centre; $10; ⊙7:15pm Tue May-Sep; ☐4) This local folkie hangout starts with a fun open-stage session (usually four acts) followed by the main attraction performing around 9pm. Local and visiting performers may be scheduled and you can check the online calendar to see who's coming up. The definition of folk here can include anything from Celtic and bluegrass to guitar-wielding singer-songwriters but you're almost guaranteed a fun time.

# 🔒 SHOPPING

**West 4th Avenue is one of Vancouver's best strollable shopping strips, especially on the stretch west of Cypress St. Nip five blocks south to Broadway for another round of good local stores and bookshops, especially west of Trafalgar St. Wherever you wander, you're never far from great coffee shops and restaurants to keep you well fueled.**

### ★KIDSBOOKS                          BOOKS

Map p282 (www.kidsbooks.ca; 2557 W Broadway; ⊙9:30am-6pm Mon-Thu & Sat, 9:30am-9pm Fri, 11am-6pm Sun; ⊕; ☐9) From *Squishy McFluff* to *The Great Big Dinosaur*, this huge child-friendly store – reputedly Canada's biggest kids' bookshop – has thousands of novels, picture books and anything else you can think of to keep your bookish sprogs quiet. There are also regular readings by visiting authors and a selection of quality toys and games to provide a break from all that strenuous page-turning.

Along with all of the usual classics and vampire-themed young-adult novels, there's a cool array of First Nations books to flick through. Looking for a great souvenir book

for a kid back home? Pick up a copy of *Mister Got To Go,* illuminating the adventures of a cat at a local heritage hotel.

### SILK ROAD TEA                           TEA

Map p282 (☎778-379-8481; www.silkroad teastore.com; 2066 W 4th Ave; ⊙10am-7pm Mon-Sat, to 6pm Sun; ☐4) Plunging into the scalding hot Kitsilano tea wars (there are two rival purveyors nearby), this new branch of Victoria's favorite fancy tea emporium combines superbly friendly staff with a lip-smacking array of hundreds of leafy varieties. Peruse the top-notch green, herbal and wellness teas and pick up a super-cool teapot to add to your suitcase-packing woes.

Accept any sample that's on offer here; it's a great way to discover a new favorite flavor. There's also a tempting range of own-brand body-care products (including a handy roll-on headache and hangover tonic). Check the website for upcoming classes and tasting events.

### THOMAS HAAS                           FOOD

Map p282 (☎604-736-1848; www.thom-ashaas.com; 2539 W Broadway; ⊙8am-5:30pm Tue-Sat; ☐9) This independent chocolatier is often bursting with locals purchasing their regular supplies of gourmet treats, such as caramel pecan squares and chili-suffused bon-bons. But the stars of the glass cabinet are the choc-encased fruit jellies (raspberry ganache recommended). A good spot for Vancouver-made souvenirs such as chunky chai and espresso chocolate bars.

And since you're buying treats for everyone back home, you deserve one yourself: a huge slab of 'dark bark' chocolate brittle topped with nuts and dried fruit should do the trick. There are also a few tables here (although they're often fully occupied) if you want to stop for a hot chocolate and a pastry treat.

### KITSILANO FARMERS MARKET            MARKET

Map p282 (www.eatlocal.org; Kitsilano Community Centre, 2690 Larch St; ⊙10am-2pm Sun mid-May–mid-Oct; ☐4) 🍃 Kitsilano's best excuse to get out and hang with the locals, this seasonal farmers market is one of the city's most popular. Arrive early for the best selection and you'll have the pick of freshly plucked local fruit and veg, such as sweet strawberries or spectacularly flavorful heirloom tomatoes. You'll likely never want to shop in a mainstream supermarket again.

KITSILANO & UBC SHOPPING

### STEPBACK                                    HOMEWARES

Map p282 (☑604-731-7525; 2936 W Broadway; ☺11am-5:30pm Tue-Fri, 10am-6pm Sat, noon-5pm Sun; ☑9) When your to-buy list includes taxidermy, vintage typewriters and retro suitcases, this brilliantly curated, highly browsable shop is the place for you. Among the new and used trinkets, homewares and accessories, look out for enamel kitchenware, leather journals and yesteryear postcards of old Vancouver and beyond. There are usually far more people looking than buying; this place almost feels like a little museum.

A great place to pick up a weird and wacky alternative souvenir.

### BARBARA-JO'S
### BOOKS TO COOKS                                    BOOKS

Map p282 (☑604-688-6755; www.booksto cooks.com; 1740 W 2nd Ave; ☺10am-6pm Tue-Fri, 10am-5pm Sat, noon-5pm Sun & Mon; ☑4) Traveling epicureans will salivate over this popular bookstore, specializing in finger-licking food and wine tomes. There are book-reading events and cooking classes in the demonstration kitchen – if you fancy rubbing shoulders with a culinary maestro, check the website schedule. There are also dinner events with chefs and writers around the city: book ahead since they usually sell out.

### ZULU RECORDS                                    MUSIC

Map p282 (☑604-738-3232; www.zulurecords. com; 1972 W 4th Ave; ☺10:30am-7pm Mon-Wed, 10:30am-9pm Thu & Fri, 9:30am-6:30pm Sat, noon-6pm Sun; ☑4) Kitsilano's fave indie music store has downsized from its double storefront but it's still easy to blow an afternoon here sifting the new and used recordings and hard-to-find imports. There's a scuzzy-carpeted, *High Fidelity* ambiance here; ask the music-nerd staff for tips on local live music and check the $2 boxes for that rare Pia Zadora record you've been looking for.

Tickets are sold here for local shows and there's also a back-of-the-shop DVD section if you need something to pop in your laptop for the flight home.

### ARC'TERYX                          SPORTS & OUTDOORS

Map p282 (☑604-737-1104; www.arcteryx.com; 2044 W 4th Ave; ☺10am-7pm Mon-Thu & Sat, 11am-6pm Fri & Sun; ☑4) Flagship branch of Vancouver's high-end outdoor gear store. Expect to pay a premium for the best water-proof jackets and weather-resistant pants here. The upside is they'll last for ages and you'll also be joining a cool group of out-doorsy types wearing a highly regarded logo. Keen to save? It also has a factory out-let store in North Vancouver (see the company's website for details).

### TILLEY                                    CLOTHING

Map p282 (☑604-732-4287; www.tilleyvancou ver.com; 1750 W Broadway; ☺10am-5:30pm; ☑9) Recently relocated to a smaller store, this family-owned BC outdoor-clothing company is ideal for that safari jacket needed for your upcoming Amazon trip. But while the hardy, own-brand clothing doesn't change much, additional labels keep the shop's line-up interesting, including Mavi jeans and Patagonia shirts. The signature item, though, is the Tilley Hat, a travel sun-protector available in many variations.

### WANDERLUST                          SPORTS & OUTDOORS

Map p282 (☑604-739-2182; www.wanderlus tore.com; 1929 W 4th Ave; ☺10am-7pm Mon-Fri, 10am-6pm Sat, noon-5pm Sun; ☑4) Divided between guidebooks, maps and travel literature on one side and an array of travel accessories on the other, this store has been inspiring itchy feet for years. While the

### VANCOUVER'S POT SHOPS

On your travels around Vancouver, you'll likely spot dozens of storefronts with names like Green Room, Herb Society and Eden Medicinal, often with their windows covered over. These medicinal marijuana dispensaries began popping up several years ago, despite a legislative gray area that makes them, by many interpretations, officially illegal. Rather than closing them down, though, in 2015 Vancouver became the first city in Canada to start regulating these businesses, issuing licenses to those meeting a strict set of criteria that includes having to be more than 300 meters from schools. Many of the original stores are digging their heels in while the city tries to regulate; keep your eyes on local newspapers for unfolding stories covering this issue.

## VANCOUVER ON TRACK FOR BOLD NEW PARK

When the City of Vancouver spent $55 million to buy a 9km stretch of disused railway line running south from Kitsilano to Marpole and the Fraser River, some locals questioned the purchase. But with the old rail lines being removed and a new park taking shape, plans are afoot to make this tree-fringed walking and biking route into the local version of New York's wildly popular High Line park. At time of research, the new **Arbutus Greenway Park** was in the early stages of preparation – removing the old rails alone is a huge task – but the project should be opened in stages over the coming years. Check the City of Vancouver's website (www.vancouver.ca) for the latest updates.

book selection is among Vancouver's best, it's the gadgets that are most intriguing. Peruse the money belts and mosquito nets, then wonder how you ever got by without quick-drying underwear.

### GRAVITY POPE
SHOES

Map p282 (☑604-731-7673; www.gravitypope. com; 2205 W 4th Ave; ☺10am-9pm Mon-Fri, to 7pm Sat, 11am-6pm Sun; ☐4) This unisex temple of footwear is a dangerous place to come if you have a shoe fetish – best not to bring more than one credit card. Quality and designer élan are the keys here and you can expect to slip into Vancouver's best selection of fashion-forward clogs, wedges, mules and classy runners.

Next door there's an adjoining fashion-forward clothing store. Called Gravity Pope Tailored Goods, it's stuffed with stylish must-have men's and women's clothing.

# 🏃 SPORTS & ACTIVITIES

### ECOMARINE PADDLESPORT CENTRES
KAYAKING

Map p282 (☑604-689-7575; www.ecoma rine.com; 1300 Discovery St, Jericho Sailing Centre; 2hr kayak/paddleboard rentals $39/29; ☺10am-dusk Mon-Fri, 9am-dusk Jun-Aug; ☐4) The friendly folk at Ecomarine offer gear rentals plus a wide range of guided kayak and stand-up paddleboard (SUP) tours from their seasonal Jericho Beach spot; they also run courses and even SUP yoga classes – check ahead before you arrive in town.

### DIVING LOCKER
DIVING

Map p282 (☑604-736-2681; www.diving locker.ca; 2745 W 4th Ave; dives from $99; ☺10am-6pm Mon-Fri, to 5:30pm Sat, to 4pm Sun; ☐4) A long-established favorite with local snorkelers and scuba divers, the Diving Locker is not just for experienced practitioners. Along with its regular series of PADI training courses, there's a great introductory scuba course ($99, including equipment) for first-timers. There are also specialist kids' camps and courses for aquatically inclined youngsters.

### WINDSURE ADVENTURE WATERSPORTS
WATER SPORTS

(☑604-224-0615; www.windsure.com; 1300 Discovery St, Jericho Sailing Centre; ☺8:30am-8:30pm Apr-Sep; 🚻; ☐4) For those who want to be at one with the sea breeze, Windsure specializes in windsurfing, skimboarding and stand-up paddleboarding rentals and courses for a variety of skill levels. Prices are reasonable (for example, one-day skimboard rental is under $25) and the venue is inside the Jericho Sailing Centre, home of the city's recreational aquatic community.

Novices are more than welcome here: the two-hour windsurfing introductory group lesson ($65) is recommended. There are also lots of classes and activities for kids.

### MAC SAILING
BOATING

Map p282 (☑604-224-7245; www.macsailing. com; 1300 Discovery St, Jericho Sailing Centre; rental per hr from $40; ☺9am-7pm Mon-Fri, noon-6pm Sat & Sun, reduced hours off-season; 🚻; ☐4) This excellent operation at the Jericho Sailing Centre caters to sailing veterans and newbies who want to learn the ropes. There are several boats available for rent – the super-fast and easy-to-sail *Hobie Getaway* is fun – and lessons (including weekday evening introductory courses) are also offered, some tailored specifically for children.

# North Shore

## Neighborhood Top Five

**❶ Grouse Mountain**
(p181) Skiing or snow-boarding the winter powder with the locals or dropping by in summer for a full day of hiking, zip-lining and bear-watching.

**❷ Capilano Suspension Bridge Park** (p181) Inching over a swaying steel-cable bridge in the heart of

the mountains, as your legs turn to jelly.

**❸ Deep Cove Kayak Centre** (p187) Sighing deeply as you slide across the glassy, mountain-shadowed waters in a kayak, seemingly a million miles from any city.

**❹ Endless Biking**
(p187) Careening down the North Shore mountain-bike trails on an adrena-line-rush bike tour.

**❺ Sewell's Marina**
(p190) Communing with the cavorting orcas, as well as lolling seals and beady-eyed shorebirds, on a face-spraying boat tour.

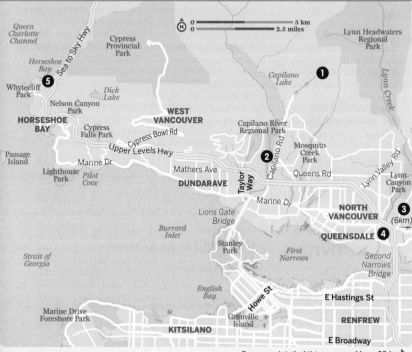

For more detail of this area see Map p284 ➡

## Lonely Planet's Top Tip

Buy a transit day pass (adult/child $9.75/7.50), which includes travel by SeaBus, if you're coming here from downtown. You'll be able to hit Lonsdale Quay Public Market, Capilano Suspension Bridge and Grouse Mountain without having to think about making the next bus before your ticket expires.

 ### Best Places to Eat

➡ Fishworks (p183)

➡ Meat at O'Neill's (p183)

➡ Burgoo Bistro (p184)

➡ Artisan Bake Shoppe (p183)

➡ Salmon House on the Hill (p184)

### Best Places to Drink

➡ Raven (p185)

➡ Buddha-Full (p185)

➡ Queen's Cross (p185)

### Best Places to Shop

➡ Shipyards Night Market (p185)

➡ Lonsdale Quay Public Market (p186)

➡ Mountain Equipment Co-op (p186)

# Explore North Shore

The North Shore comprises North Vancouver and West Vancouver, with most visitors arriving from downtown via the 12-minute SeaBus ferry trip from Waterfront Station. The Lonsdale Quay Public Market (p186) is steps from the dock and the waterfront has been reclaimed from its grungy shipyard past and now sports pleasant shoreline boardwalks. Nearby Lonsdale Ave is North Van's main thoroughfare and is hopping with restaurants and shops.

Hop bus 236 from Lonsdale Quay: it will take you to the region's two main attractions. First is the Capilano Suspension Bridge Park (about 20 minutes from Lonsdale Quay) and next is Grouse Mountain (10 minutes further along). Grouse is the end of the line, so don't worry about getting off at the right stop. You can do both these attractions in one day: best to start with Capilano (before it gets too crowded) then continue on to Grouse (where you'll want to take more time). Alternatively, both Grouse and Capilano can be accessed by free summer shuttle buses from downtown Vancouver.

To explore West Vancouver, catch bus 250 from downtown Vancouver. It'll take you through Stanley Park, over the Lions Gate Bridge and then along Marine Dr, which is the heart of West Van. A little further out than North Van, most parks and attractions here are also readily accessible via transit.

# Local Life

➡ **Alternative suspension bridge** Capilano is a huge draw for many visitors but locals prefer the smaller, less-crowded 'other bridge' at Lynn Canyon Park (p182). It's also free.

➡ **Cut-price Grouse** If you're fit you can access the attractions atop Grouse Mountain without having to pay the whole pricey gondola fee. The catch? You'll have to do it by hiking the steep, sweat-triggering Grouse Grind (p183). But you'll still have to pay the $10 gondola fee to get back down.

➡ **Farmers market** Not many North Vancouverites do their regular shopping at Lonsdale Quay Public Market (p186), but they often drop by for the May-to-October farmers market that runs on Saturdays.

# Getting There & Away

➡ **SeaBus** From downtown's Waterfront Station, it takes just 12 minutes to reach Lonsdale Quay on the transit network's ferry service.

➡ **Bus** Lonsdale Quay has a bus terminal where services depart for North and West Vancouver. Bus 236 is key: it runs to both Capilano and Grouse Mountain.

# ⊙ SIGHTS

The North Shore is home to some of Metro Vancouver's favorite outdoor attractions. But North Van, in particular, is also starting to buzz as an urban visitor lure, especially at the shoreline end of Lonsdale Ave. Save some time to wander along the waterfront here, where gritty shipyard spaces are being reclaimed for market halls and public art. This is also the home of the striking new Polygon Gallery, which was under construction during our visit; see www.presentationhousegallery.org for updates.

## ⊙ North Vancouver

### GROUSE MOUNTAIN                    OUTDOORS

Map p284 (☑604-980-9311; www.grouse mountain.com; 6400 Nancy Greene Way, North Vancouver; Skyride adult/child $44/15; ⊙9am-10pm; ℗ 🚼; 🚌236) The self-proclaimed 'Peak of Vancouver,' this mountain-top playground offers smashing views of downtown, glittering in the water below. In summer, Skyride gondola tickets include access to lumberjack shows, alpine hiking, bird-of-prey displays and a grizzly-bear refuge. Pay extra for zip-lining and Eye of the Wind, a 20-story, elevator-accessed turbine tower with a panoramic viewing pod that will have your camera itching for action.

There are also restaurants up here if you fancy dining: it's an ideal sunset-viewing spot. You can reduce the gondola fee by hiking the ultra-steep Grouse Grind (p183) up the side of the mountain – it's one-way only and it costs $10 to get back down on the Skyride. Grouse lures visitors from downtown from May to September by offering a free shuttle from Canada Place. And in winter, it's all about skiing and snowboarding as Grouse become the locals' fave powder-bound playground.

### CAPILANO SUSPENSION
### BRIDGE PARK                          PARK

Map p284 (☑604-985-7474; www.capbridge.com; 3735 Capilano Rd, North Vancouver; adult/child $40/12, reduced off-season; ⊙8:30am-8pm Jun-Aug, reduced hours off-season; ℗ 🛜 🚼; 🚌236) As you walk gingerly onto one of the world's longest (140m) and highest (70m) suspension bridges, swaying gently over the roiling Capilano Canyon, remember that its thick steel cables are embedded in concrete.

That should steady your feet – unless there are teenagers stamping across. Added park attractions include a glass-bottomed cliff-side walkway and an elevated canopy trail through the trees.

This is a hugely popular attraction (hence the summer tour buses); try to arrive early during peak months so you can check out the historic exhibits, totem poles and tree-shaded nature trails on the other side of the bridge in relative calm. On your way out, peruse what must be the city's largest souvenir shop for First Nations artworks, 'moose dropping' choccies and a full range of T-shirts and ball caps. From May to September Capilano makes it very easy for you to get here from downtown by running a free shuttle from Canada Place and area hotels. There are also often discounts on summer admission after 5pm. Check the website for full details.

### MAPLEWOOD FARM                      FARM

Map p284 (☑604-929-5610; www.maplewood farm.bc.ca; 405 Seymour River Pl, North Vancouver; adult/child $7.80/4.70; ⊙10am-4pm Apr-Oct, closed Mon Nov-Mar; 🚼; 🚌239 from Lonsdale Quay, then C15) This popular farmyard attraction includes plenty of hands-on displays plus a collection of more than 200 birds and domestic animals. Your wide-eyed kids can pet some critters, watch the milking demonstration and feed some squawking, ever-hungry ducks and chickens. The highlight is the daily (3:30pm) round-up, when hungry critters and starving hairballs alike streak back into their barn for dinner.

The top 'extra,' though, is the behind-the-scenes tour where your sprogs can learn what it's like to be farmer, from grooming to egg collecting and getting the feed ready. Book ahead: these hour-long tours are popular.

### MAPLEWOOD FLATS
### CONSERVATION AREA          NATURE RESERVE

Map p284 (☑604-903-4471; 2645 Dollarton Hwy, North Vancouver; ℗) Managed by the Wild Bird Trust of BC, this delightful nature escape is surprisingly accessible from Vancouver yet it feels like a million miles from the city. Its tangle of trees, winding paths and protected wetland beach lure woodpeckers, ospreys and bald eagles – and there are free guided nature tours the second Saturday of every month (10am).

It's a nature-lovers dream: on our visit a deer and fawn wondered languidly across the pathway.

## MT SEYMOUR PROVINCIAL PARK
OUTDOORS

Map p284 (www.bcparks.ca; 1700 Mt Seymour Rd, North Vancouver; ⊙dawn-dusk) A popular, rustic retreat from the downtown clamor, this giant, tree-lined park is suffused with summertime hiking trails that suit walkers of most abilities (the easiest path is the 2km Goldie Lake Trail). Many trails wind past lakes and centuries-old Douglas firs. This is also one of the city's main winter playgrounds.

The park is a great spot for mountain biking and has many dedicated trails. It's around 30 minutes from downtown Vancouver by car; drivers can take Hwy 1 to the Mt Seymour Pkwy (near the Second Narrows Bridge) and follow it east to Mt Seymour Rd.

## LYNN CANYON PARK
PARK

Map p284 (www.lynncanyon.ca; Park Rd, North Vancouver; ⊙7am-9pm; ♠; 🚌229) Amid a dense bristling of ancient trees, the main feature of this popular park is its **suspension bridge**, a free alternative to Capilano. Not quite as big as its tourist-magnet rival, it nevertheless provokes the same jelly-legged reaction as you sway over the river that runs 50m below – and it's always far less crowded. Hiking trails, swimming areas and picnic spots will keep you busy here as well.

The park's **Ecology Centre** (Map p284; www.lynncanyonecologycentre.ca; 3663 Park Rd, North Vancouver; suggested donation $2; ⊙10am-5pm Jun-Sep, 10am-5pm Mon-Fri & noon-4pm Sat & Sun Oct-May; ♠; 🚌227) ✎ houses interesting displays, including dioramas and video presentations, on the area's rich biodiversity. It stages talks and events for kids, especially in summer.

# ◉ West Vancouver

## LIGHTHOUSE PARK
PARK

Map p284 (www.lighthousepark.ca; cnr Beacon Lane & Marine Dr, West Vancouver; ⊙dawn-dusk; Ⓟ; 🚌250) Some of the region's oldest trees live within this accessible 75-hectare park, including a rare stand of original coastal forest and plenty of those gnarly, copper-trunked arbutus trees. About 13km of hiking trails crisscross the area, including a recommended trek that leads to the rocky perch of Point Atkinson Lighthouse, ideal for capturing shimmering, camera-worthy views over Burrard Inlet.

If you're driving from downtown, turn left on Marine Dr after crossing the Lions Gate Bridge to reach the park.

## WEST VANCOUVER SEAWALL
WATERFRONT

Map p284 (🚌250) Take bus 250 from downtown Vancouver and hop off on Marine Dr at the intersection with 24th St. Peruse the stores and coffee shops in Dundarave Village, then stroll downhill to the waterfront. Take in the panoramic coastline from Dundarave Pier, then weave eastwards along the shore-hugging Centennial Seawalk route, West Van's favorite promenade. You'll pass joggers, herons and public artworks.

After 2km, the trail comes to a halt. From here, head back up to the Marine Dr shops or weave over to Ambleside Park, where you'll find a dramatic First Nations carved welcome figure facing the water.

## FERRY BUILDING ART GALLERY
GALLERY

Map p284 (✆604-925-7290; www.ferrybuildinggallery.com; 1414 Argyle Ave, West Vancouver; ⊙11am-5pm Tue-Sun; 🚌255) FREE Housed in a cute wooden heritage building, which was once a ferry terminal when transit boats plied the waters between West Van and Vancouver, this popular waterfront community gallery is well worth a look if you're in the Ambleside Park vicinity. Shows change once or twice a month and there's a strong commitment to showcasing local artists.

Time your visit well and you can drop in for an opening reception and meet the artists themselves.

## WHYTECLIFF PARK
PARK

Map p284 (7100-block Marine Dr, West Vancouver; ⊙dawn-dusk; 🚌257) Just west of Horseshoe Bay, this is an exceptional little waterfront green space. Trails lead to vistas and a gazebo, from where you can watch the Burrard Inlet boat traffic. The rocky beach is a great place to scamper over the large rocks protruding from the beach. It's also one of the region's favorite dive spots for scuba fans. But humans are not the only divers who like this place: the park is a popular area for lounging seals.

## MOTHER NATURE'S STAIRMASTER

If you're finding your vacation a little too relaxing, head over to North Vancouver and join the perspiring throng snaking – almost vertically – up the **Grouse Grind** (www.grousemountain.com; 📖236) trail. The entrance is near the parking lot, across the street from where slightly more sane Grouse Mountain visitors pile into the Skyride gondola and trundle up to the summit without breaking a sweat.

Around 3km in total, this steep, rock-studded forest trek will likely have your joints screaming for mercy within 15 minutes as you focus on the feet of the person in front of you. Most people take around an hour to reach the top, where they collapse like fish gasping on the rocks.

Things to keep in mind if you're planning to join the 110,000 who hike the Grind every year: take a bottle of water, dress in thin layers so you can strip down, and bring $10 with you: the trail is one-way, so when you reach the summit you have to take the Skyride back down – your consolation is that you get to enjoy the summit's many attractions for free in exchange for your exploding calf muscles.

### HORSESHOE BAY                    VILLAGE

Map p284 (📖257) This small coastal community marks the end of West Vancouver and the starting point for trips to Whistler, via the Sea to Sky Hwy (Hwy 99). It's a pretty village with views across the bay and up glassy-watered Howe Sound. Cute places to eat and shop line waterfront Bay St, from where you can also take a whale-watching boat trek with Sewell's Sea Safari (p190).

This is also the home of the BC Ferries terminal for aquatic hops to Bowen Island, Vancouver Island and beyond.

## ✖ EATING

**The North Shore has plenty of dine-out options. You'll find a concentrated cluster of eateries radiating up Lonsdale Ave from the waterfront, with many more dotted around both North and West Van.**

### MEAT AT O'NEILL'S          SANDWICHES $

Map p284 (📞604-987-1115; www.meatatoneills. com; 144 Lonsdale Ave, North Vancouver; mains $4-9; ⏰11:30am-5pm Mon, 9am-5pm Tue-Thu, 9am-3pm & 6-10pm Fri & Sat; 🚢Lonsdale Quay SeaBus) A top-quality sandwich emporium fueling the local takeout crowd with satisfying all-day breakfast sandwiches and a mouthwatering array of slow-roasted meat sandwiches (the red-wine beef brisket is recommended). There's a handful of seats here if you need a pit-stop break, but your best bet is to keep on rolling down the hill to the waterfront for an alfresco lunch.

Friday and Saturday dinners here have an expanded menu that often features stews and chili. You'll also find a good selection of BC craft beers, usually including several from the North Shore.

### ARTISAN BAKE SHOPPE          BAKERY $

Map p284 (📞604-990-3530; www.artisanbake shoppe.ca; 108 E 2nd St, North Vancouver; mains $4-9; ⏰7am-5:30pm Mon-Sat; 📖230) The house-baked German-style breads here are about as far from factory-made products as possible. Be sure to pick up an ancient grains loaf (it'll keep you going all week) then indulge in some instant treats: the banana-pecan cookies and perfectly chewy pretzels. It's not just takeout; soups and sandwiches are also served at the tables in this yellow-hued bakery cafe.

If you still have room (or even if you don't), consider some eye-rollingly-good apple strudel for the road.

### FISHWORKS          SEAFOOD $$

Map p284 (📞778-330-3449; www.fishworks .ca; 91 Lonsdale Ave, North Vancouver; mains $16-32; ⏰11:30am-2:30pm Mon-Fri & 5pm-late daily; 🚢Lonsdale Quay Seabus) The patio is popular on balmy evenings but the loungey, intimate interior of this seafood-forward restaurant is an easy place to get comfortable the rest of the year. From fish and chips to fresh-shucked oysters, there's a wide range of casual and posher fishy offerings; but, if you're hungry for a feast, go for the shareable seafood platter of prawns, mussels, crabs et al.

There's a good range of by-the-glass BC wines. You can also bring your own bottle for a $25 corkage fee (there's a liquor

## NORTH SHORE'S BEST FEST

Late July is the time when everyone on the North Shore finds their party groove in one of Metro Vancouver's best community events. The weekend-long **Caribbean Days Festival** (www.caribbeandays.ca) in the city's Waterfront Park – not far from the SeaBus dock – includes a street parade; live music and dance; a food fair of epic, spicy proportions; and a popular art and clothing market. Luring thousands to the area, it never fails to put smiles on faces.

store a five-minute walk away at 132 W Esplanade Ave).

### BURGOO BISTRO                    WEST COAST $$

Map p284 (www.burgoo.ca; 3 Lonsdale Ave; mains $15-20; ☺11am-10pm Sun-Wed, to 11pm Thu-Sat; ⛴SeaBus Lonsdale Quay) With the feel of a cozy rustic cabin – complete with large stone fireplace – Burgoo's menu of elevated international comfort dishes warms up North Van's winter nights: the sausage-and-shrimp-packed jambalaya or belly-rubbing butter chicken would thaw a glacier from 50 paces. There's also a wide array of housemade soups and salads. Drinks-wise, try a boozy Spanish coffee to keep yourself merry.

You're handily close to the SeaBus terminal if you need to make it back to downtown Vancouver in a hurry.

### RAGLAN'S                   BURGERS, BREAKFAST $$

Map p284 (☑604-988-8203; www.raglans.ca; 15 Lonsdale Ave, North Vancouver; mains $12-19; ☺10am-midnight Sun-Thu, to 1am Fri & Sat; ⛴SeaBus from Waterfront Station) Friendly and funky (hence the eye-popping surfer and tiki decor), this is the most laid-back of the side-by-side, patio-fronted restaurants calling your name at the foot of Lonsdale. Expect large burgers and bulging burritos that would satisfy a biblical plague of locusts, but if it's breakfast time aim for the 'ragga muffins,' an eggs-Benedict-style dish served in several hangover-busting varieties.

Arguably the best time to come is at the end of the day, when you can slide onto the patio and work your way down a cocktail menu that feels as if it's from a beach bar in Maui. There are also plenty of vegetarian food options here.

### PALKI RESTAURANT                          INDIAN $$

Map p284 (☑604-986-7555; www.palkirestaurant.com; 116 E 15th Street; mains $13-18; ☺11:30am-2:30pm & 4:30-10pm; ☑) Don't be discouraged by the drab, gray-brick exterior of this popular Indian restaurant: inside, it's cozy and welcoming with a swish contemporary look. Budget-watchers should check out the daily all-you-can-eat buffet ($12.45), but it's worth coming back in the evening for a more considered approach. Start with a mixed platter of samosas and pakoras then graduate to the excellent lamb rogan josh.

It's a good idea to share a few dishes here – note that there's a Northern Indian feel to much of the menu.

### FEAST                                   CANADIAN

(☑604-922-1155; www.feastdining.ca; 2423 Marine Dr, West Vancouver; ☺11:30am-10pm Mon-Fri, 10am-10pm Sat & Sun; ☐250) A local favorite, this rustic-chic restaurant covers all the elevated comfort-food bases, starting with weekend brunch and extending to a dinner selection that runs from butter chicken to a delicious sourdough-crusted snapper. Service is warm and friendly and you'll often see groups of friends hanging out here over cocktails.

### SALMON HOUSE
### ON THE HILL                          SEAFOOD $$$

Map p284 (☑604-926-3212; www.salmonhouse.com; 2229 Folkestone Way; mains $28-40; ☺11am-2:30pm Sat & Sun, 5-9:30pm Sun-Thu, 6-10pm Fri & Sat ☐256) West Vancouver's old-school destination restaurant, this landmark has been luring locals for special-occasion dinners for years. But Salmon House doesn't rest on its laurels – if laurels can be defined as a gable-roofed wooden interior and floor-to-ceiling windows with sunset cliff-top city views. Instead, you'll find a menu of delectable seasonal BC seafood with serious gourmet credentials.

There are also top-notch duck and lamb dishes for those nonaquatic scoffers. And if you just want to check it out without the top-end dinner price, drop by for weekend brunch (crab eggs Benedict recommended).

## OBSERVATORY WEST COAST $$$

Map p284 (☑604-998-5045; www.observatoryrestaurant.ca; 6400 Nancy Greene Way, Grouse Mountain; mains $25-40; ☺5-10pm; 🚌236) Crowning Grouse Mountain, the fine-dining Observatory serves its garlic panisse and lamb sirloins alongside breathtaking views over Stanley Park and Vancouver's twinkling towers far below. A perfect romantic dinner venue – you wouldn't be the first to propose here – it has an excellent wine list if you suddenly need to console yourself. Reserve in advance and you'll also get free Skyride passes.

The atmosphere is more laid-back at the adjacent, pub-like **Altitudes Bistro**, which offers comfort grub of the burgers and fish and chips variety in a casual ski-lodge ambiance.

# DRINKING & NIGHTLIFE

**The North Shore isn't a great place for a destination night out, but there are some standouts worth pulling over for (with a designated driver, of course).**

## BUDDHA-FULL JUICE BAR

Map p284 (☑604-973-0231; www.buddha-full.ca; 106 W 1st St, North Vancouver; ☺8am-8pm; 🚌; 🚢SeaBus Lonsdale Quay) Completely revamped in recent years from its grungier beginnings, North Van's favorite juice bar is an inviting one-stop-shop for veggie and eco-types. Books, bath products and vegetarian wraps line the shelves flanking the communal tables, but the luscious smoothies are the reason most regulars keep coming back. Slurp a Peaceful Warrior or Buddha-buzz to feel at one with the world again.

This is a good place to fuel up for the mountain-bike trails lining the area.

## RAVEN PUB

Map p284 (☑604-929-3834; www.theravenpub.com; 1052 Deep Cove Rd, North Vancouver; ☺11am-11pm Sun-Tue, to midnight Wed-Sat; 🚌212) This welcoming Deep Cove joint effortlessly mixes barflies and 20-somethings within an inviting interior illuminated by red-glass candle holders. But it's not just about looks. The Raven serves great pizzas – prosciutto and sun-dried tomato recommended – and has a beer list with some good BC quaffs by Phillips and Driftwood, among others.

The beer selection is good enough to make this your local wherever you might live.

## QUEEN'S CROSS PUB

Map p284 (☑604-980-7715; www.queenscross.com; 2989 Lonsdale Ave, North Vancouver; ☺11am-midnight Sun-Thu, to 1am Fri & Sat; 🚌; 🚌230 from Lonsdale Quay) It's a hike from the SeaBus up Lonsdale Ave for this trad-style, gable-roofed neighborhood pub, but just think how easy it will be to roll back downhill afterwards (stop when you hit the water). Formerly the kind of place where you had the choice of Bud or Molson, it now has a tasty commitment to craft brews, many from across the region.

Food-wise, you'll find all the usual pub-grub classics. It's a good place to catch a hockey game with the locals: you'll find out just how angry those mild-mannered Canadians can get.

# SHOPPING

**Outdoor stores are a specialty here but it's not all about action. There are also plenty of food and artisan emporiums to tempt your wallet, with a browsable cluster of shops at the waterfront end of Lonsdale Ave, also home to a great summer night market. At the time of research, North Van's new Hawkers Wharf was also under construction, promising food and dining vendors in a refurbished freight-container building; see updates at www.hawkerswharf.com.**

## SHIPYARDS NIGHT MARKET MARKET

Map p284 (www.northshoregreenmarket.com; Shipbuilders Sq, North Vancouver; ☺5-10pm Fri May-Sep; 🚌SeaBus from Waterfront Station) Muscling in on the region's summertime night-market scene, North Van's is a few steps east of Lonsdale Quay. It's a fun way to spend a balmy Friday evening, with the ocean lapping nearby. Scoff grub from the many food trucks, tap your toes to live bands on the little stage and dive into the beer garden for brews from North Shore producers.

This is an easy spot to end your North Shore day out; the SeaBus back to the city is a short stroll away. If you miss the market, it also runs a permanent store filled with the work of local artisans a few steps away at 7a Lonsdale Ave.

### MOUNTAIN EQUIPMENT CO-OP
SPORTS & OUTDOORS

Map p284 (☑604-990-4417; www.mec.ca; 212 Brooksbank Ave, North Vancouver; ☺10am-9pm Mon-Fri, 9am-6pm Sat, 10am-6pm Sun, reduced hours winter; ☐211) Smaller than its Vancouver parent, this MEC branch has a friendlier, more neighborly feel. Almost everyone here – staff and customers – seems to know each other and is a member of the North Shore outdoor community. It's the perfect place to stock up on gear for your nature-loving adventures; you'll find everything from soft hiking shoes to great waterproof jackets.

You'll need to be a member to purchase from this nonprofit co-op: it's easy to arrange and costs just $5 (for life).

### UNDER THE UMBRELLA
ARTS & CRAFTS

Map p284 (☑604-971-6700; www.artisansum brella.com; 67 Lonsdale Ave, North Vancouver; ☺11am-6pm Mon-Sat, to 4pm Sun; ☐Lonsdale Quay Seabus) From stationery to kid clothes and from jewelry to cat-printed shoulder-bags, this small but highly eclectic shop is teeming with the handmade creative efforts of dozens of local artisans. Take your time to browse properly and chat to the friendly staffers who also have plenty of suggestions for others arts and crafty happenings around the region.

This is perfect place to find a souvenir that says more about the region than an orca-shaped bottle of maple syrup (although that would be cool, too).

### LONSDALE QUAY PUBLIC MARKET
MARKET

Map p284 (☑604-985-6261; www.lonsdale quay.com; 123 Carrie Cates Ct, North Vancouver; ☺9am-7pm; ☐SeaBus Lonsdale Quay) As well as being a transportation hub – the SeaBus from downtown docks here and you can hit transit buses to Capilano and Grouse – there's a popular indoor market here. Look for BC wines, slabs of fudge and glassy-eyed fish on the main floor, plus trinkets and clothing one floor up. There's also a microbrewery lounge plus a Saturday farmers market outside in summer.

If it's time to eat, the market has a food court and several other dining options. The pizza, fish and chips and housemade soup stands are all good but **Sharkey's** is the way to go; $8.95 for a heaping plate of meat and veggies that easily feeds two. The Quay is an easy jaunt from downtown, with many visitors scooping up an ice cream and lingering over the boardwalk views of Vancouver.

### PARK ROYAL
MALL

Map p284 (☑604-922-3211; www.shopparkroy al.com; Marine Dr, West Vancouver; ☺10am-7pm Mon & Tue, 10am-9pm Wed-Fri, 9:30am-6pm Sat, 11am- 6pm Sun; ☐250) It's the region's oldest mall but Park Royal does a good job of keeping up with the competition. With 280 stores (including all the usual suspects), its ever-expanding Village area emulates an outdoor UK shopping high street with strollable big stores and restaurants. The indoor area is a good option when the region's 'Wet Coast' nickname is demonstrated in full force.

Park Royal is easy to access on transit from downtown Vancouver; buses trundle over the picturesque Lions Gate Bridge and stop just outside. Fashion-wise, the new **Simons** store is worth a look; it's the only BC branch of the highly popular Quebec clothing and accessories store.

## 🏃 SPORTS & ACTIVITIES

### GROUSE MOUNTAIN
SNOW SPORTS

Map p284 (☑604-980-9311; www.grouse mountain.com; 6400 Nancy Greene Way, North Vancouver; winter adult/child $58/25; ☺9am-10pm mid-Nov–mid-Apr; ☐236) Vancouver's favorite winter hangout, family-friendly Grouse offers 26 ski and snowboard runs (including 14 night runs). There are classes and lessons available for beginners and beyond, and the area's forested snowshoe trails are magical. There are also a couple of dining options if you just want to relax and watch the snow with hot chocolate in hand.

If you're here in December, this is a great place to soak up some Christmas spirit; if you're looking for Santa in Vancouver, this is where you'll find him, along with a reindeer or two.

### CYPRESS MOUNTAIN
SNOW SPORTS

Map p284 (☑604-926-5612; www.cypressmoun tain.com; Cypress Bowl Rd, West Vancouver; lift ticket adult/youth/child $71/57/38; ☺9am-10pm

## SURFING THE SEABUS

Sashaying between downtown Vancouver's Waterfront Station and the North Shore's Lonsdale Quay, the 400-seat SeaBus (www.translink.ca) vessels easily divide the locals from the tourists. Vancouverites barely raise a glance when the boats arrive in their little docks to pick up passengers for the 12-minute voyage across Burrard Inlet. In contrast, wide-eyed visitors excitedly crowd the automatic doors as if they're about to climb onto a theme-park ride.

Once on board, it's a similar story: locals shuffle to the back and open their newspapers, while out-of-towners glue themselves to the front seats for a panoramic view of the glittering crossing, with the looming North Shore mountains growing in stature ahead of them as the voyage gets under way.

The boxy, low-slung catamarans first hit the waves in 1977. But they weren't the first boats to take passengers over the briny. The first regular private ferry covering this route launched in 1900. It was taken over and run as a public service by the City of North Vancouver a few years later, when the route's two vessels were imaginatively renamed *North Vancouver Ferry 1* and *North Vancouver Ferry 2*. No prizes for guessing what the third ferry was named when it was added in 1936. The opening of the Lions Gate Bridge, linking the two shores by road, a couple of years later slowly pulled the rug from under the ferry service, and the last sailing took place in 1958. It would be almost 20 years before a new public service was restored to the route, when *MV Burrard Beaver* and *MV Burrard Otter* hit the water.

mid-Dec–Mar, 9am-4pm, mid-Nov–mid-Dec & Apr) Around 8km north of West Van via Hwy 99, Cypress Provincial Park transforms into Cypress Mountain resort in winter, attracting well-insulated locals with its 53 runs, 11km of snowshoe trails, cross-country ski access and a family-friendly six-chute snow-tubing course. Upgraded for the 2010 Winter Olympics, the resort's newer facilities include an expanded lodge and upgrades to several runs.

Lift tickets include 20% discount off all subsequent visits. Popular with night-skiers, there's a large floodlit area here. When you're done, head to the mountain's Crazy Raven Bar & Grill for a fireplace-warmed pint of beer. And if you don't want to drive here, consider the seasonal **Cypress Coach Lines shuttle** (www.cypresscoachlines.com; return $23), which picks up in Vancouver and beyond.

**MT SEYMOUR** SNOW SPORTS

Map p284 (☑604-986-2261; www.mountsey mour.com; 1700 Mt Seymour Rd, North Vancouver; adult/youth aged 13-18/child $51/44/24; ☉9:30am-10pm Mon-Fri, 8:30am-10pm Sat & Sun Dec-Apr) This branch of the region's three main Vancouver-accessible winter playgrounds offers ski and snowboarding areas, plus toboggan and tubing courses. The snowshoe trails and tours are also popular – check out the nighttime snowshoeing and chocolate fondue tour ($57). This is usually

the least crowded snowy destination in the region, so you're likely to meet locals here.

Seymour runs a handy winter-season shuttle bus from Lonsdale Quay ($8 each way).

**DEEP COVE KAYAK CENTRE** KAYAKING

Map p284 (☑604-929-2268; www.deepcov ekayak.com; 2156 Banbury Rd, North Vancouver; kayaks per 2hr/day $39/99; ☉9am-dusk Jun-Sep, reduced hours off-season; ☒212) Enjoying Deep Cove's sheltered waters, this is an ideal – and idyllic – spot for first-timers to try their hand at paddling. Lessons and tours are available (the $65 Full Moon Evening Tour is recommended), and stand-up paddleboarding (SUP) has also been added to the mix – try it out with a two-hour introductory class ($60).

For those with a little more experience, the center also sponsors Tuesday evening race nights, as well as Wednesday night women-only social kayaking if you'd like some company out on the water.

**ENDLESS BIKING** MOUNTAIN BIKING

Map p284 (☑604-985-2519; www.endless biking.com; 1401 Hunter St, North Vancouver; ☉10am-6pm Mon-Fri, 9am-6pm Sat & Sun) The first stop for anyone looking to access North Van's brilliant bike scene. The friendly folks here can take you on a guided tour or just rent you a bike and point you in the right direction. Lessons are also available

J. A. KRAULIS/GETTY IMAGES ©

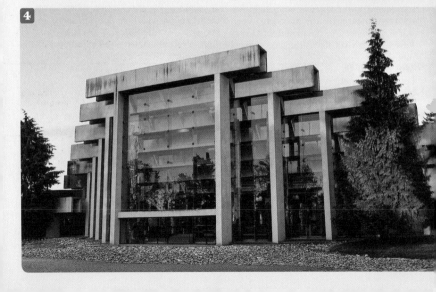

ZENNIE/GETTY IMAGES ©

### 1. Stanley Park (p52)
This 400-hectare woodland is studded with nature trails, beaches and a plethora of picnic spots – look out for scavenging raccoons.

### 2. Grouse Grind (p183)
Known as Mother Nature's Stairmaster, the Grouse Grind is a 3km verticle hiking trail that will challenge even the fittest of hikers.

### 3. English Bay (p61)
One of Canada's best urban beaches, this bay marks the start of Stanley Park and showcases Vancouver's most popular public artworks: a series of oversized laughing figures.

### 4. Museum of Anthropology (p164)
This museum hosts the most important collections of Northwest Coast indigenous art and artifacts and is located on the University of British Columbia's (UBC) campus.

LONELY PLANET/GETTY IMAGES ©

if you're a newbie and you want to learn how to negotiate all those gnarly tree roots without wiping out.

Beginners should book ahead for the Scenic Tour (from $175) which includes bike, helmet and a trundle into the wilderness for mountain and waterfront views.

### EDGE CLIMBING CENTRE                   CLIMBING

Map p284 (☑604-984-9080; www.edgeclimbing.com; 1485 Welch St, North Vancouver; ☺1-11pm Mon-Fri, noon-9pm Sat & Sun; 🚻; 🚍240) This high-tech North Van facility has a large climbing gym with more than 1300 sq m of climbing surfaces for those who like hanging around for fun. There are plenty of courses, from introductory level to advanced classes where you can learn all about diagonalling and heel-and-toe hooking. And if your kids are keen, there are age-appropriate sign-up classes for them as well.

If you enjoy this, you can drive straight from here to the Stawamus Chief in Squamish. A giant granite rock face looming over the town and studded with climbers

in summer, it's an hour's drive north via Hwy 99.

### SEWELL'S MARINA                          BOATING

Map p284 (☑604-921-3474; www.sewells marina.com; 6409 Bay St, Horseshoe Bay; adult/child $87/57; ☺Apr-Oct; 🚻; 🚍250) West Vancouver's Horseshoe Bay is the departure point for Sewell's two-hour marine-wildlife-watching boat tours. Orcas are always a highlight, but even if they're not around you'll almost certainly spot harbor seals lolling on the rocks and pretending to ignore you. Seabirds and bald eagles are also big stars of the show.

### CANADA WEST
### MOUNTAIN SCHOOL                          HIKING

Map p284 (☑604-878-7007; www.themountain school.com; 400 Brooksbank Ave, North Vancouver; ☺8am-4pm Tue-Fri) A long-established and well-respected institution, offering training and guided-excursion courses in Vancouver's spectacular outdoor backyard. Programs include climbing, mountaineering and winter camping.

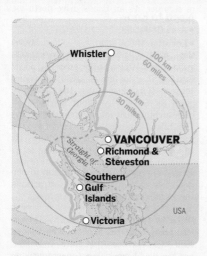

# Day Trips from Vancouver

### Victoria p192
A scenic floatplane hop or languid ferry ride from the mainland, British Columbia's historic waterfront capital fuses heritage charm, excellent attractions and a pub-tastic craft-beer scene.

### Whistler p198
The region's favorite outdoor wonderland, this gable-roofed, mountain-framed ski village offers year-round thrills including skiing, rafting and zip-lining.

### Richmond & Steveston p203
Hosting North America's best Asian dining and night night market scenes, Richmond also incorporates the pretty seaside village of Steveston, home to a couple of great historic attractions.

### Southern Gulf Islands p207
Arriving via scenic floatplane or ferry ride from the mainland, such as Salt Spring and Galiano feel as if they're million miles away from the city.

# Victoria

## Explore

With a wider-metro population approaching 380,000, this picture-postcard provincial capital was long-touted as North America's most English city. Thankfully, the tired theme-park version of old-fashioned England is no more. Fueled by an increasingly younger demographic, a quiet revolution has seen lame tourist pubs, eateries and stores transformed into the kind of brightly painted bohemian shops, coffee bars and innovative restaurants that would make any city proud. It's worth seeking out these enclaves on foot, but activity fans should also hop on their bikes: Victoria has more cycle routes than any other Canadian city. Once you've finished pedaling, there's BC's best museum, a park fringed by a windswept seafront and outdoor activities from kayaking to whale-watching.

## The Best...

→**Sight** Craigdarroch Castle (p192)
→**Place to Eat** Red Fish Blue Fish (p196)
→**Place to Drink** Drake (p197)

## Top Tip

For a meal with a difference, show your ID at security and nip inside the old-school, white-tablecloth politicians' dining room in the Parliament Buildings; it's open to everyone.

## Getting There & Away

→**Air** The delightfully scenic downtown-to-downtown floatplane services operated from Vancouver by Harbour Air (www.harbourair.com) take around 30 minutes.
→**Boat** BC Ferries (www.bcferries.com) services from mainland Tsawwassen arrive at Swartz Bay, a transit-bus ride from Victoria (bus 70).
→**Bus** BC Ferries Connector (www.bcconnector.com) buses take passengers from downtown Vancouver to downtown Victoria via the ferry.
→**Car** Drive to BC Ferries' Tsawwassen terminal, board the Victoria-bound ferry, then hit the island's Hwy 17 into Victoria (32km).

## Need to Know

→**Area Code** 250
→**Location** 112km southwest of Vancouver
→**Tourist Office** Tourism Victoria Visitor Centre (Map p194; ☑250-953-2033; www.tourismvictoria.com; 812 Wharf St; ☉8:30am-8:30pm mid-May–Aug, 9am-5pm Sep–mid-May; ☐70)

# ◉ SIGHTS

From the province's main museum to heritage houses and kid-friendly attractions, there's a full range of attractions here.

★**CRAIGDARROCH CASTLE**　　MUSEUM
Map p194 (☑250-592-5323; www.thecastle.ca; 1050 Joan Cres; adult/child $14/5; ☉9am-7pm mid-Jun–Aug, 10am-4:30pm Sep–mid-Jun; P; ☐14) One of Canada's finest stately home attractions, this elegant turreted mansion illuminates the lives of the city's Victorian-era super-rich. Lined with sumptuous wood-paneling and stained-glass windows, the rooms are teeming with period antiques, giving the impression the residents have just stepped away from their chairs. Climb the tower's 87 steps for distant views of the Olympic Mountains. Save time to read up on the often tragic story behind the family that lived here.

★**MINIATURE WORLD**　　MUSEUM
Map p194 (☑250-385-9731; www.miniatureworld.com; 649 Humboldt St; adult/child $15/10; ☉9am-9pm mid-May–mid-Sep, 9am-5pm mid-Sep–mid-May; ☻; ☐70) Tucked along the side of the Empress Hotel, this old-school hidden gem is a must-see, especially if you appreciate the craft of extremely intricate model-making. Lined with dozens of diminutive diorama scenes, divided into themes from Camelot to space and from fairyland to Olde England, it has plenty of push-button action, several trundling trains and the chance to see yourself on a miniature movie-theater screen. An immaculately maintained reminder of innocent yesteryear attractions.

**ROYAL BC MUSEUM**　　MUSEUM
Map p194 (☑250-356-7226; www.royalbcmuseum.bc.ca; 675 Belleville St; adult/child from $16/11; ☉10am-5pm daily, to 10pm Fri & Sat mid-May–Sep; ☻; ☐70) Start in the natural history gallery of BC's best museum and

say hello to the hulking woolly mammoth exhibit. From there, wander alongside evocative dioramas, then head up to the First Peoples exhibit with its fascinating mask gallery – complete with a ferret-faced white man. The museum's highlight, though, is the walk-through colonial street with its chatty Chinatown and detailed storefronts.

The museum hosts regular special exhibitions and also has a popular IMAX theater screening documentaries and Hollywood blockbusters.

### BEACON HILL PARK
PARK

Map p194 (www.beaconhillpark.ca; Douglas St; P 🚻; 🚌3) Fringed by crashing ocean, this waterfront park is ideal for feeling the breeze in your hair – check out the windswept trees along the cliff top. You'll also find a gigantic totem pole, Victorian cricket pitch and a marker for Mile 0 of Hwy 1, alongside a statue of the Canadian legend Terry Fox. If you're here with kids, consider the popular **children's farm** as well; see www.beaconhillchildrensfarm.ca.

### PARLIAMENT BUILDINGS
HISTORIC BUILDING

Map p194 (📞250-387-3046; www.leg.bc.ca; 501 Belleville St; ⊙tours 9am-5pm mid-May–Aug, 9am-5pm Mon-Fri Sep–mid-May; 🚌70) **FREE** This dramatically handsome confection of turrets, domes and stained glass is the province's working legislature and is also open to history-loving visitors. Peek behind the facade on a colorful (and free) 45-minute guided tour then stop for lunch at the 'secret' politicians' restaurant inside. Return in the evening when the elegant exterior is illuminated like a Christmas tree.

### ART GALLERY OF GREATER VICTORIA
GALLERY

Map p194 (📞250-384-4171; www.aggv.ca; 1040 Moss St; adult/child $13/2.50; ⊙10am-5pm Mon-Sat, noon-5pm Sun, closed Mon mid-Sep–mid-May; 🚌14) Head east of downtown on Fort St and follow the gallery street signs to one of Canada's best Emily Carr collections. Aside from Carr's swirling nature canvases, you'll find an immersive display of Asian art and changing temporary exhibitions. Check online for events, including lectures and frequent guided tours. Admission is by donation on the first Tuesday of every month.

### ROBERT BATEMAN CENTRE
GALLERY

Map p194 (📞250-940-3630; www.bateman centre.org; 470 Belleville St; adult/child $12.50/6; ⊙10am-5pm daily, to 9pm Fri & Sat Jun-Aug; 🚌70) Colonizing part of the Inner Harbour's landmark old Steamship Terminal building, this gallery showcases the photorealistic work of Canada's most popular nature painter, along with a revolving roster of works by other artists. Start with the five-minute intro movie, then check out the dozens of achingly beautiful paintings showing animals in their natural surroundings in BC and beyond.

### EMILY CARR HOUSE
MUSEUM

Map p194 (📞250-383-5843; www.emilycarr. com; 207 Government St; adult/child $6.75/4.50; ⊙11am-4pm Tue-Sat May-Sep; P; 🚌3) The birthplace of BC's best-known painter, this bright-yellow gingerbread-style house has plenty of period rooms, plus displays on the artist's life and work. There are changing displays of local contemporary works, but head to the Art Gallery of Greater Victoria if you want to see more of Carr's paintings. On your visit here, look out for the friendly house cats.

## 🍴 EATING & DRINKING

Victoria's dining scene has been radically upgraded in recent years. Pick up the free *Eat Magazine* to check out the latest foodie happenings. Looking for browsable

# Victoria

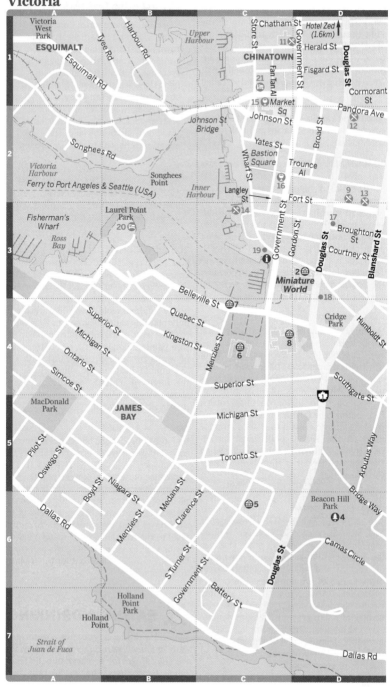

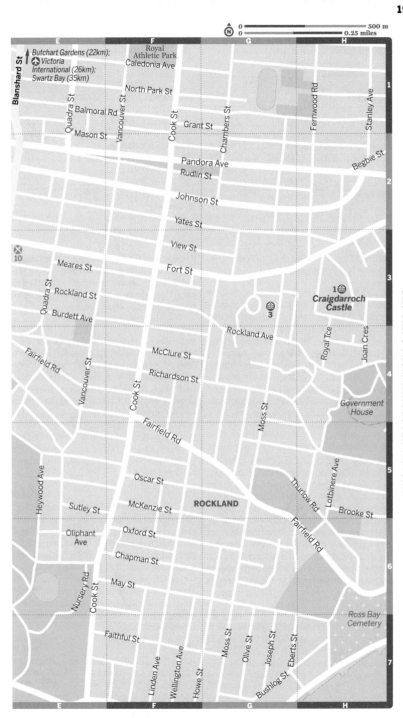

0 — 500 m
0 — 0.25 miles

Blanshard St

Butchart Gardens (22km);
Victoria
International (26km);
Swartz Bay (35km)

Royal
Athletic Park
Caledonia Ave

North Park St

Quadra St

Balmoral Rd

Vancouver St

Mason St

Cook St

Grant St

Chambers St

Fernwood Rd

Stanley Ave

Pandora Ave

Rudlin St

Begbie St

Johnson St

Yates St

View St

Meares St

Fort St

Quadra St

Rockland St

Burdett Ave

1 Craigdarroch
Castle

3

Fairfield Rd

Vancouver St

McClure St

Richardson St

Rockland Ave

Royal Tce

Joan Cres

Cook St

Fairfield Rd

Moss St

Government
House

Heywood Ave

Oscar St

Sutley St

McKenzie St

ROCKLAND

Thurlow Rd

Lotbiniere Ave

Brooke St

Fairfield Rd

Oliphant
Ave

Oxford St

Chapman St

Nursery Rd

Cook St

May St

Ross Bay
Cemetery

Faithful St

Linden Ave

Wellington Ave

Howe St

Moss St

Olive St

Joseph St

Bushlog St

Eberts St

10

# Victoria

options? Check out downtown's Fort St, the city's de facto dining row.

**CRUST BAKERY**      BAKERY $

Map p194 (☑250-978-2253; www.crustbakery.ca; 730 Fort St; baked goods $3-6; ⏱8am-5:30pm; ☐14) Arrive early for the best selection at Victoria's favorite new bakery. A fresh-baked egg, bacon and rosemary Danish should start you off nicely but be sure to fill your backpack with tartlets and top-selling cronuts, as well as chocolate and coconut bread-and-butter pudding; you may be able to trade them on the streets for ten times their face value.

**★RED FISH BLUE FISH**      SEAFOOD $

Map p194 (☑250-298-6877; www.redfish-bluefish.com; 1006 Wharf St; mains $6-16; ⏱11am-7pm; ☐70) ✐ On the waterfront boardwalk at the foot of Broughton St, this freight-container takeout shack serves fresh-made, finger-licking sustainable seafood. Highlights include jerk fish poutine, amazing chowder and tempura-battered oysters (you can also get traditional fish and chips, of course). Expanded new seating has added to the appeal but watch out for hovering gull mobsters as you try to eat.

**LA TAQUERIA**      MEXICAN $

Map p194 (☑778-265-6255; www.lataqueria.com; 766 Fort St; tacos up to $3 each; ⏱11am-8:30pm Sun-Thu, 11am-11pm Fri & Sat; ☑; ☐14) The huge, aquamarine-painted satellite of Vancouver's popular and authentic Mexican joint, this ultra-friendly spot specializes in offering a wide array of soft taco options

(choose four for $10.50, less for vegetarian), including different specials every day. Quesadillas are also available and you can wash everything down with margaritas, Mexican beer or mezcal – or all three.

**JAM CAFE**      BREAKFAST $

Map p194 (☑778-440-4489; www.jamcafevictoria.com; 542 Herald St; mains $9-16; ⏱8am-3pm; ☎☑) The locals won't tell you anything about this slightly off-the-beaten-path place. But that's not because they don't know about it; it's because they don't want you to increase the line-ups for Victoria's best breakfast. The range of Benedict varieties is popular, but we also recommend the amazing, and very naughty, chicken French toast. Arrive early or off-peak; there are no reservations.

**FISHHOOK**      SEAFOOD $$

Map p194 (☑250-477-0470; www.fishhookvic.com; 805 Fort St; mains $13-24; ⏱11am-9pm) ✐ Don't miss the smoky, coconutty chowder at this Indian- and French-influenced seafood gem but make sure you add a tartine open-faced sandwich: it's the house specialty. If you still have room (and you're reluctant to give up your place at the communal table), split a seafood biryani platter with your dining partner. Focused on local and sustainable fish supplies.

**JOHN'S PLACE**      DINER $$

Map p194 (☑250-389-0711; www.johnsplace.ca; 723 Pandora Ave; mains $9-17; ⏱7am-9pm Mon-Fri, 8am-4pm & 5-9pm Sat & Sun; ☎☑; ☐70) This friendly, wood-floored hangout is lined with quirky memorabilia, while its enormous menu is a cut above standard diner fare. They'll start you off with a basket of addictive housemade bread, but save room for heaping pasta dishes, piled-high salad mains or a pancake or Tex-Mex brunch. A near-perfect breakfast spot. Save time to study the signed celebrity photos on the walls.

### ★ DRAKE
BAR

Map p194 (☑250-590-9075; www.drakeeatery.com; 517 Pandora Ave; ⊙11:30am-midnight; ☎; ☐70) Victoria's best taphouse, this red-brick hangout has more than 30 amazing craft drafts, typically including revered BC producers Townsite, Driftwood and Four Winds. Arrive on a rainy afternoon and you'll find yourself still here several hours later. Food-wise, the smoked tuna club is a top-seller but the cheese and charcuterie plates are ideal for grazing. The washrooms are seriously tiny.

### GARRICK'S HEAD PUB
PUB

Map p194 (☑250-384-6835; www.garrickshead.com; 66 Bastion Sq; ⊙11am-late; ☐70) Great spot to dive into BC's brilliant craft-beer scene. Pull up a seat at the long bar and you'll be faced with 55-plus taps serving a comprehensive menu of beers from Driftwood, Phillips, Hoyne and beyond. There are always 10 rotating lines with intriguing tipples (ask for samples) plus a comfort-grub menu of burgers et al to line your boozy stomach.

## 🏃 SPORTS & ACTIVITIES

From outdoor action to local tours, there are many ways to explore the city and local region.

### PEDALER
CYCLING

Map p194 (☑778-265-7433; www.thepedaler.ca; 719 Douglas St; tours from $49, rentals from $10; ⊙9am-6pm, reduced hours off-season) Offering bike rentals and several guided two-wheeled tours around the city, including the Hoppy Hour Ride with its craft-beer-sampling focus.

### ARCHITECTURAL INSTITUTE OF BC
WALKING

Map p194 (☑604-683-8588 ext 325; www.aibc.ca; tours $10; ⊙10am & 1pm Tue-Sun Jul &

## VICTORIA'S VISIT-WORTHY FESTIVALS

Time your visit well and you can hang with the locals at one of these popular Victoria festivals.

➜ **Victoria Day Parade** (www.gvfs.ca) Marking Queen Victoria's birthday, this colorful street fiesta shimmies with floats, dancers and a toe-tapping complement of marching bands.

➜ **Rifflandia** (www.rifflandia.com) The city's coolest music festival sees indie bands playing at venues around the city.

➜ **Victoria International Buskers Festival** (www.victoriabuskers.com) Ten days of smile-triggering, street-performing action from local and international artists.

Aug) Five great-value history- and building-themed walking tours, covering angles from ecclesiastical to Canada's oldest Chinatown. All tours start at the downtown visitors center.

### PRINCE OF WHALES
WHALE-WATCHING

Map p194 (☑250-383-4884; www.princeofwhales.com; 812 Wharf St; adult/child from $120/95; ⊛) Long-established local operator offering several ways to check out the local whales and marine life from the water.

## 🛏 SLEEPING

From heritage B&Bs to cool boutiques and swanky high-end options, Victoria is stuffed with accommodation for all budgets. Off-season sees great deals. Tourism Victoria's **room reservation service** (☑250-953-2033, 800-663-3883; www.tourismvictoria.com/hotels) can show you what's available. Keep in mind that most downtown accommodation also charge for parking.

### HOTEL ZED
MOTEL $$

(☑250-388-4345; www.hotelzed.com; 3110 Douglas St; d from $175; ⚇☎❄☀; ☐70) Accommodation Austin Powers would love: this motel has been given a tongue-in-cheek retro makeover, complete with rainbow paintwork and free VW-van rides to downtown (a 10-minute walk away). The rooms are also fun: 1970s phones, bathroom comic books and bright-painted walls. Loaner bikes and free coffee are provided via the front desk and there's also a great diner if you're hungry.

**SWANS SUITE HOTEL** BOUTIQUE HOTEL **$$**

Map p194 (☑250-361-3310; www.swanshotel. com; 506 Pandora Ave; d from $145; 🛜📺; 🚌70) This former brick-built warehouse has been transformed into an art-lined boutique hotel. Most rooms are spacious loft suites where you climb upstairs to bed in a gabled nook, and each is decorated with a comfy combination of wood beams, rustic chic furniture and deep leather sofas. The full kitchens are handy but there's also a brewpub downstairs for liquid sustenance.

**INN AT LAUREL POINT** HOTEL **$$$**

Map p194 (☑250-386-8721; www.laurelpoint. com; 680 Montreal St; d from $260; 🌸@🛜♨️🏊; 🚌70) On the Inner Harbour a short seaside stroll from the downtown action, this friendly, art-lined and comfortable hotel is all about the views across the waterfront. Spacious rooms come with private balconies for drinking in the mesmerizing sunsets. Still owned by a local family, it has a resortlike level of calm relaxation. In-room spa treatments and bike rentals are also available.

# Whistler

## Explore

Named for the furry marmots that populate the area and whistle like deflating balloons, this gabled alpine village and 2010 Olympics venue is one of the world's most popular ski resorts. Nestled in the formidable shadow of the Whistler and Blackcomb Mountains, the village has a frosted Christmas-card look in winter. But summer visitors now outnumber their ski-season equivalents, with many lured by the area's scenic hiking, biking and thrill-popping outdoor adventures. It's surprisingly easy to get lost walking around the labyrinthine little village but you're unlikely to find yourself too far from your destination once you turn around the next corner.

### The Best...
→**Sight** Audain Art Museum (p198)
→**Place to Eat** Purebread (p200)
→**Place to Drink** Garibaldi Lift Company (p202)

### Top Tip
You can beat the crowds with an early morning (upload between 7:15am and 8am) Fresh Tracks ticket ($20), available in advance from Whistler Village Gondola Guest Relations.

### Getting There & Away
→**Bus** Services from Vancouver take two to three hours. Catch the Greyhound (www. greyhound.ca; $26), Pacific Coach Lines (www.pacificcoach.com; $55) or winter-only Snowbus (https://snowbus.com; $38).
→**Car** Take W Georgia St through Stanley Park and over the Lions Gate Bridge then follow the signs to Hwy 99 north. You'll be in Whistler in around 90 minutes.

### Need to Know
→**Area Code** 250
→**Location** 122km north of Vancouver
→**Tourist Office Whistler Visitors Centre** (Map p200; ☑604-935-3357; www.whistler.com; 4230 Gateway Dr; ☺8am-8pm Sun-Wed, 8am-10pm Thu-Sat Jun-Aug, reduced hours off-peak)

## ◉ SIGHTS

The recent opening of a dramatic new art museum isn't the only attraction worth checking out in Whistler.

★**AUDAIN ART MUSEUM** GALLERY

Map p200 (☑604-962-0413; www.audain artmuseum.com; 4350 Blackcomb Way; adult/child $18/free; ☺10am-5pm Sat-Mon & Wed, 10am-9pm Thu & Fri) BC's finest new art museum is housed in a dramatic angular building that's a landmark in itself. But inside is even better. The rooms display a jaw-dropping array of historic First Nations carvings followed by iconic paintings of the region by leading artists, from Emily Carr to EJ Hughes. There's also a strong commitment to contemporary work, with sparkling photoconceptualist images by

## SQUAMISH & AROUND

Midway between Vancouver and Whistler on Hwy 99, Squamish enjoys an incredible natural setting at the fingertips of Howe Sound. Once little more than a rough-and-ready logging town, its had a recent makeover driven by Vancouverites seeking better-priced housing, as well as development of its own outdoor activities and attractions scenes.

The biggest new attraction in the region, the **Sea to Sky Gondola** (604-892-2551; www.seatoskygondola.com; 36800 Hwy 99, Squamish; adult/child $40/14; 10am-6pm daily May-Oct, to 8pm Fri & Sat May-Sep, reduced hours in winter) takes visitors up to a lofty mountaintop promontory overlooking the shimmering, peak-framed waters of the Sound; it's a signature BC vista. If you want to see more, book a breathtaking flight tour with **Sea to Sky Air** (604-898-1975; www.seatoskyair.ca; Squamish Airport, Squamish; from $109; 9am-6pm Apr-Oct, 9am-5pm Thu-Sun & Tue Nov-Mar) at the region's tiny airport.

A few minutes' drive away, the **Britannia Mine Museum** (604-896-2260; www.britanniaminemuseum.ca; Hwy 99, Britannia Beach; adult/child $29/18.50; 9am-5pm; ) is also a popular stop. Once the British Empire's largest copper mine, it's been restored and preserved as a unique visitor attraction. The underground train tour into the pitch-black mine tunnels is a highlight here but there are also plenty of kid-friendly exhibits – including gold panning – plus a large, artsy gift shop.

Train fans should also stop just past Squamish at the excellent **West Coast Railway Heritage Park** (604-898-9336; www.wcra.org; 39645 Government Rd, Squamish; adult/child $18/13; 10am-5pm; ). This large, mostly alfresco museum is the final resting place of the legendary Royal Hudson steam engine. It also houses around 100 other historic rail cars, including working engines and the original SkyTrain car from Vancouver. If you're traveling with kids, check ahead for seasonal activities and train rides.

Activity nuts also have plenty of ways to stretch their muscles around Squamish. For mountain bikers, there are dozens of accessible forested trails to hurtle along, including the **Cheekeye Fan** trail and the **Diamond Head/Power Smart** area.

Attracting hardy climbers, the highlight of **Stawamus Chief Provincial Park** (www.bcparks.ca) is 'The Chief,' a towering monolithic rock face. You don't have to be geared up to experience its breathtaking summit vistas: there are hiking routes up the back for anyone with the energy to give it a go. Consider **Squamish Rock Guides** (604-892-7816; www.squamishrockguides.com; guided rock climbs half-day/day from $85/135) for climbing assistance or lessons.

If you're keen to stay over in Squamish, sample the quality rustic approach offered by the comfortable **Howe Sound Inn** (604-892-2603; www.howesoundinn.com; 37801 Cleveland Ave, Squamish; d $129; ). Rooms are warm and inviting and its downstairs brewpub serves up some of the best beers in the region – yam fries and Devil's Elbow IPA recommended. And if you're really keen on local tipples, hang out with the friendly folks at **Gillespie's Fine Spirits** (604-390-1122; www.gillespiesfinespirits.com; 38918 Progress Way, Squamish; noon-6pm Fri-Sun, by appointment Mon-Thu). Consider buying a bottle of Lemoncello here; it's the area's tastiest souvenir.

Jeff Wall, Rodney Graham et al. The final rooms showcase eye-popping modern First Nations works to great effect.

### SQUAMISH LIL'WAT CULTURAL CENTRE
MUSEUM

Map p200 (604-964-0990; www.slcc.ca; 4584 Blackcomb Way; adult/child $18/8; 9:30am-5pm Apr-Sep, 10am-5pm Tue-Sun Oct-Mar) This handsome, wood-beamed facility showcases two quite different First Nations groups – one coastal and one interior based. Take a tour for the vital context behind the museumlike exhibits and keep your eyes open for on-site artist demonstrations during the summer, when there are also Tuesday-night barbecue dinners. If you miss that, the on-site cafe serves tasty bannock tacos. The recently expanded gift shop offers an excellent array of BC-made arts and crafts.

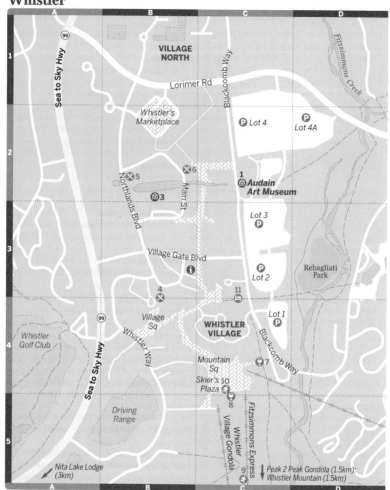

### WHISTLER MUSEUM & ARCHIVES

MUSEUM

Map p200 (☎604-932-2019; www.whistler
museum.org; 4333 Main St; suggested donation
$5; ☺11am-5pm Fri-Wed, to 9pm Thu) Tucked
into an anonymous green shed behind the
library building, this great little museum
traces Whistler development from wilderness outpost to Olympic resort. Quirky
exhibits include an original 1965 ski-lift
gondola and a 2010 Olympic torch. New exhibitions were being planned in mid-2016,
as well as a hoped-for larger venue. Check
ahead for events and add one of the area

walking tours in summer (1pm daily, by donation, from June to August).

##  EATING & DRINKING

### ★PUREBREAD

BAKERY $

Map p200 (☎604-962-1182; www.purebread.
ca; 4338 Main St; baked goods $3-6; ☺8:30am-
5:30pm) When this Function Junction
legend finally opened a village branch,
the locals came running and they've been
queuing ever since. They're here for the cornucopia of eye-roll-worthy bakery treats,

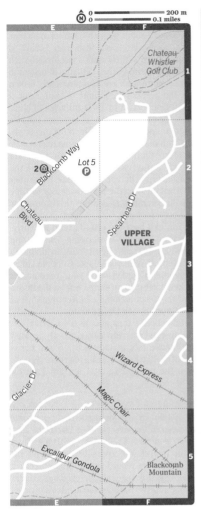

0 — 200 m
0 — 0.1 miles

# Whistler

chatty little nook that's very busy at meal-times (takeout recommended), this is the place to dive into Australia's age-old pie infatuation. Check the glass cabinet for the day's available offerings – kangaroo is included but the butter chicken is our favorite – and 'peak it' with added toppings of mashed potato, mushy peas and gravy. Add a lamington cake dessert for the full Aussie effect.

**GONE VILLAGE EATERY**   CAFE **$**

Map p200 (☏604-938-1990; www.gonevillage eatery.com; 4205 Village Sq; mains $10-12; ☺6:30am-9pm; ☏✐) This well-hidden locals' fave (just behind the store Armchair Books) serves a wide range of hearty, good-value comfort grub of the chili, pad thai and salmon burger variety. This is where many fuel up for a day on the slopes and have a Mars bar coffee when they return. There's a patio out back for summer evening basking.

Add a Howe Sound Brewing beer to the mix – just $5.50 for a real pint. There are also lots of options here for vegetarians.

**CHRISTINE'S ON BLACKCOMB**   INTERNATIONAL **$$$**

(☏604-938-7437; Rendezvous Lodge, Blackcomb Mountain; mains $28-32) A viewtastic gondola-accessed mountaintop restaurant where the swish menu combines with diners dressed in ski gear, Christine's is the best place to eat

including salted-caramel bars, sour-cherry choc-chip cookies and the amazing Crack, a naughtily gooey shortbread cookie bar. There's savory here, too; go for the hearty homity or pudgie pie.

Service is always friendly and, if you arrive just after the early morning bakeathon, you can expect the aromas to lure you into at least tripling your purchase. Wash it all down with a large coffee from Portland-based Stumptown.

**PEAKED PIES**   AUSTRALIAN **$**

Map p200 (☏604-962-4115; www.peakedpies. com; 4369 Main St; mains $7-13; ☺8am-9pm) A

during your skiing or hiking day out. Book ahead (or try to avoid the lunch rush) then dive into the smashing Keralan fish curry. Can't get a table? The adjoining cafeteria serves everything from burgers to burritos and ramen bowls.

### RED DOOR BISTRO
FRENCH $$$

(☑604-962-6262; www.reddoorbistro.ca; 2129 Lake Placid Rd; mains $22-38; ☺5pm-late) As soon as you know you're coming to Whistler, call for a reservation at this hot little Creekside eatery that delighted locals love as much as in-the-know visitors. Taking a French-bistro approach to fine, mostly West Coast ingredients means mouthwatering lamb and seafood dishes plus a highly recommended cassoulet that's brimming with everything from duck to smoked pork.

### ★ GARIBALDI LIFT COMPANY
PUB

Map p200 (☑604-905-2220; 4165 Springs Lane, Whistler Village Gondola; ☺11am-1am) The closest bar to the slopes. You can smell the sweat of the skiers or mountain bikers hurtling past the patio at this cavernous bar that's known by every local as the GLC. The furnishings have the scuffs and dings of a well-worn pub, and the best time to come is when DJs or bands turn the place into a clubbish mosh pit.

### DUBH LINN GATE
PUB

Map p200 (☑604-905-4047; www.dubhlinn gate.com; 4320 Sundial Cres; ☺8am-1am Mon-Fri, 7am-1am Sat & Sun) Whistler's favorite Irish pub, this dark-wood-lined joint would feel just like an authentic Galway watering hole if not for the obligatory heated patio facing the slopes. Tuck yourself into a shady corner table inside and revive your inner leprechaun with a stout – there's Guinness as well as Murphy's. Even better is the slightly pricey BC-craft-brew menu and regular live music, often of the trad Irish kind.

## 🏃 SPORTS & ACTIVITIES

This is British Columbia's activity central, with a huge array of winter and summer options for those who like to work up a sweat or surf a few spine-tingling thrills.

### WHISTLER-BLACKCOMB
SKIING, SNOWBOARDING

(☑604-967-8950; www.whistlerblackcomb.com; 2-day winter lift ticket adult/child $258/129) Comprising 37 lifts and crisscrossed with over 200 runs, the Whistler-Blackcomb sister mountains are also physically linked by the resort's mammoth 4.4km Peak 2 Peak Gondola. It takes 11 minutes to shuttle wide-eyed powder hogs between the two high alpine areas, so you can hit the slopes on both mountains on the same day.

More than half the resort's runs are aimed at intermediate-level skiers, and the season typically runs from late November to April on Whistler and November to June on Blackcomb – December to February is the peak for both.

You can beat the crowds with an early-morning (upload is between 7:15am and 8am) Fresh Tracks ticket ($20), available in advance at Whistler Village Gondola Guest Relations. Coupled with your regular lift ticket, it gets you an extra hour on the slopes and the ticket includes a buffet breakfast at the **Roundhouse Lodge** up top.

Snowboard fans should also check out the freestyle terrain parks, mostly located on Blackcomb, including the Snow Cross and the Big Easy Terrain Garden. There's also the popular Habitat Terrain Park on Whistler.

### PEAK 2 PEAK GONDOLA
GONDOLA

(☑604-967-8950; www.whistlerblackcomb.com/ discover/360-experience; 4545 Blackcomb Way; adult/teen/child $57/50/29; ☺10am-4:45pm) Built to link the area's two main mountaintops, this record-breaking engineering marvel gently eases goggle-eyed passengers along a lofty 4.4km gondola ride that takes around 11 minutes to complete. En route, you'll be mesmerized by the unfolding panorama of forest, snow and peak vistas – especially if you snag one of the two glass-bottomed cars. Equally popular in summer and winter.

### WHISTLER MOUNTAIN BIKE PARK
MOUNTAIN BIKING

Map p200 (☑604-967-8950; http://bike.whis tlerblackcomb.com; 1-day lift ticket adult/child $59/35; ☺May-Oct) Colonizing the melted ski slopes in summer and accessed via lifts at the village's south end, this park offers barreling downhill runs and an orgy of jumps and bridges twisting through well-maintained forested trails. Luckily, you don't have to be a bike courier to stand the knee-buckling pace: easier routes are marked in green, while blue intermediate trails and black diamond advanced paths are offered if you want to **Crank It Up** – the name of one of the most popular routes.

### ZIPTREK ECOTOURS
ADVENTURE SPORTS

Map p200 (☑604-935-0001; www.ziptrek.com; 4280 Mountain Sq, Carleton Lodge; adult/child from $119/99; ⊕) If adrenaline-rushing thrills – and screaming at the top of your lungs as you zip-line between the trees – are your bag, this is the operator for you. Several packages are available, including some aimed at kids and seniors. And if you'd rather not zip-line, there is also a great canopy walking tour through the trees.

## 🛏 SLEEPING

Winter, especially December and January, is the peak for prices, but last-minute deals are still possible if you're planning an impromptu overnight from Vancouver – check the website of **Tourism Whistler** (www.whistler.com) for room sales and packages. Most hotels extort parking fees of up to $40 daily and some also slap on resort fees, so confirm these before you book.

### WHISTLER PEAK LODGE
HOTEL $$

Map p200 (☑604-938-0878; www.whistlerpeaklodge.com; 4295 Blackcomb Way; d from $240; ☎) Brilliantly located in the heart of the village, this former Holiday Inn has been upgraded but still has some of the best rates in town (if you book far enough ahead). There's a wide choice of rooms available but full kitchen or kitchenette facilities are standard – you're steps from many restaurants if you're feeling too lazy to cook.

### NITA LAKE LODGE
BOUTIQUE HOTEL $$$

(☑604-966-5700; www.nitalakelodge.com; 2135 Lake Placid Rd; d from $240; ☎⊕) Adjoining the handsome Creekside railway station, this swanky timber-framed lodge is perfect for a pampering retreat. Hugging the lakeside, it's chic but cozy rooms feature individual patios, rock fireplaces and bathrooms with heated floors and large tubs; some also have handy kitchens. Creekside lifts are a walkable few minutes away and there's an on-site spa to soothe your aching muscles.

---

### WHISTLER'S BEST FESTIVALS

Whistler hosts some great annual events worth timing your visit for.

➡ **Winterpride** (www.gaywhistler.com; ⊙Jan) A busy week of gay-friendly snow action and late-night partying, this event keeps growing every year.

➡ **Crankworx** (www.crankworx.com; ⊙Aug) An adrenaline-filled celebration of bike stunts, speed contests and mud-splattered shenanigans.

➡ **Cornucopia** (www.whistlercornucopia.com; ⊙Nov) Bacchanalian food and wine fest crammed with parties.

---

# Richmond & Steveston

## Explore

The region's modern-day Chinatown is easy to reach via Canada Line SkyTrain from Vancouver, making for an accessible half-day of Asian shopping malls followed by a taste-trip through Chinese, Japanese and Vietnamese restaurants. And don't miss the city's historic waterfront Steveston village – a popular destination for sunset-viewing locals with a penchant for great fish and chips, and it also has a couple of great museums.

## The Best

➡**Sight** Gulf of Georgia Cannery (p205)
➡**Place to Eat** Pajo's (p207)
➡**Place to Shop** Daiso (p206)

## Top Tip

Coming from Vancouver on the SkyTrain Canada Line, alight at Aberdeen Station, then explore the streets to the next stop, Lansdowne. This is the heart of the Golden Village.

## Getting There & Away

➡**Train** Canada Line SkyTrain services zip through Richmond every few minutes, taking from 15 to 20 minutes to reach the area. Make sure you board a Richmond-

# Richmond & Steveston

N
0    2 km
0    1 mile

DAY TRIPS FROM VANCOUVER RICHMOND & STEVESTON

## Richmond & Steveston

## BURNABY

Immediately east of Vancouver via Hastings St, Burnaby – the birthplace of Michael J Fox – is a no-frills residential suburb with an elongated strip-mall feel. Luckily, there's a handful of attractions to keep you away from the shops. Check in with **Tourism Burnaby** (☎604-419-0377; www.tourismburnaby.com) for tips on what to do here.

Nestled among Burnaby's labyrinth of residential side streets, tranquil **Deer Lake Park** is crisscrossed with verdant meadow and waterfront walks, and also offers boat rentals. Nearby, the popular **Burnaby Village Museum** (www.burnabyvillagemuseum. ca; 6501 Deer Lake Ave; ⊙11am-4:30pm Tue-Sun May-Aug; ⚫) FREE re-creates the atmosphere of a BC pioneer town with replica homes and businesses of the time, and a wonderfully restored 1912 carousel. Entry is free and it's also open off-season for special Christmas and Halloween displays.

Topping Burnaby Mountain, **Simon Fraser University** (www.sfu.ca; 8888 University Dr) is the Lower Mainland's second main campus community. Visitor attractions here include the **Museum of Archaeology & Ethnology** (☎778-782-3135; www.sfu.ca/archaeology/museum.html; 8888 University Dr, Simon Fraser University; ⊙10am-noon & 1-4pm Mon-Fri; ⛽135) FREE and the **SFU Gallery** (☎778-782-4266; www.sfu.ca/galleries; 8888 University Dr, Simon Fraser University; ⊙noon-5pm Tue-Fri; ⛽135) FREE.

Brighouse-bound train in Vancouver, otherwise you'll be heading to the airport instead; you can switch to the correct train anywhere up to Bridgeport Station.

➡ **Bus** For Steveston, take the Canada Line to Bridgeport Station and switch to bus 401, 402, 407 or 410.

### Need to Know

➡ **Area Code** 604

➡ **Location** 16km south of Vancouver

➡ **Tourist Office Tourism Richmond Visitor Centre** (Map p204; ☎604-271-8280; www.tourismrichmond.com; 3811 Moncton St, Steveston; ⊙9:30am-6pm Jul-Aug, 9:30-5pm Mon-Sat & noon-4pm Sun Sep-Jun; ⛽402)

## ⊙ SIGHTS

Steveston is home to a couple of excellent museums, while Richmond hosts North America's best Asian night-market scene.

### GULF OF GEORGIA CANNERY          MUSEUM

Map p204 (☎604-664-9009; www.gulfof georgiacannery.org; 12138 4th Ave, Steveston; adult/child $10.20/6.30; ⊙10am-5pm; ⚫; Ⓜ Richmond-Brighouse, then bus 401) British Columbia's best 'industrial museum' illuminates the sights and sounds of the region's bygone era of labor-intensive fish processing. Most of the machinery remains and there's an evocative focus on the people

who used to work here; you'll hear recorded testimonies from old employees percolating through the air like ghosts, bringing to life the days they spent immersed in entrails as thousands of cans rolled down the production line. Take one of the guided tours for the full story.

### BRITANNIA SHIPYARD          MUSEUM

Map p204 (☎640-718-8038; www.britan niashipyard.ca; 5180 Westwater Dr, Steveston; ⊙10am-5pm Fri-Wed, 10am-8pm Thu May-Sep, noon-5pm Sat & Sun Oct-Apr; Ⓜ Richmond-Brighouse, then bus 410) FREE A riverfront complex of historic sheds housing dusty tools, boats and reminders of the region's maritime past, this is one of the most evocative, fancy-free historic sites in the region. Check out the preserved **Murakami House**, where a large Japanese family lived before being unceremoniously interned during the war. Ask the volunteers plenty of questions: they have some great stories to tell.

### RICHMOND NIGHT MARKET          MARKET

Map p204 (☎604-244-8448; www.richmond nightmarket.com; 8351 River Rd, Richmond; adult/child $3.25/free; ⊙7pm-midnight Fri & Sat, 7pm-11pm Sun mid-May–mid-Oct; Ⓢ Bridgeport) The larger of Richmond's two Asian-flavored night markets and the easiest to reach via transit. Expect to line-up for entry at this wildly popular summer tradition. Inside, you'll find the usual rows of blingy trinkets plus live entertainment and dozens

## FORT LANGLEY

Little Fort Langley's tree-lined streets and 19th-century storefronts make it one of the Lower Mainland's most picturesque historic villages, ideal for an afternoon jaunt from Vancouver. Aside from the fort itself, cafes, boutiques and ice cream-scoffing opportunities abound.

The highlight of a visit here is **Fort Langley National Historic Site** (☑604-513-4777; www.parkscanada.gc.ca/fortlangley; adult/child $7.80/3.90; ☺10am-5pm; ▣), the region's most important and evocative old-school landmark.

A fortified trading post since 1827, it's where James Douglas announced the creation of British Columbia in 1858, giving the site a legitimate claim to being the province's birthplace. With costumed re-enactors, re-created artisan workshops and a gold-panning area that's a kid-friendly must-do (they also enjoy charging around the wooden battlements), it's an ideal destination for families aiming to add a little education to their trips.

If you need an introduction before you start wading into the buildings, there's a surprisingly entertaining time-travel-themed movie presentation on offer. Also check the website before arriving: there's a wide array of interpretive events and activities that bring the past to life here, including book-ahead blacksmithing workshops.

You won't go hungry in Fort Langley, where there are several enticing eateries a short stroll from the fort. But if you want to hang with the locals, drop into **Wendel's Bookstore & Cafe** (☑604-513-2238; www.wendelsonline.com; 9233 Glove Rd; $8-14; ☺7:30am-10pm; ☎☑).

If you're driving from Vancouver, take Hwy 1 east for 40km, then take the 232nd St exit north. Follow the signs along 232nd St until you reach the stop sign at Glover Rd. Turn right here, and continue into the village. Turn right again on Mavis Ave, just before the railway tracks. The fort's parking lot is at the end of the street.

of steaming, hunger-abating food stalls. Fans of fish balls, deep-fried squid and bubble tea? This is the place for you.

★ **DAISO**  DEPARTMENT STORE

Map p204 (☑604-295-6601; www.daisocanada.com; 4151 Hazelbridge Way, Aberdeen Centre; ☺9:30am-9pm; ⑤Aberdeen) North America's first (and so far only) branch of Japan's favorite discount store has a cultlike following in Metro Vancouver. A visit to the large, two-floor store is as much a cultural exploration as a chance to buy temptingly low-priced stationery, rice bowls and Ultraman-type action figures, plus oddball plastic items that seem unfathomable, some of them adorned with hilarious 'Japanese English' slogans.

Give yourself plenty of time to explore the aisles here. And don't forget to add some Pocky sticks (chocolate-coated biscuit sticks) for the Canada Line ride back to Vancouver.

**RICHMOND OLYMPIC OVAL**  STADIUM

Map p204 (☑778-296-1409; www.richmondoval.ca; 611 River Rd, Richmond; ☺6am-11pm; SkyTrain, bus to Brighouse, then bus C94) The biggest new venue built for the 2010 Winter Olympics (it hosted long-track speed skating), this riverfront behemoth has since become a community sports facility shared by locals around the region. The five rings haven't been forgotten, though; the on-site **Richmond Olympic Experience** (www.therox.ca) offers a host of simulator experiences enabling you to pretend you won your own medal.

INTERNATIONAL
**BUDDHIST TEMPLE**  BUDDHIST TEMPLE

Map p204 (☑604-274-2822; www.buddhisttemple.ca; 9160 Steveston Hwy, Richmond; ☺9:30am-5:30pm; ▣403, ⑤Richmond-Brighouse) **FREE** The highlight of this classical Chinese temple complex is the sumptuous Gracious Hall, complete with deep-red exterior walls and a gently flaring porcelain roof. Check out the colorful 100m Buddha mural and the golden, multi-armed Bodhisattva figure. The landscaped garden, with sculptures and bonsai trees, is another highlight. You don't have to be a Buddhist to visit and the monks are highly welcoming if you're keen to have a look around.

# Eating & Drinking

There are several must-try fish-and-chip options in riverfront Steveston as well as a huge, taste-bud-popping array of authentic Asian eateries throughout Richmond, especially in the Golden Triangle area.

### ★PAJO'S
SEAFOOD $

Map p204 (☑604-272-1588; www.pajos.com; The Wharf, Steveston; mains $9-16; ⏱11am-7pm; SkyTrain, bus to Richmond-Brighouse, then bus 401) There's no better spot to enjoy fish and chips than Steveston's boat-bobbing wharf. Follow your nose and descend the ramp to the little ordering hatch here and you'll be greeted by a friendly face and a menu more extensive than your average chippy. Go the traditional fresh fried cod, salmon or halibut route (with secret-recipe tartar sauce), adding mushy peas for the full effect.

### PARKER PLACE
FOOD COURT $

Map p204 (☑604-273-0276; www.parkerplace.com; 4380 No 3 Rd, Richmond; mains $5-10; ⏱11am-7pm Sun-Thu, to 9pm Fri & Sat; ☎; SAberdeen) There are several popular Asian shopping malls in Richmond but, while Aberdeen Centre and Lansdowne Centre are bigger, Parker Place has an authentic-feeling food court that evokes a Singaporean hawker market, beloved of Asian-Canadian locals. Dive in for good-value noodle, fish ball and dragon's beard candy dishes; buy a few plates and share 'em at your table.

Once you're full, survey the labyrinth of surrounding retailers (you'll feel as if you're in another country) or nip outside to the food court's adjoining parking lot for a surprise: a shimmering shrine.

### SHIBUYATEI
RAMEN $

Map p204 (☑778-297-1777; 2971 Sexsmith Rd, Richmond; mains $7-14; ⏱11:30am-2pm & 5pm-9pm Mon-Sat) Inauspiciously located next to a car wash, this tiny, local favorite hole-in-the-wall serves sushi but it's really all about great ramen bowls (with no MSG) and tasty Japanese curries, served with chicken or pork *katsu* (deep-fried). It's a one-man operation so avoid peak times if you don't want to wait too long.

### LEISURE TEA & COFFEE
TEAHOUSE

Map p204 (☑604-821-9998; 8391 Alexandra Rd, Richmond; ⏱noon-12:30am Mon-Thu, noon-1:30am Fri-Sun; ☎; SLansdowne) This delightfully eclectic bubble-tea, regular-tea and naughty-dessert spot has that Asian-influenced love for European ski lodge-interiors fused with a clientele of young locals missing home (especially late at night). Go for a Taiwan-style shaved ice treat or heat up in winter with a fruit-packed peach warmer tea.

### SHANGHAI RIVER RESTAURANT
CHINESE $$

Map p204 (☑604-233-8885; 7381 Westminster Hwy, Richmond; mains $10-22; ⏱11am-3pm & 5:30-10pm; SRichmond-Brighouse) Grab a seat overlooking the kitchen window at this cavernous northern Chinese eatery and you'll be mesmerized by the handiwork that goes into folding some of the area's best dim-sum dumplings. Order plates to share – one dish per person is the usual ratio – and be careful not to squirt everyone with the juicy pork or shrimp dumplings. The servers are often not fluent in English, so keep your orders simple.

# Southern Gulf Islands

## Explore

Stressed Vancouverites love escaping into the restorative arms of these laid-back islands, strung like a shimmering necklace between the mainland and Vancouver Island. Formerly colonized by hippies and US draft dodgers, Salt Spring, Galiano, Mayne, Saturna, and North and South Pender deliver on their promise of rustic, sigh-triggering getaways. For more visitor information, see www.sgislands.com.

## The Best

➡**Sight** Salt Spring Island's Saturday Market (p209)

➡**Place to Eat** Galiano Island's Pilgrimme (p210)

➡**Place to Drink** Galiano Island's Hummingbird Pub (210)

## Top Tip

Like a mental spa treatment, the whole point of visiting this region is to wind

# Southern Gulf Islands

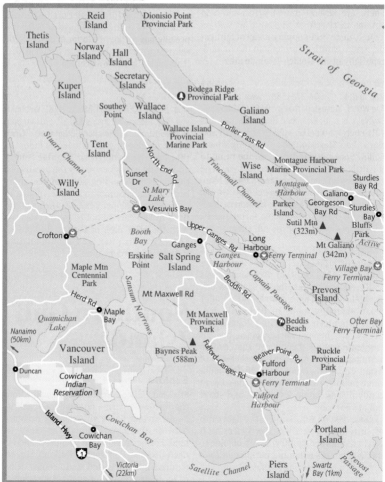

down, absorb the slower pace of life and forget about looking at your watch: island time rules here.

## Getting There & Away

➺**Air** Scenically delightful short-hop services from Salt Spring Air (www.saltspringair. com) and Seair Seaplanes (www. seairseaplanes.com) arrive from Vancouver throughout the islands. It's one of the best way to view the region before you arrive.

➺**Ferry** BC Ferries (www.bcferries.com) island-bound services depart from mainland Tsawwassen en route to each of the main

Southern Gulf Islands, with some services connecting via Vancouver Island's Swartz Bay.

## Need to Know

➺**Area Code** 250

➺**Location** Southwest from Vancouver; one to three hours by ferry or 20 minutes by plane

➺**Tourist Offices Salt Spring Island Visitor Information Centre** (☏250-537-5252; www.saltspringtourism.com; 121 Lower Ganges Rd, Ganges; ⏱9am-4pm May-Oct, 11am-3pm Nov-Apr); **Galiano Tourist Office**

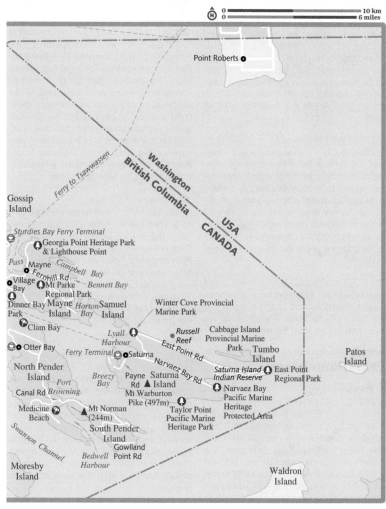

(www.galianoisland.com; 2590 Sturdies Bay Rd; ⏰10am-5pm Mon-Sat, Jun-Aug, reduced hours off-season)

## 👁 SIGHTS & ACTIVITIES

### 👁 Salt Spring Island

⭐ **SATURDAY MARKET** MARKET
(www.saltspringmarket.com; Centennial Park, Ganges; ⏰9am-4pm Sat Apr-Oct) The best market in British Columbia, this gigantic cornucopia of produce, edible goodies and locally made artworks lures everyone like a magnet on summer Saturdays. Arrive in the morning; it can be oppressively jam-packed at times. Alternatively, join the locals at the smaller produce-only Tuesday market. Everything at both markets is made, baked or grown on the island.

**SALT SPRING ISLAND CHEESE** FARM
(📞250-653-2300; www.saltspringcheese.com; 285 Reynolds Rd; ⏰11am-5pm May-Sep, 11am-4pm Oct-Apr; 🚼) This family-friendly farmstead has a strollable garden, wandering

chickens and a winerylike tasting room and shop. It's a must-see spot, producing goat- and sheep-milk chèvres, feta and Camembert style cheeses; the soft goat-cheese rounds in several flavors (the garlic one is recommended) are the farm's specialty. You can watch the handmade production through special windows but look out for glimpses of the farm's gamboling goats.

**SALTSPRING ISLAND ALES**     BREWERY

(📞250-653-2383; www.saltspringislandales. com; 270 Furness Rd; ⊘noon-5pm) Colonizing a rustic, cedar-built shack between the trees, this microbrewery's woodsy little tasting room offers a roster of all-organic brews from malty Extra Special Bitter to smooth Heatherdale Ale. There are always intriguing seasonal beers to try as well; growlers are available if you need a takeout.

**RUCKLE PROVINCIAL PARK**     PARK

(www.bcparks.ca) This southeast gem with ragged shorelines and gnarly arbutus forests has trails for all skill levels, with Yeo Point making an ideal pit stop.

## ⊙ Galiano Island

**GALIANO KAYAKS**     KAYAKING

(📞250-539-2442; www.seakayak.ca; 3451 Montague Rd; 2hr/day rental from $35/60, tours from $60) Offering kayak, canoe and stand-up paddleboard rentals to those who fancy exploring on their own, the friendly folk at Galiano also run popular guided kayak tours, including early morning jaunts, sunset tours and an immersive (not literally) six-hour Experience Galiano tour.

**GALIANO ADVENTURE COMPANY**     MOPED RENTAL

(📞250-593-3443; www.galianoadventures.com; Montague Harbour Marina; rental per hr from $20; ⊘May-Sep) For a fun way to zip around and catch as many scenic sites as possible, rent a moped from this long-established local operator, which also rents boats ($45 per hour) and has a couple of rustic cottages if you're looking for a place to stay (guests receive moped- and boat-rental discounts).

 # EATING & DRINKING

⭐**TREE HOUSE CAFÉ**     CANADIAN $$

(📞250-537-5379; www.treehousecafe.ca; 106 Purvis Lane, Ganges; mains $8-17; ⊘8am-10pm Wed-Sun, to 4pm Mon & Tue July & Aug, reduced hours off-season) At this magical outdoor dining experience, you'll be sitting in the shade of a large plum tree as you choose from a menu of comfort pastas, Mexican specialties and gourmet burgers and sandwiches. The tuna melt is a local fave, perhaps washed down with a Saltspring Island Ales porter. There's live music Wednesday to Sunday nights here in summer.

⭐**HUMMINGBIRD PUB**     PUB $$

(📞250-539-5472; www.hummingbirdpub.com; 47 Sturdies Bay Rd; mains $12-17) A beloved rustic pub nestled among the Galiano trees. Look out for wandering deer and, of course, hummingbirds, outside. Fish and chips is the mainstay of the menu but plenty of other satisfying pub grub is also available. They run their own summer shuttle bus to get you to and from the pub; check the website for schedules.

⭐**PILGRIMME**     CANADIAN $$$

(📞250-539-5392; www.pilgrimme.ca; 2806 Montague Rd; mains $16-30; ⊘5pm-10pm Wed-Mon) The delightful woodland setting will draw you through the door but the farm-to-table food is what you'll remember long after you return home: seasonal, local and even foraged. You'll find top-notch duck, seafood and beef dishes here, all lovingly prepared and served with the kind of vegetables that taste as if they've just been picked. Book ahead; this place is extremely popular.

## 🛏 SLEEPING

**OCEANSIDE COTTAGES**     COTTAGE $$

(📞250-653-0007; www.oceansidecottages.com; 521 Isabella Point Rd; d from $135) These four unique cottages are nooks of bliss. Each is exceedingly private and filled with interesting artwork and creative flourishes. We especially love the groovy little Love Shack, with its retro Austin Powers vibe.

**HASTINGS HOUSE HOTEL**     HOTEL $$$

(📞800-661-9255; www.hastingshouse.com; 160 Upper Ganges Rd, Ganges; d from $350; 📶) This

## BOWEN ISLAND

One of the best days out you can have from Vancouver – it's just a 20-minute boat hop from Horseshoe Bay but it feels a million miles from downtown – Bowen is like British Columbia in miniature. That means a sigh-triggering ferry ride to Snug Cove, a cute villagelike settlement with lots of quirky locals and lashings of outdoorsy appeal.

Stroll the Snug Cove boardwalks and drink-in the old-school ambience of dozens of wooden cottages and Tudor-look buildings. On weekends throughout July and August, there's an arts, crafts and food **market** to keep things lively. If you miss it, climb the fairly steep hill to **Artisan Square** for a loop of clapboard galleries and boutique shops – including **Cocoa West Chocolatier** (604-947-2996; www.cocoawest.com; 581C Artisan Lane; 10am-5pm May-Sep, reduced hours off-season).

Visitors used to roll in here by steamship in the 1920s and 1930s; you can hear all about these halcyon days on a fascinating excursion with **Bowen Island Tours** (604-812-5041; www.bowenislandtours.com; tours from adult/child $25/12). Alternatively, explore the breathtaking woodland trails of Crippen Regional Park and Killarney Lake – see www.bowentrails.ca for tips. Look out for Opa, the island's grandest old-growth tree, said to be centuries old, or hit the water with **Bowen Island Sea Kayaking** (604-947-9266; www.bowenislandkayaking.com; Bowen Island Marina, Snug Cove; rentals/tours from $45/$75; Apr-Sep).

Take a **TransLink** (604-953-3333; www.translink.ca) transit bus from downtown Vancouver – the 257 express bus is best – and you'll be at the Horseshoe Bay **BC Ferries** (250-386-3431; www.bcferries.com) terminal in around 40 minutes. Ferry services depart from here to Bowen Island's Snug Cove throughout the day (adult/child/car $12.35/6.20/34.85, 20 minutes, 12 daily).

smashing rustic-chic hotel with 17 rooms is just up the hill from the main Ganges action, but it feels like staying in a country cottage estate in England. The immaculate grounds are strewn with locally made artworks and the waterfront views will have your camera itching to be used. The restaurant is high-end gourmet; breakfast is recommended.

GALIANO INN — HOTEL **$$$**

(250-539-3388; www.galianoinn.com; 134 Madrona Dr; d from $249; ) One of the most popular places to sleep on the island, especially among visiting Vancouverites. Sophisticates will love this Tuscan-style villa with 10 elegant rooms, each with a fireplace and romantic oceanfront terrace. There's also an on-site spa for that extra pampering you know you need.

# 🛏 Sleeping

*Metro Vancouver is home to more than 25,000 hotel, B&B and hostel rooms – many in or around the downtown core. The city is packed with visitors in summer, so book ahead...unless you fancy sleeping against a damp log in Stanley Park. Rates peak in July and August, but there are good spring and fall deals, when you can also expect some accompanying 'Wet Coast' rainfall.*

## Hotels

Vancouver's 2010 Winter Olympics triggered a rash of hotel building, mostly in the high-end range. The Shangri-La, the Fairmont Pacific Rim and the Rosewood Hotel Georgia all opened their shiny doors, while the swanky Trump International Hotel and Tower Vancouver was being built across from the Shangri-La during research for this book; see www.trumpvancouver.com for the latest information.

Older 'it' properties such as the Opus Hotel, Loden Hotel and the St Regis Hotel have polished their appeal anew to draw attention away from the newbies, creating some healthy competition: off-season you'll find there are often seriously good rates at these signature Vancouver properties. There are also plenty of attractive midrange options, many of which offer great-value in-suite kitchens that can save you a considerable amount on dine-out costs. Consider staying downtown: there are lots of options in the area and much of the neighborhood is easily accessed on foot. Wi-fi (typically free) is common, and most properties are nonsmoking, although some still cater to visiting puffers.

## B&Bs

The closest B&Bs to downtown are in the West End, and are typically sumptuous heritage homes of the romantic, higher-end sleepover variety. Prices vary more in neighborhoods a little further out – especially Kitsilano and Fairview – where you usually won't be far from a bus or SkyTrain route that can have you downtown in a few minutes. Keep in mind that some B&Bs require a two-night minimum stay – especially on summer weekends – and cancellation policies can cost you an arm and a leg if you decide not to turn up.

## Budget Sleepovers

There are many low-cost options in the city, but keep in mind that hostels, in particular, are not all created equal. While some offer great value, others can be smelly fleapits that you'll be itching (quite literally) to get out of. Consider the popular YWCA, Samesun or HI Hostel options as well as accommodation at the University of British Columbia (UBC). There are also a couple of respectable but low-cost guesthouse-style options. When traveling off-season, your budget will likely stretch to a bargain rate at a midrange property.

## Taxes & Fees

Be aware that there will be some significant additions to most quoted room rates. You'll pay an extra 8% Provincial Sales Tax (PST) plus 5% Goods and Services Tax (GST) above the advertised rate. Also, in common with other large British Columbia (BC) cities, Vancouver charges an additional 3% Hotel Room Tax. On top of this, some hotels also charge a Destination Marketing Fee of around 1.5%. Parking fees don't help either: overnight parking, especially at higher-end downtown hotels, can be expensive, sometimes as much as $50 pr night. B&Bs usually include parking free of charge.

## Lonely Planet's Top Choices

**Rosewood Hotel Georgia** (p216) Swanky, art-lined, landmark city hotel that's been reinvented.

**Fairmont Pacific Rim** (p217) Chic new downtown sleepover with some winning waterfront views.

**Skwachays Lodge** (p220) First Nations art-themed boutique sleepover.

**St Regis Hotel** (p215) Amenity-packed boutique property with a great central location.

**Victorian Hotel** (p215) Downtown historic hotel near all the action.

**Times Square Suites Hotel** (p219) Comfortable and popular home-away-from-home near Stanley Park.

**Sylvia Hotel** (p218) Ivy-covered heritage charmer with some lovely beachfront views.

**Opus Hotel** (p220) Stylish boutique option in Yaletown; perfect for see-and-be-seen coolsters.

**Loden Hotel** (p219) Designer boutique hotel steps from the downtown action.

**Wedgewood Hotel & Spa** (p216) Classic deluxe boutique sleepover.

## Best by Budget

### $

**YWCA Hotel** (p220) Centrally located tower with comfortable rooms that offer great value (especially for families).

**Buchan Hotel** (p218) Close to Stanley Park, its smaller rooms are budget-friendly, especially off-season.

### $$

**Skwachays Lodge** (p220) New boutique hotel lined with First Nations art.

**Sylvia Hotel** (p218) Charming beachfront sleepover in the West End, overlooking English Bay.

### $$$

**Rosewood Hotel Georgia** (p216) Vancouver's top 'it' hotel for stylish overnighting.

**Wedgewood Hotel & Spa** (p216) Classic deluxe hotel dripping with elegant flourishes.

## Best Boutique Hotels

**Loden Hotel** (p219) A slick and alluring Coal Harbour property just steps from the downtown core.

**Opus Hotel** (p220) Sexy and chic hotel in the heart of Yaletown; close to many restaurants.

**St Regis Hotel** (p215) City-center accommodation with some excellent value-added amenities.

**Executive Hotel Le Soleil** (p217) Versace-esque interiors with a perfect, central location.

**Wedgewood Hotel & Spa** (p216) Classic and classy European-feel decor, plus a popular spa.

## Best Spa Hotels

**Wedgewood Hotel & Spa** (p216) Elegant, classic pampering.

**Shangri-La Hotel** (p217) Stylish contemporary Asian feel.

**Fairmont Pacific Rim** (p217) Modern waterfront property with a spa locals love.

**Century Plaza Hotel & Spa** (p216) Downtown midrange hotel with its own Absolute spa.

**Pan Pacific Vancouver** (p217) Sparkling waterfront sleepover with dedicated spa operation.

SLEEPING

# Where to Stay

| NEIGHBORHOOD | FOR | AGAINST |
| --- | --- | --- |
| DOWNTOWN | Walking distance to stores, restaurants, nightlife and some attractions; great transit links to wider region; good range of hotels | Can be pricey; streets can be clamorous; some accommodation overlooks noisy traffic areas |
| WEST END | Walking distance to Stanley Park; many midrange restaurants nearby; heart of the gay district; quiet residential streets | Mostly high-end B&Bs with a couple of additional chain hotels; can be a bit of a hike to the city center and attractions other than Stanley Park |
| YALETOWN & GRANVILLE ISLAND | Close to shops and many restaurants; good transport links to other areas | Few accommodation options to choose from |
| FAIRVIEW & SOUTH GRANVILLE | Quiet residential streets; well-priced heritage B&B sleepovers; good bus and SkyTrain access to downtown | Most options are B&Bs; few local nightlife options |
| KITSILANO & UBC | Comfy heritage houses and good UBC budget options; direct transit to downtown; on the doorstep of several beaches | Not the center of the action; scant nightlife options; can feel a bit too quiet and laid-back |
| NORTH SHORE | Better hotel rates than city center; handy access to downtown via SeaBus; close to popular attractions such as Grouse Mountain and Capilano Suspension Bridge | Away from the heart of the action; takes time to get to other major attractions |

SLEEPING

## 🛏 Downtown

Most of the city's main hotels are located downtown, many of them in the few blocks that radiate south from the waterfront. The West End is also home to some top-notch heritage B&Bs.

### SAMESUN BACKPACKERS LODGE
HOSTEL $

Map p266 (☏604-682-8226; www.samesun. com; 1018 Granville St; dm/r incl breakfast $35/100; ☻◉🛜; ▣10) Vancouver's party hostel, the popular Samesun is right on the city's nightlife strip. Ask for a back room if you fancy a few hours of kip or just head down to the large on-site bar (provocatively called the Beaver) to join the beery throng. Dorms are comfortably small, and there's a large kitchen. Continental breakfast is included.

This sociable hostel has daily events (including free tours), a large guest lounge with pool table and a large-screen TV room. It can also sell you tickets to local hockey, soccer and Canadian football games. The downstairs bar is also a good spot to catch a game, along with a few beer specials.

### HI VANCOUVER CENTRAL
HOSTEL $

Map p266 (☏604-685-5335; www.hihostels.ca/ vancouver; 1025 Granville St; dm/r incl breakfast $40/100; ☻✳🛜; ▣10) On the Granville Strip, this warrenlike hostel is more of a party joint than its HI Downtown sibling (p218). Some of the benefits of its past hotel incarnation remain, including air-conditioning and small rooms, some of which are now private, with the rest converted to dorm rooms with up to four beds. There are dozens of two-bed dorms (some en suite) for privacy fans.

Snag a back room to avoid Granville St noise issues. Kitchen facilities are limited to microwaves and toasters but a free continental breakfast is included. There's a brimming roster of social activities, including regular sightseeing tours. Location-wise, this hostel is within staggering distance of many bars and clubs.

★**ST REGIS HOTEL**   BOUTIQUE HOTEL **$$**
Map p266 (🖋604-681-1135; www.stregishotel. com; 602 Dunsmuir St; d incl breakfast $299; ➔❄@🛜; ⓈGranville) Transformed in recent years, this is now an art-lined boutique sleepover in a 1913 heritage shell. Befitting its age, almost all the rooms seem to be a different size, and they exhibit a loungey élan with leather-look wallpaper, earth-toned bedspreads, flatscreen TVs and multimedia hubs. Rates include value-added flourishes such as cooked breakfasts, access to the nearby gym and free international phone calls.

The St Regis is well located in the heart of the action, offers top-notch service and has a business center if you have left your laptop at home. Overnight parking is $30.

**BURRARD HOTEL**   HOTEL **$$**
Map p266 (🖋604-681-2331; www.theburrard. com; 1100 Burrard St; d from $229; 🅿➔🛜❄; 🚌22) A groovy makeover has transformed this 1950s downtown motel into a knowingly cool sleepover with a tongue-in-cheek retro-cool feel. The mostly quite compact rooms have been spruced up with mod flourishes and contemporary amenities such as refrigerators, flatscreens and Nespresso coffee machines. But not everything has changed: the hidden interior courtyard of Florida-style palm trees is *tres* cool.

When the new owners took over, they also added some enticing extras for guests: free-use cruiser bikes and gratis North American phone calls. Check the website for some enticing special deals. Overnight parking costs $28.

**VICTORIAN HOTEL**   HOTEL **$$**
Map p266 (🖋604-681-6369; www.victorianho tel.ca; 514 Homer St; d incl breakfast from $145; ➔@🛜; ⓈGranville) The high-ceilinged rooms at this popular Euro-style, heritage-building hotel combine glossy hardwood floors, a sprinkling of antiques, an occasional bay window and plenty of historical charm. The best rooms are in the renovated extension, where raindrop showers, marble bathroom floors and flatscreen TVs add a slice of luxe. Rates include continental breakfast, and rooms are provided with fans in summer.

The Victorian has friendly staff and an excellent location just steps from the downtown-core action.

**METROPOLITAN HOTEL**   BOUTIQUE HOTEL **$$**
Map p266 (🖋604-687-1122; www.metropolitan. com/vanc; 645 Howe St; d $369; ❄🛜❄❄; ⓈBurrard) This swish boutique property has a contemporary-cool take on style that will appeal to urban sophisticates. It's also handily located in the heart of downtown. Bold modern artworks add a splash of color to the atmospheric, subtly decorated rooms, and there's a good on-site restaurant, an indoor pool and a squash court to keep you busy. Excellent service.

Unusually for Vancouver, there are also some smoking rooms available. And if you really want to show your class, hop the hotel's downtown limo service. When you finally get back to the hotel, you can play a little pitch-and-put on the outdoor mini-golf course. Overnight parking costs $40.

**URBAN HIDEAWAY GUESTHOUSE**   GUESTHOUSE **$$**
Map p266 (🖋604-694-0600; www.urban -hideaway.com; 581 Richards St; d without bath/ ste $109/159; ➔@; ⓈGranville) This cozy but fiendishly well hidden guesthouse is a word-of-mouth favorite in the heart of the city. Tuck yourself into one of the comfy rooms (the loft is recommended) or spend your time in the lounge areas downstairs. There are laundry facilities, a computer that's free to use and loaner bikes that are also gratis. Bathrooms are mostly shared; the loft's bathroom is private.

The hosts are highly welcoming and full of suggestions for what to do in the area if you need some ideas; in fact, this feels like staying in a family house.

**MODA HOTEL**   HOTEL **$$**
Map p266 (🖋604-683-4251; www.modahotel. ca; 900 Seymour St; d from $275; ➔🛜❄; 🚌10) Moda will never be in the big league of Vancouver's fancy local boutique hotels, but that's fine because it has two key things going for it: an excellent heart-of-the-city location and better rates than its posher siblings. The mostly small rooms combine mod, 'cheap chic' flourishes with quirky heritage holdovers (the building opened in 1908). Light sleepers should avoid lower and front-facing floors.

There are three on-site drink-and-dine options (plus a liquor store), including a

**SLEEPING**

---

## ARTSY SLEEPOVERS

The **Rosewood Hotel Georgia** has arguably the city's best hotel art collection. Dominated by modern Canadian art, the hotel's public spaces have a gallery feel with abstract works by the likes of Alan Wood, Marcel Baebeau and Guido Molinari studding the walls. The highlight, though, is in the lobby and it's the only piece by a non-Canadian artist. Entitled *Internity*, the 3D work by Brit artist Patrick Hughes shifts perspective as you move in front of it and is a real eye-popper.

Over in the West End, Vancouver's self-proclaimed 'art hotel', the **Listel Hotel** (p219) has a curatorial arrangement with several local galleries and museums that means its corridors are lined with display cases of intriguing art; First Nations carvings and contemporary abstract works dominate. There's an even more dedicated First Nations art approach at **Skwachays Lodge** (p220), a new boutique hotel where every room has been designed in collaboration with a different First Nations artist.

---

popular wine bar that's perfect for a nightcap on your way back from an evening on the nearby Granville Strip. You'll also get free North American phone calls.

### CENTURY PLAZA
#### HOTEL & SPA
HOTEL $$

Map p266 (☑604-687-0575; www.century-plaza.com; 1015 Burrard St; d from $199; P☻☀⎙≋☀; ☐22) This centrally located tower sleepover combines business-hotel-style rooms (all with handy kitchenettes) with a raft of on-site amenities: there can't be many North American hotels that have both their own spa and comedy club. There's also an indoor pool and you're just a couple of downhill blocks from the Robson St shops. A handy amenity room with coin-operated guest laundry facilities was recently added.

There are many restaurants within strolling distance, but the hotel also has its own Manhattan-style Italian restaurant if you're too lazy to leave the building. Overnight parking costs $17.

### WEDGEWOOD HOTEL
#### & SPA
BOUTIQUE HOTEL $$$

Map p266 (☑604-689-7777; www.wedgewoodhotel.com; 845 Hornby St; d from $350; P☻☀@⎙; ☐5) The last word in old-world European-style luxury, the elegant Wedgewood is dripping with top-hatted charm. The friendly staff is second to none, rooms are stuffed with reproduction antiques and the balconies enable you to smirk at the seemingly grubby plebs shuffling past below. Steam up your monocle with a trip to the spa, then sip a signature cocktail in the fireplace-warmed lobby bar. The fitness

center has had a recent upgrade and is now lined with slick, state-of-the-art equipment.

### FAIRMONT HOTEL
#### VANCOUVER
HOTEL $$$

Map p266 (☑604-684-3131; www.fairmont.com/hotelvancouver; 900 W Georgia St; d $399; P☀@⎙≋☀; ⓢVancouver City Centre) Opened in 1939 by visiting UK royals, this sparkling grand dame is a Vancouver landmark. Despite the provenance, the hotel carefully balances comfort with elegance: the lobby is bedecked with crystal chandeliers but the rooms have an understated business-hotel feel. If you have the budget, check in to the Gold Floor for a raft of pampering extras.

If you'd rather not pay for internet access, join the President's Club loyalty program for free and it won't cost you a penny (this applies to all Fairmont properties). If you're staying in the city at Christmas, this place is a good option: the lobby is always beautifully decorated for the season with a phalanx of sparkling Christmas trees. Overnight parking costs an eye-popping $55, but is free for electric cars and half-price for hybrid vehicles.

### ROSEWOOD HOTEL GEORGIA
HOTEL $$$

Map p266 (☑604-682-5566; www.rosewoodhotels.com; 801 W Georgia St; d $520; ☻☀@⎙≋☀; ⓢVancouver City Centre) Vancouver's current 'it' hotel underwent a spectacular renovation a few years back that brought the 1927-built landmark back to its golden-age glory. Despite the abstract modern art lining its public areas, the hotel's rooms take a classic, elegant approach with warming earth and coffee tones, pampering treats such as deep soaker tubs and (in some rooms) sparkling downtown cityscape views.

Save time for the lobby-level restaurant. Alongside the hotel's successful resurrection, it's become one of the top places to be seen for the city's social set – and you, if you look the part. Overnight parking is from $26.

### L'HERMITAGE HOTEL
BOUTIQUE HOTEL **$$$**

Map p266 (☑778-327-4100; www.lhermitage vancouver.com; 788 Richards St; d from $315; [P][♿][❄][@][🛜][🏊][🐕]; [S]Vancouver City Centre) This discreet, well-located property is divided between longer-stay suites that attract visiting movie-industry types and guests just dropping in for the night. Whichever you are, you'll find a contemporary designer feel combined with artsy flourishes in the rooms – some of which offer full kitchens. A library-style common lounge has a secret garden terrace, and there's an adjoining Jacuzzi and lap pool.

Free loaner bikes are available on request if you fancy exploring the city's ever-expanding network of urban bicycle lanes. Overnight parking costs $28.

### EXECUTIVE HOTEL LE SOLEIL
BOUTIQUE HOTEL **$$$**

Map p266 (☑604-632-3000; www.hotellesoleil. com; 567 Hornby St; d from $350; [♿][❄][@][🛜][🏊]; [S]Burrard) One of Vancouver's most stylish boutique hotel towers, Le Soleil is lined with classical European furnishings and bold flourishes that have a chic, Versace-esque appeal. Most rooms are compact but elegantly designed (corner units have balconies), and you'll be steps from the center of all the downtown nightlife action – although those on the higher floors will feel loftily far from the bustling streets.

If you don't fancy straying too far from your room, the hotel's lobby-level bistro serves great cocktails as well as some unexpectedly excellent Indian tapas dishes. Rates include access to a nearby gym with swimming pool.

### FAIRMONT PACIFIC RIM
HOTEL **$$$**

Map p266 (☑604-695-5300; www.fairmont. com/pacificrim; 1038 Canada Pl; d from $449; [P][♿][❄][🛜][🏊][🐕]; [S]Waterfront) Near the convention center, this chic 377-room property is Vancouver's newest Fairmont. While many rooms have city views, the ones with waterfront vistas will blow you away,

especially as you sit in your jetted tub or cube-shaped Japanese bath with a glass of bubbly. Extras include gratis loaner bikes as well as a rooftop swimming pool that should monopolize plenty of your time.

Check out the wrap-around text art installation on the hotel's glass exterior. And stick around for a drink: the lobby bar is popular with local cocktail-quaffing movers and shakers. Soothe your hangover away the next day at the Willow Stream Spa, one of the area's most popular pampering options. Overnight parking costs $49.

### SHANGRI-LA HOTEL
HOTEL **$$$**

Map p270 (☑604-689-1120; www.shangri-la. com/vancouver; 1128 W Georgia St; d from $440; [P][♿][❄][@][🛜][🏊][🐕]; [S]Burrard) Occupying the lower floors of the city's tallest tower, the Shangri-La redefined opulent Vancouver sleepovers when it opened, although the new Trump Hotel that was rising across the street on our visit may challenge its lofty status. The sleek, mood-lit rooms are lined with dark-wood paneling, while detailing extras include automatic bathroom blinds so you can shower behind the floor-to-ceiling windows without startling passers-by outside. Service is of the highly attentive, first-name variety and there's also an excellent full-service spa.

### PAN PACIFIC VANCOUVER
HOTEL **$$$**

Map p266 (☑604-662-8111; www.panpacific. com/vancouver; 999 Canada Pl; d from $450; [❄][@][🛜][🏊]; [S]Waterfront) This luxe Canada

*SLEEPING* (vertical tab in right margin)

---

### HOTELS WITH HISTORY

**Fairmont Hotel Vancouver** The city's lovely, gargoyle-topped grand hotel has had several royal guests over the years.

**Rosewood Hotel Georgia** Recently restored to its 1920s golden-age glory; glam former guests include Sinatra, Dietrich and Presley (not on the same night).

**Sylvia Hotel** (p218) Ivy-covered West End landmark where Errol Flynn is said to have had more than a drink or two.

**Pan Pacific Vancouver** Glam waterfront hotel where Princess Diana and Prince Charles stayed when they were together.

**TASTY HOTEL BARS**

➡ **Loden Hotel** Slick spot for pre-dinner cocktails.

➡ **Opus Hotel** (p220) Dress to hang with the Yaletown glitterati.

➡ **Sylvia Hotel** Lovely bar views across English Bay.

➡ **Listel Hotel** Adjoined by a Canadiana-themed bar with a craft-beer bent.

➡ **Fairmont Pacific Rim** (p217) Swish lobby bar that's ideal for cocktails and schmoozing.

Place hotel starts with a cavernous lobby, complete with its own clutch of totem poles. The large rooms, many with panoramic Burrard Inlet vistas, are no less impressive; they come with decadent maple-wood furnishings and the kind of beds whose linen thread-count is off the scale. More pampering required? Hit the luxurious on-site spa, a city fave.

Stanley Park and the downtown core are minutes away on foot, while Gastown (great for nightlife) is just around the corner. Overnight parking costs from $42.

### COAST COAL
### HARBOUR HOTEL                    HOTEL $$$
(☎604-697-0202; www.coasthotels.com; 1180 W Hastings St; d $275; ⊖❄🛜🐾🐕; ⑤Burrard) A modern and popular business hotel that also lures leisure travelers with its proximity to both Stanley Park and the downtown core, the bright and breezy Coast Coal Harbour often has some great deals on last-minute hotel-booking sites. For your money, you'll get a comfortable if generic-looking room with the possibility of waterfront views through those floor-to-ceiling windows. If you need to cool off after hiking the seawall, there's also an outdoor heated pool. Overnight parking costs $35.

## 🛏 West End

### HI VANCOUVER DOWNTOWN        HOSTEL $
(☎604-684-4565; www.hihostels.ca/vancouver; 1114 Burnaby St; dm/r incl breakfast $40/100; ⊖@🛜🛗; ☐6) It says 'downtown' but this purpose-built hostel is on a quiet residential West End side street. Popular with older hostelers and families, the dorms are all mercifully small and rates include continental breakfast. Private rooms are available. There's also bike storage, a full kitchen, and TV and games rooms; plus you're just a couple of downhill blocks from the beach. At this most 'institutional' of Vancouver's three HI hostels, the front-deskers are especially friendly. Book well ahead for private rooms.

### BUCHAN HOTEL                       HOTEL $$
Map p270 (☎604-685-5354; www.buchanhotel.com; 1906 Haro St; d with/without bath $149/109; P⊖@🛜; ☐5) The great value 1926-built Buchan has bags of charm and is just steps from Stanley Park. Along corridors lined with prints of yesteryear Vancouver, its pension-style budget rooms – most with shared bathrooms – are clean, cozy and well maintained, although some furnishings have seen better days. The pricier rooms are correspondingly prettier, while the eastside rooms are brighter. The front desk is friendly.

There's also a comfy guest lounge; other extras include storage facilities for bikes and skis as well as handy laundry machines. If you're driving, there's some free parking around the neighborhood, or you can pay $10 to park overnight at the hotel (spaces limited). There are many midrange dining options nearby, including a charming Italian restaurant at the base of the building.

### SUNSET INN & SUITES                HOTEL $$
Map p270 (☎604-688-2474; www.sunsetinn.com; 1111 Burnaby St; d incl breakfast $220; P❄@🛜; ☐6) A good-value cut above most of Vancouver's self-catering suite hotels, the popular Sunset Inn offers larger-than-average rooms with full kitchens. Each has a balcony, and some – particularly those on south-facing higher floors – have partial views of English Bay. Rates include continental breakfast (with make-your-own waffles) and, rare for Vancouver, gratis parking. The attentive staff is among the best in the city.

Sunset Inn is sitting pretty a few blocks from the Robson St shopping action, popular Sunset Beach and the bustling gay village around Davie St. Handy on-site laundry for guests is also available.

### SYLVIA HOTEL                       HOTEL $$
Map p270 (☎604-681-9321; www.sylviahotel.com; 1154 Gilford St; d $199; P⊖🛜🐕; ☐5)

This ivy-covered 1912 charmer enjoys a prime location overlooking English Bay. Generations of guests keep coming back – many requesting the same room every year – for a dollop of old-world ambiance, plus a side order of first-name service. The rooms, some with older furnishings, have a wide array of comfortable configurations, but the best are the large suites, which have kitchens and waterfront views.

If you don't have a room with a view, decamp to the lobby-level lounge to nurse a beer and watch the sun set over the beach. Overnight parking costs $18.

### TIMES SQUARE SUITES HOTEL
APARTMENT **$$**

Map p270 (☑604-684-2223; www.timessquare suites.com; 1821 Robson St; d $225; P❄❖🐾; 🖵5) Superbly located a short walk from Stanley Park, this West End hidden gem (even the entrance can be hard to spot) is the perfect apartment-style Vancouver sleepover. Rooms are mostly one-bedroom suites and are spacious, with tubs, laundry facilities, full kitchens and well-maintained (if slightly 1980s) decor. Rates include nearby gym access. There's a supermarket just across the street.

Choose a back suite if you want to be away from the busy road. Up to three adults can be accommodated in each suite (all are equipped with sofa beds). Make sure you visit the shared rooftop patio: the ideal place to while away an evening with a glass of wine, it has a communal barbecue. There's often a two-night minimum stay in July and August.

### LISTEL HOTEL
BOUTIQUE HOTEL **$$**

Map p270 (☑604-684-8461; www.thelistelhotel. com; 1300 Robson St; d $265; ❖❄@🐾; 🖵5) A sophisticated, self-described 'art hotel,' the Listel attracts grown-ups through its on-site installations and package deals with local galleries. Many rooms display original artworks and all have a relaxing, mood-lit West Coast feel. Artsy types should check out the lobby sculptures for selfie opportunities, while the property's on-site bar and restaurant are arguably the best hotel drink and dine options in the city.

Check the hotel's website for its current roster of good-value, art-themed package deals. And don't worry about finding the shops on your visit: you're steps away from Robson St's retail center. Overnight parking is $29.

### BLUE HORIZON HOTEL
HOTEL **$$**

Map p270 (☑604-688-1411; www.bluehorizon hotel.com; 1225 Robson St; r $229; P❄❖@🐾🐾; 🖵5) Despite being a 1960s tower, the well-maintained Blue Horizon still feels modern. The fairly spacious suites have the kind of quality, business-hotel furnishings common in pricier joints and all have corner balconies. Those on the higher floors look across to English Bay or the mountain-framed North Shore. The revamped on-site restaurant focuses on fresh comfort food and has a street-side patio.

The hotel is right on the city's main shopping strip, so you won't have far to transport your purchases. In addition, Stanley Park is a 15-minute walk away. Parking is $17 per day.

### BARCLAY HOUSE B&B
B&B **$$**

Map p270 (☑604-605-1351; www.barclayhouse. com; 1351 Barclay St; d from $150; P@🐾; 🖵5) This magnificent bright-yellow Victorian property (built in 1904) takes a sophisticated boutique twist on the usual heritage B&B. Rather than a mothballed museum look with delicate and overly chintzy antiques, the six rooms have a sophisticated, designer feel and are lined with modern artsy flourishes. But home comforts haven't been lost to aesthetics, and several rooms have gratifyingly deep soaker tubs. Our favorite room? The lovely Haidaway, which has original First Nations artworks, a step-up bed and a large jetted bathtub. Free parking.

### LODEN HOTEL
BOUTIQUE HOTEL **$$$**

Map p270 (☑604-669-5060; www.theloden. com; 1177 Melville St; d $449; P❄@🐾🐾; Ⓜ Burrard) The stylish Loden is the real designer deal, and one of the first boutique properties in years to give Yaletown's Opus a run for its money. The chic, mocha-hued rooms have a contemporary feel, with luxe accoutrements such as marble-lined bathrooms and those oh-so-civilized heated floors. Service is top-notch; try the lobby resto-bar as well as the complimentary London taxi-cab limo service. Free loaner bikes are also available; they're perfect for hitting the nearby Stanley Park seawall. Overnight parking costs $35.

### ENGLISH BAY INN
B&B **$$$**

Map p270 (☑604-683-8002; www.englishbay inn.com; 1968 Comox St; d incl breakfast from $260; P❖🐾; 🖵6) Each of the six antique-lined rooms in this Tudor-esque B&B near Stanley Park has a private bathroom, and some have sumptuous four-poster beds. You'll think you've arrived in Victoria, BC's determinedly Olde English capital, by mistake. Rates include a lovely three-course breakfast – arrive in the dining room early for the alcove table. There's also a canopy-shaded garden for hanging out in summer. This property has been a charmer for years, with many loyal guests coming back. Free parking is available on a first-come-first-served basis, although there are only three spots.

# 🛏 Gastown & Chinatown

⭐ SKWACHAYS LODGE     BOUTIQUE HOTEL **$$**
Map p273 (☑604-687-3589; www.skwachays. com; 29 W Pender St; d from $220; ❄️🛜; ⓢStadium-Chinatown) The 18 rooms at this First Nations art hotel include the captivating Forest Spirits Suite with floor-to-ceiling birch branches and the sleek Longhouse Suite, with its illuminated metalwork frieze. Deluxe trappings, from plasma TVs to ecofriendly toiletries, are standard and there's an on-site gallery for purchasing one-of-a-kind artworks to take home. The main streets of Gastown and Chinatown are also just steps away.

With an on-site gallery, 12m rooftop totem pole and bookable sweat lodge, smudge room and artist workshop experiences, this is an inviting cultural immersion sleepover. But that's not all. Owned by the Vancouver Native Housing Society, the building's lower floors accommodate 24 live-work indigenous artist studios, each subsidized by profits from the hotel and its fair trade gallery.

# 🛏 Yaletown & Granville Island

⭐ YWCA HOTEL     BUDGET HOTEL **$**
Map p274 (☑604-895-5830; www.ywcaho tel.com; 733 Beatty St; s/d/tr without bath $93/138/160; P♿❄️@🛜📶; ⓢStadium-Chinatown) A good-value, well-located option offering nicely maintained (if spartan) rooms of the student accommodation variety. There's a wide range of configurations, from singles to five-bed rooms, plus shared, semiprivate or private bathrooms. Each room has a mini-refrigerator and guests can use the three large communal kitchens. Rates include access to the YWCA Health & Fitness Centre, a 10-minute walk away.

This is a good option for budget-conscious families; kids get a toy upon check-in. Despite the slightly institutionalized feel, the staff is friendly and helpful. And if you stay here off-season, room rates are considerably lower. Parking costs $15 per night but spaces are limited.

OPUS HOTEL     BOUTIQUE HOTEL **$$$**
Map p274 (☑604-642-6787; www.opushotel. com; 322 Davie St; d $390; P❄️🛜🐾; ⓢYaletown-Roundhouse) The Opus kick-started Vancouver's boutique hotel scene and, with regular revamps, it's remained one of the city's top sleepover options. The designer rooms have contemporary-chic interiors with bold colors, mod furnishings and feng-shui bed placements, while many of the luxe bathrooms have clear windows overlooking the streets (visiting exhibitionists take note).

A model of excellent service, the Opus has a slick on-site bar and a quality Italian restaurant, while all rooms come with loaner iPads. And if you need to get around town, you can borrow a gratis bike or hop the hotel's freebie limo service – both excellent incentives not to bring your car since parking costs from $39 per night.

HOTEL BLU     HOTEL **$$$**
Map p274 (☑604-620-6200; www.hotel bluvancouver.com; 177 Robson St; d $350; @🛜🐾🐾; ⓢStadium-Chinatown) Brilliantly located near the center of downtown (and also major sports stadiums), this newer, condo-style tower hotel offers a range of comfortably mod, kitchen-and-microwave-equipped rooms, including swanky two-level suites that you might like to move into permanently. If you've indulged too much in the local restaurant scene, there's also a morning running program for guests that's guided by a personal trainer. Free loaner bikes can also be borrowed on a first-come-first-served basis.

GEORGIAN COURT HOTEL     HOTEL **$$$**
Map p274 (☑604-682-5555; www.georgian court.com; 773 Beatty St; d $300; P❄️🛜🐾; ⓢStadium-Chinatown) This under-the-radar, European-style property has never changed its old-school approach to good service and solid, dependable amenities. Rooms have an elegant, business-hotel feel but the spacious apartment-style corner suites – with their

quiet, recessed bedrooms – are best. There's a small on-site fitness room and the hotel runs a shuttle bus around the city for guests. A good location near the city center adds to the appeal here, and if you're planning to catch a hockey, football or soccer game, the city's two main stadiums are just steps away. Overnight parking costs $23.

GRANVILLE ISLAND
HOTEL                                    BOUTIQUE HOTEL $$$

Map p275 (📞604-683-7373; www.granvil leislandhotel.com; 1253 Johnston St; d $375; P🔄✳@🛜🐾; 🚌50) This gracious boutique property hugs Granville Island's quiet southeastern tip, enjoying tranquil views across False Creek to Yaletown's mirrored towers. You'll be a stroll from the Public Market, with shopping and theater options on your doorstep. Rooms have a West Coast feel with some exposed-wood flourishes. There's also a rooftop Jacuzzi, while the on-site brewpub-restaurant has one of the city's best patios.

You're close to the seawall bike trail here (the hotel can rent you a bike) if you fancy pedaling to UBC or, in the opposite direction, Stanley Park. Car parking is outside the hotel and costs $12 per day.

# 🛏 Fairview & South Granville

DOUGLAS GUEST HOUSE          GUESTHOUSE $$

Map p280 (📞604-872-3060; www.douglas. beautifulguesthouse.ca; 456 W 13th Ave, Fairview; d from $130; P; 🚌15) A refurbished tomato-soup-hued Edwardian house in a side street near City Hall, the Douglas offers good rates (especially in winter) and the kind of laid-back feel that means you don't worry about creaky floors and knickknacks falling over. Its rooms – comfortable rather than antique-lined – include smaller units with shared bathrooms, larger doubles with private bathrooms and kitchen-equipped garden suites. Off-street parking is included. With the same owners, next door's even bigger, blue-painted **Cambie Lodge** is also worth considering.

WINDSOR GUEST HOUSE                    B&B $$

Map p280 (📞604-872-3060; www.windsor. beautifulguesthouse.ca; 325 W 11th Ave, Fairview; d incl breakfast from $120; P🔄🛜; 🅂Broadway-City Hall) This 1895 wood-built mansion has a lived-in, homey feel,

## FIVE UNDER-THE-RADAR SLEEPOVERS

**Times Square Suites Hotel** (p219) Great location near Stanely Park for this hidden-in-plain-sight property.

**Sunset Inn & Suites** (p218) Tucked into the West End but with a highly loyal following.

**Granville Island Hotel** Hidden at the quiet end of the island, with great waterfront views.

**YWCA Hotel** Downtown budget-friendly tower close to everything.

**L'Hermitage Hotel** (p217) Slick but discreet sleepover in the heart of downtown.

**Georgian Court Hotel** Steps away from everything but with a hidden back-street feel.

complete with a charming veranda and stained-glass windows. The good-value rooms vary greatly in size and some have shared bathrooms. The recommended top floor 'Charles Room' is quaint, quiet and small with a patio overlooking downtown that's shared with the neighboring room. Cooked breakfast is included, along with free off-street parking.

The Windsor is on a quiet residential street with plenty of restaurants in the vicinity. The Canada Line's Broadway-City Hall station is also a short walk away, so you can be in the heart of downtown in less than 10 minutes.

# 🛏 Kitsilano & University of British Columbia

HI VANCOUVER
JERICHO BEACH                          HOSTEL $

(📞604-224-3208; www.hihostels.ca/vancouver ; 1515 Discovery St; dm/d $34/80; ⏰May-Oct; P@🛜; 🚌4) One of Canada's largest hostels looks like a Victorian hospital but has a scenic near-the-beach location. Basic rooms make this the least palatial Vancouver HI, but it has a large kitchen, bike rentals and a recently revamped licenced cafe. Dorms are also larger here. Book ahead for the popular budget-hotel-style private rooms which come in both shared

SLEEPING

and private bathroom options. For many, this hostel delivers more of a vacation than its downtown siblings due to its retreatlike beach proximity. Unlike other HI hostels, rates do not include continental breakfast. Take bus 4 west along 4th Ave and disembark at the intersection with NW Marine Dr. The hostel is a short stroll downhill from there. It's also a 10-minute bus hop to the University of BC if you want to avail yourself of the museums and restaurants there – or just pretend you're still a student.

### UNIVERSITY OF BRITISH COLUMBIA ACCOMMODATION ACCOMMODATION SERVICES $$

Map p286 (☑604-822-1000; www.suitesat ubc.com; 5961 Student Union Blvd; r $35/119; ☺May-Aug; ☻@☎; ☐99 B-Line) Pretend you're still a student with a UBC campus sleepover. Well-maintained options include great-value student-style single rooms at Pacific Spirit Hostel as well as suites with private rooms and shared kitchens. Superior rooms with private kitchen facilities are also available, including the top-of-the-range West Coast Suites with their comfortable, hotel-style feel. Ideal for groups or budget travelers who want to be close to UBC's array of museum, garden and gallery attractions. Downtown is 45 minutes away via transit.

### CORKSCREW INN B&B $$

Map p282 (☑604-733-7276; www.corkscrew inn.com; 2735 W 2nd Ave; d incl breakfast from $215; P☎; ☐4) This immaculate, gable-roofed property appears to have a drinking problem: it houses a little museum, available only to guests, that's lined with quirky corkscrews and antique vineyard tools. Aside from the boozy paraphernalia, this lovely century-old arts-and-crafts-style home has five wood-floored rooms (we like the art deco room) and is just a short walk from the beach. Sumptuous breakfast included. A three-night minimum stay typically applies, but the owners can be flexible about this if there's availability (especially outside summer). Parking is on the street and it's free.

## 🛏 North Shore

### THISTLEDOWN HOUSE B&B $$

Map p284 (☑604-986-7173; www.thistle-down. com; 3910 Capilano Rd, North Vancouver; d incl breakfast from $185; ☻; ☐236) Located on the road to Grouse Mountain, this adult-oriented 1920s arts-and-crafts-style house is superior to most B&Bs: check out the gourmet breakfast. Among its six elegantly decorated rooms, the most palatial suite (called Under the Apple Tree) is surprisingly secluded and includes a beautiful fireplace, sunken sitting room, Jacuzzi and large windows opening onto a private patio. The owners are friendly and helpful and have plenty of suggestions for what to do in the area during your stay.

### LONSDALE QUAY HOTEL BOUTIQUE HOTEL $$

Map p284 (☑604-986-6111; www.lonsdalequay hotel.com; 123 Carrie Cates Ct, North Vancouver; d $210; P☻✳@☎; ☻SeaBus to Lonsdale Quay) This well-located North Van waterfront sleepover has upgraded its rooms to include granite bathroom counters and (in the higher-end executive suites) flatscreen TVs, new artworks and dark-wood furnishings. It's attached to the market building a short walk from the SeaBus terminal. There are numerous restaurants nearby, and you can work off any vacation excesses in the gym. If you really want to indulge, the executive suites have curved-window views of the downtown towers twinkling across Burrard Inlet.

### PINNACLE HOTEL AT THE PIER HOTEL $$$

Map p284 (☑604-986-7437; www.pinnaclehotel atthepier.com; 138 Victory Ship Way, North Vancouver; d $289; P☻✳@☎☒☻; ☻Seabus Lonsdale Quay) North Van's best hotel is an excellent option if you want to stay on this side of the water and hop to Vancouver's city center on the nearby SeaBus. Rooms are furnished with contemporary elegance, calming hues favored over bold colors. The hotel balances itself between business and leisure travelers. Harbor views are recommended. Fitness buffs will enjoy the property's large gym and pool. Lonsdale Quay Public Market (p186) is just steps away.

# Understand Vancouver

# Vancouver Today

Vancouverites are not just a bunch of bike-riding hipsters who quaff craft beer and commune with the nearby mountains. It won't be long before you've told the locals how much you love their beautiful city and they've replied that it's not all perfect. House prices have been shooting skywards here since the 1990s – those 'best places in the world to live' surveys routinely placing Vancouver near the top come with a hefty cost-of-living price tag that locals are having to deal with.

## Best on Film

**Carts of Darkness** (2008)
Documentary exploring the 'extreme sport' of shopping-cart racing among local bottle pickers.

**Double Happiness** (1994)
Generational differences in a colorful Chinese-Canadian family in Vancouver.

**Mount Pleasant** (2006)
Gentrification-themed story about moving to a changing Vancouver neighborhood.

**Delicate Art of Parking** (2003)
Documentary-style comedy about local parking enforcers.

## Best in Print

**City of Glass** (Douglas Coupland, 2000) Quirky, affectionate homage to the city by one of its leading artists and authors.

**Live at the Commodore** (Aaron Chapman, 2015) Entertaining look at the history of Vancouver's favorite live-music venue.

**The Jade Peony** (Wayson Choy, 1995) Immersive memoir about growing up in a Vancouver Chinese immigrant family in the 1930s.

**Mister Got To Go** (Lois Simmie, 2002) Delightful children's book about the adventures of a curious cat at an old Vancouver hotel.

## Livability Issues

Get any two Vancouverites in a room and it won't be long before they're complaining about house prices. Many locals will tell you they've been priced out of the market in recent years and, with rental availability also at an all-time low, the millennial generation is increasingly talking about packing up and moving on. Whether many of them will actually do so remains to be seen. But when a disgruntled resident launched the Twitter hashtag #DontHave1Million to highlight the issue in 2015, thousands joined in and the national press covered the story.

It's sometimes said Vancouver has become the victim of its own success. It's reputedly one of the best places in the world to live – according to various global surveys – and was thrust into the international spotlight by Expo '86 and then the 2010 Olympic and Paralympic Winter Games. Both showcased the scenic city to the world, triggering massive inward investment, large-scale development and sharp house and condo price rises.

The result is that lower-income areas are dissolving away faster than a bowl of artisan ice cream on a summer's day. Traditionally cheap and grungy neighborhoods such as Strathcona, Main St and Commercial Dr – areas that once housed the city's artists, bohemians and working classes – have become trendy, sought-after spots commanding eye-popping prices unheard of just a few years ago. The average price of a Vancouver single-family home was reported to be $1.7 million in early 2016. At the same time, Canadian media was covering an international survey that claimed the city was behind only Hong Kong and Sydney for housing unaffordability.

## Development or Gentrification?

The city's sprawling Downtown Eastside district – which includes Gastown and Chinatown – has been rapidly gentrifying in recent years, with old buildings repaired and repainted into living and working spaces and cool bars, restaurants and coffee shops. Heritage spaces are often saved in this process, but transforming tired old neighborhoods into hipster havens has a flip side: the locals who have called these areas home for decades – a large proportion with long standing drug, poverty or mental-health issues – don't necessarily want to leave.

There are dozens of social-housing developments in this part of the city and these will remain for years to come. While the mayor has stated several times that Vancouver is committed to ending homelessness, the Downtown Eastside continues along this tense path of development, balancing the needs of those who want improvement and those who have always lived here and don't want their homes to change. Strolling Gastown and Chinatown today, you'll likely see protesting graffiti tags occasionally applied to the newly spruced-up storefronts.

## No Fun City

In the years leading up to the 2010 Olympics, Vancouver gained a reputation for being a bureaucratic stickler that made it hard for locals to launch new events and festivals, and for existing businesses – especially those related to booze – to expand their offerings. The phrase 'no fun city' emerged to cover what many saw as a small-minded, parochial approach, despite Vancouver's claim to being a world-class metropolis. But the 2010 Games were a turning point. Locals showed they could party without causing trouble and city officials responded by trying to extend the positive vibe after the event was over. It wasn't long before a food-truck program was launched, pop-up community festivals were facilitated, and several new grassroots summer events were introduced.

The booze rules also changed for the better. British Columbia (BC) has been at the forefront of Canada's recent microbrewery surge but it took a change of policy to encourage Vancouver to catch up with and then surpass Victoria's surfeit of tasty beermakers. An excellent array of microbrewery tasting rooms has since popped up here (they're almost unheard of in Victoria) while a relaxation of other rules has delivered beer tents to local events as well as happy hours at local bars – a development that was stymied for years but which has become highly popular at city watering holes and restaurants. Dropping the 'no fun' moniker is still a work in progress, though. And locals are quick to reapply the damming label whenever they see fit.

## if Vancouver were 100 people

46 would be Caucasian
27 would be Chinese
6 would be South Asian
6 would be Filipino
3 would be Southeast Asian
12 would be other

## belief systems
(% of population)

No religious affiliation — 49
Christian — 36
Buddist — 6
Sikh — 3
Muslim — 2
Hindu — 1

# History

**Vancouverites often say there's no history here, usually in jealous reference to 'all those old buildings in Europe.' But the fact is that Vancouver has a rich and tumultuous past stretching back thousands of years. Stand by for tales of First Nations communities from more than 10,000 years ago; Spanish and English explorers who poked around the region for the first time; and an Englishman who kick-started the modern-day city with a barrel of whiskey and a pub-building project.**

**Best History Books**

........................

The Chuck Davis History of Metropolitan Vancouver (Chuck Davis)

........................

Vanishing Vancouver: The Last 25 years (Michael Kluckner)

........................

Cold Case Vancouver (Eve Lazarus)

## Living off the Land

The ancestors of Vancouver's First Nations people were in British Columbia (BC) at least 10,000 years ago, setting up camp along the coastline in areas still regarded as important First Nations lands to this day. These first people lived in villages comprising wood-plank houses arranged in rows, often surrounded by a stockade. It's not surprising that these groups settled this area: the local beaches and rivers teemed with seafood; the forests bristled with tasty wildlife, including deer and elk; and salmon were abundantly available to anyone who fancied outsmarting the odd bear for the privilege.

Several distinct communities formed. The Musqueam populated Burrard Inlet, English Bay and the mouth of the Fraser River, although they shared some of this area with the Squamish, who were largely based at the head of Howe Sound, but also had villages in North and West Vancouver, Kitsilano Point, Stanley Park and Jericho Beach. The Kwantlen controlled the area around New Westminster, while Delta and Richmond were home to the Tsawwassen. The Tsleil-Waututh-occupied much of North Vancouver, while Coast Salish tribes, such as the Cowichan, Nanaimo and Saanich, set up seasonal camps along the Fraser River when the salmon were running.

Scant evidence exists about this intriguing period in Vancouver's history: most settlements have crumbled to dust and few have been rediscovered by archaeologists. In addition, these early settlers generally maintained oral records – they told each other (often in song) the stories of their ancestors, rather than writing things down for posterity.

| TIMELINE | 8000 BC | 1774 | 1791 |
|---|---|---|---|
| | Evidence of the region's first inhabitants dates from this time; whether they arrived from Asia across the Bering Strait or were here already is contentious among historians. | The Spanish arrive in the area in search of the fabled Northwest Passage. They don't venture any further than Vancouver Island's Nootka Sound. | A little more adventurous than his colleagues, Spanish explorer José María Narváez edges into the Strait of Georgia. |

# Captain Van Hits Town

After centuries of unhindered First Nations occupation, Europeans began arriving in the late 18th century. The Spanish sent three expeditions between 1774 and 1779 in search of the fabled Northwest Passage. British explorer Captain James Cook elbowed into the area from the South Pacific in 1779. He had a similar Northwest Passage motive but when he hit the west coast of Vancouver Island he believed it to be the mainland. It wasn't until 1791 that the Strait of Georgia near what we call Vancouver was properly explored. Spanish navigator José María Narváez did the honors, sailing all the way into Burrard Inlet.

Next up was Captain George Vancouver, a British navigator. In 1792 he glided into the inner harbor and spent one day here – an auspicious day, as it turned out. When he arrived, he discovered that the Spanish, in ships under the command of captains Valdez and Galiano, had already claimed the area. Meeting at what is today known as Spanish Banks, the men shared area navigational information. Vancouver made a note of the deep natural port, which he named Burrard after one of his crew. Then he sailed away, not thinking twice about a place that would eventually be named after him.

As Spanish influence in the area waned over the next few years in favor of the more persistent British, explorers such as Simon Fraser and Alexander Mackenzie began mapping the region's interior, opening it up for overland travelers, the arrival of the legendary Hudson's Bay Company, and the eventual full entry of the region into the British Empire.

The Spanish landed here before the Brits. Captain José María Narváez named the shoreline stretch where he set foot Islas de Langara, now Spanish Banks. This early influence is reflected around the BC coastline, where islands are called Saturna, Galiano and Texada.

# Gold & Timber

In 1858 gold was discovered on the banks of the Fraser River, and more than 25,000 shiny-eyed prospectors rapidly swept in. To maintain order and control, the mainland officially became part of the British Empire at this time. James Douglas was sworn in as the governor of the region, which included Vancouver Island. In a proclamation at Fort Langley on November 19, 1858, British Columbia officially came into being.

The first lumber mills were set up along the Fraser River in 1860, and their logging operations cleared the land for farms across the region. It wasn't long before operators began chewing northward through the trees toward Burrard Inlet. In 1867 Edward Stamp's British-financed Hastings Mill, on the south shore of the inlet, established the starting point of a town that would eventually become Vancouver.

With the promise of access to a new national railway network, BC joined the Canadian Confederation in 1871. It would be another 16 years before the railway actually rolled into the region.

| 1792 | 1827 | 1858 | 1867 |
|---|---|---|---|
| The Brits join the party when Royal Navy Captain George Vancouver sails into Burrard Inlet. He stays just 24 hours before setting sail again. | The Hudson's Bay Company builds Fort Langley, the first European settlement to grace the region. | Gold is discovered on the banks of the Fraser River, prompting more than 25,000 prospectors to arrive with picks and pans. Most leave empty-handed. | John 'Gassy Jack' Deighton rows in with a barrel of whiskey and some big ideas. He opens a saloon, and a small, thirsty settlement – called Gastown – springs up near the entrance. |

# From Granville to Vancouver

In 1867, Englishman John 'Gassy Jack' Deighton rowed into Burrard Inlet with his First Nations wife, a small dog and a barrel of whiskey. He knew the nearest drink for thirsty mill workers was 20km away so he asked them to help him build a tavern. Within 24 hours the Globe Saloon was in business. And when a village sprang up around the establishment it was quickly dubbed 'Gastown.' In 1870, in an attempt to formalize the ramshackle township, the colonial administration renamed it 'Granville,' although almost everyone still called it Gastown.

Selected over Port Moody, a rival mill town, as the new western railway terminus for the Canadian Pacific Railway (CPR), the town of Granville was incorporated as the City of Vancouver in April 1886. According to legend, this name was chosen by CPR manager William Van Horne, who reasoned the new city needed a grand moniker to live up to its future as a great metropolis. He is said to have selected the name 'Vancouver' to recall the historic seafarer who literally put the area on the map.

The first piece of business for Vancouver's new council was to establish the city's first park – and so Stanley Park was born. But the city faced a less enjoyable task at the tender age of two months: on June 13, 1886, a fire lit by CPR workers to clear brush rapidly spread out of control. The 'Great Fire,' as it came to be known, took 45 minutes to destroy Vancouver's 1000 wooden structures, killing as many as 28 people (the number remains disputed) and leaving 3000 homeless.

Within hours reconstruction was under way. But this time the buildings were fashioned from stone and brick. A few months later, on May 23, 1887, Locomotive 374 pulled the first transcontinental passenger train into the city and Vancouver was back in business. Within four years, it grew to a population of 13,000, and between 1891 and 1901 the population skyrocketed to more than double that.

## Growing Pains

The railway was responsible for shaping much of the city as it exists today, with the CPR developing several key neighborhoods for new residential developments. During the first 30 years of the 20th century, the suburbs around the city also grew substantially. When Point Grey and South Vancouver amalgamated with the city in 1929, Vancouver became Canada's third-largest city – a ranking it retains today.

While the 1930s Great Depression saw the construction of several public works – the Marine Building, Vancouver City Hall, the third and present Hotel Vancouver and the Lions Gate Bridge, to name a few –

Among the reminders of early Vancouver are Kitsilano's Old Hastings Mill Store Museum and Gassy Jack's statue in Maple Tree Sq. The Byrnes Block, the oldest Vancouver building still in its original location, recalls the city's swift reconstruction after the 1886 Great Fire.

Locomotive 374 pulled the first transcontinental passenger train into Vancouver, but was left to rot on a local beach for decades after its retirement. A long-overdue campaign to restore it culminated in its unveiling in a purpose-built Yaletown home in time for Expo '86.

| 1871 | 1886 | 1887 | 1901 |
| --- | --- | --- | --- |
| With the promise of access to a new national railway network, BC joins the Canadian Confederation. Sixteen years later, the railway rolls into the region. | The fledgling town is incorporated as the City of Vancouver. Within weeks, the new city burns to the ground in just 45 minutes. | Locomotive 374 pulls the first transcontinental passenger train into a rebuilt Vancouver, and the town is back in business. | First Nations communities, who have lived here for thousands of years, are displaced from their settlements in the Vanier Park area, as colonials fell forests. |

many people were unemployed. This marked a time of large demonstrations, violent riots and public discontent.

WWII helped to pull Vancouver out of the Depression by creating instant jobs at shipyards, aircraft-parts factories and canneries, and in construction with the building of rental units for the increased workforce. Japanese Canadians didn't fare so well. In 1942, following the bombing of Pearl Harbor, they were shipped to internment camps and had to endure the confiscation of their land and property, much of which was never returned. Chinese, Japanese and First Nations people were finally given the provincial vote in 1949.

## Expo-sing the City

By the start of the 1950s Vancouver's population was 345,000 and the area was thriving. The high-rise craze hit in the middle of the decade, mostly in the West End. During the next 13 years 220 apartment buildings went up in this area alone.

In the 1960s and '70s, Vancouver was known for its counterculture community, centered on Kitsilano. Canada's gay-rights movement began here in 1964 when a group of feminists and academics started the Association for Social Knowledge, the country's first gay and lesbian discussion group. In 1969 the Don't Make a Wave Committee formed to stop US nuclear testing in Alaska, sending a protest vessel to the region in 1971. A few years later the group morphed into the environmental organization Greenpeace.

As the years passed, the city's revolutionary fervor dissipated and economic development became the region's main pastime. Nothing was more important to Vancouver in the 1980s than Expo '86, the world fair that many regard as the city's coming of age. The six-month event, coinciding with Vancouver's 100th birthday, brought millions of visitors to the city and kick-started a rash of regeneration in several tired neighborhoods. New facilities built for Expo included the 60,000-seat BC Place Stadium, which has since played a starring role in the opening and closing ceremonies of the 2010 Olympic and Paralympic Winter Games.

## Multicultural Milestones

The brewing issue of First Nations land rights spilled over in the late 1980s, with a growing number of rallies, road blockades and court actions in the region. Aside from a few treaties covering a tiny portion of the province, land-claim agreements had not been signed and no clear definition of the scope and nature of First Nations rights existed. Until 1990 the provincial government refused to participate in treaty negotiations. That

A few steps from Chinatown's Millennium Gate, Shanghai Alley was once home to hundreds of immigrant Chinese men, domiciled in cheap lodgings. With its own shops, eateries and 500-seat theater, it was designed as a one-way street that could be defended in the event of attack from locals.

HISTORY EXPO-SING THE CITY

| 1949 | 1956 | 1964 | 1979 |
|---|---|---|---|
| The region's Chinese, Japanese and First Nations peoples finally gain the right to vote in provincial elections. | The West End is rezoned for greater population density. Hundreds of wooden homes are bulldozed for apartment blocks. | Canada's gay-rights movement begins when feminists and academics create the Association for Social Knowledge, the country's first gay and lesbian discussion group. | Granville Island is developed from an industrial wasteland into one of Vancouver's most popular hangouts. A cement factory remains, to keep the faith. |

changed in December of that year when the BC Claims Task Force was formed among the Canadian and BC governments and the First Nations Summit, with a mission to figure out how the three parties could solve land-rights matters. It has been a slow-moving, ongoing process that in Vancouver's case involves the Tsawwassen, Tsleil-Waututh, Katzie, Squamish and Musqueam nations.

The 1990s saw the region become even more multicultural. Prior to the British handover of Hong Kong to China in 1997, tens of thousands of wealthy Hong Kong Chinese migrated to BC's Lower Mainland area, boosting the area's permanent Asian population by about 85% and creating the largest Asian population in any North American city. Real-estate prices rose, with Vancouver's cost-of-living figures suddenly rivaling those of London, Paris and Tokyo. Many of the new arrivals shunned the city proper in favor of the suburbs, especially Richmond. By 1998 immigration had tapered off but the city's transformation into a modern, multicultural mecca was already complete.

## Going for Gold

In the opening decade of the new millennium, Vancouver became a regular on those global surveys that designate the best places in the world to live. Seizing the initiative and recalling the success of Expo '86, the region again looked to the future, winning the bid to host the 2010 Olympic and Paralympic Winter Games.

With events staged in and around the city, and also at Whistler, a global TV audience of more than two billion gazed admiringly at picture-perfect snow-and-blue-sky vistas, while athletes from 80 countries competed for gold. And while many locals had grumbled about the cost of the Games, the entire city exploded in a 17-day mardi gras of support that surprised even the organizers.

Upwards of 200,000 Maple Leaf–waving partyers hit the streets around Robson and Granville Sts every night to hang out with overseas visitors, catch LiveSite music shows and break into impromptu renditions of the national anthem. This all-enveloping Canadian pride hit fever pitch during the men's gold-medal hockey game, when the host nation beat the US with a dreamlike last-gasp goal. For many Vancouverites, this moment was the best thing that's ever happened in the city's short modern history.

## Gentrification

After the Olympics, a new wave of development took hold in the city, especially in those areas that had traditionally seen little change in decades

| 1983 | 1985 | 1986 | 1996 |
|---|---|---|---|
| BC Place Stadium polishes its roof and opens for business, and the old courthouse building is transformed into the Vancouver Art Gallery. | The first SkyTrain line opens, creating a link between the communities of New Westminster and Vancouver. | The international spotlight shines on Vancouver as the Expo '86 world fair dominates the summer, bringing Sheena Easton and Depeche Mode to local stages. | With the Hong Kong handover to China imminent, Vancouver sees a massive influx of Asian immigrants into the city. Richmond transforms into the region's new Chinatown. |

past. One such controversial neighborhood in particular was suddenly part of these new plans. Long blighted by drugs, prostitution and a concentration of mentally ill residents, the Downtown Eastside – centered on Main and Hastings Sts – had been a no-go skid row for many years. While nearby Gastown was the historic genesis of the city, the key streets of the Downtown Eastside were also once lined with the banks, shops and bustling commercial enterprises of the region's main business district. When new development shifted the city center across to the Robson and Granville Sts area of downtown in the 1940s, though, this old 'hood began a graceless decline. City and provincial policies that concentrated services for the poor and homeless in the area didn't help, with squalid rooming houses and dodgy pubs soon becoming standard fixtures.

Politicians have made regular pronouncements about solving the area's problems since the 1990s. Current mayor Gregor Robinson promised but failed to end homelessness across the city by 2015, and a new wave of gentrification is finally changing the neighborhood. The opening of a large new housing, shops and university-campus complex on the old Woodward's department-store site in 2010 was the catalyst for change, with new businesses recolonizing the area's paint-peeled storefronts for the first time in decades. The gentrification drive is not without controversy, though. While city hipsters move into pricey loft apartments and populate exposed-brick coffee shops, the residents who have called this area home for the last few decades are feeling threatened and increasingly marginalized. In 2013 antigentrification protesters began picketing new restaurants in the area and appealing for more social housing to be part of all future plans. Finding the right balance between rampant development and support for the people who already live in the city's Eastside will be one of Vancouver's biggest challenges over the coming years.

For decades a neon-lit 'W' stood atop the old Woodward's department store. But when the building was redeveloped it was found to be severely corroded. A new one was created in its place, while the old one was preserved in a glass case at ground level.

## Real Estate Rumble

Rising housing costs haven't just been a challenge for poorer Vancouverites in recent years, though. Expo '86 and the 2010 Winter Olympics were almost 25 years apart, but their effect on the city were similar. They brought Vancouver to the attention of many more people around the world; specifically, people with money to purchase real estate. Strike up a conversation with many locals here and it's usually just a matter of minutes before they mention ever-rising Vancouver house prices that have made the city the most expensive metropolis in Canada in which to buy a home. There are several contributing factors but the result is that younger locals who are not able to splash out up to $2 million on purchasing a family home talk more than ever about leaving the city.

| 2003 | 2010 | 2013 | 2016 |
| --- | --- | --- | --- |
| BC and Ontario lead North America by making same-sex marriage legal. Vancouver becomes a hot spot for elopements. | Locals party as Vancouver hosts the Olympic and Paralympic Winter Games. Flags are waved, national anthems sung and Canada wins gold in men's hockey. | Stanley Park celebrates its 125th birthday with a mammoth free-entry party. | The Eastside Culture crawl, the city's biggest grassroots arts festival, marks its 20th anniversary. |

(Above) Stanley Park

# Green Vancouver

**It's hard to see Vancouver as anything but a green city: its dense forests and verdant, rain-fed plant life make nature an ever-present fact of life here. But beyond the breathtaking visuals, how does the city measure up to its environmental responsibilities? And – just as importantly – what can Vancouver-bound visitors do to reduce their own environmental footprint in the region without turning their vacation into a monastic, fun-free zone?**

## Painting the Town Green

Vancouver has an international reputation for being a green city, but that doesn't mean everyone here wears biodegradable socks and eats only elderly vegetables that have died of natural causes. In fact, if you stroll the Robson St boutiques or dip into a take-out coffee shop, it's easy to think that 'green Vancouver' doesn't exist at all. As with many of the city's best features, you have to do a little digging.

## VANCOUVER'S 'HIGH LINE'

Purchasing 9km of disused railway-line land that runs south from Kitsilano to Marpole and the Fraser River, the City of Vancouver is currently creating the Arbutus Greenway Park. The 17-hectare ribbonlike parkland, which cost the city $55 million in 2016, will deliver a tree-fringed cycling and walking route that aims to be a shimmering showcase of Vancouver's green credentials The hope is that the new park will create the same excitement among locals and visitors as New York's wildly popular High Line park.

Given the city's breathtaking natural surroundings, it was just a matter of time before Vancouver's residents were inspired to protect the planet, which explains why a few of them began gathering in a Kitsilano basement in 1969 to plan the fledgling Don't Make a Wave Committee's first protest against nuclear testing in Alaska. By the time their campaign boat entered the Gulf of Alaska in 1971, they had renamed themselves Greenpeace and sailed into environmental history. Greenpeace set the tone and the city has since become a headquarters for environmental groups, from the Wilderness Committee to Farm Folk City Folk and the David Suzuki Foundation.

Actions speak louder than words, however, and Vancouver's green scene is not just about protest and discussion. The city is home to dozens of large and small eco-initiatives, enabling many locals to color their lives as green as they choose. Vancouver has one of the largest hybrid-vehicle taxi fleets in North America and has a commitment to mass public transportation, including electric trolley buses and a light-rail train system. Carpooling and rideshare alternatives to traditional car hire are also big here, with Evo, Zipcar and Car2Go having a growing presence on city streets.

And while developers tout their green credentials as if they're saving the planet single-handedly, few of the city's new towers are built without key environmental considerations. Vancouver is also a leader in 'green roofs' – planted rooftops that curb wasted energy through natural evaporation in summer and natural insulation in winter. The Shangri-La Hotel tower and the giant convention center West Building next to Canada Place each have one, while downtown's Colosseum-shaped Public Library building has another. On our visit, plans were afoot to add a cafe and to open this to year-round public access.

## On the Ground

Several Vancouver accommodation options have some kind of environmental program. Opus Hotel (p220), for example, has a water- and energy-conservation scheme; the Fairmont Hotel Vancouver (p216) deploys energy-efficient lighting; and the Listel Hotel (p219) has installed its own power-generating solar panels.

Dining is also firmly on the green agenda here. Spearheaded by the Vancouver Aquarium and a growing menu of city restaurants, Ocean Wise (www.oceanwise.ca) encourages sustainable fish and shellfish supplies that minimize environmental impact. The website lists participating restaurants; and check local menus for symbols indicating Ocean Wise dishes. A similar, smaller movement called the Green Table Network (www.greentable.net) can help you identify considerate area restaurants that try to source all their supplies – not just seafood – from sustainable, mostly local, sources.

---

**Vancouver's Greenest Attractions**

Stanley Park (p52)

Stanley Park Nature House (p52)

UBC Botanical Garden (p169)

City Farmer (p1

Arbutus Greenway Park (pending) (p178)

---

Vancouver has an active plan to be the world's greenest city by 2020. Among its raft of goals, the city aims to drastically cut waste and carbon emissions, as well as improve regional ecosystems.

Vancouver has more than 300km of designated bike lanes

Vancouver recently introduced a pilot scheme to support the use of plug-in electric vehicles. The initiative, the first of its kind in BC, has seen the introduction of car-charging ports at parking lots around the city. Charging costs $1 per hour.

Sustainability also has a social side in Vancouver with Green Drinks (www.greendrinks.org), a monthly drop-in gathering for anyone interested in environmental issues. The meetings take place at Gastown's Steamworks Brewing Company bar and usually attract more than 100 regulars for beer-fueled discussions on alternative energy, global warming and the sky-high price of organic groceries. Speaking of groceries, there are lots of sustainable food-shopping options around the city, but the area's farmers markets are the ideal way to eat well and do your bit for the world. See www.eatlocal.org for listings of several area markets.

Consider hopping onto two wheels to get around the city. Vancouver has more than 300km of designated bike lanes, so you can see the sights without burning up the planet. Bike rentals are easy to come by and many operators can get you out for a citywide pedal. The city also recently launched Mobi, its new public bike-share scheme. See www.mobibikes.ca for the latest information.

## CITY FORAGING

For a cool introduction to the edible plants growing alongside us every day, book ahead for a tour with Vancouver's Forager Foundation. Promoting traditional methods of gathering food and medicine, the nonprofit organization runs illuminating tours – often including Stanley Park – for curious locals and visitors. Check the website (www.foragertours.com) for the latest tour offerings.

Fall foliage in Nitobe Memorial Garden, University of British Columbia

# Tree Hugging

It's hard not to be impressed by the towering Douglas firs in Stanley Park or the cherry blossom trees that bloom around the city in spring. But for many, fall is the best time to hang out with the trees. Burnished copper, pumpkin-orange, deep candy-apple red: the seemingly infinite colors of autumn under cloudless blue skies make this the favorite season for many Vancouverites, and it's one of the rare times you'll see locals reaching for their cameras. If you're here in October, charge up your camera, slip into comfortable walking shoes and hunt down the following pigment-popping locations.

Make a beeline for Stanley Park. Hit the seawall – by bike or on foot – to find rusty amber hues and Japanese maple reds studding the evergreen Douglas firs. If you don't have time for a full-on Stanley Park jaunt, weave towards nearby English Bay. The beach at the end of Denman St will require your camera's panorama setting. You'll find a glittering, gently rippling waterfront, backed by a stand of achingly beautiful mature trees, each seemingly a different color. Not surprisingly, this is also a great location for sunset shots. If it's raining, nip into the lounge bar of the nearby ivy-shrouded Sylvia Hotel: it faces the water, so you'll still have a great view.

Across town at Queen Elizabeth Park, weave uphill among the trees from the Cambie St entrance. Aim towards the Bloedel Conservatory dome at the summit for a spectacular squirrel's-eye view across the foliage. On a fine day, you'll also have one of the best wide-angled vistas over the glass-towered city, framed by ice-frosted mountains. And if it's time to warm up, nip inside the Conservatory where the tropical plants and neon-bright birds are guaranteed to give your day a splash of extra color.

Every June, four local neighborhoods banish their cars and turn themselves into pedestrian-only zones. Over the years, Car Free Vancouver (p140) has grown to become one of the city's most popular, family-friendly street parties, with thousands of locals rolling in for food stands, live music, craft stalls and a large serving of exhaust-free fun.

It's not all parks, of course. Many of Vancouver's older residential neighborhoods resemble spilled paintboxes of color every fall. The West End neighborhood is striped with residential streets where fall-flavored trees mix with bright-painted heritage houses: on a honey-lit, sunshine-steeped day, you can hear the photographers clicking madly here. One of the best spots is Mt Pleasant's 10th Ave, especially in the section running east from City Hall. Like a walk-through kaleidoscope, the dozens of century-old chestnut trees here create a tunnel of rich orange and yellow – above a dense carpet of fallen chestnuts that's like walking on shiny cobbles.

## Green Shoots

Many Vancouver green initiatives are at the grassroots community level and one of our favorites is the city's Pop-up Library phenomenon. Several neighborhoods across Vancouver have built their own pop-up mini-libraries for all to use. These free-to-use book exchanges sit outside on residential streets – covered, of course, to stop the dog-eared tomes suffering on Vancouver's frequent rainy days. There are at least five dotted around local communities. One of the largest is the St George Sharing Library, a double-shelved covered table a few steps from the intersection of East 10th Ave and St George St. It's always bulging with well-used paperbacks, from pulp fiction to self-published screeds on communism and the occasional Lonely Planet guidebook.

Vancouver's Fruit Tree Project Society (www.vancouverfruittree. com) deploys a green army of volunteers to harvest treats that would otherwise rot on trees around the city. Collecting hundreds of pounds of fruit every year, the goodies – typically including plums, apples, pears and grapes – are redistributed to those in need around the city.

# Arts & Culture

It's more than easy to believe that Vancouver's calf-busting outdoorsy locals must be philistines when it comes to arty pursuits – how can mountain bikers be interested in galleries, dance and literature, you might ask? But in reality, this city by the sea is a major Canadian cultural capital. With a little digging, visitors will be able to tap into the primarily grassroots scene. Ask the locals for tips and pick up a copy of the free, weekly *Georgia Straight*.

## Visual Arts

British Columbia (BC) is strongly identified with three main forms of visual arts, and each is well represented in galleries and public spaces throughout Vancouver. Historic and contemporary aboriginal works are displayed at unique institutions such as the University of British Columbia's amazing Museum of Anthropology (p164) and downtown's much

(Above) Carved masks at the Museum of Anthropology

newer Bill Reid Gallery of Northwest Coast Art (p59). Contemporary painting and photoconceptualism (often called the 'Vancouver School' of photography) are exhibited at the Vancouver Art Gallery (p57) as well as at many private galleries, including those in the Flats, an emerging new gallery district just off Main St. For further information on the local art scene, visit www.art-bc.com.

Vancouver provides plenty of opportunity to meet some of the region's creative types face to face, including one annual event that has never been more popular. Recently marking its 20th anniversary, November's partylike Eastside Culture Crawl (p93) is when hundreds of East Vancouver artists open their studios large and small for locals to wander around. It's the best art event in the city, and a firm local favorite. An even bigger celebration will likely take place when the Vancouver Art Gallery (p57) makes its long-anticipated move to a grand new downtown venue sometime over the next few years; check the website for the latest updates.

## Public Art

Vancouver has a vigorous public-art program and you'll likely spot challenging installations, decorative apartment-building adornments and sometimes puzzling sculptures dotted throughout the city. Check www.vancouver.ca/publicart for an online registry of works and some handy maps, or pick up the excellent book *Public Art in Vancouver: Angels Among Lions,* by John Steil and Aileen Stalker. It has photos of and information on more than 500 works around the city, divided into neighborhoods. Also, check the website of the Vancouver Biennale (p61), a massive public-art showcase, staged in two-year chunks, that brings monumental, often challenging, installations to the city's streets from artists around the world. The website shows where to find these works and plot your own walking tour.

Among the public artworks to look out for in Vancouver are the 14 smiling, oversized bronze figures near the shoreline of English Bay, which form one of Canada's most-photographed art installations; the five wrecked cars piled on top of a cedar tree trunk near Science World; the pixilated-looking orca alongside downtown's Convention Centre extension; the towering neon cross at Clark Dr and E 6th Ave; the silver replica of a freight shed on piles by Liz Magor, on the Coal Harbour seawall; and, of course, the quirky white-painted poodle on Main St that locals either love or loathe.

Even Vancouver International Airport is worthy of a photographic snap or two for its visual art: between the international and US check-in desks, the magnificent bronze Spirit of Haida Gwaii by Bill Reid is the terminal's focal point, while other handsome indigenous pieces dot the terminal buildings.

## First Nations Art

First Nations artists have contributed mightily to Vancouver's historic and contemporary visual-arts scene, particularly through carving. Two carvers who preserved the past while fostering a new generation of First Nations artists were Charles Edenshaw, the first professional Haida artist, who worked in argillite, gold and silver; and Mungo Martin, a Kwakiutl master carver of totem poles. Martin passed on his skills to Bill Reid, the outstanding Haida artist of his generation and the first Haida artist to have a retrospective exhibition at the Vancouver Art Gallery. His work is permanently displayed at the Museum of Anthropology (p164) and also at downtown's Bill Reid Gallery of Northwest Coast Art (p59), where exquisite works from

### Blog It

Before you hit town, jump into the indie scene via these eclectic local-music blogs:

**Van Music** (www.vanmusic.ca)

**Backstage Rider** (www.backstagerider.com)

**Vancity Music Scene** (www.vancitymusicscene.blogspot.ca)

**Winnie Cooper** (www.winnie-cooper.net)

**Groundwerk Vancouver** (www.groundwerkvancouver.com)

Dance troupe performing at annual Dancing on the Edge festival

### Vancouver Indie Movies

**On the Corner** *(2003) Fictional account of life on the Downtown Eastside.*

**Carts of Darkness** *(2008) Documentary exploring the 'extreme sport' of shopping-cart racing among local bottle pickers.*

**Double Happiness** *(1994) Generational differences in a colorful Chinese-Canadian family in Vancouver.*

**The Delicate Art of Parking** *(2003) Documentary-style comedy about Vancouver parking enforcers.*

other First Nations artists are also on display. Vancouver is also well-stocked with private galleries where you can buy authentic First Nations art from this region.

One of the world's hottest First Nations artists, Brian Jungen disassembles well-known objects and recreates them in challenging new forms, usually fusing them with traditional arts-and-crafts visuals. His most famous works are the First Nations masks made from resewn sections of Nike running shoes, and his detailed whalebone sculptures created from humdrum plastic chairs. You can see some of his work in Whistler's new Audain Art Museum (p198).

## Performance Arts

Vancouver has a strong reputation for stage performance and is especially well represented in dance and live theater.

Second only to Montréal as a hotbed of contemporary Canadian dance, Vancouver is home to dozens of professional companies. The Dance Centre is the main twinkle-toes resource in the province. Its range of activities is unparalleled in Canada, including support for professional artists, operation of Western Canada's flagship dance facility, and presentation of a huge number of programs and events for the public. Dance events are scheduled throughout the city, including the three-week-long Vancouver International Dance Festival in spring and the 10-day Dancing on the Edge event in July.

Despite losing its long-established Playhouse Theatre Company to a funding crisis in 2012, Vancouver is home to a vibrant theater scene. But rather than one or two major theaters, you'll find many smaller stages dotted around the city. The Arts Club Theatre Company (www.artsclub.com) is the city's largest theatrical troupe, and the host of fringelike smaller venues and companies include the Cultch and Firehall Arts Centre. Events-wise, plan your visit for the Bard on the Beach Shakespeare festival, the Vancouver International Fringe Festival (p109) or the PuSh Festival (p35). And if you're a fan of alfresco shows, the outdoor Malkin Bowl in Stanley Park is home to the summer season Theatre Under the Stars troupe.

## Cinema & Television

The movie industry has a starring role in Vancouver's 'Hollywood North' economy. True, not many stories are set in the city – few know that *Rise of the Planet of the Apes* and the *BFG* movies were filmed here – but the industry is home to a couple hundred productions every year. Vancouver's influential Vancouver Film School counts director/actor/ screenwriter Kevin Smith (of *Clerks* fame) among its most famed grads, while actors who have moved on to global acclaim from the city include Seth Rogen, Ryan Reynolds and Michael J Fox.

Alongside a full range of local movie theaters, Vancouver is home to many niche film festivals staged in the city throughout the year, and the giant Vancouver International Film Festival is one of the city's most popular annual cultural events. Second only to Toronto's film fest in size, it's a 17-day showcase of great flicks from Canada and around the world. The city also nurtures budding filmmakers through the likes of the Celluloid Social Club; held monthly at the Anza Club near Main St, it's a hangout for aspiring movie creatives and is open to all comers.

## Literature

Vancouver is a highly bookish city, home to a healthy round of bookstores and a large volume of literary events to keep local and visiting bookworms fully enthralled. Among the city's favorite bookshop hangouts are Macleod's Books (p75), Paper Hound (p75) and Pulpfiction Books (p142), where stacks of used tomes invite cozy browsing on rainy days. If you really want to see how serious the city is about books, visit the landmark Vancouver Public Library (p60), shaped like the Colosseum. There are plenty of ways to rub bookish shoulders with the locals at events that include poetry slams, the Word on the Street book and magazine festival, and the Vancouver International Writers Festival, where you're likely to run into every book lover in town.

Local authors past and present who have garnered international reputations include Douglas Coupland, William Gibson and Malcolm Lowry. Coupland is the city's most famous living author, with celebrated works including *Generation X, J-Pod* and his latest title: *Bit Rot.*

A strong nonfiction bent also exists within the local literary scene. In recent years two local authors have produced back-to-back wins in Canada's prestigious Charles Taylor Prize for Literary Nonfiction. Charles Montgomery's *The Last Heathen: Encounters with Ghosts and Ancestors in Melanesia* (later published around the world as *The Shark God*) led the way, followed by his colleague James Mackinnon who won for *Dead Man in Paradise*. Mackinnon also produced the excellent *Once and Future World: Nature As It Was, As It Is, As It Could Be.*

# Survival Guide

# Transportation

## ARRIVING IN VANCOUVER

Most visitors will arrive by air at Vancouver International Airport, south of the city on Sea Island in Richmond. Alternatively, US trains trundle in from Seattle to Pacific Central Station, located on the southern edge of Vancouver's Chinatown district. Cross-border intercity bus services also arrive at this terminal. Vancouver is only an hour or so from several US border crossings, so driving is a popular way to access the city from the US, while cruise ships plying the Alaska route also dock on the city's waterfront. Cross-Canada rail, bus and flight operations also service the city, which is the main gateway for accessing destinations throughout British Columbia (BC).

Flights, cars and tours can be booked online at lonely planet.com/bookings.

## Vancouver International Airport

Canada's second-busiest airport, **Vancouver International Airport** (YVR; Map p204; ☑604-207-7077; www.yvr.ca; ☎), lies 13km south of downtown in the city of Richmond. There are two main terminals – international (including flights to the US)

and domestic – just a short indoor stroll apart. A third (and much smaller) South Terminal is located a quick drive away: free shuttle-bus links are provided. This terminal services float-planes, helicopters and smaller aircraft traveling on lower capacity routes to small communities in BC and beyond. In addition, short-hop floatplane and helicopter services to and from Vancouver Island and beyond also depart from the city's downtown waterfront near Canada Place.

The main airport has shops, food courts, currency exchange booths and a tourist information desk. It's also dotted with handsome aboriginal artworks. Baggage carts are free (no deposit required) and there is also free wi-fi.

### Train

SkyTrain's 16-station **Canada Line** (see the route maps at www.translink.ca) operates a rapid-transit train service from the airport to downtown. Trains run every few minutes from early morning until after midnight and take around 25 minutes to reach downtown's Waterfront Station. The airport station is located just outside, between the domestic and international terminals. Follow the signs from inside either terminal and buy your ticket from

the platform vending machines. These accept cash, and credit and debit cards – look for green-jacketed Canada Line staff if you're bleary-eyed and need assistance after your long-haul flight. Fares from the airport cost between $7.75 and $10.50, depending on your destination and the time of day.

### Taxi

➡ Follow the signs from inside the airport terminal to the cab stand just outside. The fare to downtown, around 30 minutes away, will usually cost between $35 and $45, plus tip (15% is the norm).

➡ Alternatively, limo car services are also available close to the main taxi stand. Expect to pay around $20 more for your ride to the city if you want to arrive in style.

### Car

Most major car-rental agencies have desks at the airport, as well as multiple offices around the city. Once you're strapped in – seat belts are compulsory here – proceed east after leaving the airport on Grant McConachie Way, and follow the Vancouver signs over the Arthur Laing Bridge. Take the Granville St exit and travel north along Granville St with the mountain ahead of you. Depending on traffic, you'll be in the downtown core in around 30 minutes.

# Pacific Central Station

➔ **Pacific Central Station** (1150 Station St; ⑤Main St-Science World) is the city's main terminus for long-distance trains from across Canada on VIA Rail (www.viarail.com), and from Seattle (just south of the border) and beyond on Amtrak (www.amtrak.com). It's also the main arrival point for major intercity, including cross-border, bus services.

➔ The Main St-Science World SkyTrain station is just across the street for connections to downtown and beyond.

➔ There are car-rental desks in the station and cabs are also available just outside the building.

# Tsawwassen & Horseshoe Bay Ferry Terminals

**BC Ferries** (☎250-386-3431; www.bcferries.com) services arrive at Tsawwassen, an hour south of Vancouver, and at Horseshoe Bay, 30 minutes from downtown in West Vancouver. The company operates one of the world's largest ferry networks, including some spectacular routes throughout the province.

Main services to Tsawwassen arrive from Vancouver Island's Swartz Bay, near Victoria, and Duke Point, near Nanaimo. Services also arrive from the Southern Gulf Islands.

Services to Horseshoe Bay arrive from Nanaimo's Departure Bay. Services also arrive here from Bowen Island and from Langdale on the Sunshine Coast.

## TRANSIT TICKETS & PASSES

➔ Along with trip-planning resources, the TransLink website (www.translink.bc.ca) has a comprehensive section on fares and passes covering its combined bus, SeaBus and SkyTrain services.

➔ The transit system is divided into three geographic zones. One-zone tickets cost adult/child $2.75/1.75, two-zones $4/2.75 and three-zones $5.505/3.75. All bus trips are one-zone fares.

➔ Metro Vancouver's new ticketing system is called Compass. Buy all-access paper DayPasses ($9.75) and plastic rechargeable Compass Cards ($6 deposit) from vending machines at SeaBus and SkyTrain stations, or from designated Compass retailers around the city, including London Drugs branches. DayPasses and Compass Cards allow you access to all bus, SeaBus and SkyTrain services.

➔ After 6:30pm, and on weekends or holidays, all transit trips are classed as one-zone fares and cost $2.75/1.75. Children under five travel for free on all transit services at all times.

To depart Tsawwassen via transit, take bus 620 (adult/child $5.50/3.50) to Bridgeport Station and transfer to the Canada Line. It takes about 40 minutes to reach downtown.

From Horseshoe Bay to downtown, take bus 257 (adult/child $4/2.75, 45 minutes), which is faster than bus 250. It takes about 35 minutes.

Cruise ships, big business here from May to September, dock at downtown's Canada Place or at Ballantyne Pier just to the east.

# GETTING AROUND VANCOUVER

Transit in Vancouver is cheap, extensive and generally efficient.

➔ **Bus** Extensive network in central areas with frequent services on many routes.

➔ **Train** SkyTrain system is fast but limited to only a few routes. Especially good for trips from the city center.

➔ **SeaBus** A popular transit

ferry linking downtown Vancouver and North Vancouver.

# Train

➔ TransLink's SkyTrain rapid-transit network currently consists of three routes and is a great way to move around the region, especially beyond the city center. A fourth route, the Evergreen Line, is scheduled to begin operations in 2017 and will link the suburban communities of Burnaby, Coquitlam and Port Moody.

➔ Compass tickets for SkyTrain trips can be purchased from station vending machines (change is given; machines also accept debit and credit cards) prior to boarding.

➔ SkyTrain journeys cost $2.75 to $5.50 (plus $5 more if you're traveling from the airport), depending on how far you are journeying.

## Canada Line

➔ Links the city to the airport and Richmond.

➡ Trains run every six to 20 minutes.

➡ Services run from the airport to downtown between 5:07am and 12:56am and from Waterfront Station to the airport between 4:48am and 1:05am.

➡ If you're heading for the airport from the city, make sure you board a YVR-bound train – some head to Richmond but not to the airport.

### Expo Line

➡ The original 35-minute Expo Line takes passengers to and from downtown Vancouver and Surrey, via stops in Burnaby and New Westminster.

➡ Trains run every two to eight minutes, with services departing Waterfront Station between 5:35am and 1:15am Monday to Friday (6:50am to 1:15am Saturday; 7:15am to 12:15am Sunday).

### Millennium Line

➡ Stops near shopping malls and suburban districts in Coquitlam and Burnaby.

➡ Trains run every five to eight minutes, with services departing Waterfront Station between 5:54am and 12:31am Monday to Friday (6:54am to 12:31am Saturday; 7:54am to 11:31pm Sunday).

#### BIKE RESOURCES

➡ **City of Vancouver** (www.vancouver.ca/cycling) Route maps and bike-friendly info.

➡ **BC Cycling Coalition** (www.bccc.bc.ca) Local resources for cyclists.

➡ **HUB** (www.bikhub.ca) The locals' main bike-based resource.

## Bus

➡ Vancouver's TransLink (www.translink.ca) bus network is extensive. All vehicles are equipped with bike racks and all are wheelchair accessible. Exact change (or more) is required; buses use fare machines and change is not given. Fares cost adult/child $2.75/1.75 and are valid for up to 90 minutes of transfer travel. While Vancouver's transit system covers three geographic fare zones, all bus trips are regarded as one-zone fares.

➡ Bus services operate from early morning to after midnight in central areas. There is also a handy night-bus system that runs every 30 minutes between 1:30am and 4am. The last night-bus leaves downtown Vancouver at 3:09am. Look for night-bus signs at designated stops.

## Bicycle

➡ Vancouver is a relatively good cycling city with more than 300km of designated routes crisscrossing the region.

➡ Cyclists can take their bikes for free on SkyTrains, SeaBuses and transit buses, which are all now fitted with bike racks. Cyclists are required by law to wear helmets.

➡ In recent years, dedicated bike lanes have been created downtown and in 2016 a new public bike-share scheme called **Mobi** (www.mobibikes.ca) was introduced.

➡ Pick up a free *Metro Vancouver Cycling Map* for details on area routes and bike-friendly contacts and resources – or download it via the TransLink website.

➡ If you're traveling sans bike, you can also rent wheels (often including in-line skates) from businesses around the city, especially on Denman St near Stanley Park – home of Vancouver's most popular scenic cycling route.

## Car & Motorcycle

For sightseeing in the city, you'll be fine without a car (the city center is especially easy to explore on foot and transit routes are extensive). For visits that incorporate the wider region's mountains and communities, however, a vehicle makes life much simpler: the further you travel from downtown, the more limited your transit options become.

### Driving

➡ Seat belts are mandatory here, and there is also a ban on using handheld electronic devices while driving.

➡ Vancouver doesn't have any expressways going through its core, which can lead to some major congestion issues. Evening rush-hour traffic can be a nightmare, with enormous lines of cars snaking along W Georgia St waiting to cross the Lions Gate Bridge. Try the Second Narrows Ironworkers Memorial Bridge (known simply as the Second Narrows Bridge to most locals) if you need to access the North Shore in a hurry. Other peak-time hot spots to avoid are the George Massey Tunnel and Hwy 1 to Surrey.

➡ For suggested driving routes around the region, visit www.hellobc.com/drive. For route planning and driving conditions throughout the province, try www.drivebc.ca.

### Parking

Parking is at a premium in downtown Vancouver: there are some free spots on residential side streets but many require permits, and traffic wardens are predictably predatory. Many streets also have metered parking (up to $6 per hour).

Pay-parking lots (typically from $5 per hour) are a better proposition – arrive before 9am at some for early-bird, day-rate discounts. For an interactive map of parking-lot locations, check EasyPark (www.easypark.ca).

## Rental

Major car-rental agencies with offices around the city and at Vancouver International Airport:

**Avis** (☑604-606-2847; www.avis.ca)

**Budget** (☑604-668-7000; www.budgetbc.com)

**Enterprise** (☑604-688-5500; www.enterprisecar.ca)

**Hertz** (☑604-606-4711; www.hertz.ca)

**Thrifty** (☑604-606-1655; www.thrifty.com)

## Taxi

Vancouver currently does not allow Uber-type services. Try the following long-established taxi companies:

**Black Top & Checker Cabs** (☑604-731-1111; www.btccabs.ca; ☎)

**Vancouver Taxi** (☑604-871-1111; www.vancouvertaxi.cab)

**Yellow Cab** (☑604-681-1111; www.yellowcabonline.com; ☎)

## Boat

Waterfront Vancouver makes use of its waterways for local travel, via transit services and private providers.

## SeaBus

➡ The iconic SeaBus shuttle is part of the TransLink transit system (regular transit fares apply) and it operates throughout the day, taking 12 minutes to cross Burrard Inlet between Waterfront Station

### ARRIVING BY INTERCITY BUS

➡ Most intercity nontransit buses trundle to a halt at Vancouver's neon-signed **Pacific Central Station** (1150 Station St; ⑤Main St-Science World). It's the main arrival point for cross-Canada and trans-border Greyhound buses (www.greyhound.com; www.greyhound.ca); cross-border budget bus services on Bolt Bus (www.boltbus.com); and services from Seattle and Seattle's Sea-Tac International Airport on Quick Shuttle (www.quickcoach.com).

➡ The station has a ticket office and left-luggage lockers, and is also the city's trans-Canada and cross-border train terminal.

➡ The Main St-Science World SkyTrain station is just across the street for connections to downtown and the suburbs.

➡ There are car-rental desks in the station and cabs are available just outside.

and Lonsdale Quay in North Vancouver. At Lonsdale you can then connect to buses servicing North Vancouver and West Vancouver; this is where you pick up bus 236 to both Capilano Suspension Bridge and Grouse Mountain.

➡ SeaBus services leave from Waterfront Station between 6:16am and 1:22am Monday to Saturday (8:16am to 11:16pm Sunday). Vessels are wheelchair accessible and bike-friendly.

➡ Tickets must be purchased from vending machines on either side of the route before boarding. The machines take credit and debit cards and also give change up to $20 for cash transactions.

### Miniferries

Operators offer day passes ($10 to $15) as well as discounted books of tickets for those making multiple watery hops. Single trips costs from $3.50.

**Aquabus Ferries** (☑604-689-5858; www.theaquabus.com; adult/child from $3.50/1.75) Runs frequent minivessels (some big enough to carry bikes) between the foot of Hornby St and Granville Island.

It also services several additional spots along the False Creek waterfront as far as Science World.

**False Creek Ferries** (Map p266; ☑604-684-7781; www.granvilleislandferries.bc.ca; adult/child from $3.25/2) Operates a similar Granville Island service from Sunset Beach, and has additional ports of call around False Creek.

## TOURS

## Walking Tours

**Forbidden Vancouver** (☑604-227-7570; www.forbiddenvancouver.ca; adult/senior/student $22/19/19) This quirky company offers highly entertaining tours: a delve into prohibition-era Vancouver and a poke around the seedy underbelly of historic Gastown. Not recommended for kids. Every few months, it also offers an excellent behind-the-scenes history tour of the infamous Penthouse nightclub, a strip joint that has a rich, somewhat glamorous and sometimes seedy past. Check the website for details.

## CLIMATE CHANGE & TRAVEL

Every form of transport that relies on carbon-based fuel generates $CO_2$, the main cause of human-induced climate change. Modern travel is dependent on aeroplanes, which might use less fuel per kilometre per person than most cars but travel much greater distances. The altitude at which aircraft emit gases (including $CO_2$) and particles also contributes to their climate-change impact. Many websites offer 'carbon calculators' that allow people to estimate the carbon emissions generated by their journey and, for those who wish to do so, to offset the impact of the greenhouse gases emitted with contributions to portfolios of climate-friendly initiatives throughout the world. Lonely Planet offsets the carbon footprint of all staff and author travel.

**Architectural Institute of British Columbia** (☑604-683-8588; www.aibc.ca; tours $10; ☺Tue-Sun Jul & Aug) Local architecture students conduct these excellent two-hour wanders, focusing on the buildings, history and heritage of several key Vancouver neighborhoods. There are six tours in all, covering areas including Gastown, Strathcona, Yaletown, Chinatown, downtown and the West End. If you're visiting Victoria, tours operate there as well.

**Talaysay Tours** (☑604-628-8555; www.talaysay. com) Providing a range of authentic First Nations–led tours, including a signature Stanley Park walking option, this operator can also arrange interpretive guided kayak jaunts around the region.

**Vancouver Tour Guys** (☑604-259-7740; www. tourguys.ca; free-$10) Free neighborhood tours around Vancouver (gratuities of $5 to $10 are encouraged). Private tours are also available (including a popular beer-tasting trawl). The free tours are very popular during the summer peak so book ahead via the website.

# Bus & Boat Tours

**Vancouver Trolley Company** (☑604-801-5515; www.vancouvertrolley.com; adult/child from $45/28) Red replica San Francisco trolley cars (without the tracks) provide a hop-on, hop-off tour around the main city sites. One- or two-day options are available. Look out for Halloween and Christmas-themed tours as well.

**Sewell's Marina** (p190)

**Harbour Cruises** (p78)

# Specialty Tours

**Vancouver Brewery Tours** (☑604-318-2280; www.vancouverbrewerytours. com; tours from $75) If you're worried about over-imbibing at Vancouver's amazing microbreweries and forgetting where you hotel is, take a tour with these friendly folks. Their van will take you to three choice beermakers, samples included. A walking tour option is also available.

**Cycle City Tours** (p78)

**Vancouver Foodie Tours** (☑604-337-1027; www. foodietours.ca; tours from $50) The perfect way to dive into the city's food scene; belt-busting guided tours include a street-food crawl and a Granville Island Public Market tour.

# Directory A–Z

## Discount Cards

➡ **Vancouver City Passport** (www.citypassports.com; $25) Discounts at attractions, restaurants and activities across the city for up to two adults and two children.

➡ **Vanier Park ExplorePass** (www.spacecentre.ca/explore -pass; adult/child $36/30) Combined entry to the Museum of Vancouver, Vancouver Maritime Museum and HR MacMillan Space Centre. Includes one entry to each attraction and is available at any of the three sites.

➡ **UBC Museums & Gardens Pass** (adult/child $33/28) Combined entry to all the the University of BC's major attractions. It's valid for several months and also includes additional campus discounts.

### LISTEN LOCAL

**CBC Radio One** (690AM, 88.1FM; www.cbc.ca/bc) Canadian Broadcasting Corporation's commercial-free news, talk and music station.

**CKNW** (980AM; www.cknw.com) News, traffic, sports and talk.

**CFOX** (99.3FM; www.cfox.com) Rock and chatter.

**News 1130** (1130AM; www.news1130.com) News 24/7.

**Peak** (102.7FM; www.thepeak.fm) Popular mainstream new-rock station.

## Electricity

120v/60hz

120v/60hz

## Emergency

| Police, Fire & Ambulance | ☏911 |
| --- | --- |
| Police (non-emergency number) | ☏604-717-3321 |

## Internet Access

Most Vancouver hotels provide in-room wi-fi or (less

## PRACTICALITIES

### Maps

**Tourism Vancouver Visitor Centre** (Map p266; ☑604-683-2000; www.tourismvancouver.com; 200 Burrard St; ⏰8:30am-5pm; ⑤Waterfront) provides free downtown maps. Alternatively, the laminated *Streetwise Vancouver Map* ($8.95) is sold at many convenience stores. For free online maps, check out the Van-Map (www.vancouver.ca/vanmap) system.

### Newsapers

**Georgia Straight** (www.straight.com) Alternative weekly providing Vancouver's best entertainment listings. Free every Thursday.

**Province** (www.theprovince.com) Vancouver's 'tabloid' daily newspaper.

**Tyee** (www.thetyee.ca) Award-winning online local news source.

**Vancouver Sun** (www.vancouversun.com) Main city daily.

often) high-speed cable internet services for guests. It's usually free but check with your hotel when booking. The wi-fi icon used throughout the listings in this book indicates where free wi-fi is available. The computer icon shows where computers are offered for guests to use.

If you're toting your hardware around town and it's time to update your blog, drop into one of the many branches of **Blenz** (www.blenz.com), **Take 5** (www.take5cafe.ca) or **Waves** (www.wavescoffee.com) coffee shops for free wi-fi. The **Vancouver Public Library** (☑604-331-3603; www.vpl.ca; 350 W Georgia St; ⏰10am-9pm Mon-Thu, 10am-6pm Fri & Sat, 11am-6pm Sun; 🛜; ⑤Stadium-Chinatown) also offers free wi-fi and internet-enabled computers. You'll need an Internet Access card to use these but you can get this with one piece of ID. The City of Vancouver has also created free wi-fi services at several local community centers, including the **Roundhouse**

**Community Arts & Recreation Centre** (Map p274; ☑604-713-1800; www.roundhouse.ca; 181 Roundhouse Mews, cnr Davie St & Pacific Blvd; ⏰9am-10pm Mon-Fri, to 5pm Sat & Sun; ⑤Yaletown-Roundhouse).

If you don't have your computer with you, check your email for free in the Apple Store in downtown's Pacific Centre mall.

# Medical Services

There are no reciprocal healthcare arrangements between Canada and other countries. Non-Canadians usually pay cash up front for treatment, so taking out travel insurance with a medical-cover component is strongly advised. Medical treatment in Canada is expensive: hospital beds can cost up to $2500 a day for nonresidents.

## Clinics

The following walk-in clinics cater to visitors:

**Care Point Medical Centre** Branches at **Commercial Dr** (☑604-254-5554; www.carepoint.ca; 1623 Commercial Dr; ⏰9am-4pm Mon, Tue & Fri, 9am-8pm Wed & Thu, 9am-6pm Sat, 9am-3pm Sun; 🚌20) and in the **West End** (☑604-681-5338; 1175 Denman St; 🚌5). For additional locations, see www.carepoint.ca. Appointments not necessary.

**Stein Medical Clinic** (☑604-688-5924; www.steinmedical.com; 550 Burrard St; ⏰8am-5pm Mon-Fri; ⑤Burrard) Appointments not necessary.

**Travel Medicine & Vaccination Centre** (☑604-681-5656; www.tmvc.com; 666 Burrard St; ⑤Burrard) Specializing in travel shots; appointments necessary.

**Ultima Medicentre** (☑604-683-8138; www.ultimamedicentre.ca; Plaza Level, Bentall Centre, 1055 Dunsmuir St; ⏰8am-5pm Mon-Fri; ⑤Burrard) Appointments not necessary.

## Emergency Rooms

Vancouver's emergency rooms include the following:

**BC Children's Hospital** (☑604-875-2345; www.bcchildrens.ca; 4480 Oak St; 🚌17)

**St Paul's Hospital** (☑604-682-2344; 1081 Burrard St; 🚌22) Downtown accident-and-emergency hospital.

**Vancouver General Hospital** (☑604-875-4111; www.vch.ca; 855 W 12th Ave; Ⓜ Broadway-City Hall)

## Pharmacies

Vancouver is well stocked with pharmacies.

**Shoppers Drug Mart** (☑604-669-2424; 1125 Davie St; ⏰24hr; 🚌6)

# Money

Canadian dollars come in $5 (blue), $10 (purple), $20 (green), $50 (red) and $100 (brown) denominations. The original paper bills have been replaced with plasticized bills in recent years. Coins come in nickel (5¢), dime (10¢), quarter (25¢), 'loonie' ($1) and 'toonie' ($2) coins. The penny (1¢) has been phased out, although cash registers in most stores and businesses still include penny amounts; the price you actually pay will be rounded up or down to the nearest 0 or 5.

### ATMs

Interbank ATM exchange rates usually beat the rates offered for traveler's checks or foreign currency. Canadian ATM fees are generally low, but your home bank may charge another fee on top of that. Some ATM machines also dispense US currency; ideal if you're planning a trip across the border. ATMs abound in Vancouver, with bank branches congregating around the business district bordered by Burrard, Georgia, Pender and Granville Sts. Drugstores also frequently have ATMs.

### Changing Money

You can exchange currency at most main bank branches, which often charge less than the *bureaux de change* dotted around the city. In addition to the banks, try **Vancouver Bullion & Currency Exchange** (☑604-685-1008; www.vbce.ca; 800 W Pender St; ⓢGranville), which often offers a wider range of currencies and competitive rates.

### Credit Cards

Visa, MasterCard and American Express are widely accepted in Canada. Credit cards can get you cash advances at bank ATMs, usually for an additional surcharge. Be aware that many US-based credit cards often convert foreign charges using unfavorable exchange rates and fees.

## Tipping

Gratuities are part of the price you'll pay for visiting this part of the world. The following are typical rates:

| Restaurant wait staff | 15% |
|---|---|
| Bar servers | $1 per drink |
| Hotel bellhops | $1-2 per bag |
| Taxis | 10-15% |

# Opening Hours

Most business hours are consistent throughout the year, with the exception of attractions which often reduce their hours slightly outside the summer.

**Banks** 9am-5pm weekdays, with some opening Saturday mornings.

**Shops** 10am-6pm Monday to Saturday; noon to 5pm Sunday.

**Restaurants** 11:30am-2pm; 5-10pm.

**Coffee shops** From 8am, some earlier.

**Pubs and bars** Pubs often from 11:30am; bars often from 5pm. Closing midnight or later.

# Post

Canada Post (www.canadapost.ca) may not be remarkably quick, but it is reliable. The standard (up to 30g) letter and postcard rate to destinations within Canada is 85¢. Postcards and standard letters to the US cost $1.20. International airmail for postcards costs $2.50.

Postal outlets are dotted around the city, many of them at the back of drugstores – look for the red Canada Post window signs or head to the handy **Howe St Postal Outlet.** (Map p266; ☑604-688-2068; 732 Davie St; ⓘ9am-7pm Mon-Fri, 10am-5pm Sat; ☐6) The main downtown Canada Post branch was in the process of relocating during research for this book; its new address is slated to be 495 W Georgia St.

# Public Holidays

During national public holidays, banks, schools and government offices (including post offices) are closed, and transportation, museums and other services often operate on Sunday schedules. Holidays falling on weekends are usually observed the following Monday.

Major public holidays in Vancouver:

**New Year's Day** January 1

**Family Day** Second Monday in February

**Good Friday & Easter Monday** Late March to mid-April

**Victoria Day** Third Monday in May

**Canada Day** July 1

**BC Day** First Monday in August

**Labour Day** First Monday in September

**Thanksgiving** Second Monday in October

**Remembrance Day** November 11

**Christmas Day** December 25

**Boxing Day** December 26

# Safe Travel

Vancouver is relatively safe for visitors.

➡ Purse-snatching and pick-pocketing do occur; be vigilant with your personal possessions.

➡ Theft from unattended cars is not uncommon; never leave valuables in vehicles where they can be seen.

➡ Persistent street-begging is an issue for some visitors; just say 'Sorry' and pass on if you're not interested and want to be polite.

→ A small group of hardcore scam artists also works the downtown core, singling out tourists and asking for 'help to get back home.' Do not let them engage you in conversation.

## Taxes & Refunds

You will pay 5% Goods and Services (GST) tax on almost all purchases as well as an additional 7% PST on some purchases. These are not included in advertised prices and will be added at the checkout when you pay.

There is also a 3% hotel tax (called the Municipal and Regional District Tax) on overnight accommodation in Vancouver

Tax rebates for visitors have mostly been discontinued in recent years. Check in with the **Canada Revenue Agency** (☑902-432-5608; www.cra-arc.gc.ca/visitors) for the latest information.

## Telephone

Local calls cost 50¢ from public pay phones, but these are few and far between. If calling from a private phone, local calls are free – a gratis approach that often doesn't apply to calls made from hotel rooms.

Most Vancouver-area phone numbers have the area code ☑604, although you can also expect to see

☑778. Dial all 10 digits of a given phone number, including the three-digit area code and seven-digit number, even for local calls. In some instances (eg between Vancouver and Whistler), numbers will have the same area code but will be long-distance; at such times you need to dial 1 before the area code.

Always dial ☑1 before other domestic long-distance and toll-free (☑800, 888, 877 etc) numbers. Some toll-free numbers are good anywhere in North America, others within Canada only. International rates apply for calls to the US, even though the dialing code (☑+1) is the same as for Canadian long-distance calls. Dial ☑011 followed by the country code for all other overseas direct-dial calls.

### Cell Phones

Local SIM cards may be used with some international phones. Roaming can be expensive: check with your service provider.

### Phonecards

Prepaid phonecards for long-distance and international calls can be purchased at convenience stores, gas stations and some post offices. Beware some phonecards that advertise the cheapest per-minute rates, as they may also charge hefty connection fees for each call. Leading local phone company Telus (www.telus.com) offers a range of reliable phonecards available in retail outlets around the city.

## Time

Vancouver is in the Pacific time zone (PST/PDT), the same as the US West Coast. At noon in Vancouver it's the following:

→ 11am in Anchorage

→ 3pm in Toronto

→ 3pm in New York

→ 8pm in London

→ 9pm in Paris

→ 6am (the next day) in Sydney

→ 8am (the next day) in Auckland

During Daylight Saving Time (from the second Sunday in March to the first Sunday in November), the clock moves ahead one hour.

## Toilets

City-run public toilets are not common in Vancouver but there are many places to access the facilities if you're traveling around the city. Public libraries, departments stores, shopping malls and larger public parks all have washrooms. There are no fees to use washrooms in Vancouver.

## Tourist Information

The **Tourism Vancouver Visitor Centre** (Map p266; ☑604-683-2000; www.tourismvancouver.com; 200 Burrard St; ⏰8:30am-5pm; ⑤Waterfront) is a large repository of resources for visitors, with a staff of helpful advisers ready to assist in planning your trip. Services and info available here include free maps, visitor guides, half-price theater tickets, accommodation and tour bookings, plus a host of glossy brochures on the city and the wider BC region.

## Travelers with Disabilities

Vancouver is an accessible city. On your arrival at the airport, vehicle-rental agencies can provide prearranged cars with hand controls. Accessible cabs are also widely available at the airport and throughout the city, on request.

All TransLink SkyTrain, SeaBus and transit bus services are wheelchair accessible. Check the TransLink website (www.translink.ca) for a wide range of information on accessible transport around the region. Head to www.accesstotravel. gc.ca for information and resources on accessible travel across Canada. In addition, download Lonely Planet's free Accessible Travel guide from http://lp-travel.to/AccessibleTravel.

Guide dogs may legally be brought into restaurants, hotels and other businesses in Vancouver. Almost all downtown sidewalks have sloping ramps, and most public buildings and attractions are wheelchair accessible. Check the City of Vancouver's dedicated website (www.vancouver.ca/accessibility) for additional information and resources.

Other helpful resources:

➡ **Disability Alliance BC** (604-875-0188; www.disa

bilityalliancebc.org) Programs and support for people with disabilities.

➡ **CNIB** (604-431-2121; www.cnib.ca) Support and services for the visually impaired.

➡ **Western Institute for the Deaf & Hard of Hearing** (604-736-7391; www.widhh.com) Interpreter services and resources for the hearing impaired.

## Visas

Not required for visitors from the US, the Commonwealth and most of Western Europe for stays up to 180 days. Required by those from more than 130 other countries. However, visa-exempt foreign nationals **flying** to Canada now require an **Electronic Travel Authorization** (eTA). This excludes US citizens and those who already have a

valid Canadian visa. For more information on the eTA, see www.canada.ca/eta. For visa information, visit the **Canada Border Services Agency** (20 4-983-3500; www.cbsa.gc.ca) website.

## Women Travelers

Vancouver is generally safe for women traveling solo, although jogging alone after dark in parks and hanging out late at night in the Downtown Eastside without company is best avoided. Note it is illegal to carry pepper spray or mace in Canada. The **Vancouver Women's Health Collective** (604-736-5262; www.womenshealthcollective.ca; 29 W Hastings St; 9:30am-4:30pm Mon, 1-4:30pm Tue-Thu, 9:30am-1:30pm Fri; Stadium-Chinatown) provides advice and referrals for health issues.

# Behind the Scenes

## SEND US YOUR FEEDBACK

We love to hear from travelers – your comments keep us on our toes and help make our books better. Our well-traveled team reads every word on what you loved or loathed about this book. Although we cannot reply individually to your submissions, we always guarantee that your feedback goes straight to the appropriate authors, in time for the next edition. Each person who sends us information is thanked in the next edition – the most useful submissions are rewarded with a selection of digital PDF chapters.

Visit **lonelyplanet.com/contact** to submit your updates and suggestions or to ask for help. Our award-winning website also features inspirational travel stories, news and discussions.

Note: We may edit, reproduce and incorporate your comments in Lonely Planet products such as guidebooks, websites and digital products, so let us know if you don't want your comments reproduced or your name acknowledged. For a copy of our privacy policy visit lonelyplanet.com/privacy.

## OUR READERS

Many thanks to the travelers who used the last edition and wrote to us with helpful hints, useful advice and interesting anecdotes: Beryl Bevan, Sheldon Rempel, Stephen Bowkett.

## WRITER THANKS
### John Lee

Special thanks to Maggie for ensuring my sanity and delivering copious amounts of tea during the write-up for this project. Thanks also to our feline companion, Max, for grooming my beard on a regular basis. And cheers to my buddy Dominic for joining me on that elongated Vancouver Island road trip. Sincere apologies to all my other Vancouver friends and family for being stuck to my keyboard for so long; I'm more than ready for a beer or two now.

## ACKNOWLEDGEMENTS

Cover photograph: Lynn Canyon suspension bridge, Christopher Kimmel/Getty Images © Illustrations pp52-3 by Michael Weldon.

## THIS BOOK

This 7th edition of Lonely Planet's *Vancouver* guidebook was researched and written by John Lee. John also wrote the previous two editions. This guidebook was produced by the following:
**Destination Editor**
Alexander Howard

**Product Editor** Genna Patterson, Kate Mathews
**Senior Cartographer** Corey Hutchison
**Book Designer** Gwen Cotter
**Assisting Editors** Imogen Bannister, Janice Bird, Carly Hall
**Assisting Book Designers**

Wendy Wright, Mazzy Prinsep
**Cover Researcher** Naomi Parker
**Thanks to** Sandie Kestell, Angela Tinson, Liz Heynes, Kirsten Rawlings, Sasha Drew, Anne Mason, Katharine Marsh, Gabrielle Stefanos, Tony Wheeler

See also separate subindexes for:

🍴 **EATING P257**

🍺 **DRINKING & NIGHTLIFE P258**

☆ **ENTERTAINMENT P259**

🔒 **SHOPPING P259**

🏃 **SPORTS & ACTIVITIES P260**

🛏 **SLEEPING P260**

# Index

## DRINKING & NIGHTLIFE

## ☆ ENTERTAINMENT

## 🛍 SHOPPING

## 🏃 SPORTS & ACTIVITIES

## 🛏 SLEEPING

NOTES

# Vancouver Maps

## Sights

- Beach
- Bird Sanctuary
- Buddhist
- Castle/Palace
- Christian
- Confucian
- Hindu
- Islamic
- Jain
- Jewish
- Monument
- Museum/Gallery/Historic Building
- Ruin
- Shinto
- Sikh
- Taoist
- Winery/Vineyard
- Zoo/Wildlife Sanctuary
- Other Sight

## Activities, Courses & Tours

- Bodysurfing
- Diving
- Canoeing/Kayaking
- Course/Tour
- Sento Hot Baths/Onsen
- Skiing
- Snorkeling
- Surfing
- Swimming/Pool
- Walking
- Windsurfing
- Other Activity

## Sleeping

- Sleeping
- Camping

## Eating

- Eating

## Drinking & Nightlife

- Drinking & Nightlife
- Cafe

## Entertainment

- Entertainment

## Shopping

- Shopping

## Information

- Bank
- Embassy/Consulate
- Hospital/Medical
- Internet
- Police
- Post Office
- Telephone
- Toilet
- Tourist Information
- Other Information

## Geographic

- Beach
- Gate
- Hut/Shelter
- Lighthouse
- Lookout
- Mountain/Volcano
- Oasis
- Park
- Pass
- Picnic Area
- Waterfall

## Population

- Capital (National)
- Capital (State/Province)
- City/Large Town
- Town/Village

## Transport

- Airport
- BART station
- Border crossing
- Boston T station
- Bus
- Cable car/Funicular
- Cycling
- Ferry
- Metro/Muni station
- Monorail
- Parking
- Petrol station
- Subway/SkyTrain station
- Taxi
- Train station/Railway
- Tram
- Underground station
- Other Transport

*Note: Not all symbols displayed above appear on the maps in this book*

## Routes

- Tollway
- Freeway
- Primary
- Secondary
- Tertiary
- Lane
- Unsealed road
- Road under construction
- Plaza/Mall
- Steps
- Tunnel
- Pedestrian overpass
- Walking Tour
- Walking Tour detour
- Path/Walking Trail

## Boundaries

- International
- State/Province
- Disputed
- Regional/Suburb
- Marine Park
- Cliff
- Wall

## Hydrography

- River, Creek
- Intermittent River
- Canal
- Water
- Dry/Salt/Intermittent Lake
- Reef

## Areas

- Airport/Runway
- Beach/Desert
- Cemetery (Christian)
- Cemetery (Other)
- Glacier
- Mudflat
- Park/Forest
- Sight (Building)
- Sportsground
- Swamp/Mangrove

**265**

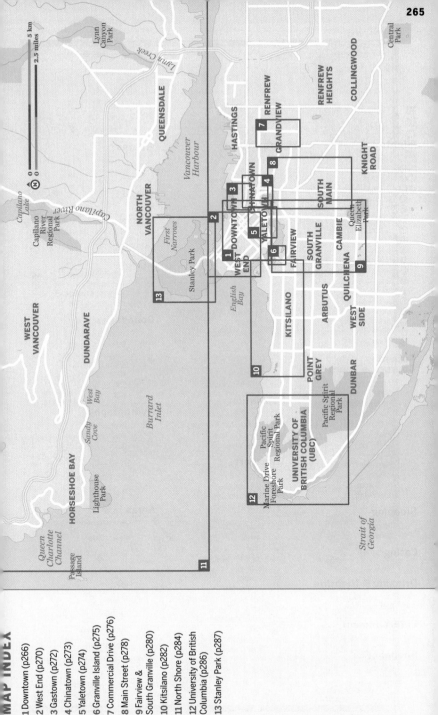

DOWNTOWN

See map
p270

Coal Harbour
Park

Cardero St

Nicola St

Broughton St

Bute St

Barclay
Heritage
Sq

Haro St

Barclay St

99
1A
**W Georgia St**

WEST
END

Nelson St

Jervis St

Cornox St

Alberni St

Robson St

Pendrell St

59

Barclay St
27

54

81

Nelson
Park

Nelson St

46

Robson
Sq

Pendrell St

Comox St

67

Bute St

Provincial
Law Courts

Burnaby St

Thurlow St

Davie St

66

Harwood St

99

71

39

16

29

34

45

37

77

Burrard St

Sunset
Beach
Park

Pacific St

Hornby St

31

Helmcken St

False
Creek
Ferries

**Howe St**

42

48

Burrard
Bridge

Granville St

**Seymour St**

Drake St

Richards St

Homer St

Beach Ave

Seabreeze Walk

Pacific Blvd

False Creek Ferry

Granville
Bridge

Broker's
Bay

**GRANVILLE
ISLAND**

David Lam
Park

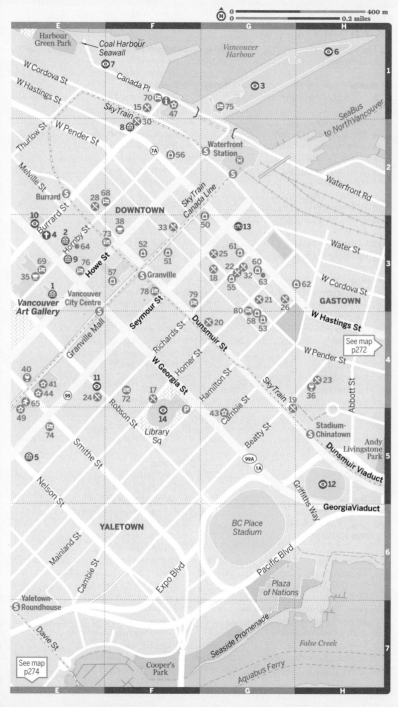

0    400 m
0    0.2 miles

Harbour
Green Park

Coal Harbour
Seawall

Vancouver
Harbour

**6**

**7**

Canada Pl

**3**

W Cordova St

W Hastings St

SkyTrain

**70**
**15**
**i**
**47**

**75**

SeaBus
to NorthVancouver

W Pender St

**30**

**8**

Waterfront Rd

Thurlow St

**7A**

**56**

Waterfront
Station

Melville St

Burrard

**28** **68**

**DOWNTOWN**

**50**

Water St

Burrard St

**10**

**i**

**4**

**2**

**73**

**33**

**STO 13**

**38**

Hornby St

**64**

**52**

**61**

**25**

**60**

W Cordova St

**69**

**9**

**76**

**51**

**22**

**32**

**63**

**62**

**GASTOWN**

**35**

**57**

**78**

Granville

**18**

**55**

**79**

**21**

**26**

Howe St

Vancouver
City Centre

Seymour St

Dunsmuir St

**20**

**80**

**58** **53**

**W Hastings St**

**1**

**Vancouver**
**Art Gallery**

Granville Mall

SkyTrain
Canada Line

W Pender St

See map
p272

**40**

**41**

**11**

**23**

**36**

**19**

Abbott St

**44**

**99**

**24**

**17**

**72**

Richards St

Homer St

Hamilton St

**43**

Cambie St

**Stadium-**
**Chinatown**

Andy
Livingstone
Park

**65**

**49**

**14**

Library
Sq

**W Georgia St**

Beatty St

Dunsmuir Viaduct

**74**

Robson St

**99A**
**1A**

**5**

Smithe St

**12**

**GeorgiaViaduct**

Nelson St

**YALETOWN**

BC Place
Stadium

Mainland St

Cambie St

Expo Blvd

Pacific Blvd

Plaza
of Nations

Yaletown-
Roundhouse

Davie St

Seaside Promenade

False Creek

See map
p274

Cooper's
Park

Aquabus Ferry

**DOWNTOWN** *Map on p266*

DOWNTOWN

**WEST END** *Map on p270*

*Key on p269*

**WEST END**

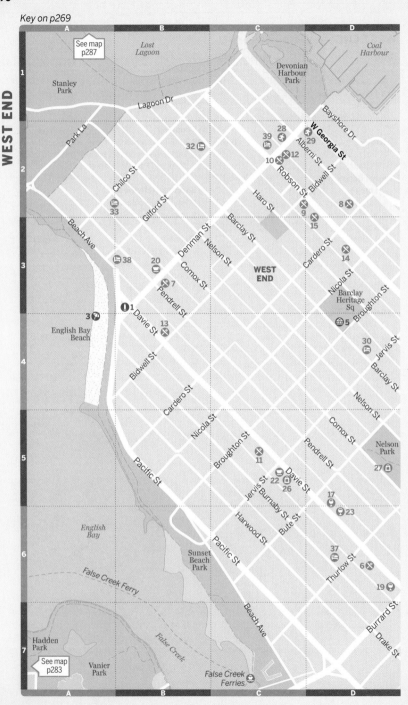

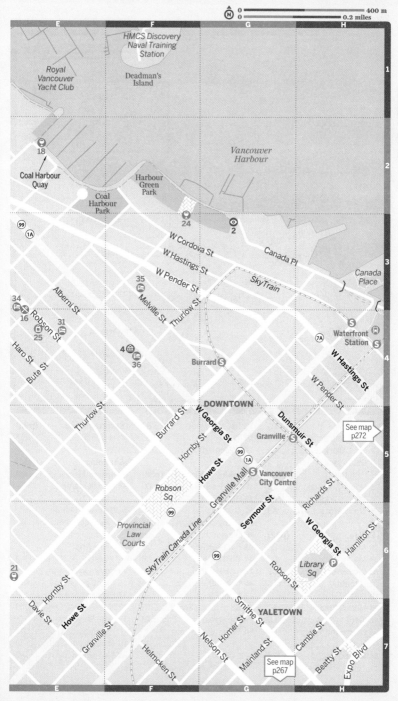

400 m
0.2 miles

Royal Vancouver Yacht Club

HMCS Discovery Naval Training Station

Deadman's Island

Vancouver Harbour

18

Coal Harbour Quay

Harbour Green Park

Coal Harbour Park

24

2

Canada Pl

Canada Place

99

1A

W Cordova St

W Hastings St

W Pender St

SkyTrain

35

Melville St

Thurlow St

Alberni St

34

16

Robson St

25

31

4

36

Burrard

7A

Waterfront Station

W Hastings St

W Pender St

Haro St

Bute St

Thurlow St

Burrard St

W Georgia St

DOWNTOWN

Dunsmuir St

See map p272

Hornby St

Howe St

Granville Mall

Granville

99

1A

Vancouver City Centre

Seymour St

Richards St

W Georgia St

Robson Sq

99

Provincial Law Courts

SkyTrain Canada Line

99

Robson St

Library Sq

Hamilton St

21

Hornby St

Davie St

Howe St

Granville St

Helmcken St

Smithe St

Nelson St

Homer St

Mainland St

YALETOWN

Cambie St

Beatty St

Expo Blvd

See map p267

GASTOWN

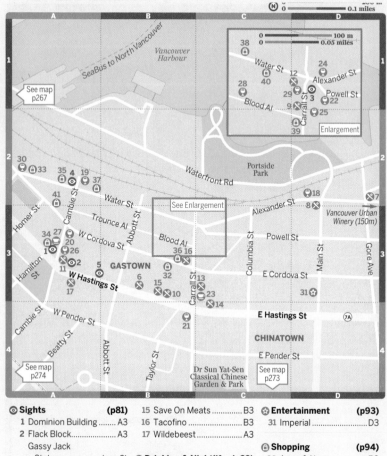

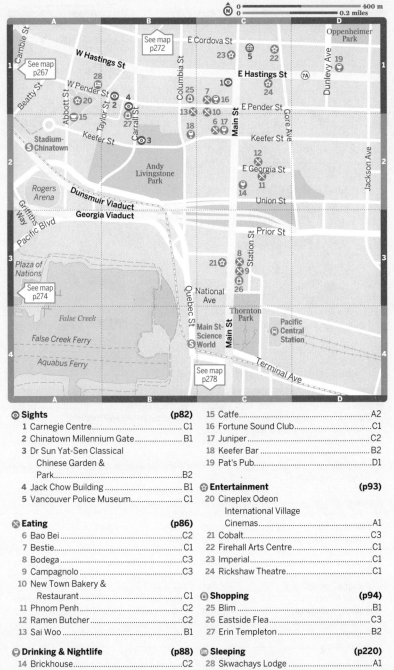

CHINATOWN

YALETOWN

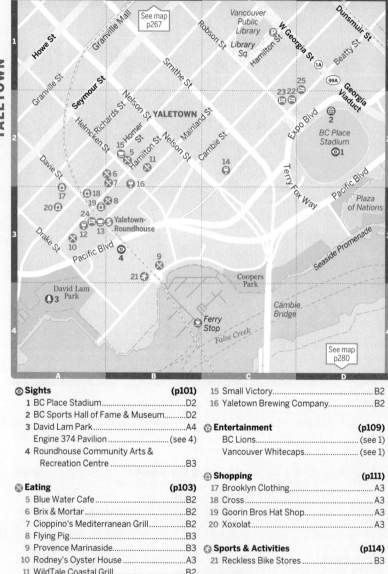

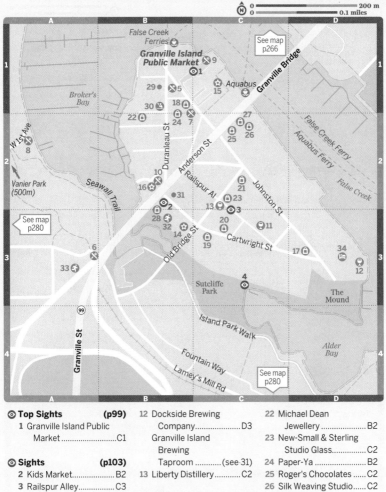

COMMERCIAL DRIVE

N

0 — 200 m
0 — 0.1 miles

23

Callister Brewing
Company (550m);
Powell Street Craft
Brewery (650m)

17

Adanac St

EAST
VANCOUVER

Doan's Craft
Brewing
Company (750m)

32

Parallel 49
Brewing
Company
(700m)

La Casa Gelato
(280m)

14

Venables St

44

29

Parker St

18
33
9

Parker St

Napier St

37
39
11

Napier St

41
4

Semlin Dr

William St

12

William St

16

Grandview
Park

7

15

1

Charles St

25
28
42

Kitchener St

Victoria
Park

Grant St

21

Grant St

Graveley St

10

McLean Dr

Woodland Dr

Cotton Dr

Commercial Dr

E 1st Ave

Victoria Dr

Semlin Dr

Clark Dr

Odlum Dr

McLean Dr

19
38
6

40

E 2nd Ave

GRANDVIEW

2

45

43

3

E 3rd Ave

5
35
24

E 4th Ave

36

E 4th Ave

McSpadden Ave

13

34
20

McSpadden
Park

E 5th Ave

E 4th Ave

E 5th Ave

E 5th Ave

30

26

E 6th Ave

E 6th Ave

E 6th Ave

Grandview Hwy N

22

8

E 7th Ave

27

McLean Ct

E 8th Ave

E 8th Ave

Commercial-
Broadway

E Broadway

31

Commercial-
Broadway

## COMMERCIAL DRIVE

MAIN STREET

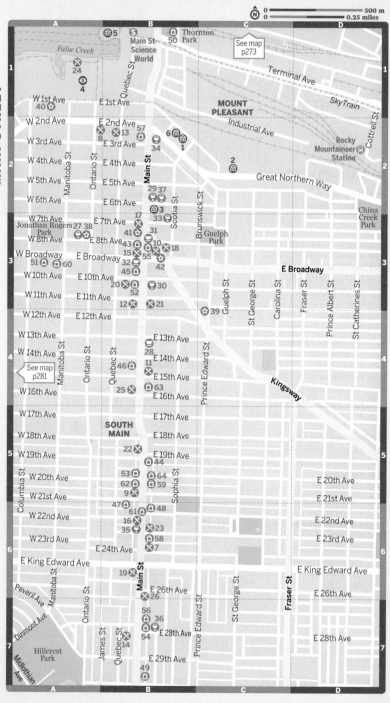

# MAIN STREET

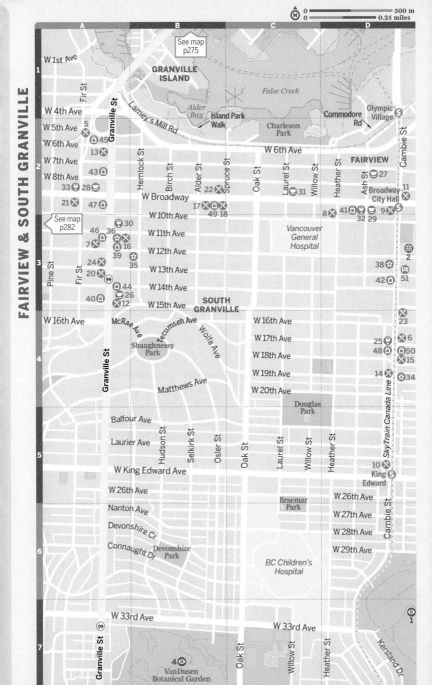

FAIRVIEW & SOUTH GRANVILLE

KITSILANO

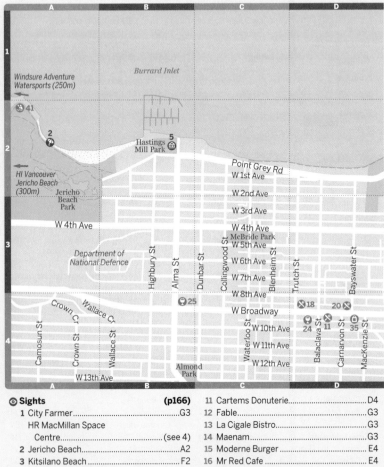

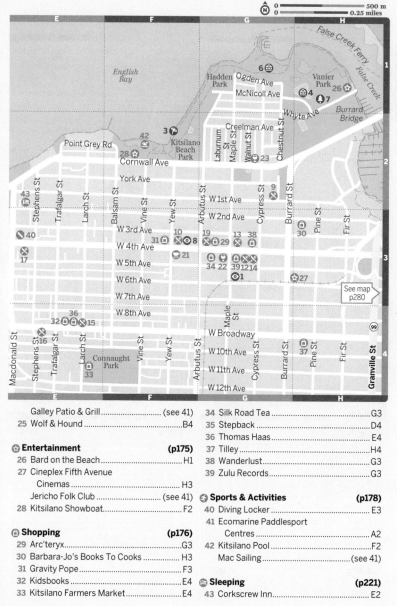

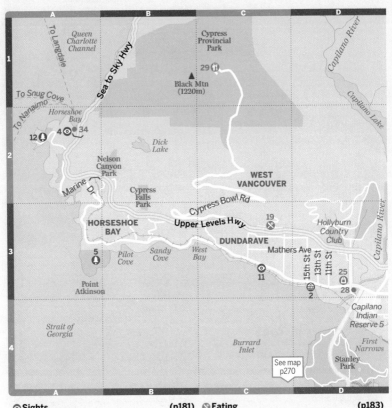

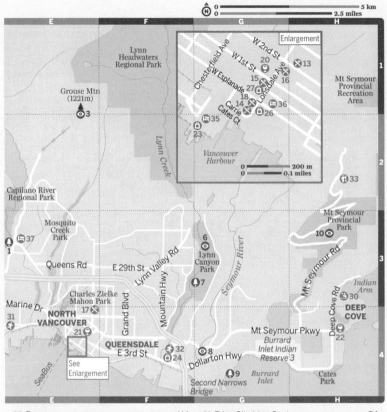

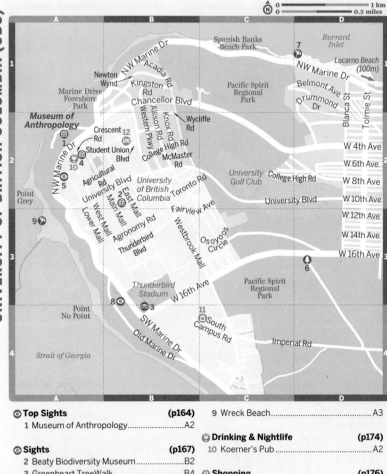

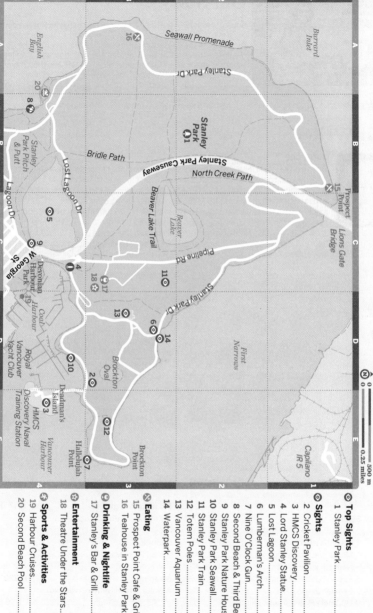

**STANLEY PARK**

## Our Story

A beat-up old car, a few dollars in the pocket and a sense of adventure. In 1972 that's all Tony and Maureen Wheeler needed for the trip of a lifetime – across Europe and Asia overland to Australia. It took several months, and at the end – broke but inspired – they sat at their kitchen table writing and stapling together their first travel guide, *Across Asia on the Cheap*. Within a week they'd sold 1500 copies. Lonely Planet was born.

Today, Lonely Planet has offices in Franklin, London, Melbourne, Oakland, Dublin, Beijing and Delhi, with more than 600 staff and writers. We share Tony's belief that 'a great guidebook should do three things: inform, educate and amuse'.

# Our Writer

### John Lee

Born and raised in the UK, John grew up in the lengthy shadow of London, then succumbed to the lure of Canada's West Coast in 1993 to begin an MA in Political Science at the University of Victoria. Regular trips home to Britain ensued, along with stints living in Tokyo and Montreal, before he returned to British Columbia to become a full-time freelance writer in 1999. Now living in Vancouver, John specializes in travel writing and has contributed to more than 150 different publications around the world. You can read some of his stories (and see some of his videos) online at www.johnleewriter.com. John has worked on around 25 Lonely Planet books, including *Canada*, *British Columbia*, *Western Europe*, *Vancouver* and *Europe on a Shoestring*.

**Published by Lonely Planet Global Limited**
CRN 554153
7th edition – April 2017
ISBN 978 1 78657 333 9
© Lonely Planet 2017    Photographs © as indicated 2017
10 9 8 7 6 5 4 3 2 1
Printed in China